THE SUNNY LAND OF FRUITS & FLOWERS

Created and Directed by Hans Höfer

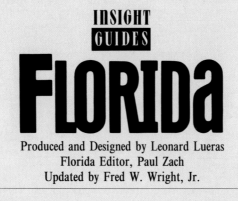

INSIGHT GUIDES

FLORIDA

Produced and Designed by Leonard Lueras
Florida Editor, Paul Zach
Updated by Fred W. Wright, Jr.

HOUGHTON MIFFLIN COMPANY

APA PUBLICATIONS

FLORIDa

Eighth Edition
© 1993 APA PUBLICATIONS (HK) LTD
All Rights Reserved
Printed in Singapore by Höfer Press Pte. Ltd

Distributed in the United States by:	Distributed in Canada by:	Distributed in the UK & Ireland by:	Worldwide distribution enquiries:
Houghton Mifflin Company	**Thomas Allen & Son**	**GeoCenter International UK Ltd**	**Höfer Communications Pte Ltd**
2 Park Street	390 Steelcase Road East	The Viables Center, Harrow Way	38 Joo Koon Road
Boston, Massachusetts 02108	Markham, Ontario L3R 1G2	Basingstoke, Hampshire RG22 4BJ	Singapore 2262
ISBN: 0-395-66174-9	ISBN: 0-395-66174-9	ISBN: 9-62421-010-1	ISBN: 9-62421-010-1

ABOUT THIS BOOK

a lovely seaside villa in the South-east Asian nation of Singapore is an unlikely birthplace for a book about Florida. But it was there, a half-a-world away from the Sunshine State that *Insight Guide: Florida* was conceived and published by Apa Publications.

Apa founder **Hans Höfer** introduced his new approach to the field of travel literature with the publication of a guide to Bali in 1970. Its surprisingly smooth blend of superb photography and interesting, colorful commentary won it immediate acclaim and an enthusiastic audience.

Apa's editorial and photographic teams are comprised of professionals who have made a living exploring the world's most exotic highways and byways.

Freelance editor **Paul Zach**, the man responsible for producing *Insight Guide: Florida*, had spent nearly three years covering Indonesia for the *Washington Post*, ABC News, McGraw-Hill World News and Reuters news agency. His expertise for handling the Florida project stemmed from three years as a staff writer for the award-winning *Evening Independent* newspaper in St Petersburg.

Zach and coeditor **Leonard Leuras** finalized plans for the Florida book over plates of Indian food in Singapore restaurants and sushi bars in Honolulu. They approached Florida as an exotic land filled with Native Americans, Cubans and Crackers, pulsing with bizarre rites like Tampa's Gasparilla pirate invasion, and alive with alligators, flamingos and other wildlife.

This edition of *Insight Guide: Florida* was prepared at Apa's Singapore headquarters under the careful direction of Höfer and contributing editor **Fred W. Wright, Jr.** It was Höfer's passion for adventurous travel combined with formal training in the Bauhaus school of the "black arts" of printing, photography and design that led him to the inspiring *bales* of Bali and the creation of the *Insight Guides*.

Leonard Leuras, a native of New Mexico, has lived in Hawaii since 1963. He produced the Insight Guides to *Hawaii, Korea, Hong Kong* and *Mexico* and was involved in the launching of Apa's Insight Chronicles series with *The Huala* by best-selling author Jerry Hopkins.

Fred W. Wright Jr. has been a writing resident of Florida for nearly 24 years. He presently freelances from his St Petersburg home, specializing mostly in cinema and theater. Wright is also a former entertainment editor of the St Petersburg *Evening Independent*.

One of the topnotch photographers of *Insight Guide: Florida* is Cuban born **Ricardo Ferro**, one-time Florida West Coast Press Photographers Association's Photographer of the Year.

Another member of Apa's "Cuban contingent," **José Azel**, contributed many obvious photographic skills to the making of *Florida*. He spent three years as photographer for the *Miami Herald* before going freelance.

Former *Miami Herald* reporter **Raul Ramirez** provided the literary component in this Apa-Cuban connection. Havana-born Ramirez joined the exodus to Miami in 1962. He drew upon his experiences as an immigrant in the Miami community to create the vivid portrait of Cubans you'll read in the "People" section.

Other major writers were **Deanna L. Thompson** and **H. Taft Wireback**, a wife and husband team working out of Tallahassee. Wireback has worked as a reporter for the *Clearwater Sun* and *Tallahassee Democratic* and has written for *Florida Trend*, the *Floridian, New Florida* and *Southern World*. Thompson has received several awards from the Florida Society of Newspaper Editors.

Freelance photographer **Pat Canova**, a native Floridian, developed her fine photographic style during years spent as a staff photographer for the *Miami News*, the *St Petersburg Times* and *Palm Beach Post*.

Photographer **Bud Lee**, a native New Yorker, has shot for *Esquire* and *Holiday* magazines, Time-Life Books and *Life* magazine, which in 1967 named him New Photographer for the Year for his coverage of rioting in Newark, N.J.

Baron Wolman, a former chief photographer

Zach

Lueras

Wright

Ferro

Wireback

of *Rolling Stone*, shot pictures for *Florida* from the Pompano Beach-based Goodyear Blimp. Wolman has worked for virtually every national magazine and presently operates his own publishing house, Squarebooks.

Cindy Rose Stiff served as a news editor with the Associated Press Miami bureau (where she directed news and feature coverage from Key West to Pensacola), with the Miami bureau of United Press International, and with the *Fort Lauderdale Sun-Sentinel*.

Photographer **Ron Smith** spent two years as a combat photographer in Vietnam and was named Military Photographer of the Year in 1968. In 1972, he became the National Press Photographers Association's Photographer of the Year.

At Palm Beach's *Post and Evening Times*, photo editor **Ken Steinhoff** and his remarkable staff contributed some of their best material. Steinhoff is the winner of more than 50 state, regional and national photography awards. His staff included **C.J. Walker**, **John Coley**, **George Milener**, **Russell Bronson** and **Steve Crowley**.

Joe Viesti has traveled the world and shot for the German edition of *Geo*, the Asian edition of *Time, National Geographic,* Italy's *L'Expresso, Signature* and *Modern Photography*, among other publications.

Back on the literary side, **Tim Rosaforte** breathed year-round life into Florida's baseball camps with his able prose. Rosaforte has covered that sport in depth – from its spring stirrings to the World Series – for the *St Petersburg Times* and presently for the *Fort Lauderdale Sun-Sentinel*. His colleague **Paul Moran** wrote about sports in Kansas, New York and Kentucky before becoming resident expert on Florida's multi-faceted gambling sports. Cheering the volume through to completion were John Anderson, who wielded an exacting copy editing pencil, and Nedra Chung, who compiled our detailed index.

St Petersburg Times columnist **Ray Holliman** dug deep into his clips for our entertaining story about Daytona's International Speedway and Florida's other speed kingdoms.

The late **Jacques le Moyne** recorded early images of the state in pen and ink. Le Moyne served as chief cartographer and artist on the French expedition to Florida of 1562 led by the explorer Jean Ribaut. Le Moyne's sketches, hand-colored by later artists, are the only known visual renderings of Florida's extinct aboriginal Indian tribes. Transparencies of Le Moyne's original work were generously provided by US Representative **Charles E. Bennett**, the veteran Congressman (since 1948) from Florida's Third District.

A thank you also for the advice and artistry of Hawaii resident **Steve Shrader** who is, ironically, a distant relative of "Swannee River" composer Stephen Foster. Shrader's work and ideas embellish many obvious and more subtle parts of this book. A tip of our Panama hat goes to Hawaii native Carol Uyeda for her multimedia montage of Florida places and to her designer friend **Vernie Miner**, who (with Shrader and Uyeda) helped power *Florida* through its final layout stages.

Others who contributed in various ways were the Florida State Museum, NASA's photo department at the Kennedy Space Center; Kennedy Space Center Tours, TWA Services, Inc.; Circus World; the John and Mabel Ringling Museums, Sarasota; Everglades National Park; Weeki Wachee and United Press International. Other assistance was provided by Madeleine Hirsiger-Carr, Majorie Green, Linda Hallman, Gary Hallman, Bill Spidle, Jo-Ann Mattey, Rob Blount, Bill Wise, Pat Tolle, Bruce Zaya, Joan Morris, Becky Smith, Bob Ardren, Mary McRory, Barbara Miller, Capt. John J. Roche, Lee and Stephen Tiger, Donna Freismuth, Toby Bruce, Lynn Bernstein, Susan Cain, Rene Kitagawa, Linda Carlock-Anderson and Paula Hawkins, Kate Masters and cartographers Jane Eckelman, Everett Wingert and Robert Campbell.

The editor would personally like to express his gratitude for the invaluable assistance and guidance of April Athey and the unfailing encouragement of Vern and Tony Zach.

—APA Publications

Wolman

Canova

Stiff

Thompson

Steinhoff

History

—by Paul Zach

14 **Come One! Come All!**

18 **Evolution of the Land**

21 **The Earliest Sun-Seekers**

25 **"Discovery" and Spanish Domain**

33 **The 18th and 19th Centuries**

42 **Florida in the 20th Century**

45 *Hurricane Andrew*
—by Joann Biondi

People

49 **Introduction**

51 **The Seminoles**
—by Paul Zach

57 **Cubans**
—by Raul Ramirez

63 **Blacks**
—by Deanna L. Thompson
and H. Taft Wireback

69 **Crackers and Yankees**
—by Deanna L. Thompson
and H. Taft Wireback

75 **Retirees**
—by Deanna L. Thompson
and H. Taft Wireback

Places

83   Introduction

CENTRAL FLORIDA
—by Paul Zach

91   Walt Disney World

105   Orlando and Its Other Worlds

THE WEST COAST
—by Paul Zach

117   Tampa

125   St Petersburg

130   To Clearwater and Beyond

139   Sarasota and Points South

SOUTH FLORIDA
—by Cindy Rose Stiff

151   Metropolitan Miami

165   Miami Beach

171   Fort Lauderdale and Points North

177   Palm Beach

186   Inland South Florida

THE EAST COAST
—by Fred W. Wright, Jr

191   The Space Coast

199   Daytona Beach

203   Old St Augustine

206   Jacksonville

NORTH FLORIDA
—by Deanna L. Thompson
   and H. Taft Wireback

213   The Panhandle

227   Tallahassee

231   Into The Pan

239 THE EVERGLADES
—by Paul Zach

THE FLORIDA KEYS
—by Paul Zach

253 Cruising Through the Keys

264 Curious Key West

Features

281 The Lure of Lost Treasure
—by Paul Zach

287 The Baseball Boys
—by Tim Rosaforte

293 Speed!
—by Ray Holliman

298 Taking a Gamble
—by Paul Moran

307 Space at the Cape
—by Paul Zach

Maps

84 Florida's Routes and Cities
90 Orlando and Central Florida
116 Tampa, St Petersburg and Sarasota
150 Miami and Vicinity
164 Miami Beach
193 Cape Canaveral
199 Daytona Beach and Ormond Beach
203 Old St Augustine
227 Tallahassee
239 The Everglades
254 The Florida Keys
266 Key West

TRAVEL TIPS

314 *Getting There*

315 *Travel Essentials*

317 *Getting Acquainted*

321 *Communications*

321 *Getting Around*

322 *Where to Stay*

330 *Food Digest*

331 *Things to Do*

339 *Culture Plus*

348 *Shopping*

349 *Sports*

355 *Further Reading*

362 *Useful Addresses*

*For detailed Information
See Page 313*

COME ONE! COME ALL!

Like a barker outside the Big Top, Florida beckons.

"Ladies and gentlemen, boys and girls. Step right up for the greatest show on earth. Guaranteed to assault your sensibilities. It's shocking! It's surprising! It's Florida!

"Meet the world's most celebrated mouse. Walk with weird and wondrous wildlife. Ride with a cowboy. Dance with an Indian. Swashbuckle with a pirate.

"Come one! Come all! To a superlative sideshow of sights, sounds and smells. A scintillating circus of sensations. A carousel

of curiosities. Right this way. Our clown will be your guide.

"Follow him on a search for the fabled Fountain of Youth. Follow him to saloons where Ernest Hemingway held court. To the Billion Dollar Sandbar where Desi Arnaz once beat out conga rhythms. And where Jackie Gleason played golf. Sail to northern reaches which look like the Deep South. Surf to southern resorts studded with pink palaces. Stroll through streets etched in Art Deco. See seaside playgrounds where the scorching sun affects people like the full moon. Indeed, even blast off for another planet.

"You've heard about her plastic flamingos. You've heard about her sequins-tailed mermaids. They're all here – and much, much more. It's decadent! It's delightful! It has kitsch! It has class! Ladies and gentlemen, boys and girls…"

Like a barker outside the Big Top, Florida beckons. And millions continue to come.

On the map of the United States of North America the most recognizable feature is the south-pointing peninsula of Florida.
> —Marjory Stoneman Douglas in *Florida: The Long Frontier*, 1967

That familiar strip of sand that juts like a hitchhiker's thumb from the Southeastern fist of the United States was not even part of the North American land mass when the continents began taking shape billions of years ago. A trench full of sea separated the

reaching the molten rocks that hardened into igneous granite rhyolite and tuff to form a solid foundation for the Florida peninsula.

Eventually, the warm seas swallowed the bedrock. Dinosaurs lumbered across the rest of the North American continent, leaving skeletons in tar pits and quarries. But the only fossils from the age of the dinosaurs ever found in Florida have been those of amphibious creatures. The oldest, a turtle, dates back to geology's Cretaceous era, 120 million years ago. An oil company turned up

mainland from an arc of steaming island volcanoes. Geologists believe these were part of the chain that developed into the Caribbean islands. Chunks of what would become Florida may even have been part of the Bahamas and Cuba before the Florida Straits evolved.

Evidence of the ancient volcanoes still exists in the jagged hill country of southern Cuba, Hispaniola and other islands, but the monotonously flat Florida landscape belies its fiery origins. Erosion and deposits of silt and sand clay buried the volcanoes a half-billion years ago. Geologists have bored as deep as 13,000 feet in some locations before

part of the turtle skeleton near Lake Okeechobee in 1955, while drilling at a depth of 9,000 feet. Other bones pegged to that aquatic period included a bizarre, shark-like mammal called the zeuglodon, ancient whales, and ancestors of the endangered manatees.

The remains of these creatures – marine shells, sand and limestone – settled on the sea bottom until, 20 to 30 million years ago, Florida slowly began to emerge from the sea. At first, it probably resembled the "Quick-sands" that color the emerald waters of the lower Florida Keys today. Later, limestone deposits thickened, reaching a depth of 18,000 feet in some areas. The sediment filled in the northern trench and the new peninsula began to brush tentatively against the underbelly of the North American continent.

Shaped by the seas: Florida was far enough south to be spared from the huge glaciers that oozed down into America during the icy Pleistocene era. In fact, the glaciers sucked up so much of the earth's water, the young peninsula swelled to nearly twice its present size. The seas at times receded 350 feet below their current level.

When the ice floes melted, the seas washed back over Florida's extended shores. The glaciers reformed, then melted again. This occurred about a half-dozen times before the Ice Age ended and the seas receded for the last time.

The pronounced tidal process chiseled a staircase of bluffs and terraces into the peninsula that today ranges from 150 feet above sea level at Okefenokee to just 10 feet at Silver Bluff. Below sea level, the continental shelf extends in a series of terraces from Florida's West Coast into the Gulf of Mexico. Geologists estimate that the last high tide that crept into Florida occurred 120,000 years ago. Continuing erosion along Florida's Gulf Coast indicates the seas are still adjusting to the last thaw of 10,000 years ago.

While the northern lands were sheathed in ice, herds of animals migrated to Florida in search of food. Vegetarians found plenty. Longleaf pine, loblolly pine, hickory and oak filled the forests of the Panhandle. Laurel, live oak, sweet gum and magnolia sprang up in forests of hardwood. Sand pine, scrub oaks, saw palmetto and rosemary blanketed the central plains while water oak, black gum, bay, cypress and cabbage palm grew in the swamps. A mixture of grasses – saw grass, wild grass, millet and bullrushes – thrived in the low-lying marshes of the south and became the Everglades. Along the coasts, tangled patches of mangroves appeared.

The Ice Age gave way to centuries of heavy rains that gushed through the scars, filling pockmarks left in Florida's brittle limestone crust by the shifting seas. Fresh water accumulated in underground pockets and burst through the thin coating to transform sinkholes into crystal freshwater springs. Mineral phosphorus, deposited by the wave action, settled in the sand and clay to give Florida a rich undercoating.

Today, drag lines strip away the surface of the land in quest of that valuable phosphate rock, a key ingredient in many fertilizers. The miners often inadvertently uncover the bones of prehistoric animal life that once flourished in Florida. So many fossils of huge, elephant-like mammoths have been found, that a model of one of these monsters glares at State Road 60 east of Bartow at the site of the Phosphate Valley Exposition. Fossils of the legendary saber-toothed tigers and mastodons also are frequent finds. Other creatures that roamed the peninsula included *synthetoceras tricornatus* (which sported a giant "wishbone" on its snout), tiny ancestors of the horse, bears bigger than the Kodiak, and vicious carnivores called dire wolves.

Fair and "Frute-Fullest": At last, just 6,000 years ago, Florida's familiar landscape took shape – an appendix of land swollen with exotic plant and animal forms. It boasts some 1,350 miles of shoreline, more than any state except Alaska. Beaches fringe about 800 miles of that. More than 30,000 lakes speckle the soil and savanna, including 730-square-mile Okeechobee, fourth largest lake in the United States. Combined with numerous rivers, like the fabled Suwannee and somber springs with names like Weeki Wachee and Homosassa, water accounts for about 4,000 of Florida's 58,000 square miles.

Because of its peculiar shape, no place in Florida is more than 60 miles from tidewater. Yet it is larger than the states of New York, Massachusetts and Rhode Island combined. Indeed, the centuries of shaping and sculpting produced a piece of property dramatically different in mood, tone and texture from the rest of the North American continent.

In 1563, an early European visitor Jean Ribaut, was enthralled by what he found.

It is a place wonderfull fertill, and of strong scituation, the ground fat so that it is lekely that it would bring fourthe wheate and all other corn twise a yeare... yt is a country ful of havens, rivers and islands of sche frutefullnes as cannot with tonge be expressed... the fairest, frute-fullest and pleasantest of all the worlde...

Preceding pages: the never-changing Everglades. Left, 10 million years ago, the Florida savanna west of Gainesville was home to bizarre creatures similar to those writhing and crawling in this colorful painting.

Florida flaunts its climate. There are so many warm, sunny days all year that the afternoon newspaper in the city of St Petersburg gives its street edition away free whenever the sun fails to shine. Life is easier, smoother. There are few cold, somber days to cloud one's mind.

Lured by the laid-back lifestyle, 10 million people have made Florida their home, the fifth-largest state population in the country. That figure is expected to nearly double by the year 2000. Another 40 million tourists flock to Florida each year to spend a few weeks or months in this mellow, yellow land.

The same sunny features that continue to attract thousands of new residents each week undoubtedly proved a strong attraction to the peninsula's earliest inhabitants as well. Most scholars subscribe to the theory that hungry Asians crossed a land bridge linking Siberia to Alaska about 20,000 years ago, probably in search of warmer, fertile lands that had not been ravaged by the killer glaciers of the Ice Age. These first Americans pushed southward through Canada, across the Rocky Mountains and Great Plains to the Mississippi River Valley. Archaeologists believe some groups reached southern Georgia and the Florida Panhandle about 10,000 years ago.

A second theory comes from archaeologists who have unearthed evidence indicating cultural similarities between primitive Floridians and Central and South American tribes. This has led to a growing school of thought that North Americans may have been migrants from the south.

Florida's "paleo-Indian" culture, wherever it may have come from, arrived with its hunting skills and found a subtropical "promised land" teeming with prey – boar, opossum, bobcat, deer, woolly bison, squirrel, and now-extinct species like mastodon, sloth and mammoth. Quail, marsh hens, ducks, geese and coots fell victim to their primitive but deadly weapons.

Digs have uncovered fluted stones, called Clovis points or Suwannee points depending

Left, the remains of Florida's aboriginal tribes, like this skeleton from an Apalachee burial mound, are found throughout the state.

upon their age and the location in which they were found. These jagged-edged flints – discovered as far south as Fort Myers on the west coast and Vero Beach on the east – resemble the arrowheads of later Indians. Hunters probably lashed them to long sticks to make spears called *atlatl*. The oldest points have been found at Warm Springs outside Venice, about 60 feet underground.

Flanked by oceans of water, these ancient Floridians inevitably waded out into the rivers, bays and lakes and found another source of sustenance – seafood. They speared tasty grouper and flounder, gathered juicy clams and oysters, snared stone crab and spiny lobster. They filled their bellies and stayed.

Prehistoric garbage heaps: By 5000 BC, aboriginal cultures known simply as "preceramic archaic" were taming the wilds of the peninsula. Primitive villages sprang up along the banks of the St Johns River. They were populated by huge, dark-skinned, straight-haired people. These early residents scraped the meat from clams, oysters and conches, then used the shells as cooking vessels, or as tools for fashioning dugout canoes to explore and fish new waters. Discarded shells accumulated in garbage heaps, known by the more respectable-sounding archaeological term "middens." As the tribes died out or moved on to new locations, time buried their traces. New people with more advanced tools replaced them, and their trash in turn wound up in new middens.

Today, construction crews gouging foundations for new condominiums, and children digging along sand banks, occasionally rediscover these Indian mounds. They provide a layer-by-layer chronology of Florida's earliest inhabitants. From the ancient spearpoints of the "paleo-Indians" deep at the lowest levels, up through shards of pottery stamped with increasingly intricate designs, to the neck ornaments and smoking pipes of later civilizations, they relate a remarkable story.

A milestone occurred in the lives of Floridians about the year 2000 BC when the red clay of the earth was first used to create pottery. It was to be another 800 years before this clay began to appear in other parts of North America.

The earliest pieces were crude, shaped like boxes or washbowls, either smooth or with simple, checkerboard patterns. As the uses to which pottery was put became more diverse over the centuries, the designs became more artistic. The etchings provide some of the first evidence of a language which linguists believe was more closely related to one spoken in South America's Orinoco River delta than to other American Indian languages. By the year 850 AD, cultures of the Gulf Coast were producing fiber-tempered works of art. The late Florida anthropologist John M. Goggin said this pottery was "thought by many to be among the finest pottery in the United States…"

cooking corn. Radioactive Carbon 14 tests indicate charcoal from those backwoods barbecues may date to 1000 BC, much earlier than the introduction of corn in the Midwest. The grain may have been introduced from South America or Mexico.

Bones in burial mounds: The most fascinating archaeological finds have been massive burial mounds that appear to have been influenced or introduced by the Hopewell cultures of Ohio and Illinois. From Matecumbe, way down in the Florida Keys, to Bear Lake in the Everglades, Malabar on the East Coast, Safety Harbor on the Gulf and dozens of sites in the Panhandle and near St Augustine and Jacksonville, the Indians created memorials

As the utensils for food preparation evolved, so did the means of obtaining the ingredients. The transition from chasing animals and fish and gathering shellfish, to planting the land and cultivating crops, occurred about 1000 BC. In digs near Lake Okeechobee, archaeologists have discovered early forms of irrigation ditches and garden plots laid on dikes above the wet savanna.

Some scientists theorize that maize, or corn, grew in south Florida before it sprouted anywhere else in the continental US. Mound excavations reveal the Indians burned lime from shells – and the only known use for lime in the preparation of food by Indians was in

to their chiefs and prominent tribesmen.

The lone skeletons of these nameless celebrities rest at the center of each mound in prone positions, facing towards the Florida sun. More skeletons, perhaps those of family members paying a last homage to their household head, rest in face-down positions above. The bones of others buried haphazardly, or in bits and pieces, are probably human sacrifices, testifying to the special position reserved for the carefully-entombed personage below. Distinctive ceramics and wooden effigies sculpted into human and bird forms, possibly prized possessions of the deceased or perhaps magic talismans to speed his ascent to heaven, also litter the burial mounds.

Florida's Indian mounds had become enormous earthworks by the time Christ began preaching his gospel in the Middle East. Canals and roadways connected some of the mounds in intricate patterns of which only the Indians knew the significance. Some scholars have remarked on similarities to the great temple-building civilizations of the Aztecs, Mayas and Incas in Central and South America. Mound-building led to empire-building by the time of the Christian era "Mississippian" culture. Located further north, this culture developed populous cities which were perched on top of pyramid-shape mounds with flattened caps.

opers' bulldozers flatten 1 to 2 percent of them each year.

Vanishing tribes: The heterogenous groups of aboriginals eventually took on distinct unifying characteristics. Historians identify six major tribal groups. The largest, the Timucuans, inhabited most of northern Florida as far south as Cape Canaveral. A related but smaller tribe called the Tocobega lived in the Tampa Bay area. Other groups included the Calusas and Mayaimi near Lake Okeechobee and in southwest Florida below Tampa Bay; the Apalachee, a sizable group, who lived in the eastern part of the Panhandle and as far north as Georgia; the Pensacola, Apalachicola and Chtot in the western Pan-

Archaeologists have been engaged in a race against modern progress in their efforts to recover irreplaceable artifacts, and valuable information about their makers, from burial mounds around Florida. According to state archaeologist Calvin Jones, researchers at one time had recorded more than 14,000 such burial sites around the state, but devel-

Left, French artist Jacques le Moyne sketched a portfolio of Florida's extinct aboriginals in 1564. Here, ancient Indians offer a stag to the sun god. **Above**, Le Moyne sketched this vision of "Floridians crossing over to an island to take their pleasure."

handle; the Ais and Jeaga of the lower east coast's Saint Lucie River region; and the Tequesta, scattered along prime Gold Coast real estate that, many centuries later, would sprout cities like Palm Beach, Fort Lauderdale and Miami.

These Indian tribes – with their highly developed civilizations, artistic and agricultural talents, and engineering capabilities – owned Florida when the first white men stumbled upon its sun-washed shores shortly after Christopher Columbus changed the course of history. These same Indian tribes had vanished from the face of the earth less than three centuries after Columbus arrived.

JUAN PONCE DE LEON, SPANISH KNIGHT, DISCOVERER OF FLORIDA,
MARCH 27, 1513.   AUTHENTIC PORTRAIT LOANED BY THE
ST. AUGUSTINE INSTITUTE OF SCIENCE AND HISTORICAL SOCIETY.

"DISCOVERY" AND SPANISH DOMAIN

Ponce de León, a Spanish adventurers, was led by the fictions of a Carib girl... to explore the country in search of a fountain famed for renovating old age. (He was not the first, nor will he be the last old gentleman to be led up and down a bootless dance by the fascinations of the fair.)
—M.M. Cohen in *Notices of Florida and the Campaigns*, 1836

Imperious Ponce de León: Credit for the European "discovery" of Florida usually goes to Spain's Don Juan Ponce de León. But an Italian with an anglicized name probably beat him here.

Genoa-born mapmaker and sea captain Giovanni Caboto, better known as John Cabot, made several voyages to Labrador and other northern points in the New World shortly after Christopher Columbus found it blocking his path to India in 1492. The voyages earned Cabot the praise of English King Henry VII, who called him the man "who found the New Found Lands."

The king also commissioned Cabot to chart the land. So John and his son, Sebastian, quietly sailed into Spanish territory in 1498. Historians believe he skirted the coast of the peninsula as far south as Cape Florida, a promontory Cabot called the "Cape at the End of April," before turning north in May. Neither Cabot nor his son ever landed here – but shortly after their voyages, crude maps appeared in Europe depicting what appears to be the Florida peninsula.

Ponce first sailed to the New World with Columbus' second expedition. After Ponce had established an outpost in Puerto Rico, King Ferdinand V rewarded him with the governorship of all Hispaniola. But Diego Columbus, Christopher's son, soon claimed that title. The king responded by giving Ponce the opportunity to become governor of a fabled island called Bimini, rumored to be a paradise flowing with waters that produced perpetual youth – if he could find it.

Left, Spanish Don Juan Ponce de León probably "discovered" Florida while searching for gold rather than a "fountain of youth." Instead, he found only death.

It was an appropriate undertaking for Ponce. The beginnings of his life remain shadowy; he may have been the illegitimate son of a nobleman of Seville. Some histories give 1460 as the year of Ponce de León's birth. That would have made him an old salt of 53 when he weighed anchor for fabled Bimini on March 3, 1513.

But it's unlikely the prospect of taking a dip in a magic fountain – even one that could wash away some of those years – was the prime motivation for his trip. Ponce had better reasons for going. In addition to gaining administrative control over Bimini and any other places he might discover, the king had promised Ponce virtual ownership of the lands, including any gold or other precious metals they might contain.

Ponce poked about in the Bahamas for about 25 days in the *Santa Maria de la Consolacion* and the Santiago. He found no trace of Bimini, but he did locate the Bahama Channel, a shortcut to the Caribbean from the Atlantic Ocean. Ponce and his crew celebrated *Pascua Florida*, the Feast of Flowers (Easter), aboard ship. Six days later, on April 2, he sighted an unknown seashore.

Ponce made landfall a few days later, somewhere between the site that would soon become the first permanent settlement in the continental United States – St Augustine – and a river now called St Johns. Some early histories say the discovery inspired Ponce to remark: "Thanks be to Thee, O Lord, Who hast permitted me to see something new." Then he christened the land in deference to the holiday season – *La Florida*. The name stuck, and was initially applied to all Spanish holdings on the North American continent.

Unfriendly natives: Further exploration led the expedition north to the St Johns River mouth, and south, where stops may have been made at Cape Canaveral and Biscayne Bay. Then the group sailed around the Florida Keys, which Ponce called *Los Martires* because the low rocky islands reminded him of a line of martyred men. That name has been forgotten, but his term for the dry patch of sand at the end of the Key stuck: *Tortugas*, the Spanish word for the sea turtles he found swarming along the beach.

After rounding the Keys, Ponce sailed up the west coast, possibly as far as Pensacola Bay. Even if he never got that far, it had become apparent to him that he had found something more than a mythical island. He did make at least one more stop at Charlotte Harbor, once called Bahia Juan Ponce, near the modern city of Fort Myers. There, he encountered Florida's natives – tall, powerful and intensely hostile.

This initial hostile encounter has led historians to suspect that earlier contacts may have taken place between Europeans and the original Floridians. Some historians speculate that slave hunters from the Spanish settlements in the West Indies had hunted Florida

together two ships, 200 men, 50 horses, and all the equipment he needed. The king commissioned him and a contingent of missionary priests to settle the "island of Florida," but to treat the Indians well, "seeking in every possible way to convert them to our Holy Catholic faith."

Ponce again put ashore near Charlotte Harbor, an event Catholic scholars consider the first authenticated instance of priests landing on the soil of the future United States. Unfortunately for the ill-fated entourage, their collective prayers proved fruitless. While laying foundations for the first shelters of the settlement, the newcomers were surprised by a group of Calusas or

Indians. Reports which maintain that Indians shouted Spanish words at astonished explorers lend credence to that theory. Others believe Indians in colonized islands had somehow sent their Florida neighbors word of their own harsh treatment at Spanish hands. In fact, during the first eight years of Spanish occupation of Puerto Rico and Haití alone, European settlers killed or enslaved more than a million of the native Caribs.

Ponce returned to Puerto Rico from that maiden voyage to plot his conquest of *La Florida*. But the king first ordered him to put down a Carib uprising in the Lower Antilles; so it wasn't until 1521 that Ponce had scraped

Mayaimis who attacked with a savage barrage of stones and arrows. Ponce vainly tried to lead a counter-attack. He and his men fought pitched battles with daggers. Blood stained the newly-consecrated soil. By some accounts, the Spanish even set snarling greyhounds on their attackers.

The Conquistadors: Despite heavy losses, the Indians never retreated. A primitive arrow hewn from swamp reed tore into the toughened flesh of Ponce de León. Six of his men also collapsed wounded around him. Survivors managed to get Ponce and the other injured into a boat. They reached Cuba, but there Ponce died. He was buried in Puerto

Rico. Instead of a fountain of youth, Ponce had stumbled into a pool of death.

Three major expeditions and several smaller ones followed Ponce into *La Florida* during the next 40 years, seeking to tame the hostile new land and its unfriendly inhabitants. All failed. About 2,000 Spaniards lost their lives in the process. Most had proudly brandished swords and donned armor to follow the battle-toughened leaders they called conquistadors.

Pánfilo de Narváez waded ashore at Tampa Bay with some 400 men on Good Friday, 1528. A red-bearded soldier, he had earned his reputation when he lost an argument and an eye to Hernando Cortéz in Mexico. He

firmly warned the Indians that if they did not obey him, and thus the King of Spain and the Pope, "I will take your goods, doing you all the evil and injury that I may be able… and I declare to you that the deaths and damages that arise therefrom, will be your fault and not that of His Majesty, nor mine, nor of these cavaliers who came with me." The

Left, Le Moyne's drawing, hand-colored by a later artist, even depicted an early form of French foreign aid that helped one Indian tribe defeat another. Like Ponce de León, Spanish conquistador Hernando de Soto, <u>above</u>, failed in his attempts to tame Florida's hostile wilderness.

Indians told Narváez exactly what he wanted to hear: there existed a land to the north called Apalachee, where they would find the treasure sought by every self-respecting conquistador – gold. Narváez set out for Apalachee on foot, ordering his ships to rendezvous with him there. He found tall forests of longleaf pine, vast plains of cabbage palm, and sparkling springs and rivers, but no gold. Occasional Indian raids and mosquito attacks took their toll. The dwindling party arrived in the Panhandle land of Apalachee exhausted and starving. Indian villagers offered them some small rations and they butchered their horses for meat. The ships never showed up. So Narváez and his men built six makeshift vessels, crawled in and set off for Mexico.

Narváez vanished along with the ships. Years later four survivors of the expedition turned up in Mexico. Led by **Alvar Nunez Cabeza de Vaca**, they had survived a shipwreck then wandered in the American Southwest for eight years before finding Mexico.

De Soto's cavaliers: Hernando de Soto, the star conquistador of his time, headed a more ambitious assault on Florida with only slightly better results. Cohen described the escapades of the handsome, 36-year-old member of Spain's *hidalgo* gentry as "poetry put in action; it was the knight errantry of the Old World carried into the depths of the American wilderness; …steelclad cavaliers, with lance and helm and prancing steed, glittering through the wilderness of Florida, Georgia, and the prairies of the Far West…"

De Soto landed at Tampa Bay in May 1539 with an impressive army of 1,000 knights and fortune hunters. They killed and enslaved Indians and penetrated the thick brush of Florida's interior, cutting their way past the present locations of Dade City, Lake City and Live Oak. Puzzled by the absence of gold and magnificent bejeweled cities such as those he had seen in Peru and Mexico, De Soto pushed on through the Panhandle to Georgia, North Carolina and the Smoky Mountains before turning west to Alabama to continue his search. Three years and thousands of miles after his arrival in North America, De Soto died from fever. His men submerged his body in the Mississippi River. Most of the conquistadors returned to Spain empty-handed but with tales of the immense, changing landscapes of the New World.

Unfortunately, the precise details of De Soto's historic expedition died along with him. As Garcilasso Inca de la Vega, the son of a Spanish nobleman and a Peruvian Inca princess, wrote in his 1609 *History of the Conquest of Florida*, "the Spaniards did not think so much of learning the situation of places, as of hunting for gold and silver in Florida."

One lasting American legend came out of De Soto's trip, however. On Tampa Bay, the conquistadors curiously scrutinized one Indian who had greeted their arrival in fluent Spanish. Under his paint, the man turned out to be **Juan Ortiz**, a soldier who had landed with Narváez and had survived capture by Timucuan Indians in a remarkable manner.

Garcilasso described Ortiz' ordeal at the hand of a Timucuan chief – or *cacique* – named Harriga:

They forced him to carry continually wood and water. He ate and slept very little, and was tormented... he began to run at sunrise, and did not stop till night; and even during the dining of the cacique *they would not suffer him to interrupt his course, so that at the end of the day he was in a pitiable condition, extended upon the ground more dead than alive. The wife and daughters of Harriga, touched with compassion, then threw some clothes upon him, and assisted him so opportunely that they prevented him from dying.*

Later, the *cacique* tried to roast Ortiz alive, but he was once again saved by the pleas of the chief's daughters:

Ortiz remained extended upon his griddle until the ladies, attracted by his cries, ran to his assistance... they took off the wretched Ortiz half burned, for the fire had already raised up on his body great blisters, of which some having broken covered him with blood... these merciful daughters had him carried to their house, where they treated him with herbs...

Ortiz finally escaped with the aid of the chief's eldest daughter. Years later, upon reading of the adventures of Ortiz, a biographer of Captain John Smith "borrowed" the scenario for his own subject and an Indian girl named Pocahontas. Smith then perpetuated the plagiarism by putting it into his own history.

Tristan de Luna y Arellano, a wealthy Spanish nobleman, tried to conquer Florida next. He was undismayed by his predecessors' inglorious failures and undeterred by the murder of three Dominican missionaries by Indians at Tampa Bay in 1549. Ten years later, his party of more than 1,500 tried to establish a settlement on Pensacola Bay. Devastated by a hurricane, desperate for food and disillusioned by de Luna's quixotic leadership, the Spaniards abandoned the attempt in 1561.

A foothold in Florida: Pirates proved to be another thorn in Spain's flesh. French, Dutch and English sailors hoisted the Jolly Roger, cruised the Bahama Channel and coastal waters of the peninsula, and preyed upon Spanish treasure galleons plying trade routes between the homeland and the New World. Brash buccaneers – one-time cattlemen from Hispaniola who cured the beef over *boucans* – plundered doubloons, pieces of eight, gold and silver, sometimes burying their booty on Florida beaches or outlying islands where 20th-century treasure hunters dig for it. Hurricanes sank other treasure-laden ships off the Florida coast.

Emboldened by Spain's preoccupation with pirates and its inability to colonize *La Florida*, **Jean Ribaut** captained a French effort to establish a settlement on the St Johns River in 1562. Ribaut built an arrow-head-shaped fort, Caroline.

That move intensified Spain's own efforts. Their purpose now was not just to gain a foothold, but also to drive out the French trespassers, whom they considered tantamount to pirates. An enormous armada under the command of **Pedro Menendez de Avilés** established a site at a promising spot on the east coast, south of the French outpost, from which to mount its defense. The day was August 28, 1565, the Feast of St Augustine. On September 8, Menendez formally broke ground for a settlement that to this day bears the name of that patron saint. It is the first permanent and oldest continuous settlement on US soil, founded more than a half-century before the Pilgrims clambered up Plymouth Rock in the north.

Well aware that Menendez planned to attack, Ribaut rushed back to Fort Caroline, assembled his forces, and tried to surprise

Right, Chief Satouriona ruled ancient Indian tribes living on the upper St Johns River and befriended French settlers at Fort Caroline.

Saturiova

Saturiova Re della Florida nell'America Settentrionale
in atto di andare alla Guerra

the Spanish. But again nature played a role in molding Florida's destiny. A hurricane grounded the French warships before they reached St Augustine. Meanwhile, Menendez had marched up the coast and seized the French fort, killing all residents except Catholics, women and children. On the way back to St Augustine, he encountered remnants of Ribaut's assault party and had all but 16 of the 150 men executed, including Ribaut, who was beheaded. The French called the location of that bloody meeting *Matanzas*, the place of slaughter.

With the French out of the way, Menendez tried to guarantee Spain's Florida claims by befriending various Indian tribes, aiding Jesuit mission development, and trying to colonize other parts of the peninsula. Of the settlements, only St Augustine would survive, and somewhat shakily at that. England's Sir Francis Drake leveled the little city in 1585. Another killer hurricane flooded the rebuilt colony in 1599. But St Augustine has endured for more than 400 years.

Menendez died in 1574 in Spain, an ocean away from his beloved Florida. An epitaph on his grave, penned by José-Maria de Heredia, serves as a fitting tribute to him and the other conquistadors who found Florida their most formidable challenge:

Glory has grooved the furrows on thy brow,
And seamed thy cheek, illustrious cavalier;
The scars of wars and scorching suns appear
On that bold front that none could force to
bow.

The end of the aboriginals: Ribaut and his mapmaker, Jacques le Moyne, provided history with a meticulous word-and-picture portrait of the Indian tribes they encountered. Ribaut wrote in a 1563 passage replete with misspellings and language nuances:

The most parte of them cover their raynes and pryvie partes with faire hartes skins, paynted cunyngly with sondry collours, and the fore parte of there bodye and armes paynted with pretye devised workes of azure, redd, and black, so well and so properly don as the best paynter of Europe could not amend yt. The wemen have there bodies covered with a certen herbe like onto moste, whereof the cedertrees and all other trees be alwaies covered. The men for pleasure do always tryme themselves therwith, after sundry fasshions. They be of tawny colour, hawke nosed and of a pleasaunt count-

enaunce. The women be well favored and modest and will not suffer that one approche them to nere, but we were not in theire howses, for we sawe none at that tyme.

In the pages of text that accompanied 42 revealing drawings, Le Moyne described some of the local customs. He indicated that the east coast groups generally seemed more curious and hospitable than their ferocious kinsmen on the west coast. He said they cultivated fields of beans, millet and maize which they stored in granaries; worshiped the sun; warred against other Florida tribes, scalping and mutilating their enemies, carrying the hair and limbs high on their spears in triumph; easily caught venereal disease;

sacrificed first-born children to their chiefs by clubbing the babies to death.

Le Moyne praised the Indians' success in hunting deer by disguising themselves in deer skins and antlers. "I do not believe that any European could do it as well," he wrote.

He vividly portrayed the heavily-tattooed chiefs and queens, who grew their fingernails long and sharpened them to points, and who painted the skin around their mouths blue. He said their gaudy attire included deer skin capes, belts made of Spanish moss, and earrings fashioned from oblong fish-bladders inflated and dyed red.

Le Moyne said that the Indians practiced a

form of primitive parliamentarianism:

The chief and his nobles are accustomed during certain days of the year to meet early every morning for this express purpose in a public place, in which a long bench is constructed, having at the middle of it a projecting part laid with nine round trunks of trees, for the chief's seat. On this he sits by himself, for distinction's sake; and here the rest come to salute him. Each, as he completes his salutation, takes his seat on the bench. If any question of importance is to be discussed, the chief calls upon his laüas *(that is, his priests) and upon the elders, one at a time, to deliver their opinions. They decide upon nothing until they have held a number of councils*

prayers or sacrifices," he reported. "However, they have temples, but they make use of them only to inter those who die, and to shut up their treasures. They erect also at the entrance of these temples, in the form of a trophy, the spoils of their enemies."

Contact with the Europeans eventually proved to be the fatal blow to the aboriginal cultures. Some fell victim to new diseases like chicken pox, measles and colds. Slave traders spirited away as many at 12,000 Indians. Many of those who resisted the European invasion died defending the lands their tribes had occupied for 10,000 years.

Coming of the Seminoles: By 1560, historians estimate the Indian population had

over it, and they deliberate very sagely before deciding.

Garcilasso also provided some insights into Indian life. He noted many similarities in customs to the Incas of Peru, particularly in their practice of putting their temples and the homes of their chiefs atop artificial mounds mounted by wooden stairways.

"The people of Florida are idolaters, and have the sun and moon for divinities, which they adore without offering them either

Left, Pedro Menendez de Avilés. **Above**, Le Moyne's drawing of the aboriginal Indians' unusual use of camouflage while stalking deer.

dwindled to less than one-fourth of its original size of about 25,000. Jesuit and Franciscan missionaries labored in Florida's humidity in their thick woolen robes, winning converts among north Florida aboriginals with a string of about 50 missions in the 17th century. But British raiders leveled all at the turn of the 18th century, driving the few remaining Timucuans and Apalachees further south. Spaniards took the last 200 aboriginals to Cuba with them when they handed Florida over to the British in 1763. By then, the Oconee Creeks, had migrated into the peninsula from Georgia. In Florida, they would become known as Seminoles.

The tide of events that rippled through Florida after the arrival of the Europeans was as extraordinary as the shifts in the seas that gave the peninsula its unusual physical shape. Flags flying over St Augustine and Pensacola changed allegiance faster than semaphore signals. Nations fought to keep Florida, then bartered it away. Through it all, it remained a frontier wilder than the Old West would ever become.

Redcoat rule and revolution: Despite its long years of occupation, Spain had only managed to settle St Augustine and Pensacola, and man a small garrison at St Marks in the Panhandle. Great Britain eyed Florida from its burgeoning northern colonies, prompting Spain to build Castillo de San Marcos to defend St Augustine. The massive earthworks and cannon repelled repeated assaults by the British including a major attack by General James Edward Oglethorpe in 1742. But just 21 years later, England acquired Florida with pen rather than sword in the First Treaty of Paris. Britain had captured Cuba during the Seven Years' War and agreed to swap Havana back to Spain for Florida.

Remnants of the Spanish quickly evaporated. The Creek tribes of Alabama and Georgia, generally friendly with the British, accelerated their migration southward. Slicing the territory into East Florida (from the Atlantic Coast to the Apalachicola River) and West Florida (from there to the Mississippi River) made British administration easier and they virtually transformed the territory into their 14th and 15th colonies.

Under Redcoat rule, Florida for the first time experienced ties with the rest of the North American continent. Spain had always operated from its flourishing Havana base. New plantations of indigo, rice and citrus, a subsequent increase in the slave trade from Africa and the West Indies, and a wave of new immigrants with Cork and Cockney accents also marked British rule in frontier Florida.

The revolutionary rumblings in Britain's

Left, General US Grant steams up the Oklawaha River in this 19th-century view of Florida. Right, Seminole Chief Billy Bowlegs.

original 13 colonies never reached Florida. British subjects in Florida remained loyal to London when rebellious American colonists turned their backs on King George III on July 4, 1776. Angry St Augustine residents even strung up effigies of American revolutionary leaders John Hancock and John Adams and burned them.

Capitalizing on Britain's preoccupation with fighting the American Revolution, Spain recaptured Pensacola and regained control of all West Florida. East Florida remained

Tory territory, its citizens donning red woolen coats and brandishing muskets to beat back three attempted incursions by American Whigs from the north.

But in the Second Treaty of Paris in 1783, only 20 years after acquiring Florida, the British gave it back to Spain. The fact that the territory had refused to fall into the American column was small consolation.

Rogues and refugees: Florida's reputation as a magnet for the homeless, the displaced and the runaway predates recent influxes of "boat people" from Vietnam, Cuba and Haiti. At the time of the American Revolution, Florida already sheltered a cross-section of the world's populations – Africans, West Indians, English, Spanish, Germans, Greeks, Sicilians, Minorcans, Creek and Choctaw Indians. All put down roots that would flourish in the subtropical sunshine. The races inevitably mixed. Blond haired, blue-eye Creek Indians appeared. Others became as dark-skinned as the slaves. It was no surprise then that the society produced men like Alexander McGillivray, William Augustes Bowles and Zephaniah Kingsley.

The son of a Scottish trader and a woman with Creek and French blood, McGillivray was a diplomatic marvel. He cultivated a working relationship between the Spanish governors of Florida, English traders, the

driven them off Indian land. His colourful adventures included an attack on the St Marks garrison, before Spain captured him and imprisoned him in Havana, where he died.

Kingsley was a flamboyant Scotsman with a hunchback and a flair for the slave trade. He imported thousands from Africa and the West Indies, trained them in the servile arts, then resold them for a handsome profit. He became a Florida legend by staunchly defending the slave system, even marrying one of his own servants and raising the half-caste children to be his heirs.

US acquisition: The second Spanish occupation of Florida fared little better than the first. British, black and Indian refugees from

United States Army, and a confederation he organized among 45,000 Indians of various tribes. This impossible alliance endured until his death in 1793. The confidence and self-respect with which he imbued the Indians never diminished.

Bowles, on the other hand, had no Indian blood, but he lived among the Creeks and married the daughter of a chief after emigrating from England. When the Spanish returned to power, he made several attempts to reestablish himself in Florida. He even contacted McGillivray and offered to supply the Creeks with weapons and ammunition to wage war against the Georgians, who had

the newly formed United States continued to trickle into the state. Georgians stirred up trouble along the northern border, forcing Spain to withdraw to the 31st parallel, the modern Florida-Georgia boundary.

In 1800, Spain ceded the Louisiana Territory to France, which in turn sold the territory to the US – foreshadowing imminent acquisition of the Florida peninsula by the Americans. The US extended its claim in 1813 to Mobile (Alabama), Florida's present western boundary. Americans in West Florida instigated a movement for independence. So in another unusual twist, the British, to whom the Spanish were allied in the War of 1812, sent troops to Pensacola reputedly to reinforce Spain's claim. This sparked concern about the return of Redcoats.

Tennessee's Andrew Jackson, nicknamed "Old Hickory" because of his stern reputation, took it upon himself to prevent the British from rebuilding their forces in Florida. He used a Creek Indian uprising in Alabama as a pretext for advancing toward Florida. He defeated the Indians at the Battle of Horseshoe Bend, then marched on Pensacola and drove out the British.

A subsequent skirmish between Americans and Indians sparked the First Seminole War of 1817–18. Spain then accepted an offer by the US to cancel $5 million in debts to Washington in exchange for the ownership of the Florida peninsula. Andrew Jackson returned to Pensacola in 1821, the first American governor of Florida.

Blood stains the Green Swamp: Andrew Jackson remained only three months as governor of Florida before returning to Washington – where he would soon exercise influence over the new territory directly from the White House. The officials he left behind quickly realized that the distance between Pensacola and St Augustine was too great to effectively manage the territory, so they consolidated government in a village of Talasi Indians, and Tallahassee became Florida's capital in 1823.

White settlers elbowed the Indians aside when founding Tallahassee, as they so often had when seizing land for farming or carving out a highway. The migration of tribes, mostly associated with the Creek confederation, had continued steadily as the aboriginals disappeared from Florida. They took over the deserted farmlands and game-filled forests. These Indians collectively came to be known as Se-mi-no-lee, a Creek word meaning "wild ones" or "runaways." Some spoke variations of the Hitchiti language, others Nuskogee.

As Whites and Indians trickled into the new territory, Florida's population nearly doubled from 34,370 in 1830 to 66,500 in 1845. Jackson's initial clash with the Seminoles proved to be only a taste of bloodier days ahead. Pressure mounted for the gov-

Left, forts like this one situated on Tampa Bay were built to protect settlements from Seminole Indian attacks. **Right**, General Andrew "Old Hickory" Jackson.

ernment to remove Florida's Indians to reservations in the west.

In 1823, Seminole tribes massed at Moultrie Creek near St Augustine. Led by Neamathla, chief of a group called Miccosukees, the Indians agreed to a compromise with the American government. Thirty-two chiefs signed a treaty calling for them to move their people and their black slaves to a 4 million-acre reserve in west central Florida, in return for payment for abandoned lands and financial aid to help them live on the new lands. Neither side abided by the provisions of the agreement. The Seminoles found the land unsuitable for agriculture and migrated there slowly, if at all. Drought aggravated

food shortages on the reservation. The US government reneged on payments. In 1830, Congress passed a removal act requiring all Indians in the east to be sent west.

The two sides met again at Payne's Landing on the Oklawaha River running through the rugged Green Swamp of Central Florida. This time, US officials managed to coax only seven chiefs into signing a new agreement, which canceled the Moultrie Creek Treaty and required the Seminoles to move to reservations in the Arkansas Territory (part of present-day Oklahoma). Most of the Seminole nation reacted angrily when the seven chiefs returned from a visit to the new reservations and reported that they had been coerced into agreeing to the move. But President Jackson issued an edict to the Seminoles in which he warned: "I tell you that you must go and that you will go."

Flanked by 10 companies of soldiers, General Duncan L. Clinch ordered Seminole chiefs at Fort King, near modern Ocala, to sign away their Florida lands. He managed to get the "X" of Micanopy, the timid chief of the nation, but few others. Florida tradition holds that an indignant young brave named Osceola plunged his knife into the document and cried, "The only treaty I will ever make is this!"

With that act, Osceola became an American hero. Though his great grandfather was a Scotsman, he publicly disavowed any white ancestry and fervently pursued the Creek culture. Historian Marjory Stoneman Douglas considered Osceola "unquestionably the greatest Floridian of his day."

Inspired by Osceola's act of defiance at Fort King, the Seminoles rebelled. A party of warriors ambushed Major Francis Langhorne Dade while he was en route from Fort Brooke (on Tampa Bay) to Fort King. The Indians killed Dade with their first bullet and massacred all but 3 of his 111 men.

The capture of Osceola: The incident touched off the Second Seminole War, a bloody 7-year struggle in which the outmanned Seminoles fought the better-armed white soldiers to a stalemate. They used the wilds of the Green Swamp to their advantage, striking at American settlements, then melting back into the marshes. The waters of the Withlacoochee and Oklawaha ran red with the white man's blood. The war cost the United States $40 million and nearly 1,500 dead. To protect themselves, the settlers built defensive forts like Lauderdale, Jupiter, Myers and Pierce.

Deception contributed to the defeat of the Seminoles. In 1837, Osceola rode into St Augustine under a white flag of truce sent him by General Thomas S. Jessup. Jessup violated his own flag by arresting Osceola. He imprisoned the great warrior, his wives, children and 116 others at Fort Moultrie in Charleston.

An army surgeon, Jacob R. Motte, described Osceola in his journal of the war years:

He was at the time of his capture about thirty five years old; and his person, rather below than above the common height, was elegantly formed, with hands and feet ef-

HUNTING INDIANS IN FLORIDA WITH BLOOD HOUNDS.

Above, stunned by the bold Seminole resistance, US troops resorted to hunting Indians with bloodhounds. **Right**, Seminole hero Osceola.

feminately small. He had a countenance expressive of much thought and cunning, and though when captured evidently sad and care-worn, the fire of his flashing eyes was unsubdued. His forehead was tolerably high, and cast in an intellectual mold – the upper portion which was generally concealed by his hair being worn low and hanging out in front expressed dignity and firmness, while the full arched brow indicated a man who thought much and intensely. His eyes were black and piercing; and when animated were full of dark fire, but when in repose they were softer than the soft eye of woman. His mouth, when relieved by a smile, wore an expression of great sweetness; and his lips were chiselled with the accuracy of sculpture.

That proud face suffered a gruesome fate. The despondent Osceola died a year after his capture, of malaria and a broken spirit. The attending doctor cut off his head, retribution for an incident in which Osceola had severed his brother-in-law's early in the war. The great granddaughter of the doctor later recalled that he used to hang Osceola's head on a bedpost in the room of his three little boys if they misbehaved. The doctor also exhibited the head in circus side shows.

Osceola's capture broke the spirit of the Seminoles. Jessup continued his trickery, capturing another 400 Indians and Chief Alligator after promising to meet with them for truce discussions. General Zachary Taylor didn't pull any underhanded punches, however, when he defeated a party of Seminole braves on the Kissimmee River in the last major battle of the war. The army rounded up Seminole men, women and children and in 1842 shipped 3,000 of them west of the Mississippi River.

Some Seminoles managed to avoid deportation by disappearing deep into the Everglades and Big Cypress swamps. There, under Chief Billy Bowlegs, they regrouped – and in 1855 massacred a camp of surveyors whom they considered trespassers. That ignited the Third (and final) Seminole War. Soldiers and settlers hunted the Seminoles like dogs for the next three years. They offered huge rewards for the capture of Indians. Bowlegs surrendered with a group of warriors in 1858 and was sent west. Others stubbornly refused to leave and evaded capture. Floridians eventually gave up the search, enabling about 300 Seminoles to remain beyond the impen-

etrable saw grass rivers of the Everglades.

Thus, the Seminoles were really never defeated. As Coacoochee so eloquently stated in a speech to his people during the war: "The white men are as thick as the leaves in the hammock; they come upon us thicker every year. They may shoot us, drive our women and children night and day; they may chain our hands and feet, but the red man's heart will always be free."

From Statehood to Civil War: After two decades of successful politicking by forces which saw benefits in joining the union, Florida became an American state on March 3, 1845. But the romance ended just 16 years later. A man's wealth in Florida was measured by the number of slaves he owned. Influential planters and landowners opposed the abolition of slavery and convinced their legislators to secede from the Union on January 10, 1861. Florida joined forces with the renegade Confederate States and went to war against the North.

The Civil War proved particularly disastrous to Florida. The new state had only barely recovered from the tragic Seminole Wars which had stunted its growth for decades. Agriculture had just begun making an impact with multiplying acres of cotton, indigo, rice, sugar and tobacco. Dr John Gorrie had put the little town of Apalachicola on the map in 1848 when he invented an ice-machine, the forerunner of modern refrigerators and air conditioners. The rugged interior of the state had begun to open by 1861 when a railroad sliced through the forests of scrub and pine and linked Tallahassee to Cedar Key on the Gulf Coast.

The Civil War halted such modest progress in its tracks. Florida mustered its miniscule population and its even smaller budget to wage war. Its participation was brief and limited, but devastating.

Union forces invaded the bustling port of Jacksonville four times. They seized most of Florida's forts. Fernandina Beach, once a haven for slave-smuggling after the US banned the practice, fell to the Union.

Inspired by the daring exploits of Captain J. J. Dickison, however, Florida's Confederate soldiers fought back valiantly. Their biggest battle occurred on February 20, 1864, when 10,000 blue and gray-clad soldiers clashed at Olustee near Lake City. The Floridians had nearly 100 men killed and more than 800 wounded, but the survivors held their ground. They stopped the advance of the Union army, which suffered twice as many casualties.

The "Cradle and Grave Company," consisting of teenagers and old men, later fell to a Union brigade in another Panhandle confrontation. But the "Baby Corp," mainly school boys, bravely turned back Union soldiers wearing hats inscribed "To Tallahassee or Hell" at a natural bridge over the St Marks River on March 5, 1865. Union soldiers never did reach Florida's capital city. But this was a hollow triumph for the Floridians. Only a month after the Natural Bridge battle, General Robert E. Lee surren-

continued to keep blacks down. In fact, until the Civil Rights Act of 1964, blacks in many parts of Florida still rode in the backs of buses and used segregated "public" drinking facilities and washrooms.

The Stars and Stripes flew over the Florida capital again on May 30, 1865. Political and economic reconstruction lurched to a hesitant start. Florida remained a wild frontier where the strong and the armed prevailed, fostering a violent streak in the state that persists today. Yellow fever, malaria and cholera also slowed settlers. Still, the sun lured northerners. Florida's population ballooned from 140,000 in 1860 to 270,000 by 1880. Among the immigrants were develop-

dered for Florida and the rest of the Confederacy at Appomattox.

The war cost Florida about 5,000 lives and $20 million in damage to its smoldering cities. The slaves were freed only in principle. The presence of Harriet Beecher Stowe (whose *Uncle Tom's Cabin* inspired abolitionists) at her cottage in Mandarin near Jacksonville notwithstanding, hooded Ku Klux Klansmen and gun-toting "regulators"

Above, Florida's Confederate troops successfully fought off the Union Army at the Battle of Olustee in 1864; it was Florida's major Civil War engagement.

ers, entrepreneurs, inventors and writers.

Hamilton Disston drained the Kissimmee and Caloosahatchee valleys, clearing the rivers for navigation and making soggy south Florida solid enough for settlement and farming. Cubans followed Vincente Martinez Ybor to Tampa in the 1880s to roll tobacco into cheroots and stogies, helping to make the name of the city synonymous with cigars.

On the East coast, a Chinese immigrant named Lue Gim Gong developed a frostproof orange that began to flourish in groves along the Indian River, laying the basis for the state's citrus industry.

Railroads and tourists: The far-sightedness

of two men of that era in particular laid the groundwork for the boom of the 20th century. They were Henry Morrison Flagler and Henry Plant. The latter constructed the Atlantic Coastline Railroad that linked Richmond, Virginia, with Tampa. At the end of the line, Plant built the ostentatious but luxurious Tampa Bay Hotel, with moorish minarets that still dominate the city's skyline. And the tourists began to come.

Flagler's Florida East Coast Railroad had an even bigger impact on the growth of the state. Beginning in 1885, he sank about $50 million into a series of hotels at locations connected by his railroad line, from the posh Ponce de León in St Augustine to the Ormond

and tourists.

The words of a growing colony of writers also fueled the move to Florida. Harriet Beecher Stowe turned from attacking slavery to extolling the virtues of the state's sunshine, crystal springs and fragrant forests. *Chicago Times* correspondent George M. Barbour, impressed by a visit to the state with General Ulysses S. Grant in 1879, wrote *Florida for Tourists, Invalids and Settlers*. The prose of poet Sidney Lanier in his 1875 work, *Florida: Its Scenery, Climate and History*, makes it easy to understand why the trickle of Florida immigrants swelled to a flood. Lanier wrote:

The Question of Florida is a question of an

north of Daytona. In 1894, his rail line abruptly ended on a desolate slip of land by the sea. Flagler dubbed it Palm Beach, built the venerable Breakers Hotel, and created a haughty haunt for the extremely wealthy.

A freeze nearly wiped out the state's infant citrus industry in the winter of 1894–95. Mrs Julia D. Tuttle, a rich refugee from Cleveland, convinced Flagler to extend his railroad further south to a strip of scrub on Biscayne Bay in 1896. Miami was born. Flagler laid tracks to Homestead in 1903, then to Key West in 1912, the year before he died. More hotels followed. So did more immigrants

indefinite enlargement of many people's pleasures and of many people's existences as against that universal killing ague of modern life – the fever of the unrest of trade throbbing through the long chill of a seven-months' winter... Here one has an instinct that it is one's duty to repose broad-faced, upwards, like fields in the fall, and to lie fallow under suns and airs that shed unspeakable fertilizations upon body and spirit.

Above, Florida railroad barons pose proudly in front of a locomotive. **Right**, 19th-century *Harper's Weekly* sketches of tourist sites in Key West.

The Naval Depot.

A Venerable Hack.

A Residence.

Green Turtle Soup.

The Custom House.
(and Fort in distance.)

The Milk-man on his Rounds.

A Key West Yacht.

Preparing Sponges for the Market.

The 19th century ended with the boom of cannons so familiar to Florida's war-weary residents. But the sound of nearby battles quickly gave way to the welcome "boom-chunk" of piledrivers. Up and down the east and west coasts, cities sprang up along the railroad tracks laid by Plant and Flagler.

Unlike previous conflicts, the Spanish-American War stimulated Florida's growth instead of stunting it. Florida's role in the war grew out of the cigar factories and Spanish cafes of the community founded by Ybor

in Tampa. The Cuban immigrants vicariously, if not actively, cheered on efforts by compatriots back in the homeland to free Cuba from Spanish control. Rebel leader José Marti rallied huge crowds in Tampa, pleading for contributions to the Cuban cause. The cause was so popular that a rising political star with the commanding name of Napoleon Bonaparte Broward – soon to become one of the state's most progressive governors – staked a claim to fame by surreptitiously supplying arms and ammunition to Cuban rebels before the US officially entered the war.

The suspicious sinking of the US battleship *Maine* in Havana Harbor in 1898 gave America an excuse to join the revolutionaries in the war against Spain. Troops poured into Florida, setting up tent cities while waiting to sail to Cuba. The army turned Tampa into a command post. Theodore Roosevelt rode into town with his Rough Riders, en route to glory at San Juan Hill. Red Cross founder Clara Barton established hospital headquarters there. A young journalist named Winston Churchill checked into the majestic Tampa Bay Hotel and had a glorious story to report. Spain was driven out of the New World at the very place it had begun its conquest four centuries earlier.

White bow ties and knickers: The victorious Americans returned to their northern homes with stories of their exciting exploits – and with glittering tales of Tampa, Miami, Key West and other Florida ports. Some returned home only long enough to gather up their belongings, family and friends before heading back to Florida. By 1920, Florida's first major boom was well under way.

Many of the characters who wheeled-and-dealed in real estate plundered Florida much as the Spanish and British had done earlier, interested only in fast fortunes. Others came, made money, stayed and formed the first solid core of state leaders.

Walter Fuller carved up St Petersburg, a sun-kissed Gulf Coast city founded by Russian railroad czar Peter Demens. In his book, *This Was Florida's Boom*, Fuller tells how he paid $50,000 for some land that he later resold for $270,000.

Glib-lipped salesmen took to wearing white bow ties and knickers as they auctioned off swampy-looking lots. Even the golden-tongued William Jennings Bryan, whose verbal skills earned him Democratic presidential nominations and the Secretary of State's job, sold real estate. Bryan's eloquence sold keys to luxury living in George Merrick's Coral Gables, the country's first planned community. It boasted regal entrance gates, pools, hotels, golf courses, zoned business districts, and alluring lots on palm-lined boulevards and canals.

Nearby, Carl Fisher dredged sand from the bottom of Biscayne Bay and transformed tangles of mangroves off the coast of Miami into a beach. In 1925 alone, 481 hotels and apartment buildings rose in Miami Beach. Over on the west coast, circus tycoon John Ringling created Sarasota, and Dave Davis dredged up islands that became enclaves for Tampa's elite.

Architect Addison Mizner picked up Palm Beach where the departed Henry Flagler had left off. His specialty was building mansions for the super-rich, inspiring Florida's passion for kitsch. His "boom Spanish" designs made homes look like wedding cakes, with pink frosting and frills. Mizner also sold $26 million worth of lots in a Venice-like setting called Boca Raton. The completion of a

velopments. That brought the madness temporarily to an end, but it was nothing compared to the stock market crash and Great Depression of 1929. Davis, Fuller and dozens of other millionaires were turned into paupers overnight. Still, the groundwork had been laid for resumed growth after the effects of the Depression wore off.

Between 1920 and 1940, Florida's population doubled to nearly 2 million. By the start of World War II, 2.5 million tourists visited annually. The population was growing increasingly urban. By 1940, more than 55 percent of the people were living in towns and cities – compared to 37 percent in 1920. Tampa attracted more industry, Miami more

highway connection through the forbidding fringe of the Everglades in 1928 further catalyzed the intense growth.

Overnight paupers: In 1926, a cold winter slowed spiraling prices. Then a hurricane whipped the peninsula, killing hundreds and bulldozing some of the flimsy housing de-

Left, a distinguished pose from the man most responsible for the growth of Florida as a tourist mecca – railroad and hotel baron Henry Morrison Flagler. **Above**, idyllic postcard images of Florida like this moonlit shot of Hollywood Boulevard north of Miami helped spark this century's tourist explosion.

sun-worshippers. More hotel rooms were built in greater Miami between 1945 and 1954 than in the rest of the states combined.

In addition to the tourist dollars, parimutuel betting on greyhounds and horses was legalized in 1931, bringing additional money to the state's coffers – and organized crime to the streets of its big cities. Members of the syndicate shuttled between profitable rackets in Miami. Al Capone found the location so convenient he moved into a fortified estate in Miami Beach.

New architectural marvels helped add dramatic dimensions to Florida's flatness. After a hurricane shredded Flagler's railroad through the Keys in 1935, engineers decided to transform the remnants into an Overseas Highway that included the Seven Mile Bridge, which sits on 544 pilings. The first span of the magnificent 11-mile Sunshine Skyway over Tampa Bay opened in 1954 – only to collapse after being hit by a freighter on its 25th anniversary in a tragic accident that killed 35 motorists. Construction of Florida Southern College, based on Frank Lloyd Wright's designs, began in 1938 in Lakeland.

Florida's greatest contribution to the future began taking shape shortly after World War II, when the War Department began testing missiles at Cape Canaveral. Florida the perilous journey from their poor country. Vietnamese fleeing the communist takeover fanned out from Eglin Air Force Base in the Panhandle to other parts of the state. And the tourists keep coming.

Illustrious emigres include entertainer Jackie Gleason, whose television show identified Miami Beach as "the sun and fun capital of the world"; the late Pulitzer prize-winning playwright Tennessee Williams of *Streetcar Named Desire* fame; the greatest player in the history of golf, Jack Nicklaus; and margarita-drinking balladeer Jimmy Buffett. Walt Disney World opened in 1971, dwarfing its California predecessor and making Mickey Mouse a familiar part of the

hosted the world's first scheduled airline service, a short hop between St Petersburg and Tampa, and in 1959 inaugurated the first domestic jet flights in the US. By that time, Cape Canaveral was well on its way to becoming the site of Kennedy Space Center. The last steps Neil Armstrong took on Mother Earth before his "giant step" on the moon in 1969 were on the sandy soil of Florida.

Cubans, Haitians and Mickey Mouse: Florida's reputation as a haven for refugees has never faltered. Fidel Castro's coup in Cuba sent waves of Spanish-speaking peoples into the state, first in the early '60s, again in 1980. Haitians also squeezed into small boats for Florida scene. Hurricane Andrew arrived in 1992, but even that didn't keep people away. They kept on coming.

Mix talking mice, moon-bound adventurers, literati and thespians, wild alligators, pouting pelicans and a hodgepodge of races; flavor it with Key limes and conch chowder; spread it on a bed of orange blossoms; add the scent of magnolias; baste in azure seas and broil under pastel skies. That's 20th-century Florida.

Above, the magnificent, but damaged, spans of the West Coast's Sunshine Skyway rise out of a morning mist. **Right**, Hurricane Andrew's havoc.

HURRICANE ANDREW

It was South Florida's worst nightmare. Just before dawn on August 24, 1992, a storm packing 160-mph winds and a 12-foot tidal wave slammed into the southern tier of the state leaving in its wake a surreal scene of devastation.

Hurricane Andrew, the worst natural disaster ever to hit the US, destroyed over 60,000 homes and left 150,000 people – 10 percent of Dade County – homeless. The category 5 hurricane, so rare that only one or two occur every century, left a 20–35 mile wide swath of damages estimated at the time at $20 billion. Over 35 people died in storm-related deaths.

Hardest hit were the rural and suburban areas about 20 miles south of downtown Miami – Homestead, Florida City, Kendall – most of which were totally destroyed. South Miami and parts of Coconut Grove and Coral Gables were also badly damaged. Along with piles of debris that once were houses, Andrew left a battlefield of wounds: schools, shopping centers, gas stations and churches demolished; cars smashed and overturned; boats damaged and blown ashore; crumpled airplanes; and a severely scarred landscape of uprooted trees.

In the days and weeks that followed, thousands of civilian volunteers from around the country, along with the American Red Cross, poured in to help. The president deployed over 20,000 US troops to the area to help deter looting, clean up the debris, and build temporary tent cities. The soldiers, many of whom had served in the war-torn areas of Lebanon and Kuwait, said that they had never seen such massive destruction. But locals complained that state and national officials, caught in a bureaucratic confusion with no one in charge, took too long before mobilizing government assistance – tens of thousands of people went for days without food, water, medical care or shelter in the 95° heat before help arrived. So desperate was the situation, that Florida City police officials hijacked a water truck that was headed for nearby Homestead.

Along with the human suffering, animals also fell victim to the storm. Thousands of dogs and cats, not allowed into the pre- or post-storm shelters, were left on the streets to fend for themselves. One Coconut Grove homeowner woke up to find a shark, washed over in the storm, floating in his swimming pool; others found fish in their television sets. Over 2,000 monkeys and baboons, used by the University of Miami and a private scientific foundation for medical research, escaped when their cages were destroyed. A nasty rumor – that the animals carried the AIDS virus and should be shot on sight – quickly spread throughout the county. Hundreds of the animals were gunned down by police and frightened, armed residents.

When the images of the hurricane hit the news media, foreign aid flowed in from around the world as if Dade County – one of the most cosmopolitan counties in the USA – were suddenly a Third World country. Canada, Japan and Taiwan all sent relief. Even President Boris Yeltsin offered to send Russian workers and machinery to help with the clean up. Despite these

offers of help, the rebuilding will likely take years.

Hurricane Andrew, however, did leave Dade County, an area often beleaguered by ethnic and racial conflicts, a more cohesive community. Residents, whether white, black, Cuban, Haitian, Guatamalan or all-American, worked together. "As one we will rebuild" was the spirit.

And fortunately, for the county's vital tourism industry, the damage wrought by Andrew to most tourist areas was minimal. Miami Beach suffered only broken windows and fallen trees; downtown Miami the same. Had the hurricane's eye hit just a few miles to the north, Miami would likely have been wiped out. Hurricane Andrew, the awesome force of nature, could have been worse. ■

PEOPLE

A settler in Florida – whether he comes as a capitalist, as a farmer, or as a laborer – can live with more ease and personal comfort, can live more cheaply, can enjoy more genuine luxuries, can obtain a greater income from a smaller investment and by less labor, and can sooner secure a competency, than in any other accessible portion of North America.

—George M. Barbour in *Florida for Tourists,
Invalids, and Settlers*, 1896

Barbour probably did not realize his enthusiastic guide book would help touch off an exodus to Florida unmatched since Horace Greeley said "Go West, young man" several decades earlier. One thing most racial and ethnic groups seem to share is a predilection for sampling paradise.

Nearly a century later, much of Barbour's assessment still holds true – and untold multitudes continue to flock to Florida. This in-migration has turned the peninsula not into a melting pot of people, but into a veritable sea of faces and faiths.

Several immigrant groups have had a particularly profound influence on Florida's development: Seminole Indians, who proudly balk at making peace with a government that drove them from their lands and who stoically carry on the legal fight to win back their property; Cubans, who like Ponce de León and his boatload of Spaniards, come from Havana in search of a dream; landed Crackers with roots dating back to 19th-century settlers; millions of Yankees newly uprooted from unpleasant northern regions; blacks, whose ancestors fled slavery; and retirees of all races and ethnic backgrounds who comprise an entire subculture seeking a place in the sun before it sets on their lives.

Other groups deserve mention: the Greeks of Tarpon Springs, the Minorcans of New Smyrna, the Japanese of Delray Beach, the Jews of Miami Beach, the Conchs of Key West. Vietnamese trickled in from Air Force bases around the state and country after their 1975 exodus from communism to Florida. There are even the carnival people of Gibsonton. Among early arrivals was boat-builder and photographer, Ralph Middleton Munroe. Around the turn of the century, he posed with friends for the picture on the preceding pages taken at his home, The Barnacle, in Coconut Grove.

This medley of people and more have made Florida sing with vitality. Indeed, this fresco of faces gives Florida's flat and monotonous landscapes shape, color and character.

Preceding pages: Ralph Middleton Munroe and friends. **Left**, retiring in the sun.

Lee Tiger hiked up his blue jeans, brushed his hand back over a head of shoulder-length hair and looked out from the boardwalk to where the saw grass met billowing clouds on the blue horizon. Then he glanced over at a *chickee* – a hut of cypress poles topped with palmetto and thatch – that had a hand-lettered menu in front advertising "Indianburgers."

"The people of the Everglades have to find a new way to exist with the modern ideas of the non-Indian world," Lee said. "This is what phase we're in now. We're in the middle of balancing out a way of existence."

Between two worlds: As a public relations chief for the Miccosukee branch of Florida's Seminole Indians, Lee has been one of the leaders in the difficult balancing act. He's part of a generation trying hard to integrate the tribe's past and future. Lee speaks a little of the language of his ancestors with elderly Indians who speak nothing else. He's had his skin pierced with sharp needles when he experienced the rites of manhood during the sacred Green Corn Dance. On the other hand, he has cut records with his rock group Tiger-Tiger and has lived apart from the reservation in the concrete New York jungle.

He ably reasoned away the tourist trappings of the Miccosukee Indian Village and Culture Center set up around tribal headquarters on a 5-mile long by 500-foot wide strip of the Tamiami Trail. "It's commercialized because we need to have cash flow here so people can have cars and go into Miami and buy food, buy shoes and whatever they need in the stores."

The village/culture center features several uniquely Florida Seminole attractions. There are refreshment stands and a restaurant where you may see young waitresses wearing Charlie Daniels Band T-Shirts over their traditional, colorful Seminole skirts. There is also an interesting model of the kind of homestead the Indians once lived in when they encamped in hammock "islands" in the Everglades harsh swamplands. The home-

Left, a smile from George Storm, the Miccosukee's tribal storyteller; and, **right**, an elderly woman ponders the present.

stead is composed of a cooking *chickee*, a sleeping *chickee* and other all-purpose *chickees* where leather-faced old women string beads and sew jackets and skirts.

The biggest ethnic action, however, takes place at a nearby alligator pit surrounded by a pack of German tourists. Over there, visitors are watching Bobby Tiger (not a direct relative of Lee Tiger) poke a pile of snoozing gators into a hissing wakefulness. Tiger nonchalantly drags one of the alligators into a sand pit where he pries its jaws apart. He

clamps the alligator's snout shut between his chest and chin and then rubs its throat – "to put it to sleep." To illustrate the hazards of his act, Tiger waves a four-fingered hand at his audience.

The souvenir stand and shop shelves are filled with items long handcrafted by Seminoles – assorted bracelets and necklaces, palmetto fiber dolls, baskets and painted wooden tomahawks. But a closer look reveals something more, a part of the renaissance that has gripped the tribe in recent years. One *chickee* contains the electrically-charged paintings of Lee's brother, Stephen. His work combines the brilliant colors and patterns historically associated with Seminole crafts in modern themes that dramatize the dual nature of the tribe's present-day existence… its struggle to come to grips with a changing world.

West of the model village, this struggle manifests itself in a modern school for Indian children, air-conditioned offices, cars and pickups bearing Miccosukee Indian license plates, and even a police department. Its chief, Tony Zecca, is an Italian from New York, but his deputies are Indian. Homes with the Everglades for backyards combine a kind of Gothic *chickee* architecture with Florida functional. Most have television antennas sticking out of the thatch roofs.

of Lake Okeechobee; and on a small plot in Hollywood.

All the Florida Indians trace their roots back to about 300 souls led into the wilderness by Chief Billy Bowlegs (or Mr William B. Legs as the US Government called him) following the Seminole Wars in the 1850s. Bowlegs himself was eventually forced to trace the "trail of tears" to Oklahoma that some 3,000 Seminoles before him had found laden with death and misery. Those who remained in Florida exhibited the same stubborn spirit that drove leaders like Bowlegs and the great Osceola. They melted into the marshes and refused to budge. The US Government eventually gave up.

D35:-SEMINOLE INDIAN WOMEN AND THEIR CHILDREN IN THE EVERGLADES .

The trail of tears: From a handful of hungry, exhausted Indians driven deep into the Everglades during the 19th-century Seminole Wars, Miccosukee numbers have rebounded to more than 550. Most still live close to their roots on the Tamiami Trail and Alligator Alley reservations, although some have turned their backs on the past in favor of Miami's suburbs.

Another 1,500-plus Indians, members of the Creek confederation of Florida's Seminoles, live and work mainly on three other reservations – the 42,278-acre Big Cypress, north of the Miccosukee land; 35,805-acre Brighton reservation, northwest

True to the name Seminole, from the Creek word for "wild" or "ones apart," they kept to themselves, living off corn, cane and pumpkins; trading alligator skins, deer hides and bird feathers; oblivious to Florida's headlong rush into the 20th century. Miccosukees congregated around the Calusa mounds near Chokoloskee, while others grouped around Pine Island near Fort Lauderdale, the Miami River, Big Cypress and the Ten Thousand Islands area. They mingled with the white man only out of necessity and without trust.

Canals cut at northern and eastern ends of the Everglades (to drain it for agriculture in the early part of his century) severely reduced fish and game populations. Some Seminoles turned to construction of the Tamiami Trail in the 1920s – and proved to be the hardiest workers. The road was a mixed blessing, bringing tourists and money, but eroding their traditions. The establishment of Everglades National Park in 1947 also had its good and bad points. It was in keeping with the Seminoles' love of the land, but it took their land out from under them.

The number of sympathetic friends in government grew, however. The Brighton, Big Cypress and Hollywood Creeks further fortified their political clout by organizing into the Seminole Tribe of Florida and a five-member council in 1957. The Miccosukees followed suit by forming a separate body in 1962. Each tribe subsequently intensified its battles with the US Government over land and money. The Indian Claims Commission awarded $16 million to the Seminoles in 1970 as compensation for land seized under early treaties, but there has been a long-running disagreement about how to split the money between Seminoles in Oklahoma and those in Florida.

The Miccosukees have declined any stake in that settlement, demanding the return of land instead. They filed suit claiming most of Southwest Florida, including the cities of Fort Myers and Naples, acreage granted them by President James Polk in a treaty in 1845. In a tentative agreement, the Miccosukees may drop that claim in return for about $1 million in cash from the state, a perpetual lease on 192,000 acres of land in Dade and Broward counties that must remain in its natural state, and the right to subsistence hunting and fishing and commercial frogging without license on certain lands.

The Indian cowboys of Brighton: Like many other Floridians in these parts, the Seminoles raise cattle here on primordial-looking land that could easily pass a screen test for an African veldt or western prairie. The Indians look more like cowboys as they chase a stray bull on horseback, then rope it in with ease. They wear Levis, thick belt buckles and western hats or truckers' caps. Only signs along State Road 721, sometimes scrawled with graffiti plugging "Indian Power," tip

Left, the rainbow-colored fashions of the Seminoles brighten up an old postcard. **Right**, a Miccosukee mans an Everglades airboat for tourists.

you off that you're on Seminole property.

"They've promoted it so well they've sold what they raised here to private buyers as far away as Arizona and Texas," says Allen Huff, who lives and works on the vast Brighton reservation. The cattle operation has been extremely successful.

The Hollywood-headquartered Seminoles and Miccosukees maintain separate existences as well as separate tribal organizations. Language has been one of the primary historical differences between these Seminoles and the Miccosukee branch to the south. The latter speak a form of Hitchiti, the others the more common Creek tongue called Muskogee. Both groups are making efforts

to put them into written forms.

Lorene Gopher, working on a dictionary at Brighton, said the task has been difficult because many of the sounds are different from those in English. She lamented the dwindling numbers of Indian children who speak their ancestral tongue. "The thing to do was to learn to speak English. So that's all they know,' she said.

The Miccosukees have had slightly better luck passing on their form of the Seminole language. Children learn it along with English in the reservation school. The tribe's efforts to preserve and promote their heritage in such forms as a public arts festival every winter and an annual Everglades Music Festival have also helped keep the native language alive.

Despite the obstacles to maintaining the languages where English – and Spanish – prevail, their impact on Florida will never fade. Place names like Chassahowitzka (hanging pumpkins), Chattahoochee (marked rocks), Okaloacoochee (little bad water), Oklawaha (crooked river), Halputtlockee (alligator eats), Panasoffkee (deep ravine), Wacasassa (some cows there) and Thonotasassa (place of flints) come from the Seminole tongues. Names like Miami, usually interpreted as "great water," and Pensacola meaning "the place where the

bearded people live," date back to the languages of Indians who lived here before the Seminoles.

Dancing in the past: A drastic step into the present was taken by the Hollywood-based Seminoles when they elected a woman as leader of their tribal council. As the equivalent of the tribe's chief, that role traditionally went to men. Betty Mae Jumper is a remarkable woman who was denied admittance to public schools in Dania and Fort Lauderdale, went to a Cherokee Indian School in Oklahoma at the age of 14, became a public health nurse at the Kiowa Indian hospital there, and returned to the Seminole reservation to make

Indian history when she was elected chairwoman in 1967. She has been credited with putting the tribe on a firm financial footing.

The Miccosukees have opted for Lee's father, Buffalo Tiger, as chairman. His parents didn't let him speak or write English when he was a child.

"We wanted no part of the white man's world. When the swamp was full of fish and game, we had all the food we needed. When we stayed to ourselves, our illnesses were simple and could be cured by our own medicines," he said.

Yet, as he himself has adapted to change, living in a home in Hialeah and operating out of a modern office, Buffalo Tiger has helped ease the transition for his people. His efforts have evoked criticism from the old who fear he has moved too fast and from the young who feel changes have been too slow.

One important link with the past that all Seminoles cling to is the annual Green Corn Dance. The late medicine man Sam Jones told *National Geographic* magazine in an interview years ago that if the dance is not held every few years, "the medicine die – and then no more Indians."

It's a ritual the Seminoles still guard jealously, rarely inviting outsiders and usually prohibiting photography. Medicine men conduct the centuries-old rites over the course of a week. Hundreds of songs are sung and chanted in the native language to the sound of rattles. Boys become men when they endure deep scratches from sharp needles.

Lee Tiger, born Shemeeyashaee, said he received his new name as part of the rites. "Being here in the Everglades this tribe is probably more traditional than most tribes throughout the country. You will find a lot of people know the dances; the songs and the corn dances are very sacred," he added.

Even more important to the Seminoles is their view of the universe as a wheel spinning slowly like the circle of logs in their ceremonial fires. It has symbolized their will to survive on their own terms, to bounce back from adversity and re-emerge even stronger to resume their fight for their rightful part in Florida's heritage.

Left, a Ralph Middleton Munroe portrait of a Seminole in front of a *chickee*. **Right**, two Seminole braves strike a pensive and classical 1890s pose.

Since 1959, Cuban refugees have descended on South Florida in waves as regular as weather fronts. They have arrived aboard commercial flights, private planes and hijacked aircraft, and as stowaways on merchant vessels. With alarming frequency, they've made the crossing on virtually anything that would float long enough to carry them through the treacherous Gulf currents separating Cuba from the Florida Keys: boats, rafts, auto inner tubes, coconuts wrapped in nets, palm leaves, even styrofoam boxes or empty gas containers lashed together.

Ten of thousands of Puerto Ricans and Central and South Americans have also settled in the Greater Miami area, but the story of Hispanic Florida today is mainly a Cuban tale. Their record in South Florida has been one of remarkable achievement in spite of continuing hardship and poverty among recent arrivals, most of whom reached Florida's shores destitute.

A reincarnation of old Havana: Nowhere is the Cuban impact more visible than in the section of southwestern Miami called Little Havana. Once a decaying neighborhood dotted by dimly lit apartment houses perennially fronted by "For Rent" signs, Little Havana is now a bustling hub that revolves around Flagler Street and the *Calle Ocho*, the Hispanic name for Southwest 8th Street.

The peeling facades and boarded-up storefronts that greeted the first waves of refugees to southwest Miami are now shiny showcase windows, busy mini-shopping centers, bookstores, cafeterias, religious goods stores, drugstores, toy shops, coffee shops and restaurants. Street signs, as in many other parts of Miami, require drivers not only to "Stop" but also to "*Parar*" at intersections. Triangular yellow signs advise motorists to "Yield" and "*Ceder*" to traffic. Neon and painted signs invite visitors to savor aromatic Cuban coffee and taste guava pastries; to buy elaborately mounted photos of John F. Kennedy, Cuban patriot José Marti, or even Ronald Reagan (flanked by Cuban and American

flags); to pause for a sugar cane juice drink, sample *moros y cristianos* (black beans and rice) and nibble on banana chips or Cuban sandwiches; and to view the latest Mexican or Spanish film (shown with English subtitles, of course).

Even if the longing gaze of many Cubans has remained fixed on their original home, their culture has exploded into the Miami scene. Theirs is a clannish, boisterous, lively island ebullience that startled the retirees in Miami Beach 20 years ago and still chagrins

some sedate American suburbanites as far north as West Palm Beach, where large numbers of Cubans have settled. Despite tragedy and hair-curling experiences, South Florida's Cubans have retained an infectious penchant for laughing at life's ebb and flow – and for doing so loudly. If Hispanic Americans have gained a reputation in parts of the US for excitability – in marked contrast to a presumed Anglo equanimity – they owe much of this lively style to their Cuban and Puerto Rican brethren in New York and Miami. Cubans are openly, unabashedly emotional. They cry and hug at separations and they laugh, weep and embrace at reunions.

Left, Cubans still blend fine tobaccos by hand to create the cigars that made Tampa famous. **Right**, daughter of a Cuban immigrant.

The emotions sometimes emerge in touching, if incongruous, ways. The septuagenarian woman descending from the airliner that brought her to Miami from Cuba via Spain – a common route these days – will drop to her knees to kiss Miami's soil. The middle-aged man, oblivious to ashes dropping onto his immaculate white *guayabera* shirt from his cigar stub, will hysterically wave his white handkerchief in the Orange Bowl to urge the Miami Dolphins football team to action. A young woman will break into sobs upon hearing the Cuban national anthem at a patriotic function for a land she left before she could even walk.

Latin rhythms and religion: Cuban music –

that complement the spoken language and reach out to touch friend or stranger in the genuine closeness of a moment – make Cuban enclaves loud, hectic, indomitable, immensely human and alive places.

Though they are not really a church-going lot, except on special occasions, the bulk of Miami's Cubans are nominally Roman Catholics, some devoutly so. Religion has therefore been incorporated into many facets of their lives. Often, in a living room corner or in a back bedroom or porch, small shrines are tucked away and dotted with candles, prints of Jesus Christ or favored saints, and a clear glass of water set out to console a departed soul or visiting spirit. A stroll

the cha cha, rhumba and mambo precursors of today's salsa – reflects the people's zeal for life, movement and color. The lesser known *boleros* – slow dance music with lyrics pegged to love themes – speak to traditional and hopelessly romantic values. This eagerness to live fast and to communicate in more than surface words is mirrored in the Cuban dialect. Their Spanish is staccato and distinct from the language spoken by other Latinos. Esses and even entire syllables are chopped off, leaving Cuban phrases to flow together ever faster. The people's demeanor – expressive eyes and faces, hands darting about in rapid, sweeping movements

through virtually any Cuban neighborhood will take the visitor to neatly kept yards flanked by small outdoor shrines with the likeness of Cuba's patron, the *Virgen de la Caridad de Cobre* (the Virgin of the Charity of Cobre). It is the *Virgen*, too, whose image is sculpted or etched on those huge gold medals dangling around many a Cuban neck.

For most, religion is a blend of Catholicism with elements of African and Caribbean native ritual, not unlike voodoo at times. The religious item stores that thrive in South Florida sell not only Catholic prayer books and imagery, but also candles, powders, *oraciones* and *novenas* (prayers) aimed at saints not sanctioned by the church, as well as other esoteric implements of faith and sacred ritual.

Like most Latin Americans, Cubans celebrate Christmas somewhat differently from Americans. After a traditional Christmas Eve meal of black beans, rice, pork roast, yucca and fried plantains, many flock to the nearest Catholic church for midnight mass (Spanish language masses are offered in dozens of South Florida churches). Christmas Day is for resting, not feasting.

It is not until Epiphany on January 6, when Hispanics everywhere commemorate the arrival in Bethlehem of the Three Wise Men bearing gifts for the newborn Jesus Christ, that toys and other presents magically appear in the living rooms of Cuban homes. It is said that one or all three of the Wise Men, camels and all, shrink to the size of ants and quietly slip into homes through cracks under doors. A form of holiday double-dipping has flourished among better-off Cuban youngsters. They manage to convince their parents that since their friends in school get visits from Santa Claus, they should get visits at Christmas as well as Epiphany.

Two months later is the biggest of all Cuban celebrations in Miami, a gigantic block party 2 miles long along the *Calle Ocho*, in the heart of Little Havana. All of Miami is invited to this mixture of cultural and religious celebration and old-fashioned Havana-style carnival, complete with strutting conga lines and Cuban dancers in full regalia.

Flights to freedom: Events like the *Calle Ocho* celebrations bring out the wide range of people that constitute the Cuban experience in South Florida. Beginning in 1959, when a small group of political and military henchmen of the deposed dictator Fulgencio Batista Zaldivar first arrived in the area, the Cuban influx into Miami has been anything but homogeneous. Almost every year has brought another new wave of refugees representing a new segment of Cuba's social, economic, political and racial strata disillusioned with Castro's communist experiment.

Although the numbers certainly were unprecedented, the 1959 influx of Latin American political émigrés seeking refuge in Miami was hardly unusual. Always a vacation land for Latin America's rich, the city also has long been a popular regrouping spot for Caribbean and Latin American revolutionaries and politicos waiting out interregnums in their rule or struggle for power. Even Fidel Castro stopped in South Florida to ponder his options before going home to overthrow Batista's bloody, US-backed dictatorship.

Castro's leftward drift, spurred by US hostility to his revolutionary regime, ironically coaxed hundreds of thousands of Cubans to flee to the US. Batista's discredited lackeys were the first to depart, followed soon thereafter by wealthier Cubans frightened by

Castro's socialist drift. A brain drain of professionals – doctors, lawyers, civil servants, journalists and old-style politicians – had begun by 1960. By 1962, middle-class technocrats, skilled workers and virtually every class of Cuban joined the exodus. By 1980, about 900,000 Cubans had left Cuba. At least half were settled in South Florida.

Guerrillas in the Everglades: For many Cubans the shock of exile, combined with language barriers and obsolete professional skills, has forced them to accept only a small share of the community's extraordinary success. Even today, the dishwasher in a Miami Beach restaurant or the man cleaning the rest

Left, a Cuban marks time to a Latin beat during festivities in Miami's Little Havana. **Right**, a local statue of the 19th-century Cuban revolutionary Antonio Maceo.

room at a southwest Miami service station may once have been a promising lawyer. A great many Cubans, especially those who turned to exile in their middle years, have not totally abandoned the dream of someday returning to a different Cuba. The lingering hopes and continuing attachment of large numbers of Cubans to the old land is reflected in the relative lack of Cuban participation in local politics and the existence of social, cultural and political organizations pegged to old Cuban institutions.

Hundreds of armed young men and some young women even go through guerrilla training in the Everglades wilderness just outside Dade County, presumably in prepa-

have been ineffective in combating terrorist activities. The local lore holds that this is partly because some of the most active terrorists were originally trained by the US Central Intelligence Agency when the CIA recruited Cuban exiles for missions in Cuba and other Latin American countries.

From pesos to dollars: But the battle that most South Florida Cubans have joined with greater success is the one to conquer the dollar. From a penniless lot – most Cubans left their country with only the two changes of clothes and one pair of shoes that Castro's men allowed – the exiled community has become an amazing economic success story. Initially, they got back on their feet with the

ration for a Cuban invasion. More recently, they have been joined by a newer group of refugees – former National Guardsmen from Nicaragua's Somoza regime.

Organizations like Alpha 66 and the clandestine Omega 7, which occasionally take their fight right into Cuba, thrived in the revival of the conservative spirit of Ronald Reagan's Washington. The zeal of some of these groups results in warfare in exile. Omega 7 and others have lashed out with bombings, beatings and assassinations of Cubans who have expressed public support of any sort of dialogue with the Castro regime. Local, state and federal authorities

help of US agencies. But, Cubans proudly point out, the doubling up of work shifts by middle-aged men and women and the relentless drive to improve their lot – often just to be able to take pictures of the new house or car and send it back to Cuba – may well account for the Cuban success of the 1960s.

In early 1981, economists estimated that the Cuban enclave of Little Havana alone generated an annual revenue of nearly $2.5 billion. Cubans owned or operated more than 18,000 businesses in Dade County, ranging from small coffee shops to hundreds of gas stations, stores, restaurants and markets, canning factories, car dealerships, garment shops, banks, savings and loans and multi-million-dollar construction and import firms. A small Cuban fishing industry thrives. Family income among Cubans has swelled to more than $18,000, just below that for non-Hispanic whites in Dade County. Before the boom spawned by the souring of Castro's revolution, only one Cuban was known among South Florida's banking elites. He was "Bebe" Rebozo, the confidante of Richard M. Nixon who later shared Nixon's notoriety after he convinced the president to be his neighbor in Key Biscayne. Today, South Florida has 16 Cuban bank presidents and scores of Cuban company directors.

But in 1980, Cuban gains were tempered

a clever way of converting embarrassment into a convenient mechanism for jettisoning some of his problems into the hands of the US – and Miami. Though comprising a minority among those who fled in the dramatic upsurge in refugees, many of these young men proved to be too unskilled and emotionally unstable to find employment or even housing in Miami's tight economy. Lumped together as Marielitos, because they left Cuba from the port of Mariel, they have been ostracized even by Miami's Cubans and are believed to be involved in a disproportionate share of violent crimes.

Stirred by the unequal treatment given to black Haitian refugees by the US, some

by several developments, particularly the forced inclusion of many mentally ill or criminally prone young men among the 125,000 refugees who fled Cuba in a mass exodus in that year's "freedom flotilla." US officials saw Castro's decision to include the problem men among the departing masses as

Left, Spanish is more widely spoken than English in parts of Miami. Thus, the *Miami Herald* obliges with a Spanish-language insert in its daily editions. **Above**, American soldiers assist a shrimp boat packed with Cuban refugees that arrived at Key West during the massive 1980 "freedom flotilla."

members of Miami's black population have been increasingly vocal and hostile towards Cubans. Some black civil rights leaders see Cubans as a barrier to the training and job opportunities that might improve the economic lot of native-born blacks and in white areas, such as the large middle-class Jewish enclaves throughout Dade County, complaints about the Cuban presence led to a successful drive to reject a referendum designating Miami as an officially bilingual city. But hostility from elements in both the black and white communities has existed all along, and it has not hindered the Cuban success story.

During the 19th century, long before it became fashionable in other social circles, blacks began migrating south to Florida. They didn't come for the sunshine or the beaches. They came to escape slavery. They crept under cover of darkness down the coast of Florida to a swampland inhabited by alligators and Indians. They fled masters in Georgia and the Carolinas.

To runaway slaves, Florida was a promised land of opportunity and freedom where, in 1860, a black might be found sitting on a jury with white men or tending to his own business affairs; where blacks owned property – $99,985 worth in 1860, according to the Federal census; where "free Negroes" blazed new ground as white plantation owners and their slaves watched in wonder.

"They represented the exception to the commonly held assumption that Negroes could live successfully only in a subordinate status," wrote Florida historian Charlton W. Tebeau.

In the 1980s, the image of Florida as a promised land for blacks lingers, despite the century of segregation, rebellion, integration and demonstrations that followed the heady days of emancipation,

"Florida blacks are told that Florida is a wonderful place," said Dr Victoria Warner, head of the sociology department of Florida A&M University (which has been the state's predominant black university since 1887). "We have to tell our graduates, 'Pack your bags and go where the opportunities are,' " said Warner. "We practically have to shove them out of the state."

The Old South: Like northern whites, many black Floridians have bought the image of Florida as a land of waving palm trees, success and the good life, Warner said.

Dr Charles U. Smith, head of graduate studies at Florida A&M and the first black county chairman of a political party in Florida, said blacks have looked on Florida as different from the rest of the South since the days

Left, a young Florida woman proudly asserts her African heritage through her dress and jewelry. **Right**, the late North Florida civil rights leader, C.K. Steele.

when runaway slaves found a haven here.

"The black population of Florida has always tended to regard itself as being different from the old South, the plantation South," said Smith. "They pride themselves on living in a more favorable climate."

One reason is geography. Not much of Florida was even settled during the confining days of slavery. Only the northern tier was dotted by cotton and tobacco plantations. Then, too, there were the governors. Leroy Collins began his term in the late

1950s as a moderate segregationist, but later gained national attention as a new, more liberal Southern governor who at least talked favorably about the rights of blacks. Reubin Askew generally is credited by historians with being the first governor to follow up talk with action by bringing blacks into government at all levels.

But that isn't to say that blacks have led charmed lives in Florida. The state was indeed part of the old plantation South, if only in its most northern reaches. In the 1860 census, 61,475 slaves were counted on the plantations of North Florida. In the years leading up to the civil rights victories of the

1950s and 1960s, Florida without question belonged to the segregationist South.

"Until 1947," recalled Smith, "blacks weren't allowed on Miami Beach after dark. Twenty years ago, in Palm Beach, blacks weren't allowed to swim in the Atlantic Ocean International waters."

Restaurants, buses, hotels, public buildings and schools were all segregated in Florida. In a May 1956 state-conducted survey, 60 percent of the parents of white high school seniors said that black youths should not be admitted to the white universities of Florida under any circumstances. For years, blacks truly lived on the "wrong side of the tracks" along the eastern coast

white Northerners has reduced that to only 13 percent. But the number of blacks in the state has more than doubled in the years from 1950 to 1980, from about 600,000 to 1.3 million. That makes Florida sixth in the US in total black population. In 1980 three-fourths inhabited urban areas – Jacksonville, Fort Lauderdale-Miami, Orlando and St Petersburg-Tampa. Sixty years ago the majority lived in rural areas.

Plantation mentality: Unlike their urban counterparts who escaped the last vestiges of the plantation system by leaving, many rural blacks still find themselves tied financially and politically to the paternalism of whites.

"It's plantation mentality that's present

from Jacksonville to Miami. Whites lived to the east of the railroad tracks, where the ocean was; the blacks inland to the west. As elsewhere in the South, outward manifestations of segregation and discrimination have faded in Florida.

"I think the biggest change is in access," said Smith. "We have access now. I think the sense of freedom is there. This is not to say that everything is good. But for many people, things have changed."

Their lifestyles, numbers and locations have also changed. In 1900, blacks constituted a large part of the state's population – 44 percent. But the influx of millions of

there," theorized Bob Hall, a doctoral student who specialized in black history at Florida State University "Whenever I'm working on a project and having trouble fantasizing the sights and sounds of slavery, I go to Gadsden County," he said, "I can hear the accents of slavery in the speech. I can see it in the attitudes of the people."

Until the late 1960s, Gadsden County in the Panhandle – nearly 60 percent black – remained tied to the era when shade tobacco was the main crop and blacks were the work force that harvested it. But one town within Gadsden has changed – Gretna, where 88 percent of the 1,448 residents are black. A white minority ruled the town until 1971. In 1981, the mayor, all five city commissioners, the city administrator and the city clerk were black.

Mayor Earnest Barkley, Jr, was part of an all-black slate elected in 1971 after a massive voter registration drive. "That's when we discovered there weren't any blacks at all on the books in Gretna," Barkley said.

Gretna isn't the oldest or the most famous of Florida's black-run towns. Eatonville in Central Florida holds that distinction. When the town was incorporated in 1888, it may well have been the first black community in the nation.

"Colored people of the United States –

for deeding land to former slaves. One suggested that the bottom half of the Florida peninsula, then virtually uninhabited, be set aside for black homesteaders. The plan called for 50,000 former slaves from Virginia to be relocated on 500,000 acres of federal land in South Florida. The scheme never materialized, but a limited homesteading program was approved.

The first black in recorded history to visit Florida is known only as "Little Steven." He accompanied Narváez on his 1527 expedition to Florida. Virtually every Spanish expedition into Florida included black soldiers. Historians agree that under Spanish rule Florida had a reputation as a place where

solve the great race problem by securing a home in Eatonville, Florida, a Negro city governed by Negroes," implored the *Eatonville Speaker* in an 1889 advertisement. In 1980, of 2,185 residents, only 30 were white.

In fact, all South Florida might have been a black community had a plan of the post-Civil War's Freedmen's Bureau worked out. The bureau, responsible for helping blacks adjust to emancipation, devised several plans

Left, Florida blacks still celebrate religion in traditional ways like this river baptism. **Above**, a handsome young Florida family.

blacks could get ahead largely unhampered by the restraints evident elsewhere in America. Both Pensacola and St Augustine had a heritage of intermarriage. Many blacks there became skilled artisans, learning crafts reserved elsewhere for white men.

Under the Seminoles: Runaway slaves who sought refuge in Florida also found the Seminole Indians and their swampy Florida existence a better way of life than the plantations. In 1838, 1,400 blacks were living with the Seminoles, only 200 of them as slaves. The Seminoles demanded little of their slaves, historians say. An annual tithe of corn to the owner was often the only requirement.

The most famous runaway, Abraham, began his life with the Seminoles as a slave, but proved such an invaluable asset that they freed him. He served as a translator and advisor to Chief Micanopy and became a leader in the Second Seminole War.

By the 1840s, white Florida planters joined their southern neighbors in becoming terrified of the threat posed to the plantation system by free blacks. They passed laws requiring all free blacks to have white guardians and ordering free black sailors to remain onboard ship while in Florida ports.

When the Civil War broke out, 1,200 blacks from Florida joined the Union Army. But more than 60,000 slaves remained on plantations. In the years of reconstruction that followed the Civil War, blacks in Florida enjoyed the fruits of a new liberalism. At one point as many as 19 freedmen served in the state legislature. More significant was the appointment of a black, Jonathan C. Gibbs, as the state's secretary of state in 1868 and later as superintendent of public instruction. Gibbs was known widely as a great orator, but after only 18 months in office he died of a seizure. Some suspected poisoning. Gibbs had so many enemies he slept in his attic with a brace of pistols.

It was more than a hundred years before another black served in the Florida Cabinet. Jesse J. McCrary, Jr, of Miami was appointed secretary of state in 1978. Earlier this century, Mary McLeod Bethune also instilled pride in Florida's black community when she single-handedly established a school, Bethune-Cookman, now a distinguished Daytona Beach institution.

Strides and setbacks: Blacks in Florida made their greatest strides toward political office in the 1970s. Governor Reubin Askew appointed blacks to the Cabinet, the state Supreme Court, the university system's Board of Regents and to important positions in other government departments.

Those appointments were major victories for blacks in Florida, who demonstrated along with the rest of the South's activists in a 1956 bus boycott in Tallahassee, and in Daytona Beach, Jacksonville and St Augustine in the 1960s. Around the state, blacks fought for the right to eat at lunch counters and to sit in the front section of public buses.

Victoria Warner, director of the sociology department at Florida A&M, remembered what life was like for her in the early 1950s in Tallahassee. In those days, she was the sole black member of the area chapter of a national social work association.

"They had to call me to ask me if I was coming to the monthly meeting," she recalled. "If I was, they would have to meet in some out-of-the way place, and they couldn't have a meal. They couldn't eat with me."

After the civil rights era passed, race relations were quiet until 1980, when blacks in a Miami ghetto called Liberty City rioted and killed to avenge the death of another black, insurance man Arthur McDuffie. Eighteen whites and blacks died in the violence.

Warner and Smith viewed the eruption in Miami as not just a race riot, but an economic protest. The small group of blacks who rioted were fed up with a system that not only – in their view – led to the death of a black man at police hands but allowed them to be beaten out of their bread-and-butter jobs by Cuban immigrants willing to take lower-than-low wages. The acquittal of four white police officers in McDuffie's death may have been the match that sparked the violence, but economic frustrations were the kindling.

But Smith can see good as well as tragedy in the incident. Blacks' insistence that they should not have to accept less than a minimum wage reflected a new pride.

Dissolving divisions: Population shifts to urban areas, however, have diluted the political force of blacks, Smith said. On the other hand, there has also been a blurring of old racial lines that have long divided blacks and whites. In the 1990s, more blacks are likely to share common goals and experiences with whites of the same economic and professional level than with blacks who live in the extremes of the socio-economic scale.

Black Floridians also have a number of encouraging role models. In addition to Florida A&M University's faculty and administration, predominantly black for years, black students can also see colleagues heading state departments, working in middle-level management in the state bureaucracy and performing other highly visible jobs.

"They're not in charge of anything much yet," said Smith. "But they're close."

Right, children help their families work at plantation jobs like sharecropping tobacco on this farm in Quincy in the Panhandle.

Florida's Crackers and Yankees *reside* in the same state, but *live* in different worlds.

That is the bottom line on the two major groups within the white population of Florida. Crackers represent the state's link with its past, its rural heritage of plantation politics and sharecropping with a few acres and a mule. Yankees are indicative of a changing Florida, of high-density subdivisions, crowded beaches and burgeoning metropolises with active nightlife.

Depending on how loosely you define the name is somewhat easier to pin down. The term began as British slang for colonists living in New England in the days before the United States won its independence from the mother country. In Florida parlance, however, a Yankee is anyone who hails from any of the northeastern or midwestern regions of the United States.

As for Crackers... some Yankee will tell you a Cracker is anyone who speaks his English with a drawl, has grits for breakfast more often than once a year, and uses the

two terms, Crackers and Yankees account for between 50 and 70 percent of the state's population. But quite a few cultural distinctions separate them. They live in different parts of the state, eat different foods, speak differently, and pursue their occupations and leisure in different ways.

The Yankee doodle dandies: So what is a Yankee and what is a Cracker, and how do you tell them apart?

Let's take Yankees first, since their nick-

Left, a native north Florida farmer relaxes atop his peanut pile. **Above**, a *Harper's Weekly* illustration of "Florida Crackers Going to Church."

contraction "y'all" to address a number of people ranging from one to hundreds. In short, anyone who gives overt signs of having been born in Dixie. Some draw the line at those native Southerners born in Georgia or Florida, descendants of the earliest settlers of those two regions.

Then there are the purists, like Florida writer Ernest Lyons in his essay, *A Florida Cracker Came Into His Own.* "Your dyed-in-the-wool, honest-to-God, genuine Florida Cracker traces his family back to the Indian wars," Lyons wrote. "Their folks were here when Colonel Zachary Taylor and his troops fought chiefs Wildcat, Alligator and Sam

Jones at the battle of Okeechobee in 1837.

"The Florida Cracker is as closely rooted to his pine and palmetto ranchland as the Tennessee mountaineer to his blue hills. He may rise to be a supreme court justice or a governor but his heart stays at the ranch with his cows, catch-dogs and rattlesnakes. His ancestors made their own salt from the sea, their own homespun from patches of cotton, ran wild hogs and wild cattle, lived off the land."

Lyons got even more specific. He said the truly genuine Florida Cracker has a surname like Platt, Carlton, Rowell, Hendry, Bass, Cash, Alderman and Whiddon.

So, depending on exactly whose defini-

Laird said social and political philosophy has a lot to do with a native Floridian's acceptance and even willingness to be known as a Cracker.

"The proud Crackers think of themselves as the common people, opposed to privilege and special interests," Laird said.

One of the first recorded usages of the word was in *The Life and Death of King John*, a 1590 play by William Shakespeare. "What Cracker is this same that deafs our ears with this abundance of superfluous breath?" asks the Duke of Austria in the play.

In those days, a Cracker was a storyteller of no mean accomplishment. And that apparently is why the nickname was originally

tion you accept, Crackers can encompass a rather broad or exceedingly narrow slice of humanity. They can be anyone with strong roots in the South, someone hailing only from the extreme southeastern part of that region, or a very exclusive group of those born and bred in the Sunshine State.

But visitors to Florida should be careful when they use the nickname. It has been interpreted in some quarters to mean "poor, white trash," so some native Floridians are touchy when called Crackers. Florida author Allen Morris advised his readers that it was wise to use the nickname with a quick smile.

Still, Florida scholar Angus McKenzie

bestowed on the roughhewn ancestors of the present-day Platts, Hendrys and Whiddons. "I should explain to your lordship what is meant by Crackers, a name they have got by being great boasters," one British observer reported to his superior in the period before Florida gained statehood.

Other theories on how the nickname evolved involve corn and cowboys. The vegetable theory says the nickname was bestowed upon native Floridians because they cracked their corn to make grits. In the other concept, Crackers won their title because Florida ranchers had a habit of making loud snaps with their cattle whips.

"Cowboys on horses shouting at the tops of their lungs and whips cracking like pistol shots," said Laird, telling of one such cattle drive he saw during his youth in North Florida. "It was a sight to see and hear, and those Crackers were something."

Whatever the source, the nickname stuck. Its early recipients carved a bountiful lumber, farming and ranching domain out of the semi-tropical jungle that once was inland Florida. Today, some of their descendants live in those same inland enclaves on land passed down directly from those hearty ancestors, often working at agricultural enterprises begun by their forefathers.

The invasion of the Tin Can Tourists: The

Florida's average citizen would be 27 years old instead of 35, because many of those who migrate from the north are retirees. Indeed, at last measure, Florida's death rate was 11 per thousand, 16 percent higher than America's national average.

Much of the groundwork for the population surge was laid by a pair of Connecticut Yankees, Henry B. Plant and Henry M. Flagler, who built the railroads that sparked a land and building boom. During that boom, many Northerners got their first peek at the state. Called Tin Can Tourists, they came by train or auto, stayed in impromptu tent cities and ate from tins. Many liked what they saw and adopted a vision of Florida that eventu-

mass influx of Yankees changed the face of Florida from predominantly rural and sparsely populated to an urbanized state. Things would be different in Florida were it not for the population shift of the last four decades, the mass migration from the North to the Sunshine State. Florida would have thousands fewer people than Minnesota. As it is, Florida has more people than Minnesota, North Dakota, Nebraska and South Dakota *combined*.

Left, Plant City citizens mimic their portraits in a John Briggs'mural. **Above**, an all-purpose cap shades a stroller from the Miami Beach sun.

ally emerged as its popular image in less tropical regions of the US – a sunny playland where the lifestyle was more pleasant than back home. Nonetheless, many returned to the North, convinced that Miami was a nice place to visit but a lousy place to live.

A large percentage of Miami's new residents were folks with a Cracker heritage of their own. As late as 1940, a full 40 percent of the white males in the Miami area had been born in Georgia. World War II marked the watershed. Hundreds of thousands of Yankees were assigned to military bases near Jacksonville, Pensacola, Tampa and other Florida cities. Many servicemen came right back to Florida after the war, fueling an 81.5 percent growth rate during the 1940s.

That set the stage for the massive growth of the next three decades. Now, 30 percent of the state's population hails from the Northeast or Midwest, while only 22 percent come from southern states other than Florida. The top states feeding Florida's ongoing population boom are New York, New Jersey, Ohio, Michigan and Illinois.

The relocated northerners don't share much of a common ethnic heritage. In that, they differ from Crackers, who usually have a strongly developed sense of place keyed to their upbringing in the rural South. But Yankees have remade South Florida in the image of the crowded Northeast.

If the newcomers are a polyglot of ethnic origins, they do seem to share one important thing – that vision of Florida implanted in the national consciousness during the land boom of the 1920s. "I thought the whole state would be like one of those picture postcards of Miami Beach," said one woman who relocated from the North in the mid-1970s. "I was pleased to discover that wasn't true, but I think some small part of me still sees the state in those terms."

The Northerners tend to concentrate in the Atlantic or Gulf coasts of the peninsula. The last two census evaluations show all 10 of the state's fastest-growing regions are in coastal and peninsular Florida.

That trend has produced crowded neighborhoods, crowded streets, crowded restaurants and crowded beaches.

Despite the crowding, Yankees remember why they came to The Sunshine State. "I'll never go back," said Russ Chilcoat, a native of landlocked Pennsylvania. "I like living near the water, the sand, the surf."

Native Floridians are harder to pin down on the subject of what they love about their state. "It's my home," said one lifelong Florida resident. "I was born and raised here and it's just my home and I love it."

"I don't like that there are tall buildings on the beach where I grew up," said Pat Hendry, a native of Daytona Beach. "We used to have just cottages there," Often the product of a small town, the Florida Cracker shows signs of feeling threatened by the newcomers.

"It seems like they are a completely different kind of people," said one county official in the Panhandle. "I think their way of opera-

tion and their background is totally different. It's a faster lifestyle, and I kind of like things the way they used to be."

Subtle differences: So there are some tensions between the Yankees and Crackers. Crackers feel that the changes are happening too quickly and are not necessarily for the better. Yankees feel that Crackers are too wedded to the outmoded folkways of another place and time. Friction between the two groups is rare, but it sometimes shows in small ways.

"There is an obvious sense of pride among natives," wrote Florida publisher and editor Harris Mullins. "They usually refrain from throwing their distinction verbally in the

face of non-natives. They inject it subtly by reference."

Somewhat tongue in cheek, Mullins outlined basic differences between the two groups by noting that natives: never go swimming after Labor Day, dislike Miami Beach, live within 12 minutes of the office, dislike crowded beaches, real estate taxes, crisply cooked vegetables and lamb, but love pork, cool days, politics, and doing business with their old friends.

Above, a tourist sprouts a familiar set of ears. **Right**, a mascot dear to University of Florida Crackers and Yankees – the Florida Gator.

The post-war baby boom made big news in US demographics in the 1950s. But Florida experienced another kind of population surge, one that didn't crowd hospital delivery rooms. It needed no obstetricians or pediatricians, and it didn't send the state's educators scurrying to build more kindergartens.

Florida's demographic phenomenon was a far removed grandparent boom. It was the mass migration of retirees to the Sunshine State, a trend that began more than 50 years ago and continues.

This in-migration of senior citizens has reshaped Florida, transforming former villages like Clearwater and Fort Myers into overnight metropolises, creating a demand for dozens of service industries, and making retirement checks one of the state's major sources of cold cash. It also has given Florida the nation's highest concentration of elderly residents. That distinction, when combined with the influx of honeymooners, has earned Florida a dubious reputation as a "land of the newlywed and the nearly dead."

End of the rainbow?: Of the state's 12 million residents, nearly 2 million are 65 years old or older. That means one of every five Floridians is a senior citizen.

"Florida's population mix is what the rest of the country can expect in 2010," said John Stokesberry, director of Florida's programs to aid the elderly. "The rest of the country won't have so high a concentration of older citizens until the second decade of the 21st century, when the baby boom generation reaches 65."

In 15 of Florida's 67 counties, more than a third of the populace is over 60. Senior citizens number more than 40 percent of the residents in five of those counties. In Charlotte County on the state's southern Gulf Coast, retirees account for an astounding 52.5 percent of the population.

And the trend shows no signs of abating. If anything, it is gathering steam. Stokesberry estimated that in recent years Florida has

attracted between 15,000 and 18,000 older citizens every month. "Sometimes it seems overwhelming," he said.

Indeed, it appears that Ponce de León's search for the Fountain of Youth may not have been in vain. Many retirees find Florida a place where they can enjoy a pleasant place in the sun. And tales of chronically ill people going on to live long lives in the state are legion. Take the case of genius inventor, Thomas Edison, for example. Doctors said he was in bad shape before he began winter-

ing in Florida at age 38, but he lived on and continued to inventively reshape the world until age 84.

The retire-to-Florida syndrome has become part of the national mythology, particularly in the Northeast and Midwest; it's a final installment of an American Dream that helps so many adults get through their homebuying and childrearing years.

For millions of working Americans, Florida is their just reward for decades of labor in the landlocked and seasonally cold northern states. Retirement here is what they promise themselves on all those snowy winter mornings when the car refuses to start, and during

Left, a senior swinger swats a hit in St Petersburg's unretiring Kids and Kubs baseball league. **Right**, Florida's senior citizens even ride motorcycles.

those endless business meetings when the boss refuses to listen to reason. It has been that way since the 1930s when Florida began to attract its first influx of retirees.

"That's when electronic cooling became generally available, fans and eventually air-conditioning," noted Dr William G. Bell, director of Florida State University's gerontology center. "Before than, year-round retirement in Florida really wasn't very practical. It was just too hot here." But Bell added that the state's warm climate is an attribute that has traditionally lured the elderly.

Financial factors: There are also strong and pressing financial reasons for Florida's popularity among retirees.

nomic strata and a distinct area of the US. "There's no mystery to that," Bell explained. "People tend to go where they will feel at home, where they expect to find others with similar backgrounds."

So, retirees from the Midwest flock to the central Gulf Coast, from Tampa Bay south to Fort Myers. Often, these people are former white-collar workers with secure pensions and conservative political bents.

Retirees from the urban Northeast usually go to extreme South Florida, the Fort Lauderdale and Miami areas. Their politics are usually more liberal than their Midwestern counterparts. A sizable number of them are Jewish, and many are former blue-collar

"Florida probably is one of the top 10 states in terms of favorable tax conditions," Stokesberry said. The state has no income tax and it offers homeowners partial exemptions from property taxes; in addition, it levies a smaller tax on inheritances than most states. "A lot of people come down here for those financial reasons alone," he said.

In the early years, the bulk of retirees settled in Miami Beach and St Petersburg. But, in the last two decades, retirees have grouped throughout South Florida, particularly along the Gulf and South Atlantic coasts. Each section of Florida seems to draw its senior citizens from a different socio-eco-

workers and trade-union members.

But where does the wealthy retiree go, the person who couldn't care less whether the Social Security check arrives on time, who buys General Motors stock but who drives about – or is chaufeured – in a Rolls? That person retires to Palm Beach.

Jacksonville is popular with black retirees. It is also preferred by military retirees, a distinction it shares with the Pensacola area.

Retired life in Florida varies according to individual tastes… and the money one has to pursue those tastes. Some buy homes in subdivisions specifically oriented toward the elderly – well-manicured blocks of suburban housing similar to those back home, except, of course, for the palm trees.

Other new retirees rent an apartment, or rent or buy a mobile home in a trailer park catering to older people. Purchasing a condominium apartment is another option that has gained popularity in the last decade. The standard condominium is a tall apartment building with dozens of one or two-bedroom units. Residents own their apartments and pay a monthly fee for upkeep of common grounds, which give them freedom from maintenance worries.

To the shuffleboard court by adult tricycle: Not all of Florida's retirees are full-time residents. Some come during the winter, and return North in the spring. Their migratory habits have earned them the nickname "snowbirds," because they follow northern fowl that fly South for the winter.

And what about the lifestyle in that house, apartment or trailer? Again, it's a matter of choice and economics. Some throw themselves into a hobby, some secure part-time employment, and some just while away the hours in the warm sun.

There are several traditional symbols of retirement communities. One is the tricycle, which is popular because it handles more easily than a two-wheeler, while still providing ample exercise.

Another is lawn bowling and shuffleboard courts. Most cities with sizable retirement populations have acres of them. Lawn bowlers knock down pins on grassy services with smaller, lighter balls than those used on wooden lanes. Shuffleboard requires that players shove a disc down a concrete court to score points. Both involve little strain or exertion and allow ample opportunity to socialize.

Seniors clubs and "adults only" neighborhoods are also prevalent. The former are social organizations restricted to people 55 or older. Big band music of yesteryear is featured at weekly dances. Card games and fashion shows fill other free-time. "Adults only" cater to elderly people who want to escape noisy children and the changing proclivities of the modern world. Most bar children from living on the premises, although

Left, Sunday morning strollers on a St Petersburg street corner. **Right**, another golden ager preaches patriotic politics.

grandkids can visit. Sun City Center near Ruskin on the West Coast is a prime example of a planned activities community designed for thousands of elderly who retire there.

Silver-haired politicians: Political activity is another important aspect of Florida's retirees. Many find local politics a hobby and go on to become mayors and councilmen in their communities. This syndrome has helped mold the elderly into a potent state political force. Write off the candidate for Florida governor who does not court the senior citizen vote by making regular campaign stops in the condominium clusters and mobile home parks.

The Silver-Haired legislature, a collection of over-60 seniors elected by their peers,

gathers annually in the state capital. They don't have the power to pass laws, but make influential recommendations to the real legislature regarding ways of improving laws affecting Florida's senior citizens.

Many retirees have the money to back up their political convictions, but pockets of destitute old men and women do, of course, exist. St Petersburg's downtown area has become known as "The Battle Zone" because those who inhabit its cheap tenement homes and dilapidated hotels are easy prey for muggers and thieves. Miami's South Beach has such a huge number of penniless and lonely old folks dumped there by heartless children and relatives that some call it "God's Waiting Room." But impoverished retirees are the exception. Retirement income pumps $12 billions annually into the state. Nearly a third of Florida's real estate transactions involve the elderly. More than 75 percent of the homes headed by retirees are owned by them.

So, with money, political clout and leisure activities aimed at their age group, retirement in Florida is the perfect answer for everyone approaching the sunset years. Right? Wrong! Many ultimately find that Florida just isn't for them. They get depressed by the self-imposed segregation of hundreds of thousands of old people. They

freedom from the work-a-day world a renew a college career he abandoned in 1912. He obtained his master's degree in history from Florida State University in the mid-1970s, and then, at 92, became the oldest man in history to earn a doctorate.

"I was 80 when my son suggested that our business could do just as well without me as with me, and I wasn't sure what the future held for me," Conner said. "Going back to school was the best thing I ever did."

Other retirees turn to sports they never had the time to conquer in their youth. St Petersburg's Kids and Kubs play in a unique baseball league where the aged, not the young, have the edge in spring tryouts. You must be

miss their home towns and the opportunity to mingle with the young and vigorous.

"I don't like it here," said one dissatisfied retiree from Iowa. "It's too hot and there isn't anything to do. I've lived in some fine places in my life and this just isn't one of them."

"Retirement to Florida sometimes produces a lemon instead of a juicy orange," wrote essayist Ernest Lyons.

Lyons and other experts advise retirees to rent or travel in Florida for a year until they decide if it's right for them. Experts also advocate that the elderly pursue some project or leisure interest that will keep life meaningful. Virgil Conner, for example, used his

at least 75 years old to qualify for a team. One player was still swinging at age 95.

So, indeed, many of the elderly do find happiness here – that pot of golden sunshine at the end of the rainbow. And there's one sight in Florida more moving than any brilliant sunset or spectacular seascape. It's the poignant scene of elderly couples holding hands while strolling on the beach, nuzzling each other on a park bench or stealing kisses in a darkened movie theater.

Above, bench-warming passes the time for some aging Floridians. **Right**, others join in a communal adult trike hike at their mobile home park.

PLACES

There's just too much to see waiting in front of me,
And I know that I just can't go wrong
With these changes in latitudes, changes in attitudes.
—Jimmy Buffett

With those words, Florida-based balladeer Buffett put his guitar-pickin' finger on a fundamental reason for Florida's popularity as a retreat for routine-weary Americans. No other place in the continental United States lies in more southern latitudes. Some folks have become so addicted to the tranquilizing effects of Florida's balmy climes, they return year after year for another dose. It's the national sedative.

Nature laid the groundwork for this annual people invasion by providing the beaches and forests. Then man added hotel and amusement complexes. Now, it's a rare corner of Florida that doesn't have at least a gator farm or orange juice stand within jogging distance.

Yet Florida is much too big, much too diverse to swallow in one gulp. The following pages have been designed to give you Florida in smaller sips.

The state has been subdivided into seven sections. The Central Florida tourism hub revolves around Walt Disney World but extends as far south as Sebring, north to the Ocala National Forest and west to Lakeland. The beach-fringed West Coast has Tampa-St Petersburg as its nucleus, Marco Island as its southern end and Cedar Key at its northern tip. South Florida is anchored by Metropolitan Miami (whose urban tentacles stretch to Fort Pierce), but is bounded by acres of rural lands and towns like Homestead in the south and Palmdale to the west. The East Coast strip stretches from Melbourne to Jacksonville. North Florida encompasses the Pensacola to Tallahassee Panhandle region as well as the "pan" – Gainesville, Cross Creek and the rugged Big Bend country. The Everglades includes the Big Cypress Swamp. The travel section winds up in the Florida Keys, crowned by their uncommon capital, Key West.

Preceding pages: roadside rest stop. **Left,** road hawg.

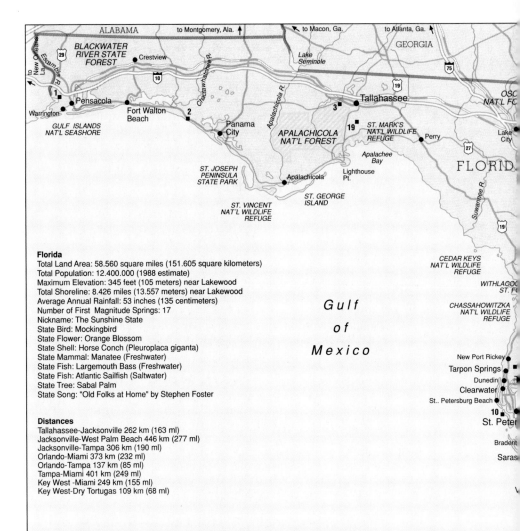

ALABAMA → to Montgomery, Ala. ← to Macon, Ga. to Atlanta, Ga. →

GEORGIA

BLACKWATER RIVER STATE FOREST

Crestview

to New Orleans, La.

Escambia R.

29

10

Chactawhatchee R.

Lake Seminole

Apalachicola R.

75

19

1

Pensacola

Warrington

GULF ISLANDS NAT'L SEASHORE

Fort Walton Beach

2

Panama City

Tallahassee

3

19

ST. MARK'S NAT'L WILDLIFE REFUGE

Perry

APALACHICOLA NAT'L FOREST

Apalachee Bay

Lake City

27

FLORIDA

ST. JOSEPH PENINSULA STATE PARK

Apalachicola

Lighthouse Pt.

ST. GEORGE ISLAND

ST. VINCENT NAT'L WILDLIFE REFUGE

Suwannee R.

19

OSC NAT'L FO

CEDAR KEYS NAT'L WILDLIFE REFUGE

WITHLACOO ST. F

Florida

Total Land Area: 58.560 square miles (151.605 square kilometers)
Total Population: 12.400.000 (1988 estimate)
Maximum Elevation: 345 feet (105 meters) near Lakewood
Total Shoreline: 8.426 miles (13.557 meters) near Lakewood
Average Annual Rainfall: 53 inches (135 centimeters)
Number of First Magnitude Springs: 17
Nickname: The Sunshine State
State Bird: Mockingbird
State Flower: Orange Blossom
State Shell: Horse Conch (Pleuroplaca giganta)
State Mammal: Manatee (Freshwater)
State Fish: Largemouth Bass (Freshwater)
State Fish: Atlantic Sailfish (Saltwater)
State Tree: Sabal Palm
State Song: "Old Folks at Home" by Stephen Foster

Distances

Tallahassee-Jacksonville 262 km (163 ml)
Jacksonville-West Palm Beach 446 km (277 ml)
Jacksonville-Tampa 306 km (190 ml)
Orlando-Miami 373 km (232 ml)
Orlando-Tampa 137 km (85 ml)
Tampa-Miami 401 km (249 ml)
Key West -Miami 249 km (155 ml)
Key West-Dry Tortugas 109 km (68 ml)

Gulf

of

Mexico

CHASSAHOWITZKA NAT'L WILDLIFE REFUGE

New Port Rickey

Tarpon Springs

Dunedin

Clearwater

St.. Petersburg Beach

10

St. Peter

Bradent

Saras

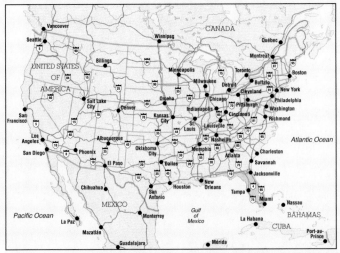

Vancouver

Seattle

CANADA

Winnipeg

Québec

Montreal

87

UNITED STATES OF AMERICA

Billings

Minneapolis

Toronto

Boston

Milwaukee

Detroit

Buffalo

New York

Salt Lake City

Omaha

Cleveland

Chicago

Pittsburgh

Philadelphia

San Francisco

Denver

Kansas City

Indianapolis

Cincinnati

Washington

Richmond

St Louis

Louisville

Los Angeles

Albuquerque

Oklahoma City

Nashville

San Diego

Phoenix

Memphis

Atlanta

Charleston

El Paso

Dallas

Savannah

Atlantic Ocean

Chihuahua

Houston

New Orleans

Jacksonville

San Antonio

Tampa

Miami

MEXICO

Gulf of Mexico

La Habana

Nassau

BAHAMAS

Pacific Ocean

La Paz

Monterrey

CUBA

Port-au-Prince

Mazatlán

DRY TORTUG

18

Guadalajara

Mérida

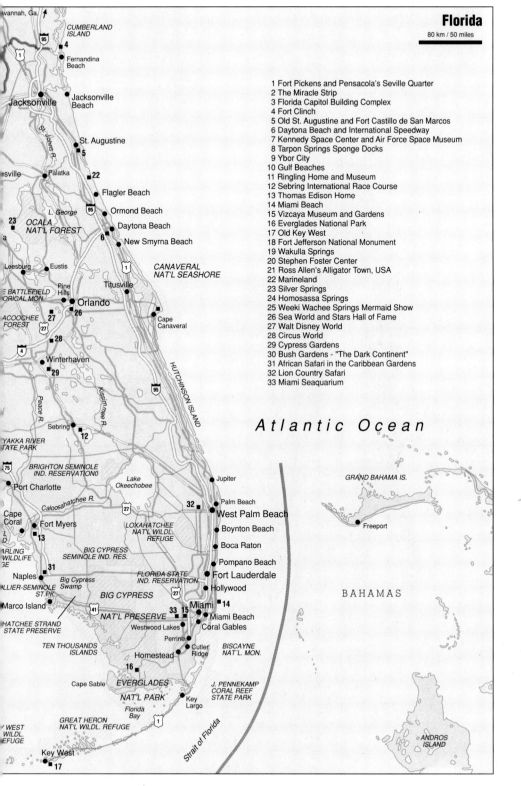

Florida

80 km / 50 miles

1 Fort Pickens and Pensacola's Seville Quarter
2 The Miracle Strip
3 Florida Capitol Building Complex
4 Fort Clinch
5 Old St. Augustine and Fort Castillo de San Marcos
6 Daytona Beach and International Speedway
7 Kennedy Space Center and Air Force Space Museum
8 Tarpon Springs Sponge Docks
9 Ybor City
10 Gulf Beaches
11 Ringling Home and Museum
12 Sebring International Race Course
13 Thomas Edison Home
14 Miami Beach
15 Vizcaya Museum and Gardens
16 Everglades National Park
17 Old Key West
18 Fort Jefferson National Monument
19 Wakulla Springs
20 Stephen Foster Center
21 Ross Allen's Alligator Town, USA
22 Marineland
23 Silver Springs
24 Homosassa Springs
25 Weeki Wachee Springs Mermaid Show
26 Sea World and Stars Hall of Fame
27 Walt Disney World
28 Circus World
29 Cypress Gardens
30 Bush Gardens - "The Dark Continent"
31 African Safari in the Caribbean Gardens
32 Lion Country Safari
33 Miami Seaquarium

Atlantic Ocean

BAHAMAS

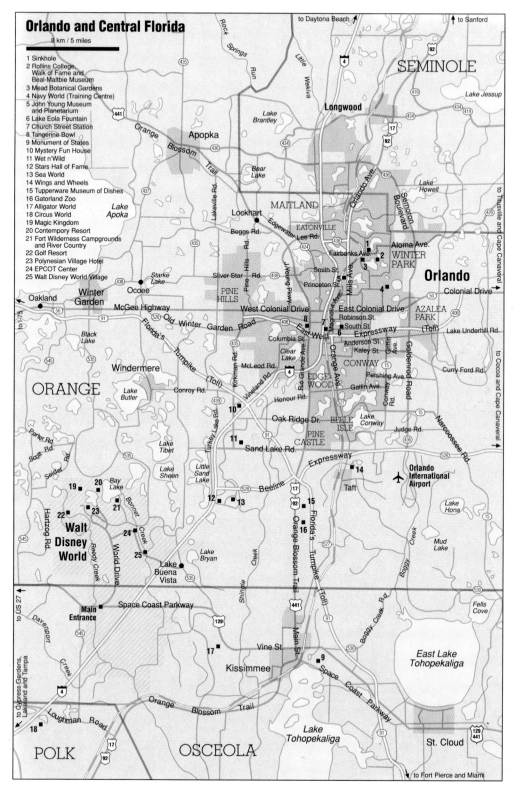

Orlando and Central Florida

8 km / 5 miles

1 Sinkhole
2 Rollins College,
  Walk of Fame and
  Beal-Maltbie Museum
3 Mead Botanical Gardens
4 Navy World (Training Centre)
5 John Young Museum
  and Planetarium
6 Lake Eola Fountain
7 Church Street Station
8 Tangerine Bowl
9 Monument of States
10 Mystery Fun House
11 Wet n'Wild
12 Stars Hall of Fame
13 Sea World
14 Wings and Wheels
15 Tupperware Museum of Dishes
16 Gatorland Zoo
17 Alligator World
18 Circus World
19 Magic Kingdom
20 Contempory Resort
21 Fort Wilderness Campgrounds
  and River Country
22 Golf Resort
23 Polynesian Village Hotel
24 EPCOT Center
25 Walt Disney World Village

The lake-studded, river-creased acres of Central Florida have long lured tourists seeking escapes from reality. They came to walk in gardens hung with Spanish moss and brimming with flowers, to gaze at tropical fish through sheer spring water, to eye mounds of lethargic alligators an arm's length away. Then, a famous Hollywood mouse set up shop in the neighborhood. The resulting explosion of tourist attractions was unmatched in volume and variety. Droves of new visitors have flocked to Central Florida to experience self-contained worlds of pleasure that use new technology to tease and massage the senses. Simple joys like fishing have made room for computers that can resurrect long-dead presidents and trainers who teach killer whales to play basketball. Simple and complex diversions abound. Pick an orange from a tree or hike through a cypress swamp. Ride a rocket through dark hills in space or a roller coaster through citrus groves. The choice is yours.

WALT DISNEY WORLD

In 1967, the Florida legislature created an entity in its heartland unlike any place else in the state – or on earth, for that matter. It granted a private corporation the privilege to turn 27,400 acres – 42 square miles of land, twice the area of Manhattan – into a kingdom, complete with corresponding powers.

The kingdom takes its name from a waterway bordering the land – the **Reedy Creek Improvement District**. But that unpretentious moniker belies the influential nature of its enterprise. Reedy Creek is a governmental unit with full power to enact and enforce building codes, construct roads, carve out canals and lakes and enforce the law with its own security team.

Within Reedy Creek, two cities called **Bay Lake** and **Lake Buena Vista** each have their own mayor, hold elections and meet all requirements of Florida municipalities. Despite occasional criticism of its vast powers, Reedy Creek has pioneered advanced technology systems most cities only dream of employing. It utilizes the water hyacinth to treat waste water. It has the world's first totally electronic phone system. It boasts the world's fifth largest navy, carrying 10 million people a year on more than 400 ships, including such uncommon vessels as submarines, stern wheel steamboats, jungle launches and European swan boats. Its land transport system revolves around a noiseless, elevated, air-conditioned and computerized monorail.

Florida statutes call it the Reedy Creek Improvement District. The world knows it as the **Walt Disney World Vacation Kingdom**.

It claims to be the world's top tourist attraction – and, in fact, outdraws all but a handful of entire countries. More than 240 million people visited between 1971 and 1985 which would make it the world's sixth most populous nation if they had all gone on the same day.

Major new editions keep adding to the spectacle. The biggest addition is the new **Disney-MGM Studios Theme Park**, which will compete with Universal Studios in nearby Orlando for tourists and film-making dollars. The full-size working studio allows visitors to see stars in action, tour backlots and sound stages and enjoy one-of-a-kind Disney shows and adventures based on the glamour of Hollywood.

When Mickey Mouse observed his 60th birthday in 1988, Walt Disney World celebrated with **Mickey's Birthdayland**, where the party continued non-stop. A 60-foot-high balloon of Mickey himself marked the site of Mickey's house that includes **Mickey's Memory Room**, full of films and souvenirs of Mickey's film career which spans more than three score years.

Preceding pages: beauty and the beach; 5,000 Disney World members toasted the parks 10th anniversary.

The continuous expansion of Walt Disney World means new rides, new adventures, and new hotels almost constantly. In 1989, the theme park added **Pleasure Island**, a 50-acre water adventure area with flumes, slides, surfing and snorkeling, as well as another place for visitors to stay, the **Grand Floridian Beach Resort**.

The legacy of a legend: The vastness of Walt Disney World stuns most newcomers, particularly those familiar with its predecessor in California, Disneyland. It is literally the heart of Florida's tourist industry. Most tourists who circulate through the arteries of the state's highway system pass through Walt Disney World at some point – before being pumped out again to other extremities. Its offspring include Sea World, and Hotel World. Even the US military advertises its Orlando recruiting facility as **Navy World**, a macho place where spectators can watch armed forces demonstrations, then enlist. The legendary Walt Disney had selected Central Florida as early as 1963, but kept plans secret until property could be purchased. His associates conducted an undercover operation of CIA proportions, even traveling to Florida via circuitous routes. When Walt made the first public announcement of his plans in Florida in 1965, some local land that had been selling for $200 an acre immediately shot up in value to as much as $200,000 an acre. Walt died in December, 1966, but his successors fulfilled his dream. They put 9,000 people to work on his plan. Walt Disney World opened in October 1971. Only the dropping of an atom bomb could have wrought greater, more immediate changes in Central Florida.

Critics argue that some changes have been for the worse. Others praise Walt Disney World for bringing a profitable, but clean, industry to the region. They give the organization high marks for designating one-third of its area as a wildlife reserve, landscaping other areas in keeping with Florida flora and even banning billboards from its district – a move many government bodies have refused to consider. Walt Disney World

Mickey looks over the start of a new era during Disney World's construction.

produced benefits and problems, but one wonders what would be left of Florida's tourism industry today if Mickey Mouse hadn't moved in.

A monorail ride into the Grand Canyon: It takes 4 to 5 days of non-stop moving to wander through most of Walt Disney World's attractions. A 5-day World Passport is recommended to thoroughly enjoy the best of Magic Kingdom and the EPCOT Center.

The logistics of moving from one end of the kingdom to the other make it more convenient to dig in at either the 1,047-room **Contemporary Resort** or 644-room **Polynesian Village** on the grounds. The latter offers outdoor luaus, a tropical rain forest in the lobby and flaming tiki torches around a pool with its own waterfall. The monorail whisks you right into the lobby of the futuristic Contemporary, a few steps from your room. Walkways overhang the **Grand Canyon Concourse** of restaurants, shops and the monorail below. A tall mural composed of 18,000 separate tiles depicts the kind of life to be found at different levels of the real Grand Canyon.

Rooms on one side of the Contemporary overlook **Bay Lake**. Engineers completely drained it and discovered tons of white sand on the bottom which they used to create beaches. They refilled the lake and stocked it with fish during construction. Rooms on the other side look out upon the **Seven Seas Lagoon**, a man-made lake connected to Bay Lake by a water bridge constructed over a highway. Disney engineers insisted on building the expensive water bridge over the road instead of an automobile bridge over the water to preserve the integrity of their landscapes.

Prices at both hotels flanking the **Magic Kingdom** are higher than hotels outside the park, but as many as five people can stay in each room, split the cost, and make their stay economical as well as convenient. However, reservations must be booked well in advance – years in the case of some popular holiday dates. Officials say the slack periods are September, October, early November and December, January, and

A monorail streaks into the Contemporary Resort Hotel.

May. Fridays and Sundays are usually the least crowded days, unless they occur during a holiday period.

The **Disney Inn** has another 288 rooms and the Fort Wilderness campground has 1,190 sites for trailers or tents. Further removed, but still in the kingdom, are 3,558 rooms in seven hotels operated by major chains with branch properties at **Lake Buena Vista**. If you want to spend your vacation out on a limb, try the **Treehouses**. Lake Buena Vista also offers Vacation Villas, Fairway cluster villas and Club Lake Villas.

Otherwise, Interstate 4 between the Walt Disney World exit and Orlando is wall-to-wall with less expensive accommodations. Many have shuttle service to Disney World. Nearby, US 192 offers 9,000 more units.

After exiting I-4, you'll find it's still a long drive to the gates of the World. Tune in to the Disney radio network for current Disney World information. Unless you're staying at a hotel within, continue through the gates into one of 12,000 parking spaces. Make a mental note of your section. Each is named after a Disney character, so just ask the kids if you forget. It's still a tram ride to the ticket windows where you'll find a variety of prices. The most economical provide passes to all attractions for several days. Then you can ride a monorail or ferryboat to Walt Disney's masterpiece – the **Magic Kingdom**.

When you enter and find Mickey Mouse etched in flowers in front of the railroad depot, put aside notions that what you are about to experience is for the sake of the children. Adult visitors outnumber youngsters 4-to-1.

The depot is a time machine that transports you to **Main Street, USA**, a thoroughfare straight out of a Norman Rockwell painting. The shop facades of Federal and Victorian era architecture give it the ambience of an Eastern seaboard resort at the turn of the century.

A hot, lather shave before dinner at the Castle: Merchandise in the maze of shops ranges from stuffed animals, records, books and souvenirs of Disney creations to a corner camera shop where you can buy anything from Instamatics to professional Nikon equipment – and get ailing cameras fixed free. In keeping with the time warp, there's a **Main Street Cinema** (featuring silent film classics) and a barber shop where you can still get a hot lather shave and facial massage. Magic shops, candy stores, china shops, tobacco emporiums and more line a street that looks up toward the centerpiece of the Magic Kingdom – the **Cinderella Castle**.

It is breathtaking at first sight, a crown jewel of a creation that doesn't look real. Its gold-crested spires float 181 feet above a moat. The fairy tale architecture is a composite of European castles at Fontainbleu and Versailles and the chateaux of the Loire Valley. But the principal inspiration was a Bavarian castle built by mad King Ludwig. The attention to detail in the design commands study: gargoyles sculpted right to the top reaches that tourists never see; interior columns embellished with carved birds and mice from the animated Cinderella film classic. Mosaics of scenes from the movie adorn the walls. An Italian artist spent 18 months creating them from 500,000 individual Italian tiles made of gold leaf and distinctive colored glass.

A winding staircase in the black hall ascends to the Arthurian **King Stefan's Banquet Hall**. Meals are reasonably priced but you must make a reservation early in the day.

Close encounters of the crowded kind: The paths to the six themed lands of the Magic Kingdom radiate outward from the park in front of the castle like the spokes of a wheel. To maximize enjoyment and minimize encounters with the routinely huge crowds (9,000 people even showed up the day Hurricane David drenched the state), arrive when the gates open. Failing that, wait until after noon when traffic thins out. The beginning and end of the day are best for getting into attractions without a long wait. Midday is better for shopping and sightseeing – and avoiding the hot Florida sun.

You can save treadwear on your feet by touring the Magic Kingdom systematically walking from Adventureland to

Left, a runaway mine train rumbles down Thunder Mountain.

Frontierland, Liberty Square, Fantasyland and Tomorrowland – or vice versa. There's more in these places than meets the eye, so pause to admire the details. Each world takes its theming seriously, right down to what employees call "generic landscaping." Notice the mesquite trees imported from the southwest US for the **Pecos Bill Cafe** in Frontierland. And the souvenirs. You can buy genuine Paul Revere silverware in **Liberty Square**, including service sets worth up to $13,000.

Enchanted birds: Enter **Adventureland** over a wooden bridge festooned with Tiki-type effigies. The immense tree that houses the **Swiss Family Robinson residence** is actually 200 tons of concrete and steel with a 90-foot wide spread of limbs sprouting 800,000 plastic leaves (all made by a single family in Mexico).

The **Enchanted Tiki Birds** pavilion, patterned upon architectural styles of the islands of Bali and Borneo, is the exotic roost for singing tropical birds. Disney "imagineers" have brought them to life using a complex, computer-controlled system called Audio-Animatronics. It combines voices, music and sound with three-dimensional figures that move realistically.

The **Jungle Cruise** provides a vicarious trip for would-be Indiana Joneses down what may be a tributary of the Amazon River. The **Pirates of the Caribbean** boats you back to the days when buccaneers plundered the West Indies, including a trip through the middle of a cannon battle between an enormous pirate ship and a fort.

"Authentic dirt": It's only a short walk around a corner to the Old West – **Frontierland**. Here, full-size Mississippi stern wheelers and a realistic 2-acre sculpture of an Arizona desert scene stand out. The latter is the stage for the **Big Thunder Mountain Railroad** ride, which trundles past redstone buttes, canyons, and bubbling geysers at 30 miles an hour.

If everything looks dusty, don't fault maintenance. "We try to make things look authentically dirty," an operations official said. One new supervisor ordered the attractions cleaned up, but when superiors discovered her over-zealous mistake, she was asked to return them to their original state.

The line for the **Country Bear Jamboree** moves excruciatingly slowly, so wait until it's short. It has Audio-Animatronic action with a barnful of bears who "sing" country music standards like "Tears Will be the Chaser for My Wine" and "All the Guys That Turn Me On Turn Me Down." Watch the facial expressions on the buffalo, moose and elk mounted on the wall.

Where past presidents come alive: The most impressive use of Audio-Animatronics is **Liberty Square's Hall of Presidents** where "imagineers" have resurrected past presidents and cloned those still living. A 15-minute movie on a 120-degree screen chronicles the history of the American Constitution. Then a curtain rises on an eerie scene. Each "president" acknowledges his spotlighted introduction with a nod or wave. The illusion of life is maintained throughout a speech by Abraham Lincoln. His colleagues scratch their noses, chat, nervously tap their feet and even yawn in the background. The Lincoln figure alone is capable of 47 separate body actions and 15 head motions and expressions.

The architecture of Liberty Square also incorporates idiosyncrasies of early America. The window shutters have been tilted at angles so that they seem to be mounted on the leather hinges used in the 18th century and the "antique" windows are warped and full of air bubbles. The **Diamond Horseshoe Revue** has a saloon with an old-fashioned variety show; be sure to reserve seats before 9.30 a.m.

On a rise overlooking **Tom Sawyer Island** broods the **Haunted Mansion**. Its horrors far outclass those of any carnival rides with similar names. After an introductory scare in a room that "stretches," doom buggies carry you through corridors loaded with special effects. At one point, you see a party of transparent ghosts that you would swear are made from genuine ectoplasm.

By submarine and spaceship: Fantasyland pays tribute to characters popular-

Right, a caped specter pipes "spirituals" in the Haunted Mansion.

ized in Walt Disney animated classics such as *Snow White, Cinderella, Dumbo, Peter Pan* and *Pinocchio*. World travelers will enjoy trying to place familiarly-costumed dolls from the hundreds that populate **It's a Small World**.

Spacy submarines styled on those dreamed up by Jules Verne highlight **20,000 Leagues Under the Sea**. Here, the Animatronic fish include a giant squid that attempts to swallow your ship. Another slow-moving line.

Finally, there's **Tomorrowland**. Since its inception at Disneyland in the 1950s, many of its concepts have materialized; "Todayland" might be a more appropriate name. The structure that looks like an oversized tent with spires is **Space Mountain**. Disney's unique concept of keeping visitors entertained while standing in line stands out here. You enter through a cooled tunnel lined with diverting window displays until you arrive in the rarified atmosphere of a distant planet where meteors and asteroids careen overhead. Compact rockets take you on a roller-coaster ride in the dark. You can't see the hills and turns ahead, a situation that intensifies the thrills and illusions of hurtling through outer space. Expectant mothers and people with heart conditions are wisely advised not to board. Real astronauts and Jordan's King Hussein have been among distinguished space riders.

In the underground: A fascinating part of the park, off-limits to visitors, exists right under your feet. The Magic Kingdom is built above more than a mile of catacombs called **The Utilidor System**. This is the brains and brawn of the Kingdom. Disney World officials rarely provide glimpses into this private domain to preserve the illusion of fantasy above. Rest assured that thousands of people labor below to assure the amazing efficiency above.

Eventually, Walt Disney realized his Walt Disney World was just a few stages short of being a utopian city of the future. He resolved that the second phase of his Florida masterpiece would be just that – a planned community that would bring people together in an ideal envi-

A rocket ride above Tomorrowland

ronment. With an investment that grew to nearly one billion dollars, the Disney corporation went ahead with the largest private construction projects in the US to date. Futuristic buildings of glass and metal rose above 600 acres of reclaimed swampland. In October, 1982, **EPCOT Center** – the "thinking man's theme park" – opened a new Disney era.

EPCOT Center: EPCOT Center was a dream typical of the ambitious genius of Walt Disney. Shortly before his death, Disney announced plans to build an Experimental Prototype Community of Tomorrow (hence, the acronym EPCOT). He envisioned it as a domed city with a controlled climate free from pollution where a permanent population of 20,000 would live and work.

The men who succeeded Disney decided to go ahead with their founder's plans, but changed the concept of EPCOT from an actual city to a sophisticated theme park to make it a viable financial venture. Still, the task of building Disney's dream city proved monumental. Engineers, architects, craftsmen and building materials were imported from China, Europe, Japan and other corners of the earth. More than 250,000 shrubs and 12,000 mature trees were shipped in from places as distant as Nepal. Nineteen acres of emerald "show grass" were laid.

Visitors familiar with the Magic Kingdom will find a new atmosphere in EPCOT Center. There are no thrill rides here. Disney cartoon characters do not flit and parade through the streets. Even Mickey Mouse has been barred from EPCOT Center.

What visitors will find is an educationally-oriented complex, twice as large as the Magic Kingdom. The technological achievements surpass those of the sister park. Advanced systems utilizing laser beams and holograms have proven too complex for even their creators to explain to laymen. These innovations of tomorrow and the nations of today comprise the two distinct theme areas of EPCOT Center – **Future World** and **World Showcase**.

The dramatic gateway to EPCOT

A monorail cruises past Spaceship Earth in the EPCOT Center.

Center and to Future World is a monolithic sphere nearly 17 stories high called **Spaceship Earth**. It stands on three mammoth legs that elevate the unusual structure to 180 feet at its highest point. Disney imagineers said it was the first geosphere ever constructed.

Inside Spaceship Earth, the Bell System presents a time machine trip into the past, present and future that depicts man's progress through the evolution of communications. You exit into **CommuniCore**, the heart of Future World, where hands-on activities enable you to see, touch and hear the immediate future. **EPCOT Computer Central** focuses on the role of computers. From Spaceship Earth, you can fan out to others parts of Future World.

Future World: Future World consists of six other attractions (proceeding clockwise from Spaceship Earth around Communicore).

• **The Universe of Energy**, sponsored by Exxon, offers a journey into a three-dimensional reaction of prehistoric days alive with the sights and sounds of dinosaurs, earthquakes and erupting volcanoes. The trip dramatizes the entrapment of fossil fuels in the earth. Eighty thousand solar cells on the pavilion's roof power six theater cars that carry 100 passengers at a time.

• Ride through the human body in **Wonders of Life** by Metropolitan Life Insurance Co., with a microscopic tour of the human immune system. Cranium Command features a new gang of Disney characters, called "Brain Pilots," who dramatize the mind's functions.

• **Horizons**, a General Electric presentation previews family lifestyles of the 21st century in a city, on a desert farm, in a floating undersea environment and in a space colony. It winds up in an eight-story "Omnisphere" that immerses you in images of the future.

• General Motors transports you through the **World of Motion**. Humorous scenes trace the progress of locomotion. You visit early innovators in transportation including a "Used Chariot" lot.

• The boundless realms of creativity

Visitors explore a "tunnel of light" in EPCOT's Journey Into Imagination.

are explored in **Journey Into Imagination**, rapidly becoming the most popular attraction. Sponsored by Kodak, new Disney characters called Dreamfinder and Figment escort you through the worlds of art, literature, science and technology, film and other pursuits.

• Kraft's **Land Pavilion** is the biggest Epcot attraction. It covers 6 acres with explorations of the worlds of nutrition, food production and harvest. You visit a tropical rain forest, a desert, an American prairie and a controlled environmental farm.

Future World also contains EPCOT's fascinating addition, a pavilion called the **Living Seas**, which takes visitors to a Sea Base at the bottom of a vast saltwater tank.

World Showcase: A broad, pink sidewalk encircling the lagoon in the centre of EPCOT connects Future World to World Showcase. Miniature replicas to ten foreign countries and the US have been built.

• **Mexico** is dominated by an **Aztec pyramid**. A **River of Time** boat ride tours the country's past. The **San Angel Inn** offers authentic cuisine.

• A stormy river ride through the Maelstrom highlights **Norway**, with a turbulent Viking river voyage and a visit to an authentic Norwegian village.

• **China's** striking feature is a scaled-down reproduction of Peking's **Temple of Heaven**. A Circlevision 360 film provides a dramatic glimpse into modern China. Artifacts on display include several of the famous terra-cotta horses from Xian and blocks from the Great Wall of China.

• In **Germany**, activities center around a year-round Octoberfest. Stores sell genuine Hummel figures and Hutschenreuther porcelain.

• **Italy** unfolds around a replica of the bell tower at **St Mark's Square** in Venice. The original **Alfredo's** restaurant of Rome caters to the appetite.

• The **American Adventure** provides an amazing look at the history of the US, hosted by Audio-Animatronic figures of Ben Franklin and Mark Twain. The Franklin figure actually walks.

A replica of Peking's Temple of Heaven graces EPCOT's China.

• A great vermilion *torii* gate graces the entrance to **Japan**. Inside is an exquisite five-story **pagoda** fashioned after the 8th-century Horyuji temple.

• Nine tons of hand-cut North African tile are featured in the Koutoubia minaret at **Morocco** as a detailed replica of a prayer tower stands guard.

• A scaled-down **Eiffel Tower** looms over **France**. Of course, there's a restaurant, **Les Chefs de France**.

• The **United Kingdom** features a **Rose and Crown pub** with a polished mahogany bar, a dart board, steak and kidney pie and Guinness stout.

• The **Hotel du Canada**, modeled after Ottawa's Chateau Laurier, rises from the landscapes of EPCOT's **Canada**. Another Circlevision 360 movie transports visitors to the Great White North.

Activities ad infinitum: The **Main Street Electrical Parade** twinkles through the streets at times. Dragons and boats float over the Seven Seas Lagoon in the **Electrical Water Pageant** most evenings. A shower of fireworks caps each summer night and holiday period.

Other features:

• Shopping is themed to attractions and areas. You won't find shoddy merchandise or cans of Florida Sunshine. Instead, you will find genuine Hummel figurines and imports from around the world in the **Walt Disney World Village** complex in Lake Buena Vista.

• **Discovery Island** in Bay Lake, reached by boat, has a Disney World anomaly – living birds and tropical plants in a serene wildlife sanctuary.

• **River Country** invites you to tube down rapids and skim down twisting 260-foot slides.

• **Ford Wilderness Resort** has campgrounds with nighttime entertainment at the Pioneer Hall.

• The **Empress Lilly Riverboat**, named in honor of Walt's wife, features three complete restaurants and a nightly Dixieland singalong.

• A **Topiary** of sea serpents, Brahma bulls, camels, mushrooms and cartoon characters is shaped from creeping figs, ligustrum, podocarpus and other plants.

Below, Bay Lake in Disney's kingdom. Right, fireworks end another day at the Cinderella Castle.

ORLANDO AND ITS OTHER WORLDS

The bulk of Central Florida's other theme parks owe their existence to the presence of Walt Disney World. They make the state the only place in the world where a person can pet a porpoise, shake hands with a knight and visit a movie set, all in the same day.

Sea World's name sums up its offerings. This is the home of dancing penguins, prancing seals, performing water spouts, a man who skis on the backs of dolphins, and a killer whale that preens on command. Water skiers perform amazing feats on the lake each day. A tunnel carries you through a poolful of sharks. New attractions include the elaborate 2½-acre Cap'n Kids World, a $1.75 million playground. Nearby is the **Florida Festival**.

Universal Studios brings Hollywood to Florida in grand style with a working movie studio and sets, complete with guided tours and rides, and some spectacular special effects – King Kong roaring, Jaws snapping and even E.T. charming young and old.

King Henry's Feast and **Mardi Gras** are two food-and-festivities attractions on International Drive. Both offer fixed menus and a fun theme atmosphere. King Henry's Feast puts visitors in the court of King Henry VIII, with jesters, jugglers and fair maidens. Mardi Gras has a Cajun flavor and often features live Dixieland Jazz music.

Wet 'N' Wild is one of a host of water parks. Here, swimming is secondary to activities such as skimming down slides, some of them 60 feet high and 400 feet long; bobbing in a wave-making pool; and belly-flopping painlessly into a bubble machine. A new feature is Raging Rapids, a 400-foot-long ride in inner tubes down cascades.

The Mystery Fun House updates old carnival tricks for the joy of young and old, and features one of Florida's most extravagant miniature golf courses.

Boardwalk and **Baseball** features a combination of themes – carnival-style

Left, at Sea World, a man water skis on the backs of dolphins. **Below**, Shamu, the killer whale, takes a bow.

rides including a soaring roller coaster and baseball memorabilia, featuring a batting machine.

The grandaddies of them all: Long before Disney World, two attractions contributed to Florida's image as a tourist mecca. The Dick Pope family cultivated moss-draped cypress, fields of flowers, pools and grottoes on the edge of a lake in Winter Haven in the 1930s, added water ski shows in 1942, and called it **Cypress Gardens**. Four performances of the world famous show have been given every day since 1946. Esther Williams came to film underwater music spectaculars in the 1950s. The gardens have aged gracefully and continue to draw crowds to walk among Southern belles and serene, shaded walks. World water skiing champions gather to compete here each June. Recent additions include the Southern Crossroads and Living Forest.

Northeast of Ocala, ABC Broadcasting's leisure division has dressed up one of Florida's greatest natural attractions with gardens. Early Indians venerated the area known as **Silver Springs** as a shrine to the water gods.

Glass bottom boats glide over translucent waters teeming with rainbow-hued fish. More than a half billion gallons of water have flowed from the spring daily for the past 100,000 years or so. The boats' captains relate stories about parts of the spring named **Devil's Kitchen, Bridal Chamber** and **Blue Grotto**. Another boat takes you on an hour cruise through a real, wildlife-filled jungle. The **World of Reptiles** includes demonstrations of snake-handling where experts drain venom from rattlers. The exhibit was established by the late, renowned Ross Allen who could pet deadly vipers without being bitten.

To avoid paying an admission fee, you can put your own boat or canoe into the water downstream and cruise up to the springhead. But less-crowded springs abound in the state. In fact, 17 of the 75 first-magnitude springs in the US are here, flowing at rates of 100 cubic feet or more per second. There are also 49 second-magnitude springs and count-

Below, Dick Pope Sr with Tampa's "Anna Tampana" at his Cypress Gardens. Right, a Florida spring.

less lesser ones. This accounts for all the canoes you see overhanging car roofs and inner tubes piled in car trunks.

Once sleepy Orlando reborn as a boom-town: The main beneficiary (or victim, depending on your point of view) of Central Florida's acres of theme parks has been the city of **Orlando**. Once a sleepy town content to bob along on ripples spawned by surrounding citrus industries, it has turned into a mega-lopolis. It once had only 5,000 hotel rooms. Now, there are more than 64,000 units here, more than you'll find in Honolulu or Miami Beach. It remains one of the fastest growing metropolitan areas in the US.

Most of the breakneck building is concentrated to the west. Downtown Orlando is rapidly beginning to lose its quiet demeanor, however, as high-rise buildings fill the skyline. It gleams in sun-splashed plazas on **Lake Eola** which offers horse-drawn carriage rides around its edges at night, and a fountain that dances during the day and lights up at night. Historians believe the city got its name from a soldier named Orlando Reeves who was killed by an Indian arrow while protecting an early settlement here.

Two new shopping centers – the **Church Street Market** and the **Church Street Exchange** – sit back to back, side by side, offering upscale boutiques and shops. On the third floor of the Exchange is the world's largest game arcade, with roller-skating waitresses to serve you while you play your quarters.

If you are on your own, start at **Orange Avenue** for a look at the La Belle Epoque architecture of the **Kress Building**, the Classic Egyptian revival style **First National Bank Building**, circa 1929, and the Art Deco **McCrory's Five and Dime** built in 1906. Three soft-textured red brick buildings on **Church Street** exemplify the early Victorian style of the 1890s. This is the street where the building renaissance began with **Rosie O'Grady's Goodtime Emporium** complex in the old **Orlando Hotel** across from **Church Street Station**. Note the bulbous, turned column on the corner of the old train station balcony, considered

one of the best examples of Richardsonian Romanesque in the south. **Phineas Phogg's Balloon Works** in the O'Grady's complex of bars, restaurants and shops offers morning "champagne balloon flights" over Central Florida. **Lili Marlene's Aviators Pub and Restaurant** is in the old Strand Hotel.

Sinkhole city: The charm of suburban **Winter Park** has always been a magnet for knowledgeable tourists. But the city inadvertently became an international attraction in 1981 when a sinkhole opened up in the middle of town. It swallowed a foreign-car repair shop and six cars, parts of two streets, the deep end of the local public swimming pool and the home and yard of Mae Rose Owens. Winter Park residents took up a collection to buy the poor woman a new place. When it stopped sinking, the hole was nearly 350 feet across and 100 feet deep and had devoured 2½ acres. A mini-tourist industry also grew around it. Pawn shops and gas stations sell T-shirts, caps and photographs of "Sinkhole '81." Located north of Fairbanks Avenue near Denning Drive, there has been talk of trying to fill it in, but it will probably become just another local lake. Most of Florida's lakes started out as sinkholes.

Otherwise, Winter Park has **Rollins College**, built in 1885 and bordered by a **Walk of Fame** with 800 inscribed stones from the birthplaces and homes of famous people, and a large sea shell collection in the **Beal-Maltbie Museum**. Park Avenue's **Little Europe** encompasses expensive shops and boutiques. The largest arts festival in the southern US is held in the park in the town center each March.

Pleasant, unpretentious **Central Florida Zoological Park** is tucked into natural landscaping at the junction of US 17 and 92 in Sanford, north of Orlando.

Steak and oranges: Next to sunshine, sand and sea, Florida prompts thoughts of citrus. Some groves have given way to sea shows and such, but Florida still grows more than 70 percent of the nation's oranges and grapefruit worth about $3.3 billion annually. This is the center of citrus country. Neat, parallel rows of rounded trees disappear in every direction. **Polk** and **Orange** counties together account for upwards of 125,000 acres of Florida's 697,000 acres orange and grapefruit-bearing acres.

Citrus trees, native to the Far East, came to Florida with early Spanish expeditions. Commercial production began in the last part of the century when a Chinese immigrant, Lue Gim Gong, developed a cold-resistant variety that bears his name and still grows along the **Indian River**. Lue was honored by the citizens of his adopted home in **De Land**, north of Orlando. Today, citrus remains the city's sustenance, but De Land is more renowned as the site of **Stetson University**, a namesake of the hat manufacturer. Nearby, **Hontoon Island State Park** is accessible by boat from SR44. It includes a Timucuan Indian ceremonial mound.

On a clear day, you can see 2.7 million orange trees, about a third of Florida's crop, from the top of the **Florida Citrus Tower** on US 27 in **Clermont**, northwest of Disney World. You can buy fruit from a packing house adjoining the tower, and you'll learn that the sweetest oranges aren't necessarily orange. In fact, some growers dye the fruit to make it more attractive to northern buyers who might balk at a green orange. Citrus stands flourish along the backroads of Central Florida. Some even permit you to take your pick right from the trees. Winter Haven has the **Florida Citrus Showcase** and **Lake Wales** touts its **Donald Duck Citrus World**.

A fragrant time to drive these rolling roads is spring, when the white blossoms hanging on the trees saturate the air with sweet smells. The fruits swell from their limbs in autumn. Farmers watch the weather closely in winter. In spite of Florida's warm reputation, early morning temperatures from December through February occasionally plunge below freezing and send farmers into the fields with smudge pots and sprinklers to try to keep the chill from killing the fruit. Record cold spells in 1983 and 1985 caused severe damage.

A mountain of oranges at a Central Florida juice factory.

Ten miles east of Disney World, the city of **Kissimmee** (accent the second syllable) is the capital of another major Florida crop – cattle.

Kissimmee cowboys: Florida ranks among the top 10 beef producing states in the country. Some 200 ranches flourish in the flat scrub innards of the state. Ranch hands with spurs on their boots and grime on their faces ride horses and rope Brahma bulls here as skillfully as any Western cowboy.

Kissimmee is the headquarters of the **Florida Cattlemen's Association**. If you're not picky about the tablecloths and down-home service, you can eat some of the best beef in the country here. Cook-outs coincide with Wednesday cattle auctions. Cowboys compete in the Silver Spurs Rodeos in February and in July, and a second major rodeo is held in February. February is also the month for the annual Kissimmee Valley Livestock Show.

Geographers and geognosts should visit **Lakefront Park** for a look at the **Monument of States**, a 50-foot tall irregular quadrilateral step-pyramid with 21 tiers. It's composed of more than 1,500 stones from every state and 21 foreign countries.

Lesser known, but equally offbeat, is the **Tupperware International World Headquarters**. Visit its **Museum of Dishes** and take home a set.

Ranches of a different kind monopolize the mellow hills around **Ocala**, in the northwestern part of the region. Past champions such as Carry Back, Foolish Pleasure, Needles and Affirmed hail from here. It's a horse lover's heaven.

Hundreds of thoroughbred horse farms along US 301 and its arteries make for a dramatic drive through grassy, fenced landscapes. They offer stable space, stud service, training and various breeds for sale. Only California and Kentucky have more professional paddocks. You can park your car and watch breaking and training in the fall. Paintings of famous Florida steeds line the **Hall of Fame** at the **Florida Thorough-bred Breeders' Association** in the **Golden Hills Golf and Turf Club**

Pursuing the fox in Ocala thoroughbred country.

on US 27, some 7 miles west of Ocala.

Florida horses began making news in 1956 when Needles, born at **Ocala Stud Inc.** and bred at **Bonnie Heath Farm**, won the Kentucky Derby. The limestone-based soil, pure air and water spurred a dynamic growth of farms after that. Most recently, Arabians have entered breeding arenas here.

Many ranches welcome visitors. Try **Fairview Farm** near **Candler**, which exercises horses in a lake; **Just a Farm** near **Dunnelon; Flamingo Farm** at **Reddick**; and **Another Episode Farm** near **Fellowship**. Check in at the office or residence and be sure to close the gates behind you.

Enter lush **Ocala National Forest** via State Road 40, east of the city. "The Big Scrub," as locals call it, is a subtropical wilderness noted for the world's largest stand of sand pine and a large deer herd. Check with wilderness officials to determine the best deer and bear hunting seasons.

Canoeing and tubing are also popular here. Best bets are **Alexander Springs**, bubbling 78 million gallons of clear, cold water a day, and **Juniper**. It's better to test them on weekdays when crowds are small. If you don't have a canoe or inner tube, try swimming. The largest developed recreational area in the forest is **Salt Springs** on SRs 40 and 314. Its canoe path flows through **Lake George** to the **St Johns River**.

The historic **Oklawaha River** marks the western boundary of Ocala National Forest. Old sketches depict a journey here by General Ulysses S. Grant. The tiny town of the same name on **Lake Weir** made history on January 16, 1935. That was when 15 FBI agents pumped an estimated 1,500 bullets into a lakeside cottage and into the infamous Kate "Ma" Barker and her son Fred. Her criminal gang had terrorized the country by kidnapping, killing and stealing. Locals will point out the house, which still stands, but it's private property – and the bullet holes have been patched.

If you are looking for scenery, follow State Road 19 which runs north-south through the forest to tiny **Umatilla** and

Kissimmee cowboy, chaw in cheek.

Eustis at the southern boundary. About 1,300 of Florida's 30,000 lakes speckle this county, aptly called **Lake**. Hikers can test their stamina on the forest's **Florida Hiking Trail**.

Just south is **Lake Apopka**, second largest in the state. The neighboring city of **Apopka** got its name from the Indian word for "Potato-eating place."

Lake Wales, at 250 feet above sea level, is one of the highest folds of earth in Florida. Even higher than Lake Wales is a 205-foot tower of marble and coquina atop **Iron Mountain**. Dutch immigrant Edward Bok, an early editor of the *Ladies Home Journal*, donated this **Singing Tower** to the state in 1929. He is buried at the foot of it. The tower's 53-bell carillon rings out concerts.

Spook Hill haunts Fifth Avenue in **Lake Wales**. Turn off your car motor at the bottom of the steep drive, put it into neutral, and your car will appear to roll back uphill. **Masterpiece Gardens** here has a 300,000-piece mosaic copy of "The Last Supper." Another local religious spectacular is the **Black Hills Passion Play** at the amphitheater. Led by sturdy septuagenarian Josef Meier, it runs from February through March. The place to dine and sleep in the area is **Chalet Suzanne** at US 27 and 27A. Its rooms have Moroccan, Mexican, Italian and Indian furnishings.

US 27 south from Lake Wales leads to a city which is famous only for auto racing – **Sebring**. The city's population of 7,500 swells by tens of thousands annually in March during the 12 hours of the Sebring endurance test race.

Off US 27 west of Sebring, drive into the steamy jungles of **Highlands Hammock State Park**. It has excellent hiking trails through cypress swamps. Head west on SR 70 to **Arcadia** (more cowboys and big rodeos), then north on US 17 to **Bartow**. It marks the center of a controversial industry that has taken its toll on the environment, but bolstered the state's economy. Whether you turn east or west on State Road 60, you will pass lunar-like landscapes of sand mountains and craters filled with slime or stinking water. This is Bone Valley, the heart of the phosphate mining industry.

Florida produces 25 percent of the world's phosphate, which is a chemical byproduct of alluvial wastes washed into the sea in prehistoric times. These waste matters settled under the soft soil as the seas receded. Most phosphate is turned into agricultural fertilizers vital to food production.

Phosphate officials argue that the industry contributes $3 billion a year to the state's economy. But because of the industry's obvious effect on land and rivers, phosphate producers have a public relations problem. You can probably arrange a tour of mines and reclamation efforts through the **Florida Phosphate Council** office in Lakeland.

Draglines frequently dig up fossils of incredible Pleistocene era animals such as mammoths, saber-toothed tigers and giant sharks – hence the name Bone Valley. Some skeletal remains are on display at the **Bone Valley Exposition**.

Goodbye, Frank Lloyd Wright, and so long, Central Florida: Lakeland, north of Bartow, is another blue-collar city. Of main interest to tourists is **Florida Southern College** at McDonald Street and Ingraham Avenue. Students study within the world's largest collection of buildings designed by Frank Lloyd Wright. He began showcasing his "organic architecture" here, considered futuristic at the time, with construction of the **Annie Pfeiffer Chapel** in 1938. Maps providing a self-guided tour of these functional works of art can be obtained at the administration building. Visit the esplanade between buildings and marvel at its colored-glass squares that provide at rainbow of sunshine.

Now that you have seen Central Florida, whet your appetite for one of the best feasts of southern home-cooking this side of Atlanta. Follow the signs on I-4 to Branch Forbes Road and **The Branch Ranch** restaurant. The Branch family converted their home into dining rooms in 1956 and have fed legions of fans ever since. Order a main course of fried chicken, prime rib, even lobster, then endless plates of okra, fried eggplant, squash and cornbread will pile up before you. You'll leave Central Florida with a happy stomach.

Right, an archaeologist inspects a dig near a slime pit site created by phosphate mining.

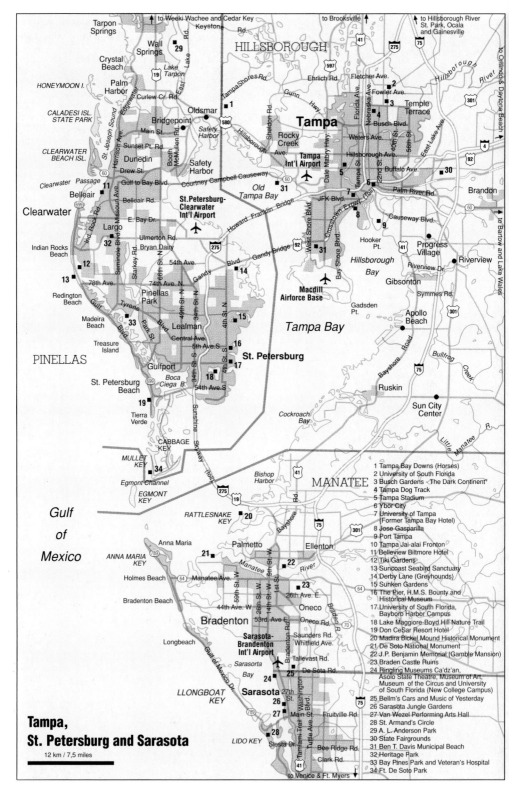

Tampa, St. Petersburg and Sarasota

12 km / 7,5 miles

1 Tampa Bay Downs (Horses)
2 University of South Florida
3 Busch Gardens - "The Dark Continent"
4 Tampa Dog Track
5 Tampa Stadium
6 Ybor City
7 University of Tampa (Former Tampa Bay Hotel)
8 Jose Gasparilla
9 Port Tampa
10 Tampa Jai-alai Fronton
11 Belleview Biltmore Hotel
12 Tiki Gardens
13 Suncoast Seabird Sanctuary
14 Derby Lane (Greyhounds)
15 Sunken Gardens
16 The Pier, H.M.S. Bounty and Historical Museum
17 University of South Florida, Bayboro Harbor Campus
18 Lake Maggiore-Boyd Hill Nature Trail
19 Don CeSar Resort Hotel
20 Madira Bickel Mound Historical Monument
21 De Soto National Monument
22 J.P. Benjamin Memorial (Gamble Mansion)
23 Braden Castle Ruins
24 Ringling Museums Ca'dz'an, Asolo State Theatre, Museum of Art, Museum of the Circus and University of South Florida (New College Campus)
25 Bellm's Cars and Music of Yesterday
26 Sarasota Jungle Gardens
27 Van Wezel Performing Arts Hall
28 St. Armand's Circle
29 A. L. Anderson Park
30 State Fairgrounds
31 Ben T. Davis Municipal Beach
32 Heritage Park
33 Bay Pines Park and Veteran's Hospital
34 Ft. De Soto Park

The Gulf of Mexico caresses the fine, bleached sand of Florida's West Coast. It undulates gently, or not at all, often flat as a sheet of plate glass on humid summer days. Its tranquility contravenes the clamor on its shores. Newcomers and developers have laid siege to this once placid part of the state. From the metropolitan Tampa/ St Petersburg nucleus north to New Port Richey and south to Fort Myers, the West Coast has begun to resemble the waterfront wall of windows characteristic of the Miami to Palm Beach strip on the East Coast: retirement farms and youth-oriented singles complexes, stilt houses and stucco mansions. With them have come professional sports, massive malls – and anything else anyone is looking for. There are even some lingering bits of Old West Coast in fishing villages around Cedar Key and spots south of Naples.

TAMPA

The aroma of fine cigars still flavors some of the old brick-lined alleys of **Tampa**. Yet there's youthful new vigor in the air as well. Emerald office towers soar above one side of the **Hillsborough River**. The imposing spires of the old Tampa Bay Hotel-turned-university grace the other side. But for all its obvious appeal, tourists usually rush through Tampa on the interstate en route from Suncoast beaches to Disney World and company, or come to spend only a day at Busch Gardens or an evening at an excellent restaurant. Tampa certainly deserves much closer attention.

Part of the problem is that the average tourist expects a sandy beach and the sea to be part of his Florida vacation package. Tampa proper can't provide that. A pretty but polluted **Tampa Bay** and the Pinellas County peninsula lie between the city and the Gulf of Mexico. The big, bird claw of a bay bustles with international freighter traffic, carrying 51 million tons of cargo annually. It has made Tampa the nation's seventh largest port. She exports phosphate from nearby mines, citrus from area groves, cattle from Florida ranches, seafood, even yachts. At the **Twiggs Street docks**, watch the banana boats unload and see the state's largest shrimp boat fleet bring in their catch at **Hooker's Point** at the end of Bermuda Avenue.

The blue-collar workers remain the backbone of the city. They roll out 3 million cigars a day from Ybor City factories, stir vats of Schlitz and Busch beer at two major breweries, grow strawberries, pilot tankers, and pack seafood. But the brisk market in office buildings underscores an influx of white-shirted attorneys, architects and entrepreneurs.

Tampa's population of nearly 300,000 is third only to Jacksonville (whose numbers are inflated by its unusual county-size boundaries) and Miami. But it's the center of a rapidly merging multi-city megalopolis of over a million people.

Spanish roots: The Spanish influence here is subtler, more elegant than that of the barrios of Miami's later Cuban influx. The deep Spanish roots date way back to the landing of Pánfilo de Narváez in 1528. Settlement began much later with the establishment of Fort Brooke in 1824, one of a series built to keep tabs on the Seminole Indians. But like the East Coast cities, Tampa developed when railroad tycoon Henry B. Plant extended his narrow-guage South Florida Railroad to the Hillsborough River in 1884.

In emulating the East Coast's Henry Flagler, Plant built the **Tampa Bay Hotel**. Its incongruous silver minarets topped by Islamic crescents still lend character to the city's skyline today. Plant added Oriental rickshaws to carry guests around the opulent grounds, wicker chairs on the cool verandas and imported antiques. The hotel now houses the administrative offices of the **University of Tampa** on Kennedy Boulevard. You can visit the **Henry Plant Museum** off the lobby. It contains his collection of late Victorian era furniture and art objects. In spite of the structure's Middle Eastern appearance, it's another tribute to Tampa's Spanish lineage, a model of The Alhambra in Granada.

The Cuban connection: About the time Plant was building his railroad and hotel, Vincente Martinez Ybor was moving his cigar factory away from labor problems in Key West. Today, **Ybor City** no longer pulses with the color and excitement of its Cuban heyday: when crowds gathered at cockfights in the alleys and to hear Cuban freedom fighter José Marti make fiery speeches to recruit rebels and contributions for his revolution against Spain; when Teddy Roosevelt rode into town on his horse, Texas, flanked by his dog, Cuba, and the Rough Riders, before galloping to glory on San Juan Hill near Santiago; when prostitutes plied their wares on "Last Chance Street" near the docks to sol-

diers awaiting transfer to the Spanish American War.

Still, street vendors peddle deviled crabs and Cuban coffee. Some perfectionists still roll fine tobacco into finer cigars. Ybor City has even been getting a facelift that may bring back shouts of "Cuba Libre!" – if only from the local bars. The very building around which the enclave grew, Ybor's cigar factory, has been the centerpiece of plans to spur restoration of other classic buildings.

Take Interstate 4 to the Ybor City exit, then head south on 21st, west on 10th and south again to 14th Street. At this cigar-making site, built in 1886, hundreds of workers used to sit at long benches inside, tediously shaping prized cigars while a "reader" sat on a platform above entertaining them with selections from poetry, books and newspapers. It kept workers happy and production high. Italian and German immigrants joined the move to this "Cuba City" to cash in on its economic vitality.

Automation eventually put most of the cigar factories out of business. En-

Cigar-making at an Ybor City factory, circa 1910.

trepreneurs rescued Martinez' handsome building, restored its iron grillwork, oak and heart-pine interiors, and cleaned its red-brick exterior. They have added restaurants and shops where you can still buy a good cigar or treasures from Tampa attics. You can lunch with local businessmen at the rustic **Rough Riders** restaurant under old photographs of Teddy and his men. At the **Stemmery**, added in 1902 for curing tobacco leaves and removing stems, you can still see *puros* (cigars) made by hand.

Seventh Avenue has more shops. Some sell lacy Spanish fabric. Connoisseurs consider the Cuban sandwich at the **Silver Ring Cafe** Tampa's best. Atmosphere and more Spanish food is the specialty of the landmark **Columbia Restaurant** at 22nd Street. Built in 1905 by Casimiro Hernandez, the 11-room, 1,600-seat structure has been run by his son-in-law, Cesar Gonzmart, since 1953. There's a Latin Flamenco floor show, strolling violinists, and dishes like chicken and yellow rice and garbanzo bean soup. Gonzmart's son, Richard,

Street scene in modern Ybor City.

has opened a popular **Cafe and Warehouse** with coffees and jazz. Also popular and classic is the **Spanish Park** restaurant, several blocks away at 3517 East 7th.

Pirates – Gasp! – invade downtown Tampa: Downtown Tampa's gleaming new skyscrapers, including a $93 million office and **Hyatt Regency Hotel** complex, are the West Coast's biggest. Nearby, the low-slung **Franklin Street Mall** allows you to window-shop unmolested by automobile traffic. The facades of **Hayman Jewelry Co., Adams' City Hatters** and **Butler Shoes** showcase Florida's ubiquitous 1930s Art Deco look. The restored **Tampa Theater** here unreels movie classics, foreign films and occasional live shows.

Tampa Museum behind **Curtis Hixon Convention Hall** presents changing art and culture exhibits. You can watch University of Tampa students practice crew racing along Hillsborough River. South of downtown, Bayshore Boulevard offers a waterside drive from the foot of Platt Street Bridge. Joggers jam its sidewalk, speculatively called the world's longest. If the barge docked here resembles a pirate ship, that's because it is.

Tampa's Rites of Spring occur every February when its businessmen and bigwigs exchange their tailored suits, brougham shoes and briefcases for puffy-sleeved shirts, buckled boots, pistols and sabers – even nose rings and scars – and board the *José Gasparilla* which launches for the annual Gasparilla Invasion from the Tampa Yacht Club, and berths the rest of the year at the Platt Street Bridge at Bayshore Boulevard. The ship, commissioned in 1954, has three masts which tower 100 feet above the deck. With the aid of a few early morning beers, some pirates climb to their crows' nests. They raise 300 flags in an explosion of color, blast cannon salutes, and weigh anchor for the mouth of the Hillsborough River flanked by hundreds of smaller craft with their own swashbuckling crews.

Upon landing, Ye Mystic Krewe of Gasparilla swarms into the streets of Downtown Tampa where hundreds of thousands of spectators watch them lead a parade. The mayor surrenders the city and declares a holiday. Buccaneers fling gold doubloons and blank shells from their pistols to adoring throngs in an all-day procession.

The first Gasparilla Invasion was held in 1904. It grew out of the Gulf Coast's reputation as a haunt for bloodthirsty buccaneers, particularly a dubious character named José Gaspar who, believers say, plundered, tortured and raped his way up and down the coast. Although history books sometimes record how José led a mutiny aboard the Spanish ship, *Florida Blanca*, in 1785 before becoming a pirate, no public or private records prove his existence. Gaspar was more likely the invention of a Marco Island mullet fisherman named Johnny Gomez, about 1870. Gomez claimed to have sailed with Gaspar and the tales helped his booming business in buried treasure maps.

Busy February also means the annual staging of the Florida State Fair at its permanent exhibition sites off Interstate 4 east of Tampa. In addition to livestock, plant and horse competitions and commercial exhibits, it features an enormous midway chock-a-block with thrill rides, carny games and freak shows.

The world's largest wine cellar?: Gourmands will find Tampa's restaurants among the best in Florida. One dining must that has earned a full page story in *Playboy* magazine is **Bern's Steak House**, four blocks north of Bayshore at 1208 S. Howard Avenue. Its claustrophobic baroque decor, likened to the interior of a funeral parlor by some, may not appeal to all, but the selection of beef and wines will. The quality steak is aged and hand-turned 5 to 8 weeks, fine gourmet points that are explained on a menu that gives the vital statistics of each cut and a choice of weights and thickness (from a *petit filet* to a 60-ounce sirloin that serves six). Gert and Bern Laxer grow their restaurant's vegetables on their own organic farm, free from chemical sprays and additives. Caviar is flown in fresh regularly. Cress seeds, imported from London, add the right touch to salads.

But it's his wine list that makes Bern's place so extraordinary. About half a million bottles, representing some 7,000 varieties of wine, clog his cellars. This collection is thought to be the largest on-hand stock of wines maintained by any restaurant in the world. An abridged version of the encyclopedic list stands on the table, but ask for a peek at the complete volume. You may have to brace yourself to lift it. Inside, you'll find rare vintages like a Lafite 1841 for around $3,100 and a Gruaud Larose 1833 for just $4,100 per magnum.

A more average meal in even odder surroundings may be eaten at **Crawdaddy's**, on the bayside street next to the gold-mirrored international headquarters of the Shriner's off Courtney Campbell Causeway. Don't be put off by the dirty washing on the clothesline, the chickens and barnyard smells, or the fact that the crooked building looks like it's about to tumble into Tampa Bay. Instead, feed on fried alligator and dance in the spacious disco.

From the windows of Crawdaddy's

Ye Mystic Krewe aboard the *José Gasparilla*.

you can watch planes climb into usually clear skies from **Tampa International Airport**, a hub for traffic from Europe, the Caribbean, Mexico, South America and most of the US. This slick and extremely efficient facility has been voted the best airport in the nation by the Airline Passengers Association for the ease with which you can walk from stacked parking lots to ticket counters and on to shuttle cars that whisk you from the terminal's lobbies to gateside and back. At the southern point of the city, many of the country's combat pilots earn their wings at **MacDill Air Force Base**.

On Fowler Avenue in northeast Tampa, the **University of South Florida** serves 25,000 students on a campus that offers a planetarium and fine arts gallery for visitors. Its large arts faculty has become a leader in new visual forms, as exemplified by a sculpture called "Collected Ghost Stories from the Workhouse" by the noted Alice Aycock, with its controversial blend of moving wheels, bottles and spinning platforms.

Beer lovers may wish to take a guided tour of the **Joseph Schlitz Brewing Co.**, easily recognizable on 30th Street not far from campus by its silos painted to resemble giant beer cans.

On Busch Boulevard, the brewers who bring you Budweiser have outkitsched Schlitz by transforming the grounds around their plant into a miniature Africa – sort of – alive with wild animals, snake charmers and tropical birds.

The African connection: The 300-acre theme park that has evolved around Busch Brewery and Gardens is billed as **The Dark Continent** – to the dismay of black residents who had hoped that unenlightened term had gone the way of George Wallace. The name has stuck, however, and the initial racial furor has subsided. The attraction now entices more tourists than any other Florida theme park except Disney World and Sea World.

It all started simply as **Busch Gardens**, a patch southwest of the factory where families used to stare at flamingoes, converse with parrots and drink

A summer storm slows traffic on a Tampa superhighway.

free beer (limit three to a customer) at the **Hospitality House** after a tour of the brewery – where barrels of hops are turned into beer and squirted into bottles and cans traveling at breakneck speed on incredible conveyor belts.

The Busch family added an **Old Swiss House** restaurant, then some wild animals for people to watch while dining. Then someone who realized the Florida terrain could pass for an African plain brought in more animals, constructed a train and monorail to cruise the grounds, and soon discovered people would pay admission for a close look at zebras, giraffes, elephants and tigers who run free of zoo bars. Taking a cue from Walt Disney, Busch entered the theme park competition without looking back. Its animal area became the **Serengeti Plain** and a pond in its midst was named **Lake Tanganyika**. They called the small animal farm **Nairobi** and a section with a theater and log flume **Stanleyville**.

Newer additions include sanitized versions of **Morocco**, the **Congo** and **Timbuktu**. A large hall that looks like a Foreign Legion outpost is the **Festhaus** and entertains the hot and hungry with an air-conditioned Octoberfest year round. Anyone expecting to visit Africa in Florida shouldn't quibble about finding a German oasis in Timbuktu.

There are also the inevitable thrill rides: the neck-twisting Python, the back-wrenching Scorpion, the Ubanga-banga bumper cars, the nauseating Mamba, and the African Queen jungle cruise which the park ballyhooes as having live animals, *not* plastic ones.

After a steamy day in the jungle, you can refresh yourself in the body flumes, lagoons and waterfalls of **Adventure Island** across 56th Street (for a separate admission charge).

Tampa panders to all people. The greyhounds match muscled strides at **Tampa Track**; horses do the same at **Tampa Bay Downs**. The Tampa Bay Buccaneers butt heads with other professional football teams at **Tampa Stadium** whenever the Tampa Bay Rowdies aren't getting their North American Soccer League kicks in the grass there.

High-flying Buccaneers collar a Cowboy.

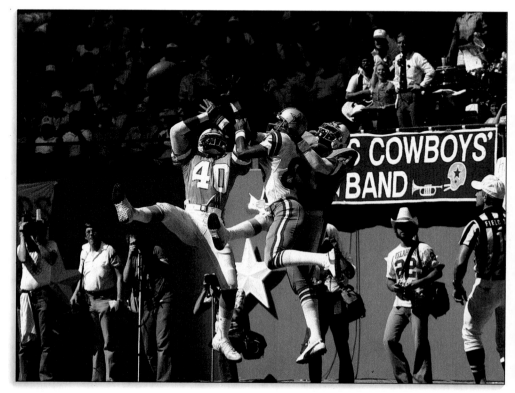

Strip joints beckon voyeurs on late-night **Dale Mabry**.

Showtown, USA: Take US 41 south along Tampa Bay for a look at the industrial side of the state. Here, the stacks of chemical factories edge the water instead of palm trees. The road crosses a bridge over the **Alafia River** into **Gibsonton**. The **Giant's Fish Camp** is a clue to what you will find in this campy town. Fat men, bearded ladies, dwarves, the Alligator-Skinned Man, the Acrobatic Half Girl – you might see them all shopping for groceries.

The city's proximity to Sarasota, where John Ringling lived and assembled his fabulous circuses early this century, attracted them. Most of these "show people," as they prefer to be called, live here from November to May when they are not on the road.

Whatever you do, don't stop your car and stare, but it's all right to mingle and chat with them at the **Showman's Bar**.

The naked and the plucked: North of Tampa, nature lovers of the au naturel species will find one of the nation's oldest and largest nudist colonies – **Lake Como** in **Lutz** on US 41. The camp has made Tampa a leader in the anti-clothes movement and spawned a developing **Paradise Lakes** condominium complex for the naked in **Land O'Lakes Navajo Lodge Health Resort** in nearby **Port Richey** and at unofficial, clothes-optional spots like **Beer Can Island** off **Davis Island** in Tampa Bay. **Zephyrhills** boasts more than a bizarre name. It hosts the world parachuting championships. Six miles south of town, **Hillsborough River State Park** has 3,000 forested acres and a scary suspension bridge.

Further north on US 41, **Brooksville** is the hub of a natural wonderland. The 20-mile scenic **Dogwood Trail** takes you through **Chinsegut Hill National Wildlife Refuge** and **Withlacoochee State Forest**. The **Dade Battlefield State Historic Site** is at the north end of the forest, near **Bushnell**. It's a memorial to Major Francis L. Dade and his 100 men who were massacred here at the start of the Seminole Wars in 1835.

South of Brooksville, **Masaryktown** still celebrates Czechoslovakian Independence Day, the last Sunday of October, with native foods and dancing. Czechs settled here in 1925. Neighboring **Spring Hill** has earned its place in the Guinness Book of World Records as the site of the annual World's Chicken Pluckin' Championship.

North of Zephyrhills on State Road 52, the city of **St Leo** is almost totally owned by the non-profit **Saint Leo College**, the **St Leo Abbey**, a Benedictine monastery and the **Holy Name Priory**. Nuns and monks regularly get elected to the city commission.

Three bridges connect Tampa to the Pinellas County resorts across the bay. The **Howard Frankland** (15,782 feet long) is the longest and most traveled because it's part of I-275. The excitement of the long ride over water dissolves, however, when a car breaks down midway, especially if it's yours. There are no emergency lanes. Alternatively, the **Gandy Bridge** is a more pleasant means of getting from Tampa to St Petersburg and back.

Gibsonton resident fondles his performing pet.

ST PETERSBURG

St Petersburg has always been the antithesis of Tampa. It's a slow-paced resort city with a reputation for catering to large numbers of fixed-income elderly. But with the booming changes sweeping the Suncoast, even sedate St Pete has begun shedding its old image. Downtown buildings are taking on new facades, while restaurants and lounges reach out for a younger, upwardly mobile crowd. The American Stage Company continues to offer live theater intermixed with foreign films at its Central Avenue stage and the summer afternoon band concerts in Williams Park are drawing an enthusiastic younger audience these days.

The opening of a **Bayboro Harbor** branch of the **University of South Florida** marked another milestone in Downtown St Petersburg's revitalization. The college kids have found the old hotels and boarding houses near

campus economical and share them with the aged. The university library is named after the late owner of the Times Publishing Company, Nelson Poynter, a leader in the city's growth. Poynter's publications, housed in editorial offices on First Avenue South and 50th Street, include the nationally-respected, Pulitzer Prize-winning *St Petersburg Times*. The company has pioneered the use of eye-catching graphics and quality color photographic reproduction on newsprint while maintaining high journalistic standards in its editorial columns and news reports.

The loveliest and most eye-catching feature of Downtown is its **Bayfront**. The **Municipal Marina** offers a variety of sailboats at their moorings, many with exotic names like **Vanity's Fair** and **At World's End**, from ports around the world.

An inverted pyramid at the end of The Pier juts out into Tampa Bay from Second Avenue North. It encompasses a popular restaurant with romantic views, an observation deck on top and

Left, The Pier on St Pete's Bayfront. Below, colorful Sunken Gardens.

an array of shops and displays. The approach on The Pier offers a scenic stroll and a panorama of nature, from diving pelicans to jumping mullet, while seagulls cry overhead for a tossed tidbit.

The classic lines of world-class competition yachts add class to docks at the **St Petersburg Yacht Club** each February. Champion helmsmen like Atlanta Braves owner Ted Turner and Americas Cup winner Dennis Conner come to town along with magnificent craft like *Tenacious, Williwaw* and the *Kialoa.* The occasion is the running of the Southern Ocean Racing Conference (SORC). The tradition began with a St Petersburg to Havana race in 1930. That ended in 1959 when Fidel Castro took over Cuba. Since 1961, the sleek yachts have sliced through 370 miles of surf to Fort Lauderdale, then on to Nassau. Several weeks of short competitions, fine-tuning, testing and, of course, partying, precede the main event, then the yachts tack out to an area off **Pinellas Point** where a series of gunshots marks the start of each class.

Doting on Dali: During its current renaissance, St Petersburg has also received a sorely-needed cultural transfusion. In fact, a neat, spacious building adjacent to the USF Bayboro campus houses one of the world's largest collection of paintings by the late Spanish surrealist, Salvador Dali. The **Dali Museum**, opened in 1982, contains a total of 93 oils, 200 watercolors and drawings, and 1,000 prints by the noted artist. They are displayed on a rotating basis.

The collection was assembled over a 40-year period by a wealthy Cleveland, Ohio plastics machinery designer, A. Reynolds Morse, and his wife, Eleanor. Experts have estimated the total value of the art works at $35 million.

Guided tours through the collection – and the offbeat career of Dali – begin at regular intervals in the lobby. From the museum, it is a short drive north to St Petersburg's Bayfront.

While along the waterfront, keep an eye out for a small, brick building near the foot of Second Avenue North. It's a public restroom called affectionately by

Meditating at the Dali Museum.

locals "Little St Mary's." Legend has it that an architect for St Mary Our Lady of Grace Church a few blocks south of there used the same blueprints when commissioned by the city to design a public facility.

Next door, the **St Petersburg Historical Museum** contains Indian artifacts from the significant Weedon Island and Safety Harbor cultures. The **Museum of Fine Arts** on Beach Drive has European, Oriental and American art. Historical homes open for tours in the area are the **Grace S. Turner House, Lowe House** and **Haas Museum**, all in the 3500 block of Second Avenue South. **Beach Drive** has taken on a continental look with expensive shops and the **Plaza Mall. Peter's Place** here is among the state's finest gourmet restaurants.

The **Al Lang Field** south of Beach Drive is the spring training home of the St Louis Cardinals. The **Bayfront Center** has hosted diverse entertainments – from the annual filming of the Ringling Brothers and Barnum and Bailey Circus television special to annual sold-out performances by Lawrence Welk and his troupe, to Broadway shows. Even Bob Dylan has played here.

North of The Pier, the impressive, sand-colored building on the horizon once catered to wealthy patrons. The **Vinoy Hotel** now caters to vagrants and vandals. Its windows are broken and the paint is cracking, but there has been talk of restoring it. West of the bayfront, green benches still line the streets of downtown as they have since 1907.

Mirror Lake is a shady place for pensive moods. A geyser-like fountain spouts at programmed intervals. On its northern edge, you'll hear the crackle and shush of shufflers at play at the world's largest shuffleboard club. Adjoining the courts is the **Shuffleboard Hall of Fame**. Here, such greats as Mae Hall and Lucy Perkins have been enshrined. The **Coliseum** on Fourth Avenue N. features ballroom dancing to the sounds of Big Band-era orchestras.

Free outdoor concerts often sound off at the **William's Park Bandshell**, a pigeon feeder's paradise. This bandshell and all of downtown marches to the beat of All-American high school bands every March.

Of bands and boats: When invited to participate in St Petersburg's Festival of States, high school musicians throughout the country spend their winters selling oranges and hawking concert tickets to raise money for the trip south. They jam downtown hotels four to a room, warm up their tubas and trombones while dangling their feet in Tampa Bay, and participate in prestigious competitions for the Mayor's and Governor's Cup which highlight a week of festivities. More than 100 bands take part in a parade that closes the festival.

It was the extension of Peter Demens' Orange Belt Railroad into the Pinellas Peninsula that gave birth to St Petersburg. Demens, the Russian exile who named the city for his birthplace in 1888, shaped it with the aid of Detroiter John C. Williams. Its reputation as a health spa lured elderly Yankees early on. Hollywood director Robert Altman filmed his little-seen movie *Health* here.

Progressive residents have been try-

Dali's depiction of sails and saints.

ing to shake their city's image as a haven for the old and ill. Early this century, they dreamed up a "purity league" that demanded the city outlaw "shocking bathing suits" in hopes the publicity would draw young people wanting to see the suits. "Doc" Webb opened "The World's Largest Drugstore" – a fore-runner of modern shopping complexes, that included a floor full of talking plastic mermaids and live dancing ducks – and held beauty contests on the premises. Eventually, St Petersburg settled into a cluster of neighborhoods: **Snell Isle** with its winding streets and gaudy mansions; the **Northeast's** brick streets and Spanish-Mediterranean homes; the **Pink Streets** near Pinellas Point; and **The Jungle** (in jungles on **Boca Ciega Bay** that are so thick you can barely see the old estate through the vines and trees).

Other points of interest include **Sunken Gardens** on Fourth Street, a once water-logged sinkhole drained and landscaped by George Turner 70 years ago. Tropical birds and exotic plants still make it one of the state's better garden attractions. The **Boyd Hill Nature Trail** skirts **Lake Maggiore** off Ninth Street.

Other fine parks are **Lake Seminole, Sawgrass** and **Bay Pines**. The latter, on the piney grounds of a Veterans' Administration Hospital, often plays host to rare and nesting bald eagles. Historic homes have been renovated and moved to **Heritage Park** at Walsingham and 125th Street in neighboring **Largo**.

The regal structure across from Pasadena Golf Course, once the Rolyat Hotel, now encompasses the classrooms of **Stetson Law School**.

On the southern fringes of the city, **Mullet Key** is the site of the area's finest park – **Fort De Soto**. The series of penny ante toll booths, thoroughly irritating and incomprehensible, should not deter you from a drive to this oasis of calm in a West Coast sea of development. You can scramble around the historic fort, watch huge tankers ease into Tampa Bay from the beach, and also pitch your tent here overnight.

Finger-fill houses in St Pete's Shore Acres.

The Bayway itself was once a magnificent drive across **Boca Ciega Bay**, with unobstructed views of sand, sea and fowl. That changed in the '70s when developers crammed in condos.

Tierra Verde, on the way to Fort De Soto, is another island once lush with mangroves and wildlife. It is now lush with condos and homes. In fact it was so primitive a paradise, that at one time an eccentric chap by the name of Silas Dent built himself a palm frond hut and lived the life of "the happy hermit" here, existing on fish and fowl, playing his banjo and rowing across the channel to the nearby settlement of Pass-a-Grille in his Santa Claus suit, to the delight of local children. Dent became such a living legend that his death, at the age of 76 in 1952, warranted an obituary in the *New York Times*.

The Gulf beaches: The long, narrow islands clinging to the west coast of Pinellas County resisted mass intrusion by developers longer than the lower East Coast islands. However, thoughtless landowners and construction crews have made up for lost time over the past few decades. Early settlers confined themselves to Pass-a-Grille, at the southern end of Long Key, now known as **St Petersburg Beach**, and north at **Sand Key** in the vicinity of **Indian Rocks Beach**. It's hard to imagine today, but flamingos, wild boars, sea turtles, deer and alligators were once more common sights in these islands than people. Today there are more than 30,000 full-time residents, a total swelled by tens of thousands during the holidaying spring.

Turn left when the Bayway ends to **Pass-a-Grille**. The pink palace in front of you is the **Don Cesar Hotel**. It's had its ups-and-downs since T.J. Rowe erected it in the 1920s. Scott Fitzgerald and his wife Zelda are said to have been among its illustrious guests. The army bought the building for use as a hospital during World War II, but it was restored and reincarnated into a hotel in 1973.

The Don marks the southern boundary of a wall of big beach hotels. South of it, Pass-a-Grille still retains some of its fishing village charm.

The Don Cesar Resort Hotel.

TO CLEARWATER AND BEYOND

North on Gulf Boulevard, an endless procession of hotels, condominiums, fast food restaurants, T-shirt shops and concrete are barely distinguishable from one another in what's left of the scenery. Property owners have inexplicably fought for high density zoning from here to Sand Key, burying the beauty so many come to Florida to find, then wondering why real estate values here don't match those in more sensibly planned communities like Longboat Key near Sarasota.

Fortunately, this strip still boasts some of the state's best beaches, but their sands are behind all those buildings so you will have to use "public access" paths to get to most of them.

Points of interest in St Petersburg Beach run from the inescapable – the **London Wax Museum** – to the pleasantly surprising – the "early diner" architecture of the **Pelican Diner** on the corner of Gulf Boulevard and A19A. To continue the drive up these beaches, turn north onto Blind Pass Road from A19A. It runs back into Gulf Boulevard and onto **Treasure Island** (which early settlers named after hearing of treasure chests buried here). No treasure has ever been found. **Sunset Beach** harbors an ever-increasing number of stilt houses facing the Gulf. Otherwise, it is more of the same – buildings. The municipal beach here is an extraordinary wide piece of sand. A drawbridge connects Treasure Island with **Madeira Beach**, also known as "Mad Beach." **Bird Key**, east of the span in **John's Pass**, is a roost for birds, but for an insight into what happens to them when they come up against the motors, fishing lines and deliberate cruelty of modern man – proceed north to the **Suncoast Seabird Sanctuary** in **Indian Shores**.

The Bird Man of Florida: Birds can't pay for hospital visits, but that hasn't stopped Ralph Heath from catering to them. He depends on contributions from bird-lovers the world over to tend the sick

Anglers dangle lines off a Clearwater Beach pier.

and injured, a cause that has made him a celebrity on TV programs like ABC's *20/20* and in the old "Profile" ads for Dewars scotch. (Heath never drank Dewars.) In fact, word of his Suncoast Seabird Sanctuary has flown so far that Heath finds injured fowl actually flying or limping into his clinic of their own accord. He also boats in search of birds who may have gotten hung up in fishing lines and were mauled, accidentally or intentionally, by thoughtless humans. You can visit his fascinating sanctuary without charge, but have a generous heart when you pass one of the contribution boxes.

Healthy peacocks strut around the grounds of **Tiki Gardens**, an oasis of "Polynesian" kitsch tucked among the forest of condominiums in Indian Shores. The Gardens offers items collected by its original developer, Frank Byars, during trips to Hawaii and the South Pacific. There's also **Trader Frank's** Polynesian-style restaurant.

The Intracoastal Waterway butts against the edge of Gulf Boulevard as you enter **Indian Rocks Beach.** The Gulf is only yards away to the west, a reason why this sliver is called "The Narrows." The railroad once brought Tampans right to this beach resort, so many older families still own weekend retreats here. You can fish for shark from the **Big Indian Rocks Pier**.

Gulf Boulevard proceeds north past the big gulf-front homes of **Belleair Beach** to the tip of **Sand Key**. Once a desolate sand spur thick with Norfolk pines, its natural beauty has been all but obliterated by highrises.

Another sandy resort, one that is increasingly popular among travelers from Canada, Great Britain and West Germany, basks in the sun that almost always shines on **Clearwater Beach** across the toll bridge from Sand Key. Its long, wide beach, blinding white in daylight, even has a few dunes. You'll find patches of sea oats shimmying in the gulf breezes, but don't pick or trample these endangered, protected plants.

Condos and a cult: Across landscaped **Memorial Causeway**, Clearwater

Antique decor at the Kapok Tree restaurant.

proper rests on a bit of bluff. It is the government seat of Pinellas, Florida's most densely-inhabited county. Clearwater evolved around Henry Plant's classic, wooden **Belleview Biltmore Hotel** which opened in 1897. It still stands, flanked by a few modern additions, on the bay behind two rolling golf courses. This colossal heart-pine structure is listed in the National Registry of Historic Places.

Another old hotel, the Fort Harrison, is no longer open to the public. Instead, it has become the "flag" headquarters of the controversial **Church of Scientology**. This California-based group, founded in the early 1950s by science-fiction writer L.Ron Hubbard, claims several million adherents throughout the world. Its foothold in otherwise conservative Clearwater has caused much concern among residents.

For an overall look at the city, try Gulf-port artist Steve Smith's aerial mural atop the city Utilities Building at Chestnut and Prospect. Smith has also painted a postcard mural that decorates the lobby of St Petersburg's main library. The Clearwater offices of the *St Petersburg Times* provide a look at the future, being powered by a windmill and layered solar panels on the roof.

Connoisseurs of kitsch may want to follow the droves of tourists who patronize the **Kapok Tree** restaurant on McMullen-Booth Road on the Tampa Bay side of the city. The routine here is to sip a tall Planter's Punch while strolling through 18th-century baroque Italian gardens and fountains out back. A loud-speaker will summon you to dine in one of several garish rooms. Afterward, take a scenic drive along parallel Bayshore to quaint **Safety Harbor**. A small, interesting history and fine arts museum south of Main Street has been built here near a Timucuan Indian mound.

Scots and Greeks: Early Scottish immigrants established the community of **Dunedin** north of Clearwater. A squeal of bagpipes fills the air every March when a kilted and tartan-clad band kicks off the annual Highland Games festival.

Cross **Hurricane Pass** by boat from **Dunedin Beach** to **Caladesi Island State Park**. It is a pocket of tranquility away from the traffic and piledrivers on the mainland – 1,400 acres of cabbage palms, yucca plants and sand. Get an eagle's-eye view from the 60-foot observation tower.

You will have to grit your teeth and bear the drive north up US 19, by far one of Florida's most abominable boulevards. Mobile home parks, malls, country music parlors, condominiums, billboards, signal lights and traffic clash in an unnerving drive that gives one second thoughts about pushing onward. More pleasant, but also slow, is Alternate 19. Both highways emerge in another of those Florida incongruities, a city that would look more at home in Greece's Aegean Sea.

Tarpon Springs sprang up on the Anclote river around the turn of the century when Peter Demens brought in his railroad. With Key West's sponge beds dwindling, John Corcoris summoned his brothers and friends from the Aegean islands to test the beds around

Tarpon Springs shipbuilder.

132

Tarpon Springs. They found them rich in sponges. Tarpon Springs soon stripped the title of "Sponge Capital" away from Key West.

Corcoris pioneered the use of old, copper-helmeted diving suits to hunt for sponges in deeper waters. These early outfits, clumsy and poorly made, sometimes became shrouds for the brave young Greek divers who wore them. But the industry grew into a multi-million dollar business. It began to ebb in the 1940s when red tide disease ruined some of the beds. Later, the introduction of inexpensive, synthetic sponges virtually shut down the industry.

But that Greek heritage still drives this colorful city. Most visitors head straight for the historic sponge docks along **Dodecanese Boulevard**, perhaps more accurately called shrimp docks now. Spongers still man a few boats and you may spot some cleaning their catch on deck. Tourists can also board a boat for a demonstration of sponge-diving – although there are rumors about that the divers stuff a sponge inside their suit before diving to ensure that they will "bring one up."

You can buy genuine sponges from the sea here in a variety of forms – either wool sponges, wire sponges, finger sponges or loofahs for body massages. A **Spongerama** exhibits items and photos from earlier sponging days. Most of the historic **Sponge Exchange** itself, built in 1907 to provide a place for storage and auctions, has fallen to the tides of time and demolition experts. The owners of the popular **Louis Pappas' Riverside** restaurant (delicious food in spite of the crowds and off-the-wall architecture) began demolishing the Exchange in 1981 to make way for another mall full of souvenir shops. Some members of the city's 20,000 strong Greek community, appalled at the prospect of losing this link with their past, got a court order to stop the wrecking ball in mid-flight. The State Legislature, meanwhile, deliberated belatedly whether to buy the Exchange, as a historical site. But the Pappas' had already battered a large portion of the storied

A diver and crew prepare to plunge for sponges in the 1930s at Tarpon Springs' docks.

walls into rubble before being stopped. People draped black cloth along the boulevard in a gesture some said would put a curse.

Curse or not, their restaurant is thriving. Big Greek salads, *mousaka, baklava* and other native dishes are served along with fresh seafood. Or try some of the holes-in-the-walls in this part of town where the food is usually more delightful than the decor. **Zorba's** is the best place if you want to watch belly dancers.

In addition to sponge-diving, boat-building has always been big business in Tarpon Springs (as it is in most of Pinellas County). Small builders like **Peer Lovfald Marine** here concentrate on customized yachts, while shipbuilding giants like **Irwin Yachts**, **Gulfstar** and **Watkins Yachts** have larger assembly plants in some of the neighboring communities.

St Nicholas Greek Orthodox Cathedral on Pinellas Avenue in downtown Tarpon Springs dates to 1943. Its neo-Byzantine walls are chock full of icons, including a statue of the Blessed Mother that has been said to shed tears at times. The **Universalist Church** on Grand Boulevard has a collection of paintings by the late landscape artist, George Inness, Jr. Prime time in the city is the Feast of the Epiphany in January when the Greek Orthodox archbishop comes to town to bless local waters and toss a crucifix into **Spring Bayou**. Boys aged 16 to 18 dive into the chilly winter waters to retrieve it and earn extra blessings for themselves and their families. A dove, symbolic of the Holy Spirit, is released to begin a *glendi* with Greek food, music and dance.

Near Tarpon Springs on US 19, **Innisbrook**, one of the plushest resorts in the country, offers accommodations on package plans in the midst of three championship golf courses, tennis courts and rolling, wooded splendor. **A.L. Anderson Park** on **Lake Tarpon** is a pretty place for a picnic.

Mermaids of the spring: A collection of burgeoning new communities and snoozing old ones alternate the rest of

Epiphany Rites, St Nicholas Greek Orthodox Cathedral.

the way up the West Coast. **New Port Richey**, which grew at a 75 percent clip during the 1970s, sports the worse traits of rapid urbanization with its jammed highways and indiscriminate development. It also holds the *Guinness Book of World Records* mark for throwing the largest barbecue, a distinction the local Sertoma Club attempts to surpass annually at its Chasco Festival on the banks of the **Pithlachascotee River**.

The number of cars and convenience stores thin out as you cross into **Hernando County**. Since 1947, live mermaids have played in the waters of **Weeki Wachee Spring** here, on US 19. It is just beyond the 110-foot long, 48-foot tall concrete dinosaur that looms over Harold and Dana Hurst's Fina gas station. Named by Indians for the "winding waters" of its snaking river that flows to the Gulf, **Weeki Wachee** sprang from immeasurable depths. Navy frogman Newton Perry found its waters so clear he used them to stage underwater shows. He taught young women the techniques of breathing through hoses

Harold and Dana Hurst at their "prehistoric" service station.

so they could remain far below the surface for long periods of time. Then he dressed them in mermaid costumes and a famous attraction was born.

The Weeki Wachee mermaids perform strenuous acrobatics about 16 feet underwater, which you watch through plate glass windows. The park also offers a cruise down the river past a rain forest (where sprinklers provide the precipitation) and a pelican orphanage for 60 recovering patients from the Suncoast Seabird Sanctuary. Weeki Wachee also delights in those plastic sculptures so characteristic of old Florida, including King Neptune and family. The only beach in the vicinity is a small patch at **Pine Island Park** on the western tip of County Road 595. Crabbers and fishermen prefer the pier at **Bayport Park**.

US 19 here becomes a more pleasant drive north. You may even be lucky enough to see your car's headlights reflected off the eyes of a deer late at night. The next town of any consequence, **Chassahowitzka**, marks the entrance to a national wildlife refuge of

the same name. A remnant of the region's relocated sweets industry is the **Yulee Sugar Mill Historical Memorial**. **Homossassa** (Indian for "the place of pepper trees") **Springs** has been turned into another tourist attraction, but is not quite as commercialized as **Silver Springs**.

In **Crystal River**, you can swim with a herd of manatees, the docile, but endangered, mammals that resemble a cross between an elephant and a walrus. Some say the best way to attract them so you can pat their backs is by humming "The Star-Spangled Banner" into a snorkel. More than 100 springs keep **King's Bay** filled, while the **Crystal River State Archeological Site** marks the center of a huge ceremonial ground for Indians who lived here about 1,600 years ago. About 450 graves have been opened here and have yielded important relics of that era. North of Crystal City, locks of the unfinished **Cross Florida Barge Canal** adjoin US 19. They are a symbol of one victory environmentalists can claim. Shippers have tried to engineer construction of a canal connecting the Gulf of Mexico to the Atlantic Ocean since 1818. Work finally began in the 1930s. It proceeded, with many interruptions, until conservationists, worried about damage to the Oklawaha River, convinced President Nixon to halt the canal construction in 1971. The state cabinet eventually voted to abandon the project in 1976.

Head west on State Road 24 for the 25-mile drive to Cedar Key, a sleepy resort which served as one of the busiest ports and the largest city in the state only a century ago. Manufacturers made pencils from the cedar trees that gave this group of small islands their name. Even Florida's first big railroad line terminated here. A severe hurricane leveled the town in 1896 and it never regained its former importance. The **Cedar Key State Museum** documents the port's short-lived prominence.

Cedar Key remains a favorite destination of seafood lovers who flock to its small restaurants that serve up turtle steak and deviled crab with swamp cabbage salad. Thousands cross the scenic bridges to the island for a Sidewalk Art Festival in April and a Seafood Festival each October.

Towards the southern latitudes: The **Sunshine Skyway** staples the Pinellas peninsula to the southern stretches of the West Coast. Total tollbooth-to-tollbooth length is about 11 miles, with a central bridge more than 4 miles long and 250 feet above the water. The height enables oil tankers and fertilizer freighters to pass underneath en route from the Gulf to the Port of Tampa. But even those specifications, thought sufficient when the first span opened in 1954, have not been able to accommodate today's enormous ships. On a stormy, May 9 morning in 1980, a phosphate freighter rammed the southbound span of the Skyway. The metal grill roadbed – and a bus, cars, and a truck that had been crossing it – plunged into the bay, killing 35 people.

Now a beautiful, golden span stretches over the blue waters, past the remnants of the old bridge with its gaping maw. The new bridge features a main span supported by twin, fan-like arrangements of cables, and this unusual style of construction makes the Sunshine Skyway well worth its $1 toll each way, and ranks it as Florida's first suspension bridge. Nevertheless, the Skyway is likely to remain haunted by the accident and other incidents that have tarnished its history.

A Coast Guard cutter called the *Blackthorne* rammed another freighter near the bridge only months before it fell. The cutter sank and crewmen died. A memorial to the men of the *Blackthorne* can be visited in a park north of the bridge. The top of the Skyway has also been a favorite jumping-off spot for suicides.

Terra Ceia Island, immediately west of the Sunshine Skyway, is the site of the **Madira Bickel Mound Historic Memorial**, believed to have been occupied by primitive Indians from the time of the birth of Christ until the 17th century. There is a burial mound about 20 feet high that was used during the Weedon Island archaeological period from AD 700 to 1400.

Right, a mermaid sparkles amid the seashells at Weeki Wachee.

SARASOTA AND POINTS SOUTH

South of the Sunshine Skyway, signs point the way to the **J.P. Benjamin Memorial** in **Ellenton**. This white, frame Southern mansion has 18 pillars surrounding the front veranda and sides. It was built by Major Robert Gamble Jr. around 1845 (making it the oldest home on Florida's West Coast). The major once employed some 300 slaves on a 1,500-acre sugar plantation on the grounds. Gamble provided refuge here after the Civil War for the Secretary of State of the defeated Confederacy, Judah P. Benhamin. He later escaped to England. Don't be surprised that Florida has chosen to honor a war fugitive with a memorial: the birthday of Confederate President Jefferson Davis is celebrated as a state holiday.

Ellenton has also attracted a growing number of residents, permanent and seasonal, who subscribe to the Mennonite faith. These men with their distinctive hats and beards and women wearing old-fashioned bonnets and dresses have brought a flavor to the city usually associated with Pennsylvania Dutch country and the Amish areas of Ohio and Indiana.

US 41 continues south through **Palmetto** and crosses the **Manatee River** into **Bradenton**. The river is named for the sea mammal, but heavy boat traffic has decimated its numbers here. During the high spring season, automobiles inch along US 41 in solid lines that often stretch all the way from the Skyway to **Fort Myers**. The opening of Interstate 75 has begun to alleviate some of that heavy traffic.

A national monument at the mouth of the Manatee commemorates the landing of Hernando de Soto in 1539. Modern day conquistadors (actually local businessmen) reenact the landing each March during a week of festivities in Bradenton. The helmets worn by de Soto and crew were forged in Germany from molds used during the days of the legitimate de Soto and the swords were

Left, Renaissance statuary in the Ringling courtyard. Below, the circus king's home, C'ad'zan.

forged from imported Toledo steel. A contingent of prominent people from Spain regularly attend the show. The highlight is a pageant at the memorial that traces the exploits of the ruthless, but courageous, conquistadors.

Settlers didn't put down roots on the river until about 300 years after de Soto's arrival. Among them was a sugar planter, Joseph Braden, who gave the town his name. The ruins of **Braden Castle** are off State Road 64. The city fringes remain agricultural with tomato farms and packers, citrus groves and processors. At US 41 on 26th Avenue East, you can watch oranges and grapefruits bounce along conveyor belts while workers sort them into chutes for packing. Owner Bill Mixon ships more than 100,000 crates a year.

Cultural Sarasota, a city the circus built: You can reach **Sarasota** via US 41 South, but the island chain across **Sarasota Bay** provides a more pleasant approach. Take State Road 64 west from Bradenton to **Anna Maria Island**, then head south on Gulf Drive. You will pass through weathered **Bradenton Beach** and posh **Longboat Key**, getting good peeks at azure Gulf waters all along the way. The drive runs snack into **St Armands Circle**, a ring of expensive boutiques and restaurants named after its original, French owner. But the man for whom the intersecting boulevard is named, circus master John Ringling, left a more indelible imprint on Florida, from Venice to Gibsonton to Barnum City's Circus World. The street patterns and Italian statuary here on **Lido Key** are circus elephants.

The hub of Ringling's world lies back up US 41, past the lilac-colored, shell-shaped **Van Wezel Auditorium** and the **Sarasota Jungle Gardens** on Bayshore Road to glittering **C'ad'zan**, a museum of art and the circus, and the **Asolo State Theater**. Flush with a fortune from his "Greatest Show on Earth," and lucrative investments in oil, railroads and real estate, Ringling brought in artisans, stone, tapestries and art from around the world. The 30-room mansion, patterned after the Doges' Palace in Venice, Italy,

The adventures of The Three Musketeers at Asolo State Theater.

was completed in 1926 as a gift to his wife, Mabel. *C'ad'zan* means "House of John" in Venetian. Tour the cavernous living room with its tapestries and Aeolian pipe organ, then walk through the landscaped grounds that are studded with fat banyan trees.

Ringling collected so much art he decided to erect a museum to put it in. He patterned the adjoining edifice after a 15th-century Florentine villa. It now contains one of the world's most important collections of works by the Flemish painter, Pierre Paul Rubens, in its large Baroque art section. A magnificent bronze cast of Michaelangelo's David dominates the courtyard. A less imposing building houses the circus museum with memorabilia from Ringling's three-ring extravaganzas.

The Ringling influence transformed Sarasota into the cultural nerve center of Florida. A prime example of that function is the nationally-renowned **Asolo State Theater** company which performs an annual selection of plays in an 18th-century Italian theater. The interior was dismantled piece-by-piece at a castle in Asolo, Italy, then shipped here in 1950 and reassembled behind the art museum.

Special events also add to the excitement of the Ringling complex. An arts and crafts festival attracts hundreds of exhibitors and thousands of buyers from around the country each year. More unusual, but in keeping with Ringling's eccentricities, is a Medieval Fair held each March. The setting lends itself to performers who resurrect the days of King Arthur. Knights in armor joust on the bay. Cone-capped maidens frolic in the gardens. Craftsmen shear sheep, spin flax and carve flutes. Roving minstrels spin lusty ballads.

You will find a human chess match where live actors and athletes engage in axe-wielding, sword-swinging, mace-mashing combat with frightening reality.

The University of South Florida's **New College** campus north of the museum has several buildings designed by architect I.M. Pei. The school emphasizes the liberal and performing arts.

Knights shine in armor prior to a joust at Ringling Museum's annual Medieval Fair.

Van Wezel offers operas, symphony and ballet. Writers, notably, the late John D. MacDonald, have found inspiration here. MacDonald wrote the popular Travis McGee novels that have sold more than 23 million copies.

Nature lovers, too, will find inspiration at **Myakka River State Park** on Stater Road 72. It is a wildlife refuge larger than Disney World and kept as close as possible to its pristine state. You can tour it by car or bicycle over a scenic 7-mile road or aboard guided boat and train tours.

Other Sarasota sights include **Bellm's Car and Music of Yesterday**, the **Marie Selby Botanical Gardens** on South Palm Drive, and the **Lionel Train and Seashell Museum** on US 41. Golfers may be interested to learn that Scotland's Col. John Gillespie built the nation's first golf links here in 1886.

Clown town: Sarasota's circus legacy has spilled over into **Venice**, 20 miles south on US 41. All three rings winter here in quarters on Airport Avenue and stage combined dress rehearsals of the national touring companies before they hit the road each year.

A large, hangar-like building on the grounds serves as the hallowed halls of the **Ringling Clown College**. About 5,000 applicants vie for 60 spots in its celebrated classes each year. After a 9-week course, about half the class graduates to professional clowndom in one of the road shows or at Circus World. Ex-clown and college director Bill Ballentine explained that "We found the clown art form was slowly dying for a lack of new talent. In the past, we would hold auditions, but most persons who responded just didn't have any talent. We then decided to see if we could train our own."

Venice was planned early in Florida's development and still boasts wide streets and parks. **Warm Mineral Springs** on US 41 and San Servando Avenue, 12 miles south of Venice, touts the therapeutic value of its 87° waters that contain sodium, sulfate, chloride and other natural chemicals. Warm Mineral Springs has in addition hosted im-

Sarasota: local high school students show their skills on the trapeze.

portant archaeological digs that have produced evidence of some of Florida's earliest residents.

Punta Gorda and **Port Charlotte**, still small, provide a change of pace from the rapid growth to the north and south. **Ponce de León Park** commemorates the landing place of the father of Florida, fatally wounded during an Indian attack. The old city dock has been transformed into a **Fisherman's Village** specialty mall. The **American Police Hall of Fame** and **Museum** in **North Port** exhibits murder weapons and electric chairs for those with a morbid sense of curiosity.

Swarms of ghosts of pirates and Spanish explorers inhabit **Charlotte Harbor**. You can cross a toll bridge at **Placida** to **Gasparilla Island** where the notorious, but imaginary, José Gaspar was rumored to have ruled. **Boca Grande**, in mid-island, is a retreat for the wealthy from up and down the West Coast. They pull into port in their yachts while cruising the Gulf.

Playground of a genius: You can double back to US 41 or Interstate 75 south to the **Fort Myers/Cape Coral** area, the fastest growing metropolis in the nation during the 1970s, when the combined population of the cities grew by 94.2 percent. It is still growing, the influx consisting mainly of Northeasterners who come to cash in on retirement lots purchased during their workings years.

The population surge adds more meat to stories about the incredible foresight of inventor Thomas Edison who predicted in 1914 that "There is only one Fort Myers, and 90 million people are going to find it out." Edison, however, managed to beat the rush when he built a winter estate here in 1886 at the age of 39. Doctors warned him his health was failing and advised him Florida's climate might help. It did. Edison lived until the age of 84 and produced some of his greatest post-light bulb inventions here. Edison perfected phonographs, motion pictures, the teletype and many of his other patented inventions in his Florida laboratory. He tried using bamboo that he found on the banks of the

SORC race entries sail past Fort Myers.

Caloosahatchee as light bulb filaments and experimented with the vulcanization of rubber from goldenrod grown in his gardens here.

The **Edison Winter Home and Museum** sprawls across both sides of McGregor Boulevard (State Road 867) beautified by the royal palms planted by Edison. The home and guest house, among the first pre-fabricated buildings in the US, were constructed in Maine and brought to Fort Myers by four schooners. Tropical gardens engulf the homes. Native Florida palms and satin leaf figs, calabash trees from South America, cinnamon trees from India and Malaysia – some 6,000 species were collected by Edison at a cost of about $100,000. Florida's first modern pool – built in 1900 with Edison's own Portland cement and reinforced with bamboo – has never cracked or leaked. In this paradisiacal setting he invented the future and entertained famous friends like next door neighbors Henry Ford and Harvey Firestone. Edison even offered to light up his new town with electrical installations, but the townspeople refused for fear the lights would keep their cattle awake at night.

Across the street, a museum contains photographs, personal items such as Edison's gold watch, a collection of automobiles, and a treasure house of inventions, including 170 photographs with huge, handpainted speakers and, of course, dozens of light bulbs. A strip of tin foil 5 inches wide and 18 inches long – the world's first record – still plays "Mary had a Little Lamb." The laboratory in back of the museum has been closed indefinitely because of concern about the stability of some of the aging chemicals inside. A banyan tree brought by Firestone from India in 1928 has grown into Florida's largest, with a circumference of 400 feet. Mrs Edison deeded all to the city in 1947 to be maintained as a shrine to her husband who died in 1928. A Pageant of Light tribute to the inventor illuminates the city each February.

Fort Myers is also the end of the line of **Shell Factory** billboards you have undoubtedly seen alongside highways during your Florida travels. It is a shell supermarket crammed with sea souvenirs. For an excursion into the Everglades without mounting a full-scale expedition, the **Everglades Jungle Cruise** takes you up the **Caloosahatchee River** to the edge of the vast wilderness on a 3-hour tour. The river was the main highway to Fort Myers in the days when the city still served as a stockade in the Seminole Wars fort network. More hardy adventurers can take the **Lazy Bones Shanty Boat Cruise**, a 5-day expedition all the way to Lake Okeechobee with side excursions on swamp buggies and airboats. Fort Myers is also the gateway to two islands where you can commune with nature within arms length of modern amenities.

Shunting for shells despite the "Sanibel Stoop": Area residents long fought construction of a causeway linking **Sanibel** and **Captiva Islands** to the mainland. The case went all the way to the Supreme Court. But the bridge builders won and since 1963 thousands of cars have driven right onto these fragile showcases of nature. Uncontrolled development threatened to turn Sanibel and Captiva into two more uninteresting specks heavy with highrises, until 1974 when Sanibel seceded from **Lee County**, set up its own city government, put a near halt to further growth, and even managed to keep out highrises.

Thus, you will find air-conditioned homes and hotels, restaurants, a few shopping centres, even a playhouse. But Sanibel also has the **J.N. "Ding" Darling National Wildlife Refuge**, named for the early environmentalist and newspaper cartoonist. A highlight of the 5-mile dike drive through the refuge is the sight of crimson-winged roseate spoonbills coming and going in the mornings and evenings in groups as regimented as air force squadrons. Their spatulate bills enable them to scoop up food from the shallow pools. That's the best way to differentiate them from flamingos. Anhingga "snake" birds, Louisiana herons, gulls, sanderlings, willet and vultures are among the hundreds of other birds that make the refuge home. Across the street, submerge yourself in nature at the **Sanibel-Captiva Conservation Foundation**.

Fortunately for the peace and well-being of the wildlife, these preserves are usually of secondary importance to tourists that descend on Sanibel. The island's reputation is built on its beaches which are usually so thick with shells you can't see the sand. Tides toss them up by the ton. And shelling is a science practiced by bent-over people afflicted with a local syndrome called the "Sanibel Stoop." Only Jeffreys Bay in Africa and the Sulu Islands in the Philippines are considered better for shelling. Of course, neither of those distant shores attracts the legions of collectors lured by Sanibel. In an attempt to restrict the practice and prevent Sanibel from becoming a shell of its former self, the city council allows only two live shells of each species to be taken per person. Early morning, and the hours after storms and heavy tides, are the best time to hit the beach armed with a wire mesh scoop and bucket. At those times you may find your feet sinking into the mounds of mollusk casings. You have now become a shunter (short for shell hunter).

Shunt for shells like the rare royal Florida miter, golden olive and spiny oyster, and you may find avid collectors offering their shirts for your finds. More common are the queen and horse conchs, murex, limpet, left-handed whelk, paper nautilus, cowrie, jewel boxes, jingles, tulips and lion's paw. A shelling checklist purchased anywhere on the islands will enable you to identify your finds.

The outside-in world of the Koreshans: Cross the bridge over **Blind Pass** to Captiva. Here, according to stories, José Gaspar hid his loot and held young girls captive – hence the island's name. The hitch in the story is that Spaniards christened the island long before Gaspar's alleged reign. The **South Seas Plantation** at the north end features low-slung, Polynesian-style villas textured to the terrain, plus tennis courts, a marina and the whole works.

The next point of interest on US 41 south memorializes one of the state's most unusual pioneer settlements. Reli-

Shell hunters indulge in "The Sanibel Stoop."

gious visionary Cyrus Reed Teed brought his followers from Chicago in 1894. He preached that the earth was a hollow sphere with the sun in the center and life covering the inner walls. A restored village at **Koreshan State Historic Site** in **Estero** demonstrates how Teed "proved" his theories and how his commune shared property and practiced celibacy. The movement never quite caught on, but the Koreshan newspaper, *The American Eagle*, and a magazine, *The Flaming Sword*, are still published by descendants of Teed's followers.

Gateway to Alligator Alley: The drive from Sanibel along State Road 901 through **Fort Myers Beach** and **Bonita Beach** is slow but scenic. It will get you to **Naples**, another of those sparkling, little Florida towns in the midst of a population explosion. It is being dissected into subdivisions filled with mobile homes, waterfront suburbs and condominium complexes.

Naples is laid out tidily with scrubbed avenues that end at excellent **Gulf Beaches**. Train buffs will enjoy **Naples Depot's** restored old rooms and boxcars turned into shops. The legendary *Orange Blossom Special* once stopped here. Former Clevelanders may want to pay a nostalgic visit to the **African Safari Park** in the **Caribbean Gardens** where Jungle Larry Tetzlaff and wife, Safari Jane, have set up winter quarters. Tetzlaff was a regular on the *Captain Penny* television show in that Ohio city. His animal collection has been gathered during expeditions around the world.

Naples is also the gateway to the Everglades and a boundary of the **Big Cypress Swamp**. There is an excellent nature center on Merrimue Drive on the **Gordon River**. In Naples, US 41, also known as the "Tamiami Trail" (short for Tampa-Miami), curves west into the vast river of grass. Laid out by rugged laborers who weathered yellow fever in the 1920s, the road still crosses some rugged territory to Miccosukee Indian camps and the **Redlands** vegetable acreage before turning into Little Havana's Calle Ocho in Miami. The other, newer route across the swamp is the unswerving **Alligator Alley** toll road.

A popular annual event on Radio Road west of the Naples Airport on the waist-deep **Mile-O-Mud Track** has captured national attention – the World Championship Swamp Buggy Races. Souped-up hunting half-tracks roar from the starting line in a cloud of goop. The race course is flooded with water for two weeks before the race to assure it is in the worst possible shape. First run in 1949 to signal the opening of the Everglades hunting season, the track also hosts events like the traditional dunking of a "Mud Duchess."

Marco Island eagles: Marco Island was another gorgeous Florida seascape caught in a tug-of-war between environmentalists and developers. The latter won. But they have pledged some concessions to nature. Some consider that the new developments are among the state's better planned communities. Developers have even erected artificial bald eagles' nests in the shadow of the condos in hopes of encouraging the birds to remain. Evidence, they say, that they will try to strike a balance between the needs of modern man and nature.

The quiet, old village of **Marco** at the north end of the island and **Goodland** in the southern tip still retain cottages and recall pleasant memories of an older Florida. Archaeological digs in the vicinity have turned up important carvings, tools, face masks and weapons used by Calusa Indians who lived here as long ago as 500 BC.

Offshore and south of Marco Island, a labyrinth of mangrove splotches known as the **Ten Thousand Islands** beg to be explored by boat. Some consist of no more than a few trees. It is safer to take a guide, however, as expert navigators have been known to get lost in the tangle of islands. They melt into the sea at the western edge of **Everglades National Park**. **Collier-Seminole State Park**, 6,423 acres of virgin marshland marking the meeting of Big Cypress and the Everglades, lies just west of Marco Island. There is restricted canoeing, camping, and fishing in most of the park. Beyond is **Everglades City**, a last outpost on the edge of a kingdom still ruled by wildlife.

Good Life at South Seas Plantation, Captiva.

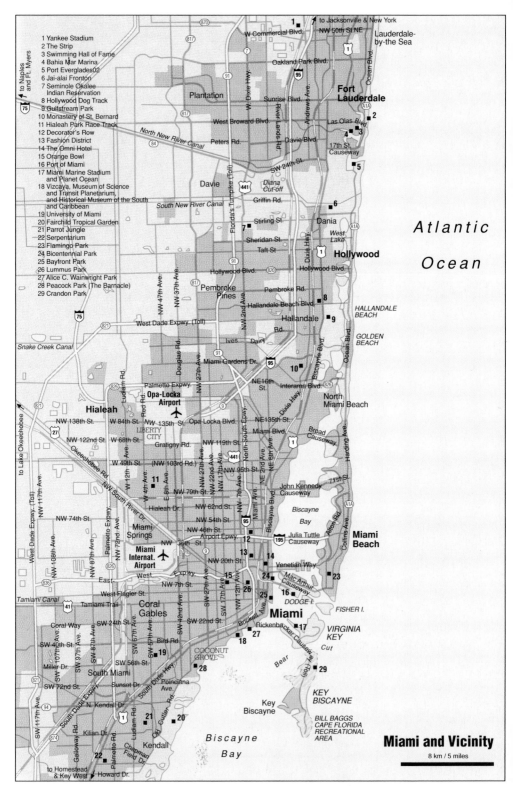

Miami and Vicinity

1 Yankee Stadium
2 The Strip
3 Swimming Hall of Fame
4 Bahia Mar Marina
5 Port Everglades02
6 Jai-alai Fronton
7 Seminole Okalee
  Indian Reservation
8 Hollywood Dog Track
9 Gulfstream Park
10 Monastery of St. Bernard
11 Hialeah Park Race Track
12 Decorator's Row
13 Fashion District
14 The Omni Hotel
15 Orange Bowl
16 Port of Miami
17 Miami Marine Stadium
   and Planet Ocean
18 Vizcaya, Museum of Science
   and Transit Planetarium,
   and Historical Museum of the South
   and Caribbean
19 University of Miami
20 Fairchild Tropical Garden
21 Parrot Jungle
22 Serpentarium
23 Flamingo Park
24 Bicentennial Park
25 Bayfront Park
26 Lummus Park
27 Alice C. Wainwright Park
28 Peacock Park (The Barnacle)
29 Crandon Park

Atlantic

Ocean

to Jacksonville & New York
NW 50th St.NE
Lauderdale-
by-the-Sea

Fort
Lauderdale

W Commercial Blvd.
Oakland Park Blvd.
Sunrise Blvd.
Las Olas Blvd.
Davie Blvd.
17th St.
Causeway

Plantation
West Broward Blvd.
Peters Rd.
North New River Canal

Davie
South New River Canal
Griffin Rd.
Stirling St.
Sheridan St.
Taft St.
Hollywood Blvd.

Diana
Cut-off

Dania
West
Lake

Hollywood

Pembroke
Pines
Pembroke Rd.
Hallandale Beach Blvd.
Hallandale
Rd.

HALLANDALE
BEACH

GOLDEN
BEACH

Snake Creek Canal

West Dade Expwy. (Toll)
Ives   Dairy
Miami Gardens Dr.

Opa-Locka
Airport

Hialeah
LIBERTY
CITY

NE16th
St.
Interama Blvd.

North
Miami Beach

NW 138th St.   W 84th St. NW 135th St. Opa-Locka Blvd.   NE135th St.
NW 122nd St. W 68th St.   Miami Blvd.
Gratigny Rd.
W 49th St.   (NW 103rd Rd.)   NW 119th St.
NW 95th St.
E 8th St.   NW 79th St.
Hialeah Dr.   NW 62nd St.
NW 54th St.
NW 46th St.
Airport Epwy.
NW 36th St.
NW 20th St.
NW 7th St.

Broad
Causeway

John Kennedy
Causeway
71st St.

Biscayne
Bay

Julia Tuttle
Causeway

Miami
Beach

Hialeah
Miami
Springs
Miami
Internat.
Airport

Venetian Way
MacArthur
Causeway

DODGE I.
FISHER I.

West Flagler St.
Tamiami Trail
Coral
Gables

Coral Way
Bird Rd.

Miami

Rickenbacker Causeway
VIRGINIA
KEY
Cut

Coconut
Grove

South Miami
Sunset St.
Poinciana
Ave.

N. Kendal Dr.

KEY
BISCAYNE

Key
Biscayne

Biscayne
Bay

BILL BAGGS
CAPE FLORIDA
RECREATIONAL
AREA

Kendall
to Homestead
& Key West   Howard Dr.

to Naples
and Ft. Myers

to Lake Okeechobee

Tamiami Canal

Miami and Vicinity

8 km / 5 miles

The area known as South Florida – the state's lower east coast region – is a microcosm of the entire state. It has the biggest cities and some of the smallest, the best public beaches and some private ones walled in by mansions or condominium blocks. There are cowboys and Indians, Crackers and Yankees, Cubans and Haitians. The varied landscape features multi-level superhighways and dirt lanes; rows of mobile homes and fields of sugar cane; skyscrapers, swamps and farmland. From metropolitan Miami full of designers, Art Deco and models, to peaceful Vero Beach and Lake Okeechobee, South Florida has it all.

METROPOLITAN MIAMI

Miami and its famous sister city, Miami Beach, have shared a meteoric transition from mosquito-infested swamp and palmetto scrubland to subtropical megalopolis. From an aircraft approaching Miami International Airport, you can look down at the Everglades and glimpse the past – a soundless sea of saw grass. Now look again and gaze upon the fast-pulsed cacophony of the present – a white-washed, high-rise skyline, set starkly against the aquamarine of Biscayne Bay.

Your first encounter echoes the accolades of travel brochures. Here are wall-to-wall beaches, balmy weather and around-the-clock nightlife. Even Hurricane Andrew, which in 1992 ripped through the suburbs of Coconut Grove and Coral Gables, could not puncture the dream. But under the banks of cauliflower clouds, you will also find a major international finance center and growing commercial complex, buoyed by the Latin-flavored cultural diversity of Greater Miami and the Art Deco success story of Miami Beach.

From fishing village to phenomenon: Problems have in the past tarnished Miami's sparkle. Fickle northern tourists years ago began spending their vacation dollars in other parts of Florida. $15 million in beach restoration counters the erosion of storms and tides. Rampant urban growth has consumed farms. An outbreak of racial violence has rocked a city once smug in its desegregation

process. And an uncontrolled influx of Cuban and Haitian refugees has taxed Miami's stability.

Nevertheless, the history of Miami remains an American Cinderella story. Miami was only a fishing village on the edge of a vast wilderness when it was incorporated as a city in 1896. Railroad magnate Henry M. Flagler even voiced doubts about the city's future when his first train chugged into town. But his Florida East Coast Railroad triggered phenomenal growth all along the Gold Coast. In gratitude, the major street bisecting Miami now bears his name. So does a dog-racing track and a savings-and-loan company. A marker in Bicentennial Park on Biscayne Boulevard honors Flagler at the site of the original port of Miami, built to service early steamships.

The history of surrounding Dade County predates Flagler's appearance, however. The first white man believed to have lived in the area was a shipwrecked Spanish sailor enslaved by Tequesta Indians living at the mouth of the Miami River. In his memoirs, the sailor wrote about a place the Indians called the "Lake of Mayaime." Historians speculate that the name meant "very large" and was a reference to Lake Okeechobee, northwest of modern Miami. Somehow, the word Mayaime evolved into Miami, the Tequesta word for "sweet water."

Later, many of the settlers who manned Fort Dallas to keep Seminole Indians at bay early in the 19th century stayed on in the area. The site of the fort became the exclusive address of Julia

Preceding pages: Christo's Surrounded Islands, Biscayne Bay, 1983.

Tuttle, one of the first Yankees to flee cold Cleveland winters for Florida's warmth. She convinced Flagler to extend his railroad to the banks of Biscayne Bay, sending him orange blossoms in the middle of winter when a freeze caused citrus losses upstate. Tuttle's former home site is now a parking lot fronting the DuPont Plaza Hotel at the southern terminus of Biscayne Boulevard in downtown Miami. The city moved the barracks of **Fort Dallas**, stone by stone, to Lummus Park on North River Drive on the Miami River in 1924.

Biscayne Boulevard spills into **Brickell Avenue**, named for Mary and William Brickell. In the 1870s, they owned all the bayfront land from the Miami River south to Coconut Grove. During the boom that followed Flagler's railroad down the East Coast, the wealthy constructed handsome homes here along the bay.

Today, searching for the past among the concrete offices and condominiums of burgeoning Brickell Avenue is like trying to find a mountain in South Florida. But there is a 14-room stone house in the 1500 block patterned after the 14th-century Priory St Julienne in Duoy, France. It has three towers, wrought-iron gates and dormer windows. Isolated mansions such as this one, trapped among the modern highrises, hint at the grace that was Brickell Avenue at the turn of the century when the woods were so dense, timid residents refused to venture out after dark.

Only one small public section remains of wooded **Brickell Hammock** in **Alice C. Wainwright Park**, a block south of the Rickenbacker Causeway intersection. Pirates once camped in the area, but today the park hosts weekend weddings. It even sports a "hill." Some 100,000 years ago, when Miami was covered by a shallow sea, fast currents rolled up little balls of limestone. This limestone rock now crops out in a 2-mile ridge parallel to the bayshore. Geology books call it Miami oolite.

Also near Wainwright Park is **Villa Serena**, former residence of famed orator and politician William Jennings

Cruise ships, power boats and even aircraft converge at the Port of Miami, the world's busiest.

Bryan. The two-story, Spanish-style home, built in 1915 at 3115 Brickell Avenue, is not open to the public.

The growth and prosperity spawned by the railroad also breathed life into the mangrove islands and scrublands surrounding the city's core. Miami Beach, Hialeah, Opalocka, Coral Gables and other suburbs flourished. Land promotion turned into speculation. Property changed hands several times, sometimes the same day and always at higher prices. But a combination of the 1926 hurricane and the Great Depression ended Miami's first growth phase.

Gradual improvement in the economy and the establishment of new business opportunities kicked off Miami's modern period of expansion in the 1930s. Commercial aviation transformed the city into an international destination. Modern **Miami International Airport**, connected to the city center via a pair of fast expressways, offers air routes to most corners of the world.

Thousands of servicemen trained in Miami Beach during World War II, housed in hotels-turned-barracks and beaches that doubled as drill fields and rifle ranges. Many of these servicemen returned with their families after the war. Some used the GI Bill to attend the **University of Miami**. Founded in 1925, the school floundered when the crash came but rebounded with the injection of military blood. Located in Coral Gables, the University is noted for its medical school, marine science department and the **Lowe Art Museum**.

The coming of the Cubans: Miami hogged national headlines in the 1950s during the US Senate Committee hearings on organized crime. The city had once attracted mobsters like Al Capone, whose home still stands at 93 Palm Island, north of the MacArthur Causeway. He bought the house during the Roaring '20s from Clarence M. Busch of the beer family, and died in it in 1947.

By the 1960s, both **Biscayne Bay** and the **Miami River** suffered from the scars of rapid growth. The area was panned nationally as a "polluted paradise." Environmentalists attracted community

Cheerleaders at the University of Miami.

interest toward cleaning up the waters and blocked location of new industrial plants. Government planning was centralized in a Metro body with countywide powers to improve control over unrestricted development and pollution.

Following the pattern of other metropolitan areas, established white residents fanned out into the suburbs while the inner city, already heavily black, attracted hundreds of thousands of refugees who fled Cuba after Fidel Castro seized power in 1959. The influx dissolved some racial barriers, but the poverty of black ghettoes worsened and black resentment deepened while the Cubans prospered. The economic schism contributed to an eruption of violence in Liberty City, a predominantly black area of northwest Miami, while the Republican National Convention camped out at Miami Beach in 1968.

Trouble peaked in 1980 when 18 people died in riots that caused $200 million damage. Another influx of Cuban "boat people" that year had added to Miami's problems, particularly since many of the 125,000 refugees unleashed by Castro came from Havana's prisons. Jobless and penniless, some returned to their old criminal habits, adding another unwanted face to Miami's mural of urban unrest. In 1980, 243 homicides made Miami's murder rate the highest per capita in the United States.

For all its warts, Miami is a cosmopolitan mix of Americans, Canadians and Europeans who contribute to a cultural exchange rivaling that of New York City. The unprecedented rise of Miami Beach as a style capital and mecca for bright young things put Miami back on the map. Designers and other artistic visitors flocked to the beach.

Hurricane Andrew, which gave a devastating blow to the beautiful homes and swaying palms of Coconut Grove and Coral Gables, miraculously left most of the beach area unscathed. Miami, always a refuge for forward-thinking people, is back with a vengeance.

Downtown Miami: A black monolith called the **Omni** and a brightly lit edifice called the **CenTrust Tower** stand

Left, interstate tangle in downtown Miami. Below, the cosmopolitan population mix on a downtown street.

in stark contrast as centers of Miami's renaissance. The CenTrust Tower, with its 47 floors, stands as one of the tallest office buildings this side of Chicago and lights up the Miami night sky. The 20-story Omni hotel draws a healthy share of free-spending South and Central Americans and the 150-plus stores in its two-level mall give them plenty of opportunity to part with their money.

East of the Omni are the offices of the **Miami Herald**, one of the country's largest newspapers. South of it, below the Interstate 395 bridge, is **Bicentennial Park**, a good vantage point from which to watch and photograph cruise ships docking or leaving their terminals on **Dodge Island**. Access to the island is further south on Biscayne Boulevard. Here you will find the **Port of Miami**, the world's leading cruise-passenger facility. It caters to enormous pleasure craft with names like *Carousel* and *Sovereign of the Seas*.

South of the Port Boulevard entrance lies **Bayfront Park**, a brief respite from the hustle of downtown Miami. Here is the **John F. Kennedy Memorial Torch of Friendship**, symbolizing friendly relations between Miami and Latin America with an 18-foot shaft topped by a perpetual flame. Other monuments in the park honor Christopher Columbus; José Martí, liberator of Cuba; José Cecello del Valle, who wrote the federal constitution of Honduras; and Ruben Dario, Nicaraguan poet. There's also a monument near a brand new amphitheater to the 1986 **Challenger Shuttle** disaster. In addition, a $100 million **Bayside Marketplace**, featuring entertainment and waterfront shopping, has been added in recent years.

Construction of new buildings and multi-million-dollar entertainment complexes are changing the look and energy of downtown Miami. In addition to the **Metro-Dade Cultural Center**, a Mediterranean-style complex that houses the **Center for Fine Arts**, the **Historical Museum of Southern Florida** and the main public library, there is the **Gusman Theater for the Performing Arts**. Designed in Rococo style, this ornate center features high-class entertainment – opera, ballet, symphony – as well as top headliners.

The **Miami Arena** also features entertainment in the form of professional basketball as well as pop music and rock concerts and special events, such as touring circuses and ice shows. The Arena is sited in Overtown, north of the core of the downtown sector.

New "Old Havana," English spoken: Across from the park, a line of hotels borders the busy commercial district. If you can manage to pick your way through the crowds of Latin American tourists in the lobby of the rejuvenated **Everglades Hotel**, ride the elevator to the pool and sun deck on the roof for a panoramic view of the city.

Other downtown sites include the blue-delft-tiled mosaic on the **Bacardi Art Gallery** building, from the same people who bring you rum, in the 2100 block of Biscayne Boulevard. The brass onion-shaped dome of the **Assumption Ukrainian Catholic Church** at 58 N.W. 57th Avenue lends a touch of the East to the city. There's also a bit of the Mideast

The Virgin of Charity presides over this street in Little Havana.

in the bakeries, shops, churches and restaurants of Lebanese, Syrians, Greeks and Palestinians along S.W. Third Avenue in the vicinity of the Rickenbacker Causeway exit from Interstate 95.

For all its diversity, the heart that has kept Miami healthy during the past 20 years is a Hispanic one. Old Havana didn't disappear when Castro took Cuba in 1959. It just moved, lock, stock and barrel to Florida. Don't be surprised if the bellboy at your hotel addresses you in Spanish before trying English. Gas station attendants will often only smile if you speak to them in any language *but* Spanish. Shopkeepers hang signs advising potential customers "English Spoken." A trip to Miami is like vacationing in a foreign port.

Hialeah and Coral Gables have both become Spanish-speaking enclaves, but **Little Havana** remains the core of the community. Wedged between downtown Miami on the east and Coral Gables on the west, and roughly bounded by W. Flagler Street on the north, and S.W. 22nd Street on the south, Little Havana promotes itself as a chic Latin quarter with cosmopolitan airs.

S.W. Eighth Street, here known as **Calle Ocho**, is Little Havana's main street. It is alive with cigar-chomping men in crisp, white *guayaberas* (the cotton shirt of the tropics), quaint fruit stands, unique boutiques and factories where employees still roll cigars by hand. If you want to try strong, aromatic Cuban coffee, stop at one of the many sidewalk coffee counters. They also sell *churros* – long spirals of sweet dough, deep-fried. Watch them being made, then sprinkle with sugar, dip in a cup of Cuban chocolate, and devour.

An ideal way to visit Calle Ocho is to drive its 30-blocks, picking out sections you find interesting. Then park and stroll. Bear in mind, it's a one-way street where traffic flows to the east, so if you are coming from downtown, drive west on S.W. Seventh Street before cutting back. Older Cubans enjoy company, so don't be afraid to strike up a conversation. They have fascinating stories to tell about their escapes from a Communist

A festive flamenco floor show enlivens *Les Violins*.

homeland. In **Antonio Maceo Park**, you'll find men, and sometimes women, intent on games of dominoes. Bus stop benches in Little Havana are tiled, and lamp posts are Spanish-style.

Four businesses along Calle Ocho operate as combination retail fish markets and seafood restaurants. At least one offers fresh fish selections from a retail case, cooked to order. **La Concha's** speciality is fresh shellfish cocktail, while **La Mar Pescaderia** features *ceviche*, an appetizer of raw fish that actually "cooks" in a special lemon juice marinade. Shrimp is one of the main attractions at **Los Piratas**. Try them with fried plantains, a delicious way to eat bananas. The oldest fishmonger restaurant is **El Pescador**. Here you can get *sopa marinero*, which has become so popular it could qualify as Miami's version of the traditional *bouillabaisse* of Marseille.

Other than seafood, you can try **Fritas Domino** for a Cuban hamburger or *frita* served with pencil-thin French fries inside a bun. The **Versailles** offers about the best Cuban sandwich in Little Havana, although **Casablanca** is also popular. The ingredients aren't special – crispy Cuban bread; boneless, processed ham cured in boiling sweet water and baked in sugar; slow-boiled pork; imported Gruyère cheese; pickles and butter. But there's an art to putting the sandwich together to get the right blend of tastes.

Of shrines and gas stations: A popular way for Cubans to show their devotion to a particular saint is by erecting shrines in their front yards and even at their businesses. You'll find many on the lawns of neat houses if you venture into the side streets bordering Eighth Street. The most revered patron is Saint Lazarus, a hero to the Cubans because of his ability to endure poverty and pain.

One shrine incongruously decorates a corner of Armando Tundidor's gas station at 1599 W. Flagler Street. **La Virgen de la Caridad del Cobre** sits on a revolving pedestal in a wrought-iron cage right under the Phillips 66 sign. Almacenes Felix Gonzalez, at 2610 S.W. Eighth Street, sells a full line of religious statues for a wide range of prices.

A shrine particularly important to the Cuban exiles is **Ermita de La Caridad** near a Catholic high school at 3805 S. Miami Avenue. Inside a cone resembling a spaceship, a Spanish-language tape explains that the shrine's shape symbolizes the Virgin of Charity's mantle and the six columns stand for the six provinces of Cuba. The hectagonal cement block beneath the altar was made with rock, water and dirt from Cuba. The priest's chair is carved from a Cuban palm tree and the church faces the old country across the seas. "Pray for Cuba," pleads the voice.

A more blunt reminder of the homeland is the Bay of Pigs monument at the **Cuban Memorial Plaza** on 13th Avenue, the site of many commemorative ceremonies. Each March all of Miami is invited to a block party called Open House Eight, a sort of Cuban Mardi Gras. Another important celebration is the Three Kings Parade on the first or second Sunday of January, which includes nearly 100 floats and marching units, some with flamenco dancers.

Within the overwhelming Cuban community, close inspection will also turn up a Little Buenos Aires, a Little Managua, a Little Bogotá, a Little Quito and a Little Caracas. These myriad quarters have shaped Miami into a melting pot of Central and South American cultures.

Fashions and furnishings: Bargain hunters attracted to things French like Yves St Laurent, Pierre Cardin and Christian Dior styles – will revel in Miami's **Fashion District**. But shoppers must be willing to search for what they want along N.W. Fifth Avenue between N.W. 24th and 30th streets. You must know what quality you're seeking, and the cost of the retail item, in order to make a good buy. At times, you might find entire rows of designer clothes marked off as much as 50 percent. Few of the outlets have fancy trappings and some do not accept credit cards. Lower prices for lesser brands can be found at factory outlets scattered along N.W. 20th Street, between 17th and 27th avenues. All in all, this busy area comprises the nation's second largest fashion district.

Decorator's Row is another hidden shopping treasure, a tree-line 10-block area frequented by Rolls-Royces and monied customers. It centers on N.E. 40th Street between N. Miami Avenue and N.E. Second Avenue. Even if you can only afford to window-shop, the displays will update you on the latest trends in furniture and accessories for the home and office. Most showrooms are open to the public, but some have signs reading "to the trade only." That means a designer must refer or accompany you, but only the haughtiest store-keepers will turn you away if you arrange a call from an architect, or produce a card of introduction from a major furniture store or designer.

Visiting Vizcaya: You can visit Miami's southern reaches via Brickell Avenue. Unfortunately, this area was slammed by Hurricane Andrew's 160-mph winds, demolishing most of the trees. After Brickell turns into Federal Highway, take a left into S. Miami Avenue. On the bayside is the grand gate-way to **Vizcaya**, an Italian Renaissance villa and gardens built by International Harvester magnate James Deering in 1916. A winding road through an exotic jungle leads to the edifice *National Geographic* magazine once described as "a triumph in recalling the Golden Age of art and architecture… a repository of Italian decorative art, unexcelled in America."

In addition to the palatial home filled with fine period furniture, textiles and sculpture, Vizcaya (Basque for "elevated place") has 10 acres of formal gardens that, pre-hurricane, closely resembled the European original. In Biscayne Bay opposite the gardens, Deering anchored a sculptured stone barge. It was used as a clandestine dock for unloading shipments of illegal liquor.

Across Miami Avenue from Vizcaya is the **Museum of Science** and **Space Transit Planetarium**. The Planetarium has an entertaining laser show which uses light beams, color imagery and music to take you on a trip through a black hole. The **Historical Museum of**

The villa and gardens at Vizcaya.

Southern Florida once also on Miami Avenue, has moved to the Metro-Dade Cultural Center on Flagler Street.

Continue down South Miami until it becomes Bayshore Drive and you wind up in **Coconut Grove**. The oldest settlement in the area, "the Grove" developed a reputation as a winter resort for northerners as early as the turn of the century. For years, its Peacock Inn was the only hotel in town. Built in 1880, it overlooked Biscayne Bay from the rock ridge above modern day **Peacock Park** on McFarlane Road near South Bayshore Drive. A marker in the park commemorates the hotel.

The catalyst for settlement of the Grove was naval architect and photographer Ralph Middleton Munroe. He built a house called **The Barnacle**, now a historical museum at 3485 Main Highway. The Barnacle was originally a one-story building of materials salvaged from shipwrecks. Instead of constructing a new home to accommodate his growing family, Munroe jacked the entire house up on stilts and built a new first floor underneath in 1895.

Meanwhile, a colony of blacks moved in and inspired the Bahamian-Key West-style "gingerbread" architecture of the area. You can still admire these early homes on **Charles Avenue**. At the west end of the street, the gravestones of pioneers dot the **Charlotte Jane Stirrup Memorial Cemetery**. The character of the area is changing to upscale, however, with an increasing number of salons featuring the latest European fashions interspersed with vintage clothing and antique shops and sidewalk cafés.

Goombay in the Grove: All kinds of colorful characters cruise the sidewalks of the Grove on roller skates, bicycles, skateboards, even feet. The Goombay Festival each June, where musicians prefer to play the horse conch and kazoo to the guitar, is a prime time to visit.

A well-marked bike patch can be used for touring the Grove. Pedal past woodworking, candlemaking and pottery shops to Main Highway. The shops give way to churches and schools.

Off Main Highway is the **Plymouth**

Wheeling through the Grove.

Congregational Church, built in 1897 to resemble a Spanish mission. The area's first schoolhouse is also located here, at 3429 Devon Road, built by early settlers from the wood of wrecked ships. Continue south on the bike path, then turn left on dead-end St Gaudens Road. You are now officially in **Coral Gables**, a city built by dreamers.

George Edgar Merrick planned this remarkable community which sprang up almost overnight during the first Florida boom. He would still be pleased today at its refined cultural atmosphere. The city derives its name from Merrick's own gabled mansion of coral. Florida writer Rex Beach sized up Merrick: "At heart, he was a writer, a poet, an artist. But fate with a curious perversity decreed that he should write in wood and steel and stone, and paint his pictures upon a canvas of spacious fields, cool groves and smiling waterways…"

Merrick's stately plan, only slightly amended, still controls the arrangement of the winding, often confusing streets and the architecture of the houses. He dictated that Coral Gables' homes should have a Mediterranean flair, later adding a dash of France, Holland, South Africa and China – although he had never been outside of the United States. A tour of Coral Gables, therefore, can turn out to be a trip around the world. Book a visit on a tour bus, or lead yourself with a self-guiding pamphlet available at City Hall on the western end of the shoppers' street called **Miracle Mile**.

Merrick paid William Jennings Bryan a salary of $50,000 a year to promote his city from a floating platform in the **Venetian Pool** at Almeria Avenue and Toledo Street. Once a stone quarry, the pool is now a tropical paradise of islands, caves, rock towers, cascades and arched bridges open to the public.

The main entrance to Coral Gables is **La Puerta del Sol** ("The Sun Portal") at Douglas Road and Tamiami Trail. Merrick designed its water tower, town clock and belfry to mimic a Mediterranean town square. Coral rock gates adorn other entrances to the city. A resort hotel Merrick built for $10 million flanks

Coral Gables' Venetian Pool.

the western edge of the city: the **Biltmore** has a tower patterned after the Cathedral of Seville, but it fell into disrepair during the Depression. It has been totally renovated but again experienced financial difficulties in the early 1990s.

To Key Biscayne: It can take up to an hour to cross the **Rickenbacker Causeway** in weekend traffic, even though it looks navigable on a map. Along the route, you'll find the **Miami Marine Stadium** where you can watch pop concerts at twilight from the grandstand overlooking the lagoon, or from a boat. Flipper, the porpoise, and Lolita, the killer whale, are the lures of the **Seaquarium**.

Two of hundreds of islands that surround the southern tip of Florida, Key Biscayne and Virginia Key are sedimentary barrier islands, strung north to south, parallel to the South Florida mainland. They began as sandbars, millions of years ago. As ocean waves and winds piled limestone and quartz on top of hard coral rock, islands emerged, a barrier between the Atlantic Ocean and the mainland for that same water and wind.

Crandon Boulevard runs into Key Biscayne, which was the site of the Florida White House during the Nixon Administration. The most popular spot is the lighthouse in **Bill Baggs Cape Florida State Park**. In 1836, Seminole Indians trapped the keeper and his aide in this tower, then tried to burn them out. A keg of gunpowder hurled from the top put an explosive end to the Indians' efforts: a patrolling ship heard the discharge and came to the rescue. The five-room keeper's home has been restored to its original form.

Developers have discovered Key Biscayne, but a quiet tempo still prevails. Shops are more retro than trendy, delivering the basics with old-fashioned service; the hardware store will still sell you one nail or one screw. There are few traffic lights on Key Biscayne, and even fewer traffic jams.

Readily accessible from Key Biscayne by boat are the **Spoil Islands**. Fourteen dot Biscayne Bay, providing peaceful settings for camping, fishing or lazing in the sun. They were formed from rock and sand pumped from the bay bottom to deepen ship channels. Miami Beach developer Carl Fisher enlarged one, **Monument Island**, to honor Henry Flagler, and installed a column similar to the Washington Monument, flanked by four statues symbolizing prosperity, industry, education and pioneers. Pop artist Christo immortalized some of these same islands by "wrapping" them in enormous sheets of neon-pink plastic in May 1983, an endeavor he called *Surrounded Islands.*

Nightlife is scattered from one end of Miami to the other from the venerable **Crazy Horse Saloon** in North Miami Beach where men take it all off, to **Les Violins Supper Club** downtown, where strolling violinists are followed by a Cuban floor show.

Another attraction includes the **Monastery of St Bernard**, south of the park near Snake Creek. Moorish, Jewish and Christian slaves carved its stones from hills near Zamora, Spain. You can still see the symbols in the rock – stars of David, crescents and crosses. The bulk of the structure was built in the 12th century. Newspaper magnate William Randolph Hearst bought it from Spain and planned to reassemble it at his San Simeon castle in California. Instead, he sold it to a group who rebuilt the monastery here. While in the area be sure to see **Metrozoo**, a cageless zoo with many native Florida species.

Miami's major annual sporting event is the **Orange Bowl** football game when major college teams clash under the light of the moon around New Year's Day. **New Joe Robbie Stadium** is the home of the Miami Dolphins National Football League team.

Greater Miami has more to offer than most resort areas – from mad metropolitan nights to mellow mornings on the beach. Despite previous negative publicity, the city continues to thrive and boom. A $22 million Miami Free Trade Zone, similar to zones at Port Everglades and Orlando, solidified its position as the American capital of Central and South American business. Further development of Watson Island is promised, once municipal minds can agree.

A "love boat" at the Port of Miami.

163

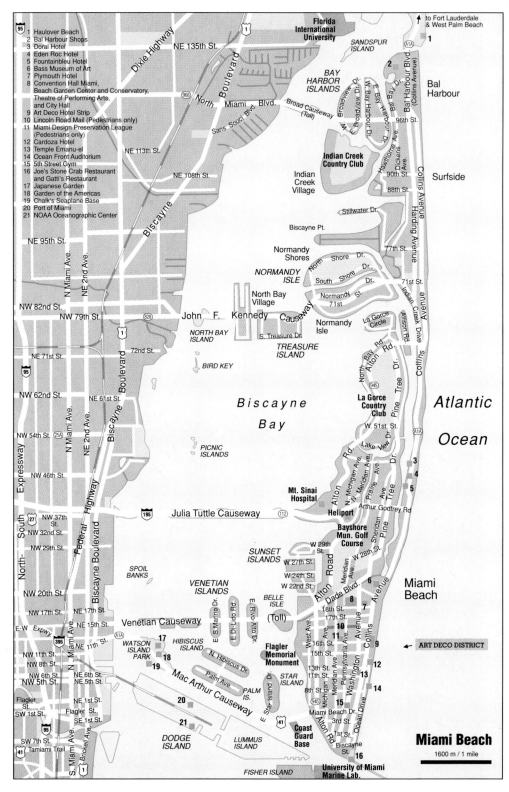

1. Haulover Beach
2. Bal Harbour Shops
3. Doral Hotel
4. Eden Roc Hotel
5. Fountainbleu Hotel
6. Bass Museum of Art
7. Plymouth Hotel
8. Convention Hall Miami,
   Beach Garden Center and Conservatory,
   Theatre of Performing Arts,
   and City Hall
9. Art Deco Hotel Strip
10. Lincoln Road Mall (Pedestrians only)
11. Miami Design Preservation League
    (Pedestrians only)
12. Cardoza Hotel
13. Temple Emanu-el
14. Ocean Front Auditorium
15. 5th Street Gym
16. Joe's Stone Crab Restaurant
    and Gatti's Restaurant
17. Japanese Garden
18. Garden of the Americas
19. Chalk's Seaplane Base
20. Port of Miami
21. NOAA Oceanographic Center

to Fort Lauderdale
& West Palm Beach

Florida
International
University

SANDSPUR
ISLAND

BAY
HARBOR
ISLANDS

Bal
Harbour

Broad Causeway
(Toll)

Indian Creek
Country Club

Surfside

Indian
Creek
Village

Stillwater Dr.

Biscayne Pt.

Normandy
Shores

North   Shore   Dr.

NORMANDY
ISLE

South   Shore   Dr.

North Bay
Village

Normandy   St.

71st

Normandy
Isle

La Gorce
Circle

NORTH BAY
ISLAND

John   F.   Kennedy   Causeway

TREASURE
ISLAND

S. Treasure Dr.

BIRD KEY

B i s c a y n e

B a y

La Gorce
Country
Club

Atlantic

Ocean

W. 51st. St.

PICNIC
ISLANDS

Lake View Dr.

Mt. Sinai
Hospital

Julia Tuttle Causeway

Heliport

Arthur Godfrey Rd.

Bayshore
Mun. Golf
Course

Miami
Beach

SUNSET
ISLANDS

W. 29th
St.

W. 27th St.

W. 24th St.

W. 22nd St.

VENETIAN
ISLANDS

BELLE
ISLE

(Toll)

ART DECO DISTRICT

Venetian Causeway

HIBISCUS
ISLAND

WATSON
ISLAND
PARK

N. Hibiscus Dr.

Flagler
Memorial
Monument

Palm Ave.

STAR
ISLAND

PALM
IS.

Mac Arthur Causeway

E. Star Island Dr.

Coast
Guard
Base

DODGE
ISLAND

LUMMUS
ISLAND

FISHER ISLAND

University of Miami
Marine Lab.

Miami Beach

1600 m / 1 mile

SPOIL
BANKS

SW 7th St.

Tamiami Trail

Flagler
St.

SW 1st St.

Flagler St.

SE 1st St.

NW 5th St.

NE 5th St.

NW 6th St.

NE 6th St.

NW 8th St.

NW 11th St.

NE 11th St.

E-W   Expwy

NW 17th St.

NE 15th St.

NE 17th St.

NW 20th St.

NW 29th St.

NW 32nd St.

NW 37th
St.

NW 46th St.

NW 54th St.

NW 62nd St.

NE 61st St.

NE 71st St.

NW 79th St.

NW 82nd St.

NE 95th St.

S. Miami Ave.

Brickell Ave.

Biscayne Boulevard

Federal Highway

South   North-   Expressway

N Miami Ave.

NE 2nd Ave.

N Miami Ave.

NE 2nd Ave.

72nd St.

Biscayne

Boulevard

NE 108th St.

NE 113th St.

Sans Souci Blvd.

North   Miami   Blvd.

Dixie Highway

NE 135th St.

Broadview Dr.

W. Bay Harbour Dr.

E. Bay Harbour Dr.

W. Broadway Dr.

E. Broadway Dr.

Bal Bay Dr.

Bal Harbour Blvd.
(Collins Avenue)

96th St.

Hawthorne Ave.

Dickens Ave.

90th St.

88th St.

Collins Avenue

Harding Avenue

77th St.

71st St.

Indian Creek Avenue

Allison Rd.

North Bay Rd.

Alton Rd.

Pine Tree Dr.

Collins Avenue

Pine Tree Dr.

Alton Rd.

N. Michigan Ave.

W. Meridian Ave.

Prairie Ave.

Sheridan Ave.

Pine Tree

Meridian Ave.

W. 28th St.

Dade Blvd.

Alton Road

18th St.

16th St.

15th St.

13th St.

11th St.

8th St.

West Ave.

Michigan Ave.

Meridian Ave.

Pennsylvania Ave.

Washington Ave.

Collins Avenue

Ocean Drive

Miami Beach Dr.

3rd St.

1st St.

Biscayne St.

17th St.

Alton Rd.

MIAMI BEACH

Since Carl Fisher shaped it out of a rattlesnake and rodent-infested sandspur and cut Lincoln Road through dense mangrove using circus elephants in 1915, golden days in Miami Beach have come, gone and come again. Once the dream-vacation mecca of every red-blooded American, it fell into disrepair as families spurned it for central Florida and Walt Disney World during the 1970s. Now, like a dowager snoozing on the porch of a South Beach hotel, the city has awakened to the voices of a new generation of visitors, including young American families and tourists from Europe and Central and South America.

Dredging ships have already put the beach back where it belongs behind the solid wall of overblown hotels along Collins Avenue. Plans are in the works to tear down everything south of Sixth Street and erect a modern resort development. Preservationists began campaigning for restoration of the Beach's unmatched collection of F. Scott Fitzgerald-era Art Deco hotels, with remarkable success. Parks have been cleaned up and improved. South Beach is now the place to be – and be seen. Nowhere more so than on South Beach are the boundaries between trendy and tacky so well fused. Tacky is trendy here: kitsch is cool. And the beach beckons all year round.

"Miami Beach," as one observer put it, "has had more comebacks than Peggy Lee." And here it is again, with a vengeance and a bang, this time driving a souped-up retro convertible and sipping a pale pink cocktail.

Gateway to the beach: Several causeways span Biscayne Bay between the mainland and Miami Beach. Interstate 195 crosses the Julia Tuttle Causeway, then runs into Arthur Godfrey Road. Venetian Way links the islands of the same name before turning into Dade Boulevard. But the most entertaining route is via Highway A1A over MacArthur Causeway.

The familiar skyline of the "sun and fun capital of the world."

First stop is **Watson Island Park**, named after three-time Mayor James Watson, who came to Miami in 1898. Here, you'll find a helicopter base offering air tours of the city. The oldest airline in the world, **Chalk's Flying Service**, makes trips to the Bahamas aboard amphibious planes.

Watson Island also offers landlocked tourists a stunning view of the coming and going cruise ships that use the port across the bay. These liners, large and small, draw a steady stream of onlookers. And city-ward, the view of Miami from Watson Island offers a big-city skyline of high-rise condos mixed with a few surviving palm trees.

A1A enters the city at Fifth Street, an inauspicious introduction to the beach. Virtually everything south of the street, with its decaying old buildings, might be demolished and replaced with new hotels, a canal system and marinas.

Unfortunately, the revitalization may take away such landmarks as Chris Dundee's **Fifth Street Gym**, where Muhammad Ali trained for early cham-

pionship bouts, and **Joe's Stone Crab Restaurant**, 227 Biscayne Street, a local institution where in season you can dine on the delectable claws some people consider tastier than lobster. **Gatti** Italian restaurant next door holds the distinction of being the oldest restaurant on the beach. It opened in 1925.

You'll notice a proliferation of Stars of David painted on Jewish synagogues in the area. The beach has always attracted Jewish retirees who while away their last years with fellow spirits in front of the old, crumbling hotels and rooming houses.

Art Deco dreaming: North of Fifth Street lies the **Art Deco District**, more than 80 blocks and 800 buildings surrounding **Flamingo Park**. These were the first 20th-century structures to be listed on the National Register of Historic Places. At first, you may see them as a collection of pastel hotels and tenement houses that have seen better days. If that is the case, drop by **Miami Design Preservation League** headquarters at 1244 Ocean Drive. Someone there will be happy to

Some spacy spires and glass blocks in the trim Art Deco District.

open your eyes to the streamlined racing stripes, porthole windows, glass-block construction, pipe railings with geometric patterns, rounded corners, ribbon windows, and bands of pastel pinks, oranges, limes, blues and yellows that give these creations of the 1930s a funky, contemporary style.

For a sample of what this group has achieved battling powerful politicians who argued for demolition of these buildings in favor of sterile new ones, visit the renovated **Cardozo Hotel**, 1300 Ocean Drive. **Stuart's** offers trendy dishes and stylings, and a stunning ocean view. The menu is a mix of "burgers and seafood," and the cafe's motto is: "If you don't see it on the menu, ask anyway. If we've got it, we'll fix it."

On the same street, the **Leslie** and the **Park Central** and **Cavalier** are some of the many buildings that have undergone facelifts. All look across the Ocean Front Promenade of Lummus Park. The beach has pink Deco lifeguard headquarters that are still in use.

Don't neglect to explore the interiors

of these magnificent old structures. You'll find esoteric murals of flamingos, and etched glass mirrors and windows with sea nymphs, mermaids and tropical birds. The **Amsterdam Palace** on Ocean Drive is built around a patio that a Busby Berkeley set designer could have made.

Significant structures in Art Deco motif, also called Streamline Moderne, are too numerous to list. Notables include the Ocean Drive stretch highlighted by the **Avalon**, the **Edison**, the **Clevelander**, the **Adrian** and **Royal Palm** hotels; the soaring, futuristic spire of the **Plymouth** on 21st Street that reminds one of the flared rears on '50s automobiles; the curvilinear corner architecture of the **Warsaw Ballroom** and tangerine stripes of the **Essex** on Collins Avenue; the nautical windows and neon of **Hotel Neron** on Drexel Avenue, now a municipal police station featured on TV's *Miami Vice*; the Middle Eastern eclectic dome of **Temple Emanuel** on Washington Avenue; and the **Spanish Village**, Española Way,

whose Moorish arcades and hidden courtyards undoubtedly catered to the likes of Cuban entrtainer Desi Arnaz and other conga players.

The definitely Deco **Washington Storage Building**, 1001 Washington Avenue, is under renovation to be a museum of decorative arts from the 1920s. If anything could have brought back the crowds that so successfully filled Miami Beach's avenues with life, it is this preservation and restoration of these Art Deco masterpieces, found nowhere else in such numbers. They are an attraction as alluring as Old Town in Key West or Greenwich Village in New York City.

Into the 1950s and beyond: Driving north on Collins Avenue is like taking a time trip through 20th-century architectural periods. You go from the colorful 1930s to the drabber, but occasionally ostentatious and always monstrous, constructions of the 1950s. The granddaddy of that era is the **Fontainebleau**, now enjoying new popularity under Hilton management after a $25-million facelift.

Its pool has an island in the middle with eight palm trees, and waterfalls that cascade over the heads of swimmers. Bars and restaurants lurk around every bend of the tropically-landscaped grounds. If you're not staying in one of its 1,224 rooms, you can park at **Indian Beach** and stroll over for a look.

Next door, the **Eden Roc** has also been spruced up. So have the **Sans Souci**, the **Seville Beach** and the **Versailles**.

Collins Avenue eventually caves into a canyon of concrete: condos on the west, the **Clarion Castle Hotel and Resort** and other hotels on the Atlantic. This depicts the 1960s method of cramming maximum people into waterfront compartments.

To view the rich in their natural habitat, swerve over to **North Bay Road**. Its developer, Carl Fisher, memorialized in **Fisher Park**, set aside this corner of Miami Beach for the wealthy and lived at 5020 North Bay Road. Celebrities like Chris Dundee and Barry Gibb (of the Bee Gees) now live in this area. Gibb buys, upgrades and sells million-

Deli-dwellers at lunch, Miami Beach.

dollar-plus mansions along the stretch. His current 12-bedroom house is at 4820 North Bay Road.

Many of these show places went up between 1922 and 1924 and incorporate the lavish details of that period. They sport balconies, Corinthian columns, and stucco reliefs with vegetable motifs. Number 4750 has a brick lookout tower and wishing well. Others have servant quarters built over the entrance gates. If you pedal into the area on a bicycle, don't let the guard at the gatehouse put you off. The public is legally entitled to ride through.

Collins Avenue continues north through **Surfside**, passing **North Shore Ocean Park** – an oasis of sea grapes and roofed pavilions with a boardwalk for pedestrians and bicycles. **Bal Harbour** encompasses the most modern hotels and an exclusive shopping center with expensive retailers like Neiman Marcus, Saks Fifth Avenue, Gucci and Cartier.

Across the bridge over Baker's Haulover Cut is **Haulover Beach Park** with 2 miles of beach, sightseeing cruises, helicopter rides, surfing, golf and deepsea fishing.

Before leaving Miami Beach, visit one of its many delicatessens for a bowl of matzoh ball soup, blintzes or pastrami on rye. **Wolfies, Pumperniks** and the **Delicacy Shop** are landmarks. Kosher restaurants, butcher shops and Torah treasure stores with Hebrew religious books are other evidence of the Jewish influence here.

In addition to the retirees, Miami Beach includes recent arrivals from the Soviet Union, plus many Israelis and even Cuban Jews. The religious customs of these immigrants range from passive to ultra-orthodox in beards, black hats and prayer shawls.

Few visitors realize that beyond the close-packed resorts and residents of Metropolitan Miami lie rich agricultural fields that put Dade County among the top 100 producing counties in the United States. Many farms encourage people to "pick-your-own" during the growing season, especially in the area known as "The Redland" in the Everglades south of Miami.

It takes a lot of fertilizer to enrich the clay-like soil, but off US 1 near **Homestead** and **Florida City** is the nation's "winter vegetable basket" laden with potatoes, tomatoes and strawberries, peas, cucumbers, limes and avocados.

But unfortunately it was here, in the prosperous agricultural areas of South Dade County, that most of the destruction and damage caused by Hurricane Andrew in August, 1992, occurred. Slowly, some of these important agricultural lands are being restored, but for the most part Florida City and Homestead will be undergoing major rebuilding and replanting for years to come.

One of the few post-Andrew points of interest that remain, not surprisingly, is a sturdy, whimsical place called **Coral Castle**. Located on US 1, better known as Dixie Highway, just north of Homestead, Coral Castle was built by a 97-pound Latvian immigrant named Edward Leedskalnin between 1925 and 1940. This bizarre castle contains rock furniture, a sundial and a finely-balanced 9-ton swinging gate.

A sexy stroll down Miami Beach.

FORT LAUDERDALE AND POINTS NORTH

There are three basic ways to drive north from Miami. Interstate 95 is fast and free, but incomplete. The Florida Turnpike is fast, but expensive. Neither of those superhighways make for a particularly interesting drive. Highway A1A, on the other hand, takes forever to drive as it skirts the east coast. It's occasionally scenic, occasionally overwhelmed by the high-rise condominiums and hotels which blot out views of the Atlantic Ocean, and it's always crowded – but it's rarely boring. You'll have to cut back inland to US 1, wherever A1A runs into unbridged inlets. But the reward for enduring the traffic lights and detours will be some memorable rides through big and little seaside resorts. Several beg for long stops.

A sophisticated fort: When you see the sophisticated beauty of the beaches and resorts of Fort Lauderdale, it will seem inconceivable that it was a dismal swamp, unfit for habitation, less than a century ago. A wooden fort built here during the Seminole Wars, and named after Tennessee volunteer Major William Lauderdale, rotted for two decades after troops left in 1857 before significant development occurred – construction of a House of Refuge for shipwrecked sailors. For the most part, it remained a mangrove swamp that hid runaway slaves and desperate army deserters. Henry Flagler's railroad again changed that. In 1911, the city was incorporated.

Its swampy coast kept construction off the famous beach until men were farsighted enough to keep the sands open to the public, and situate hotels and businesses on the far side of A1A. Today, a drive along that beach highway stirs the senses. The 6½ miles of open beach are undoubtedly the city's primary attraction.

To transform the mangrove swamp into prime real estate, Charles Green Rodes resorted to "finger-islanding" – dredging up a series of parallel canals and using the fill to create long peninsulas between them. It was the same system used in a certain Italian city, and it earned Fort Lauderdale the nickname, "Venice of America." The town boasts more than 350 miles of natural and artificial canals, inlets, rivers and bays bordered by lovely homes.

Downtown Fort Lauderdale is neat and clean, brandishing boutiques with imported toys, paintings and sculpture. Stop at **The Chemist Shop** for ice cream. Try the chili for lunch on a brisk winter day. At **The Fly Shop**, you may find Sandy Carroll fabricating fly-fishing lures that look like Christmas tree ornaments and hear earnest advice about fly-fishing in salt water with a wide array of man-made bait. The shop offers over 300 choices of lures and specializes in custom-built fly rods as well, and Sandy says what works in salt water often lures fresh water trout and bass too.

A small park under giant oak trees along New River commemorates the massacre of William Colee's family by Indians during the Second Seminole War in 1836. Nearby is the historic restoration area, **Himmarshee Village**. It's mainly a shopping district, but craftsmen show off their talents. **King-Cromartie House** dates to Fort Lauderdale's earliest times.

Discovery Center in the **New River Inn** is a living museum where children can touch, feel and see how and why things work. The floors and staircase of the inn were built of steel-hard pine in 1905. Not even the very large President Grover Cleveland broke things when he sat down. The "hurricane-proof" hostelry had hot baths in iron tubs and running water as early as 1909.

Spring break on The Strip: Las Olas East runs into the honky-tonk area simply called "**The Strip**." Connie Francis' song and the 1960 movie *Where the Boys Are* romanticized this beachfront stretch as the magnet for college students on Spring Break. Today, it faces stiff competition from Daytona Beach up north, but Fort Lauderdale still lures tens of thousands of collegians bent on celebrating the Rites of Spring, sometimes at the expense of property and the locals' nervous system.

Left, sportsmen in pursuit of prize-winners – a familiar Fort Lauderdale sight.

The forerunner of "spring migration" was the Collegiate Aquatic Forum, a unique winter attraction when it started in 1935 at the city-owned casino and pool. College students told their shivering classmates about the sun and beach – and they came, first in a trickle, then in waves. Fort Lauderdale has since constructed a new world-class public-pool to replace one of Spanish design built on heavy pilings in 1928. Alongside is the **Swimming Hall of Fame** with lore and memorabilia from 107 nations. Among the exhibits is a lifelike statue of the most famous Tarzan, Johnny Weissmuller.

The 1960 beach-party movie featured The Strip and a bar called the **Elbo Room**, a place where you won't find any during Spring Break. It has become such an institution that radio stations around the country called there for first-person reports on 1979's Hurricane David. Nevertheless, its demise has been rumored for years and current hearsay has it being replaced with another McDonald's. **The Button, Stagger Lee's, Durty Nelly's** and **Nards** are among countless other nightspots (whose names are subject to annual change) popular during Break.

The Strip lost its sparkle during the 1970s. Authorities enacted zoning laws aimed at Spring Breakers, teenage runaways and drug peddlers. New bars that were not part of hotels were banned, fortune tellers, ball-playing and frisbees. Food and alcoholic beverages are banned outside throughout the entire city. The kids still come, but their behavior has been tempered somewhat.

The city also still sponsors free concerts, and hotels toss free beer parties and offer cut-rate rooms to students in March and April. After all, the students pump some $80 million into the area annually during those few weeks.

Recently, Commercial Boulevard's glittering, high-octane "**New Strip**," Oakland Park's neon-lit lounge capital, has captured some of the Fort Lauderdale business.

Boats and more boats: Spring Break or not, Lauderdale attracts night-clubbers.

Student stomping grounds, the corner of Las Olas and A1A.

About 30,000 drop into Broward County bars on a typical weeknight. Among the more subdued and long-standing is **Stan's** on the Intracoastal Waterway. A favorite of families and tourists since 1956 has been **Bob Thornton's Mai Kai**, where imported Polynesian dancers perform while you sip a banana daiquiri in a tropical garden.

Fort Lauderdale claims to berth more pleasure craft than any other Florida city. Many tie up at Bahia Mar, a marina full of magnificent yachts. The area had a House of Refuge and Coast Guard station before being transformed into a luxury marina in 1949. Picking up on the theme, the **Yankee Clipper** hotel nearby closely resembles a cruise ship.

The real things sail from **Port Everglades**, at the eastern end of State Road 84 in the southern part of the city. Once a shallow landlocked lake, the port was opened to the Atlantic when a channel was blasted in 1928.

Other Lauderdale sites include **Ocean World**, another of Florida's myriad fish shows, next to the Marriott Hotel on East 17th; a **Seminole Indian Village** on State Road 7 at Stirling Road; and **The Jungle Queen**, a paddleboat that navigates the New River, setting out from the Bahia Mar Yacht basin, and where passengers can enjoy dinner or evening cruises on the water.

The town of **Davie**, to the southwest, offers airboat rides into the fringes of the Everglades from **Sawgrass Recreation Area**, which is close to Alligator Alley and US 27.

Dania and **Hollywood** are smaller towns with lovely beaches that you hit before reaching Fort Lauderdale en route from Miami. Dania Beach Boulevard harkens back to the days when mangroves grew by the roadside and still had plenty of room to flourish and multiply. It leads to a beach and to the **Dania Fishing Pier**. Just north is **John U. Lloyd Beach Recreation Area**, 244 acres of barrier island.

Hollywood was founded by a Californian, but bears no resemblance to its West Coast namesake. The major draw is the oceanfront boardwalk, the only

Sailboarding along the South Florida seaboard.

place in South Florida where you can eat and drink at open sidewalk cafés on the ocean and find home-cooked meals in old wooden guest houses. The city's West Lake section is one of South Florida's last coastal mangrove areas and harbors pelicans and spoonbills.

Up the coast on A1A: The beach drive north from Fort Lauderdale is particularly rewarding. Each resort seems to melt into the next until you hit **Pompano Beach**. For the next 25 miles the road brushes the shoreline and butts against the Intracoastal Waterway.

Although it has grown rapidly as a resort and condo community, Pompano is still a major agricultural center with one of Florida's largest wholesale vegetable markets. Long before the sun rises each morning during the winter growing season, the **Pompano Beach Farmers' Market** buzzes with growers, vegetable brokers and homemakers bartering for the best prices on a variety of produce.

The Pompano Beach Air Park is home to the Goodyear Blimp, which you are allowed to see but not touch – or go up in.

The **Deerfield Island Park**, one of 288 parks in Brevard County, can be reached only by boat and offers a nature trail, tennis and 55½ acres of solitude.

The area's premier restaurant is **Cap's Place** in **Lighthouse Point**. Follow N.E. 24th Street and Yacht Club signs from Federal Highway to Cap's Dock. The *S.S. Dramamine* will take you to the island restaurant and bar. If it's not docked, blink your car lights and wait until it arrives. Cap Knight, a Spanish-American war veteran and occasional rum-runner, opened the Club Unique here in the 1920s on some beached barges and a derelict dredge. Guests boated to the hideout to gamble and defy Prohibition. Notable guests included the Duke of Windsor, Franklin D. Roosevelt, Jack Dempsey and Winston Churchill. The ramshackle atmosphere remains.

Bill Stewart's Riverview Restaurant, under the causeway bridge on Hillsboro Boulevard, has a similar history and atmosphere. It was converted from packing house to casino in the 1930s. Gangsters sometimes frequented the place and Al Capone had begun transactions to buy the triangular island across the way – until he was busted for income-tax evasion. The island, now a pristine park that can be visited by boat, still bears Capone's name.

Continuing north past the miles of towering dwellings that edge A1A, **Boca Raton** is soon reached. Eccentric architect Addison Mizner envisioned a fleet of gondolas romantically plying a man-made canal through town. But the waterway was never completed and the only gondola shipped from Italy disintegrated during the Depression. However, the filled-in ditch became in time one of Florida's most attractive streets, winding **Camino Real**, whose tall palms grace the attractive route to the **Boca Hotel and Club**.

Originally known as the Cloister Inn, the hotel is considered one of Mizner's greatest achievements. The loggias, archways, tiled patios and sculptured fountains of the original section convey the opulence of the 1920s. Boca Raton grew up around the hotel, acting as its service village for many years.

Boca Raton's posh veneer even surpasses that of Palm Beach in one respect – it fields a better polo team. Only Prince Philip's dashing British group and the expert horsemen of Argentina are thought to be better than these. The action occurs every Sunday from January through April.

Delray Beach is a pleasant, inexpensive alternative to the plush resort cities to the north and south. Its **Morikami Park Museum** offers changing exhibits dealing with Japanese art and a *bonsai* display of dwarf trees.

One of the world's largest circulation, but least influential, newspapers has put **Lantana** on the map. It's the headquarters for the lucrative *National Enquirer*, the supermarket "scandal sheet" that dishes up weekly doses of soapy stories about celebrities.

Lantana is linked with its northern neighbor, **Lake Worth**, which straddles a lake of the same name and is actually a salt-water lagoon.

Right, primed for polo at Boca Raton.

PALM BEACH

Enclave of enormous wealth and power. The poshest of the posh. A haven for the idle rich. These are some of the things that have been said about South Florida's most fabled city, **Palm Beach**.

If you are not extremely wealthy, you may not like the vibrations that emanate from this island. You can practically smell money growing here. Its residents may, in turn, look upon you with disdain. Tourists are tolerated, although not exactly welcomed. But if you keep a low profile and keep your eyes from bulging out of your head at the displays of excessive wealth, it's a fascinating side trip.

A few words of caution: leave your camera in the car, don't stare at the regulars at Petite Marmite, don't try to ogle mansions over the ficus hedges, and don't ask the prices of the diamond necklaces on Worth Avenue. The cost probably exceeds your mortgage. And

remember, it's against the law to park most anywhere, to own a kangaroo or any other exotic animal, or to hang a clothesline.

In the fields of the rich: In his enlightening literary portrait, *Palm Beach*, author-resident John Ney told the story of a young Junior Chamber of Commerce type bragging at a Palm Beach party. "I'm one of those under-40 millionaires!" the man boasted, startling an established resident of Palm Beach who involuntarily replied, "I was a millionaire before I was born!"

The moral of the story is that it's impossible to ride into Palm Beach and blend in with the surroundings, so don't even try.

Unless you prefer to gape at empty mansions undergoing beauty treatments and garden manicures, visit during the "social season" – an indeterminate period of time that falls somewhere between Thanksgiving and Easter. That's when you'll see the pretty people who, yes, actually live in – or at least decorate – the palatial dwellings.

The annual migration of money ignites a round of galas, teas, charity balls and political cocktail parties in election years. People willing to pay up to $1,000 a plate can get invited to some of the prestigious, glittering balls. But it may take a larger donation to get into one of the exclusive political gatherings.

Appropriately, a boatload of Spanish sailors with 100 cases of wine aboard stumbled upon the barren strand in 1878. They sold their cargo, including 20,000 coconuts, to a shrewd islander for $20. The islander sold two coconuts for a nickel to his neighbors. They planted them in the sand and, *voila*, the beach got its palms. Not long afterward, Henry Flagler and his railroad rolled into town. He liked it, built a home and transformed Palm Beach into a personal playground for himself and his wealthy, fun-loving friends. Addison Mizner added his ostentatious architectural touches, his Spanish spires, courtyards, plazas and arcades.

Astors, Goulds, Vanderbilts, dukes and duchesses followed Flagler into town. They stayed at the Royal Poinciana, one of the largest wooden buildings ever constructed and the largest resort hotel of its time. Black men pedaled them around the grounds aboard "Afromobiles," and a feature attraction was Cakewalk Night, where black dancers competed for a big white cake, then entertained richly-dressed guests with spirituals. The hotel has long since been dismantled, but its ghost lingers.

Post's Place and pampered poodles: You can leave Florida – and enter Palm Beach – by proceeding north on Highway A1A. You can't miss it. The garish strings of 7-Elevens and neon hotel signs vanish. Clean, uncluttered streets of class take over. The structures behind the high walls of concrete and ficus are not museums, just second homes to Palm Beachers. If you suddenly feel conspicuous among the Mercedes and Jaguars in your battered Pinto or rented Honda Civic, visit Classic Motor Tours on Poinciana Plaza. They'll ride you through this monied maze in a 1958 Rolls-Royce Silver Shadow.

An opulent bathroom fit for a sheik.

South Ocean Boulevard runs right past the Moorish estate of the late cereal heiress, Marjorie Merriweather Post. It's called Mar-A-Lago, and is now owned by Donald Trump. You can see its highest tower north of the Southern Boulevard Bridge. Its 17 acres, complete with nine-hole golf course and 117 rooms, has been valued at a cool $20 million, minimum. At 702 South Ocean Boulevard is a home formerly owned by the late Beatle, John Lennon. Next door is a mansion that once belonged to Woolworth Donahue, heir to the dime store fortune.

Turn left into Worth Avenue. It has been likened to London's Bond Street, Rome's Via Condotti and Paris' Faubourg St Honore. Here Courreges, Hermes, Gucci and other shops open onto courtyards and winding vistas. Try not to exhibit astonishment.

Show up at least a half-hour before noon to get a table at **Petite Marmite**, where you can eat shoulder-to-shoulder with celebrities if you don't mind paying dinner prices for lunch. The photo

case has a picture of John Lennon having dinner there with his wife, Yoko Ono, and actor Peter Boyle. Younger heirs gravitate to **Chuck and Harold's** on Royal Poinciana Way with its Parisian-style sidewalk café.

The Esplanade is a two-story klatch of shops surrounding a courtyard with another popular lunch spot, **Café l'Europe**. To find out who partied where, pick up a copy of *The Palm Beach Daily News*. (It may be all you can afford to buy here.) Note that it is printed on paper especially treated to prevent ink from smudging expensive hands or outfits.

Most of the exotic-looking animals heeling like military cadets at their masters' sides are probably dogs. John Ney once wrote:

It is correct to have any sort of dog, comme il faut *to have a small dog like a corgi or pug, and* de rigueur *in certain circles to have a toy poodle. The poodle is such an important demonstration of conspicuous consumption that many people who have no money at all haul*

Ice tea attire at Palm Beach's Colony hotel.

poodles around in their cars as the easiest and cheapest way of pretending that they are really loaded, but it rarely works.

Behind and beyond the ficus hedges: Flagler's old home, built in 1901, is now a museum to one of Florida's prime movers. He and his third wife lived in it for only four years. The rooms and most original furnishing have been restored, and one of Flagler's railroad cars is on display in the backyard.

Another memorial to Flagler regally sprawls across the street. **The Breakers** has weathered booms, busts and even two fires, but remains one of the nation's first-class resorts. Stately Venetian arches lead into the lobby, comfortable sofas and Persian carpets line the rambling hallways, and the Circle Dining Room has an immense circular skylight, cathedral windows and bronze chandelier. Another cavernous old hotel, **The Biltmore** (north of Royal Poinciana Way), is now a condominium.

The northern reaches of Palm Beach have more of the same. Just beyond 1075 N. Ocean Boulevard is the compound of the Kennedys. There hasn't been a street number visible for years. Look for a garage with servants' quarters above. Mizner himself designed the American-Spanish hacienda in 1923, and Joseph Kennedy purchased it 10 years later.

Here, a young Senator John Kennedy wrote his best-selling *Profiles in Courage* after a stint in World War II. He later wintered in Palm Beach after becoming President, but John Ney wrote of a local prejudice against this neighboring "royal family."

During the 1980s Palm Beach enjoyed a renaissance fueled by an influx of wealthy scions from abroad. Prominent newcomers included French shopping center tycoon Robert de Balkany and his wife, Princess Maria Gabriella of Savoy, the Duke of Doudeauville, Krupp fortune heir Arndt Krupp von Bohlen und Halbach and Prince Yuka Troubetskoy, who long dominated the French Riviera social scene.

If you keep driving north on Ocean

The flags and fountains about The Breakers, Palm Beach's five-star resort.

Boulevard you will eventually run out of road. Park in a metered space, if you can find one, and take the short hike to the wooden clock on the Palm Beach Inlet. If you make it early enough you'll witness a sunrise all the money around you can't buy.

With champagne and cold duck hawked from a canopied cart instead of hot dogs and beer, it's obvious that polo is not akin to a Sunday afternoon baseball game. Palm Beach's pet sport is played at nearby **Palm Beach Polo and Country Club** and Boca Raton's **Royal Palm Polo Club**. Here, some of the top matches in the world have attracted players as illustrious as Great Britain's Prince Charles. You must be either rich or an expert with a wealthy sponsor to participate. But it costs little to watch from your car or camper. More than 20 area polo fields host matches from October to July.

Back in the "Real World": West Palm Beach, across Lake Worth, was conceived as an asterisk by its rich patron Flagler. It was reserved for servants, gardeners and other peons who toiled to keep Palm Beach from crumbling while their employers partied, shopped, played polo, and made more money. In fact, Palm Beach still parks its garbage trucks around here.

The drab downtown has no pretensions, but may prove a refreshing change from the rarified air of Palm Beach. And it has things the beach hasn't – including a new Palm Hotel, with convention facilities and international-standard service, at Okeechobee and Australian boulevards.

Nearby **Belle Glade** and **Clewiston** have come into their own as commercial centers for the forests of sugar cane that dominate much of Palm Beach County. They produce enough sugar to supply more than 15 million Americans for an entire year. Try suckling the delicious sap right out of the cane.

Construction, real estate and banking are other major Palm Beach County industries. **Palm Beach Gardens** is headquarters for the Professional Golfers Association (PGA), which has given

Polo players tumble at Palm Beach.

its initials to one of that town's main thoroughfares. The PGA operates a housing development with four championship golf courses and a **Gold Hall of Fame**. Palm Beach Gardens is also home of the National Croquet Association, which holds international tournaments each year.

Fifteen miles west of downtown is **Lion Country Safari**. The well-fed lions have grown lazy, but it's thrilling to watch one lead a parade of cars or see a giraffe peering in your window. Keep your windows closed, though.

You can pick your own oranges at **Anthony Groves** on State Route 7. Some 17,000 citrus trees bloom here in the winter. **Knollwood Groves** south of Lake Worth offers wagon train rides.

Smokey the Bandit and his dinner theater: Highway A1A curves back to the beach over Blue Heron Boulevard. You can follow it through the high-rises of **Singer Island** all the way to **Jupiter**. Although considerably south of Kennedy Space Center, this town once was a terminal for the Celestial Railroad, which took its name from the stations it served – Juno, Neptune, Mars and Venus, as well as Jupiter. Flagler bypassed this peninsula with his railroad, so it has remained less developed. A monument in Jupiter marks the site of the abandoned Celestial track.

A red brick lighthouse juts from a mound at Jupiter Inlet. Climb it for a view of the Gulf Stream – a veritable river in the Atlantic Ocean – then quench your thirst at **Harpoon Louie's** across the water. Barefoot mailmen once began their long trek from here to Miami. Visit the home of Harry DuBois on the shell mound for insights into those days.

Jupiter is famous as the hometown of Burt Reynolds. His dad once served as the town sheriff and still operates the **Burt Reynolds Ranch Tack and Feed Store** on Jupiter Farms Road off Indiantown Road.

Burt and his wife Lonnie Anderson are frequently seen in the area. The **Jupiter Theater**, formerly the Burt Reynolds Theater, stages top plays with stars like Sally Fields, Farrah Fawcett, **The way to catch a wave at Sebastian Inlet.**

Carol Burnett, Martin Sheen and occasionally, Burt himself.

The mansions of **Jupiter Island** house millionaires who don't like Palm Beach. But the owners are equally wary of tourists. You will find no hotels, convenience stores or gas stations here. Police pull over any vehicles that stray off public roads into narrow, private drives. Photo-electric beams along the roadways tell police the direction of a vehicle at night. Still, it's worth a look. Turn off US 1 to State Road 707 through an archway of overhanging trees.

Australian pines, tall palms and bushy fuchsia hide most homes. Expensive yachts huddle along the shore. In 1961 a circuit court judge upheld restrictive zoning laws here when he said Jupiter Island "was cut from one mold and its counterpart cannot be found elsewhere. Many people would consider it dead – but it is very much alive with genteel living, friendship and compatibility. The town doesn't want what many others have, but many others would be better off if they had more of what this town

has and wants to keep – seclusion, solitude and tranquility."

Trapper Nelson and Jonathan Dickinson: In Martin County, to the north off US 1, **Jonathan Dickinson State Park** preserves the last wild river in southeast Florida. You can paddle your canoe along the upper Loxahatchee River past alligators half-submerged in the water, and rarities like the bald eagle. Trapper Nelson's camp upriver can be reached by canoe or via the *Loxahatchee Queen* river cruise. Trapper was a folk hero who opened a zoo here where he wrestled alligators and devoured raw possum. His property made him a millionaire, but health officials closed the zoo and he retreated into isolation, discouraging visitors with his shotgun. Police found him dead with a bullet in his head, and some suspect foul play because he had held up an important multimillion dollar land deal.

Dickinson Park rolls through tall sand dunes that peak at Hobe Mountain, an 86-foot sand pile with a 22-foot observation deck. It is the highest point above

Teeny bikinis compete for whistles and prizes in Jupiter.

sea level in South Florida. Jonathan Dickinson was shipwrecked here in 1696. Indians stripped him, but he escaped to St Augustine.

The **St Lucie River** splits into two forks at **Stuart**. This stream and the **Caloosahatchee River** form the **Okeechobee Waterway**, used by thousands of craft annually. The *MV East Chop*, run by **Hyline Cruises** of Stuart, takes you into wilderness on the St Lucie Canal locks, through orange and lemon groves to Lake Okeechobee, and back.

Turtles attract tourists to **Jensen Beach**. Large loggerheads and green sea turtles crawl out of the ocean at night each May to lay eggs in the sand.

Hutchinson Island has rocky cliffs where **Gilbert's Bar House of Refuge** can be visited. High on stilts on Highway A1A, it is the only one still standing of six lifesaving stations for sailors built more than 100 years ago. Locals call the outcroppings along this beach, unusual for Florida, "worm rocks."

Look for Florida's largest Chinese vegetable plantation, the **Sang Yick Farm**, west of **Hobe Sound**. It does no retail business but you'll find exotics like bok choy, woo, okra and long beans growing here.

The inn that drifted in: Fort Pierce concentrated on the shipping and processing of Indian River citrus products for decades, but it now also draws its share of tourists to resorts and luxury campgrounds. Within the city's limits is the **Savannahs Wilderness Area**, akin to the Everglades. The drives up State Road 707 or Highway A1A to the city are particularly scenic.

Vero Beach's landmark is a rickety-looking complex called the **Driftwood Inn**. Eccentric entrepreneur Waldo Sexton fashioned it from just that. Its newer additions have gone condo, but visitors can snack in its dining room or stroll through this impromptu architectural jumble perched like a shipwreck on the tideline. So improbable is the construction of weather-beaten timbers, it looks as if a simple tug might bring the whole thing down. Yet it has withstood high waves and fierce hurricanes ever since the 1930s.

Each bedroom in the original section is unique. An assortment of unmatched windows on one side adds to the odd appearance. Cannons from Spanish ships stunk offshore, hand-painted ceramic tiles, ornate church windows, rusting iron chains, and bells, bells, bells hang in the halls and rooms. Sexton loved bells. Appropriately, a statue of Miguel de Cervantes, author of *Don Quixote*, greets you at the main entrance. It's carved from a single piece of walnut.

Another Sexton creation, the **Ocean Grill**, serves dinner a stroll away up the beach. Its bar extends over the beach where windows mist with sea spray. Also in Vero Beach, the **Indian River Island Sanctuary** can be reached by a footbridge at the end of Dahlia Lane.

Thirteen miles north of the city near **Sebastian** in the Indian River is **Pelican Island**, the nation's oldest wildlife sanctuary. Established in 1905, the 7,000-acre refuge is the breeding place for that awkwardly built bird that flies so gracefully. Rent a boat for a close look, but obey signs warning: "Stay Off the Island."

Sebastian Inlet Park on the ocean is considered excellent for fishing. **McLarty State Museum** is on the site of an old Spanish salvage camp. Archaeologists believe an Indian mound near the inlet may contain the skeletal remains of some of the first European settlers of Florida. Researchers think shipwreck survivors may have lived with the Ais tribe at least three years before the founding of St Augustine. Documents in Spanish archives indicate that two men picked up by a French ship testified to their capture by the barbaric tribe in 1562. Researchers say a large cross of conch shells found over the grave of a chief of the extinct tribe indicates someone had introduced the Indians to Christianity.

Florida's best, and virtually only, surfing action is on the East Coast's Atlantic waves. The implacable Gulf of Mexico provides little surf (except during hurricanes) and caters to windsurfers instead. Most non-wind enthusiasts "hang ten" in the wavey regions from Sebastian Inlet to Daytona Beach.

Hot-air balloon cruises are one way to see South Florida.

Inland South Florida

Inland southern Florida revolves around enormous **Lake Okeechobee**. This is Florida Cracker country, as lazy and laid back as other sparsely settled spots in the United States. Cowboys and Indians raise cattle and sugar cane, fish and hunt. Migrant workers come and go. Travel the main routes like US 27 up through the Everglades and cane fields from Miami, US 441 or 90 from West Palm Beach. You'll find ghost towns and wisps of towns. Veer off onto some of the smaller roads, if you can find any. You might see a Seminole roping a calf or a Jamaican immigrant cutting cane.

The "Big Water": Lake Okeechobee's name comes from an Indian word meaning "big water." Okeechobee is 750 square miles of crystal waters, Florida's largest lake and the second largest freshwater body within the boundaries of a single state. It has been both a blessing and a curse to the people who live nearby.

Early settlers to LaBelle and Clewiston watched two hurricanes spin flood waters from the lake over their fields and homes. More than 1,800 persons died during the destruction, but an exact body count proved impossible.

A system of dikes, pumping stations, spillways and canals has tamed Okeechobee and helped turn some surrounding mucklands into an agricultural paradise of vegetables and sugar cane. Fish camps and resorts punctuate the lake's perimeter. Okeechobee is the centerpiece of a water-control district stretching from Orlando to Miami. The US Corps of Engineers controls the level of water; some environmentalists contend it is to the detriment of the Everglades. Both the Everglades and South Florida's cities have been threatened with drought in recent years by the dwindling water level of the lake. Excessive pumping for the booming population growth along the Gold Coast have been sucking it dry.

You won't see mighty Okeechobee from US 27 as you drive from Belle Glade to Clewiston. The 35-foot-high Hoover Dike, which took 40 years to build, obscures the view.

Chewiston is headquarters for the US Sugar Corporation, the south's largest sugar mill. The **Clewiston Inn** is a homey hotel you would expect to find in such a city. Try fried gator meat and catfish at **Tony's Glades Restaurant** or give in to an interminable procession of signs along western US 27 imploring you to eat at the **Old South Bar-B-Q Ranch**. The annual Swamp Cabbage Festival here brings out country-western bands and cloggers, who take part in an energetic, arm-waving, stomping dance from the mountains that has become popular here.

Moore Haven, on the Caloosahatchee River, caters to truckers and bass fishermen. Here, a lock allows access from the lake to Fort Myers, 50 miles west. This is the final link in a chain of waterways connecting the Atlantic Ocean to the Gulf of Mexico.

Up State Road 78 toward the town of **Okeechobee**, you'll pass by the **Calusa**

Tractor-pull contests highlight South Florida's agricultural heartland.

186

Lodge, a resort for hunters and fishermen whose trophies adorn its restaurant walls. Even the wild boars were bagged nearby. Seminole Indians often lunch here, not far from the **Brighton Indian Reservation**. These early Florida inhabitants have used their land for cattle farming and turned it into big business.

Okeechobee is the largest town on the north shore of the lake, another center for vegetables grown on thousands of acres of drained muckland. The city holds a Speckled Perch Festival the second Saturday of March, drawing thousands to a fish fry. Labor Day brings in the Cattlemen's Association Rodeo. The Rodeo Bowl itself is east of the lake near **Indiantown**.

Sucking sap from a cypress knee: West of Lake Okeechobee, US 27 travels to two old-time attractions that entertained early tourists. **Gatorland** will allow the kids a close-up look at snakes and other reptiles, peacocks and raccoons. You may well be the only customers, so prepare to enjoy a personalized visit.

A line of tree limbs beg you to stop at Tom Gaskins' **Cypress Knee Museum**, just north of Fisheating Creek in **Palmdale**. Gaskins began collecting knees, the gnarled roots that poke from the ground around the trees, in 1934 when he noticed their natural shapes resembled dolphins, insects, bears, people and even famous faces. Customers began buying them as souvenirs of Florida's wilder side. Gaskins will show you how he peels and preserves the knees, how you can make a meal from them by sucking on the nutritious sap, and how they grow along the catwalk he himself built through an oak and cabbage hammock and a cypress swamp (now drying up) adjoining his workshop and showroom. Across US 27 he has preserved some of his favorite finds in a museum. There you will find the "Mona Lisa," "FDR," "Joseph Stalin," and several "Madonnas."

Instead of the standard Mickey Mouse ears or bushel of oranges, you may wish to take home a cypress knee, a glass-top tree table, a turkey call or some driftwood from Gaskins' place.

An aviator cropdusts sugar cane near mighty Okeechobee.

A drive uphill, north from Melbourne, along Florida's East Coast, is a pleasure trek that retraces the tourist migration routes that fed the rush to the Gold Coast playgrounds of Miami and Fort Lauderdale. Down the East Coast tens of thousands of Florida's first tourists poured in a steady flow along the Atlantic, leaving small oases every dozen miles or so. Eventually, they struck roots in the lower eastern portion of the state, a slice of Florida that for many years was virtually the only spot for tourists.

Yet, the Melbourne-to-Jacksonville strip of East Coast Florida has all the trademarks of tourism, all the strata of the eras of the good years and the bad years, all the topography of generations of visitors who came and made the state a mecca for leisure money. To retrace that route is to experience a trip back and forth through time. Depending on how you want to cover the 200 or so miles, you can experience Florida in terms of Yesterday, Today or Tomorrow.

There are three land routes north from Melbourne – the old, rustic, weaving and sometimes frustrating A1A that snakes along the coast line, often within tantalizing sight of the shimmering Atlantic Ocean; a more traditional but rather random US 1 that also leads straight up the coast, sometimes bypassing some of the smaller towns, but allowing a continual view of Florida in all its sparkle and bangles; and finally the route of Tomorrow, Interstate 95, which ribbons along clean and untouched, fast and four-laned, leaving the motorist with quick and unclear visual impressions of a landscape that whizzes by in a sameness of trees, cars and interchanges.

THE SPACE COAST

Melbourne is an ideal place to start. It is surrounded, like the petals of a flower, by a sampling of communities that have all the age and nostalgia of Old Florida, the shiny and startling newness of New Florida, and the brash technology of Future Florida.

While Melbourne as a community dates back to the 1970s, the land was long home for the first Floridians – Indians of the Ais and Timucuan Tribes.

The first homesteader to make the Melbourne area his home was a surveyor commissioned after the Civil War to determine if the Florida Territory was suitable as a colony for thousands of newly freed slaves. His report was unfavorable, but his personal opinion was just the opposite – he settled in Florida, first in an area that is now downtown Miami, later in a place he called "Eau Gallie." He took the name from the French word *eau*, meaning

Preceding pages: the drive-on beach of Daytona. Left, the launch pad at Kennedy Space Center.

"water," and the Chippewa Indian word *gallie*, meaning "rocky," which he chose for the ledges and foundations of natural coquina rock – a soft, whitish limestone made up of broken sea shells and corals and used as a building material throughout Florida.

By 1893, the Florida East Coast Railroad extended its southern tip to Eau Gallie. After that, growth was steady until the post-World War II construction of Patrick Air Force Base, now also home for a seaside missile display. In 1890, a second nearby community was born and named Melbourne; in 1969 Melbourne merged with Eau Gallie.

Today's Melbourne offers the standard amusements and distractions – at least seven public golf courses, fresh and salt-water fishing, museums, bicycle trails, a variety of parks and nature trails, even a zoo in an orange grove. **Houser's Zoo**, where you'll find more than 100 animal species, from a Kodiak bear to a Florida puma, is worth a browse.

The **Brevard Art Center and Museum** has a nice touch for visitors – a "please touch" gallery for the visually handicapped, and the local Chamber of Commerce offers a tour covering some 50 historical sites such as early churches, homes, hotels and trysting pathways favored by yesteryear's young loves.

The **Florida Institute of Technology** in Melbourne is the home of a botanical garden with more than 300 species of palms, ferns and other tropical foliage that flourish along a quiet stream. It's free and open from dawn to dusk.

The mixture of the modern and the natural continues throughout this section of East Coast Florida. A few miles north of Melbourne is **Rockledge**, one of the oldest winter resorts on the East Coast, first established in 1837 and named for the ledges of coquina rock which look out over the **Indian River.** This area is noted for old and beautiful residential homes.

Just north of **Cocoa Beach** on A1A is the city of **Cape Canaveral**, which includes **Port Canaveral**, a deep water port that gives Central Florida access to shipments of oil, cement, lumber and fish. A bit more unusual is the occasional berthing there of atomic submarines, which dock while undergoing Polaris and Poseidon missile launch tests. Nearby are missile-tracking ships that accompany the nuclear subs.

Gateway to the stars: Midway between Cocoa and Cocoa Beach is **Merritt Island**, flanked by the **Banana River** on one side and the Indian River on the other. Here again is an odd blend of the old and the new. The island includes a well-kept air strip, facilities for private aircraft and the largest, most modern shopping mall in this part of Florida.

North and east of the malls and air strips is the **Merritt Island National Wildlife Refuge** that shares a common boundary with the **John F. Kennedy Space Center**.

You can visit the Space Center via the NASA Parkway, State Road 405. At the main gate, visitors receive a pass that permits entry to the **Visitors' Center**, which is a veritable museum of America's space program.

The Visitors' Center is also the launch-

The Vehicle Assembly Building looms over Kennedy Space Center and the Merritt Island Wildlife Refuge.

ing point for tours of the vast Kennedy complex. Air-conditioned buses transport you to the enormous **Vehicle Assembly Building**, one of the world's largest in volume, the space shuttle launch pads and to other sites of interest. For more details on Kennedy Space Center, turn to our feature "On Finding Space at the Cape."

For Tomorrow fans, there are spaceships and rockets poking into the blue Florida sky. You can view 10-story high Titan missiles at close range at **Patrick Air Force Base**. Such displays appear at several points fronting directly on A1A. But the Kennedy Space Center remains the biggest paean to flight and its spectacle is unmatched.

Because of the curvature of the Florida coastline, these launch centers project well out into the Atlantic. When such vehicles are launched here they roar down the **Eastern Test Range**, pass directly by local beaches while still at relatively low altitudes, and provide spectacular views of the Space Age all along the Melbourne area coastline.

Below right, join the space race.

Appropriately, the Merritt Island refuge is one of the nation's premier sanctuaries of the creatures that taught man to fly. The refuge is a natural habitat for more than 250 species of birds, many in danger of extinction.

The freedom of the wildlife on Merritt Island makes an indelible impression on visitors, particularly since it sits right next to a man-made world of new and artificial flight.

Among the endangered species taking refuge here is perhaps the most exciting of all Florida birds – the southern bald eagle. Its large nests – some more than 10 feet thick and 6 feet in diameter – may be seen in the tall slash pines along the refuge's roads. In the past, between 15 and 20 pairs of bald eagles may have nested at Merritt Island; today, no more than five pairs are regularly nesting there.

Birdwatchers estimate that as many as 70,000 ducks use the refuge during the winter months. This winter tourist population includes some 23 species that migrate to the refuge from their

northern nesting grounds each year. One native, the Florida mottled duck, also nests here.

Fathoms of fish: As on most of Florida's East Coast, offshore waters are famous for their abundance of trout, redfish, drum, crevelle jack, sailfish and snook. The beaches of the Space Coast provide fine offshore fishing for surf casting; indeed, record catches have been lured right from **Canaveral Pier**, a manmade promontory that reaches 825 feet into the Atlantic Ocean at Cocoa Beach. Deep-sea fishing provides a different breed of potential catches: grouper, flounder, mackerel and kings, among others. There are limits on the size and number of fresh and saltwater fish and on certain shellfish and crabs that you are allowed to catch.

One bizarre sea creature that you won't need a rod and reel to catch is the walking catfish. It is exactly what its name implies, using sturdy pectoral fins near the head to lift itself out of the water. They squirm snake-like over lawns and roads along the East Coast and Central Florida. A native of Southeast Asia that escaped from fish farms near Boca Raton in the early 1960s, these walking catfish have gills that enable them to breath on dry land.

There's one last feature to Melbourne that you might want to take in if you're there between June and August full moons. On the deserted beaches south of the bright lights and heavily populated cities, a phenomenal night spectacle takes place when giant sea turtles return to the beaches, scoop out their nests and lay thousands of ping-pong-ball-sized eggs. Three turtle species bury their eggs here. The most common is the loggerhead, averaging 200 to 300 pounds, but sometimes topping the scale at 500 pounds. It is one of the sea's oldest creatures, dating back as far as 10,000 years.

Occasionally the leatherback, which averages 700 pounds, and a few 130-pound green turtles come ashore too. But most of the turtles here are loggerheads, who spend nearly their entire lives at sea and return to land only to lay

A resident of Merritt Island comes in for a landing the envy of any astronaut.

their eggs under the cover of darkness.

These turtles and their eggs are protected by federal law; they cannot be touched or hindered. But you *can* view their egg mounds, each containing perhaps as many as 100 eggs. Note the tortuous paths in the sand made by these huge parent turtles. When their babies hatch, 7 to 8 weeks later, they make the trek toward the surf. Many never make it, falling prey to seagulls, raccoons, the hot sun and large fish in the water. Predators also destroy many nests.

Melbourne's northern neighbor, **Cocoa**, offers a calmer, more leisurely contrast to the hustle and bustle of the Kennedy Space Center. Cocoa boomed in population with the coming of the Space Age, yet the community manages to retain a certain picturesque charm.

The city was first named Indian River City when it was founded in 1882 because it sits on the west edge of that baylike river. But the US postal authorities said that name was too long for use as a postmark. When word arrived at Willard Store that a new name was needed, someone suggested "Cocoa" – picked from the front of a box of Baker's Cocoa that had just been brought in with the freight. The name stuck.

The tranquility of old-fashioned **Cocoa Village** in downtown Cocoa remains. The streets are lined with flowering planters and specialty shops where visitors can view a potter at his wheel, a leathersmith making belts, antiques being restored, and artists at work.

Acres of cattle: West of Melbourne is the huge **Deseret Ranch**, acquired by the Church of Jesus Christ of Latter Day Saints during the 1950s. It encompasses 316,000 acres – that's 44 miles in one direction and 29 in the other. It's so big that *all* roads leading from Melbourne and its vicinity to Walt Disney World cross the ranch at some point.

Deseret Ranch's main products are beef cattle, timber and citrus. The ranch has about 2,000 acres of citrus trees and more than 5,000 head of Brahma cattle, animals particularly suited to Florida's climate because they are the only breed with sweat glands. They are also more

An infant survivor of the Melbourne turtle march.

resistant to many diseases that can diminish typical English breed herds.

Aside from all that cattle and citrus, Deseret also has 275 or so head of horses – and communities of deer, turkey, quail, panthers, bears, alligators and, no doubt, snakes. There are plans to construct a tourist center at Deseret Ranch. In the meantime, groups are welcome – with advance notice.

As you observe the acres of cattle in Florida, you may wonder why they are always followed by longlegged white birds with yellow bills. These cattle egret feed on grasshoppers and other insects stirred up as the cattle plod along.

Indian River country: As you continue northward from the Space Coast, the seaside again begins to look like early Florida. There are fewer condominiums and more houses nestled in dunes and shrouded in sea oats, palmetto bushes and scrub. On up US 1, through **Mims**, **Scottsmoor** and **Oak Hill**, the return route takes you along the **Canaveral National Seashore** on the right and the **Intracoastal Waterway** left.

Before getting there, though, you first enter **New Smyrna Beach**, a small but charming community with a wide, flat and firm beach that invites motorists to leave the hot asphalt and concrete ribbons of man for a leisurely drive along some of the smoothest sand in the world.

New Smyrna Beach offers 8 miles of drive-on-it, park-on-it, sunbathe-on-it beaches. It's considered the world's safest beach because of tremendous rock ledges 25 to 40 miles offshore in the Atlantic that prevent dangerous ocean undercurrents which can pull an unwary wader off his feet and out to sea.

New Smyrna Beach is one of the oldest settlements in America. Shell mounds around the city indicate that early Florida Indians lived there, generation after generation. Historic **Turtle Mound**, which overlooks both river and ocean, is the highest point on the coast for miles around.

Records show that the Indian village of Caparaca once stood on the site of what is now New Smyrna Beach, and historians claim that in 1513 Ponce de

A grasshopper and its enemy.

León, buffeted by a storm off what is now Cape Canaveral, found refuge and fresh wood and water here before being attacked by Indians and forced to retreat back to his ship. Called Rio de la Cruz (River of the Cross) by the Spanish and later nicknamed "The Mosquitoes," for obvious reasons, the inlet was officially named **Ponce de León Inlet** in 1926.

The first colony of settlers came to the area in 1767. This group, led by Dr Andrew Turnbull, a Scottish physician, included 1,500 Greeks, Italians and Minorcans looking for a new land to raise fruit, indigo, maize, sugar cane, cotton and rice. Dr Turnbull named his colony New Smyrna, in honor of his wife's birthplace in Greece. The colony disbanded in 1777 because of a shortage of funds and political intrigues.

Yet, during the 10 years it existed, a system of irrigation and drainage canals was built and is still in use today. The ruins of coquina wells, foundations and indigo vats – still visible – indicate the wide scope of activity by the colonists. Check out the **Turnbull ruins** and the **Sugar Mill ruins**, built in the 1830s and torched by rampaging Seminole Indians a half-century later.

It is a lovely drive down A1A past luxury stilt houses to the windblown dunes and sea oats that mark the entrance to the **Canaveral National Seashore**. Beyond are 25 miles of primitive beach and shoreline uninhabited by man. Stop at **Turtle Mound** where 600 years, worth of oyster shells were piled up by ancient Indians. More than 100 plant species have taken root here. It's an interesting climb to the top.

Curiosity-seekers may wish to ask directions to **Canova Street** before leaving New Smyrna. Here lies another of Florida's numerous oddities – a grave on an island in the middle of the street. It is the final resting place of the 16-year-old son of a pioneer citrus grower who died while hunting in 1860.

Detour back on A1A en route to Daytona for a look at Ponce's Inlet and its 175-foot, red brick lighthouse. It is a hot, hard climb to the top, but the trip is well worth it.

A Cracker cowboy cools off his cattle.

DAYTONA BEACH

North of New Smyrna Beach lies even more driveable sand, more beach, more amusement centers, more boardwalk, more dunes, more beer, more discos, more of everything. It's a mecca sought by college students during Spring Break. It is *where the boys and girls are* every Easter – **Daytona Beach**.

Actually, Daytona is a year-round mecca for young and old. It has 23 miles of firm, flat beach that is up to 500 feet wide at points, most of it open to cars. The speed limit is a patient 10 mph. A small fee to drive on the beach has reduced the number of people who have been killed in car accidents here.

In contrast to the current beach pace, Daytona began as a place for speed. Between 1902 and 1935, no less than 13 land auto racing records were set on the beach by speedsmiths such as Barney Oldfield and Sir Henry Seagrave. Sir Malcolm Campbell personally broke

Left, kitsch "art" dives over a Daytona swimsuit shop.

existing records five times, including the 286-mile-per-hour record made in his famous *Bluebird*.

In the 1950s Southern stock car racers began to compete on an oval track dug from the dunes at Ponce Inlet on the south end of the beach. In 1959, as cars became faster and crowds of spectators bigger, auto racing moved to the asphalt, high-banked **Daytona International Speedway**. Now, every January the International Motor Sport Association stages its championship finals at the Speedway, a race-track considered by many to be the world's fastest. Stock car speeds of more than 180 miles per hour are common.

Other perennial raceday favorites include the GOODY's 300 in February and Firecracker 400 every July, and a spate of racing every February that includes a NASCAR 200 and the main event – the Daytona 500. Motorcycle races are also held every March and October.

The roar of race cars is a long and audible leap over centuries from Daytona's quiet beginning. This town was briefly settled in 1767, but in the early 1800s English settlers from the Bahamas developed vast indigo and sugar plantations along the **Halifax River**, a waterway which blends with the Intracoastal Waterway and flows through the city.

From the area's hammocks, live oak was cut, floated down the river and loaded onto schooners to be taken to England for shipbuilding. During the Seminole War of 1835 the Indians were victorious, so no white man remained in what is now Daytona Beach until the late 1800s when settlers return to the area and the community was named Daytona after its founder, Mathias Day.

Migration, student-style: An altogether different sort of exploring goes on every spring. This in-migration, of exam-weary, sun-starved college students, has been going on for years. Indeed, Daytona Beach seems to be edging out Fort Lauderdale as *the* place for college Spring Break madness and a lucrative reputation that can mean millions of dollars to any Florida beach commu-

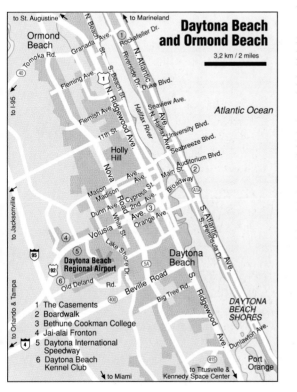

Daytona Beach and Ormond Beach

3,2 km / 2 miles

to St. Augustine
to Marineland
Ormond Beach
N. Beach Ave.
Granada St.
Rockefeller Dr.
Tomoka Rd.
Riverside Dr.
N. Atlantic
Fleming Ave.
Duke Blvd.
N. Beach St.
N. Ridgewood Ave.
Seaview Ave.
Halifax River
Atlantic Ocean
Flemish Ave
11th St.
N. Halifax Ave.
University Blvd.
Holly Hill
Seabreeze Blvd.
Nova Ave.
Main St.
Auditorium Blvd.
Mason Ave.
Broadway
Madison
Dunn Ave. Cypress St.
2nd Ave.
Road
White St.
Ave.
Orange Ave.
to Jacksonville
Volusia
Lake Shore Dr.
Daytona Beach
S. Atlantic
S. Peninsula Dr.
Ave.
Daytona Beach Regional Airport
Old Deland Rd.
Beville Road
S. Ridgewood Ave.
Big Tree Rd.
DAYTONA BEACH SHORES
to Orlando & Tampa
Dunlawton Ave.
Port Orange
to Miami
to Titusvelle & Kennedy Space Center

1 The Casements
2 Boardwalk
3 Bethune Cookman College
4 Jai-alai Fronton
5 Daytona International Speedway
6 Daytona Beach Kennel Club

nity. It's estimated that between the first week of March and Easter more than 400,000 students visit.

Aided by the theme parks near Orlando, Daytona seems also to put out more of a welcome mat for the student, with cut-rate prices on many of the city's 16,000 hotel rooms, free beer parties and lots of friendly smiles.

During a typical peak Spring Break, one of the top disco spots along the beach's blocks-long boardwalk – aptly named **Top of the Boardwalk Discotheque** – may see as many as 700 to 800 students walk through the doors each night, despite a maximum capacity of only 250. The **Boardwalk** also offers a selection of amusement centers, arcades, and rides.

There are also places like **Finky's**, a Texas-theme club on Grand View Avenue near Seabreeze, 701 South, a popular lounge with live disc jockeys, laser shows and video screens. All contribute to Florida's pervasive carnival atmosphere. College students have found the bizarre streets of neon and glitter tacky enough for their spring tastes – and easier to reach than Fort Laudedale further down the coast. Many hotels, however, require a damage deposit by student guests.

Rockefeller's retreat: A few miles north, you can visit what was once considered a "Millionaires' Colony." This is **Ormond Beach**. Its beginnings, however, were modest. No one is exactly sure who the first settlers here were. Some say, a bit romantically, that they may have been victims of shipwrecks which were prevalent along the coast in the 1600s.

In 1804 Spain offered grants of land to English colonists living in the Bahamas. Among those who accepted such grants was Capt. James Ormond, who acquired a tract on the Halifax River. Another was Charles Bulow, whose plantation was destroyed in the Seminole Wars. Remnants of Bulow's sugar mill can be seen north of the city.

Climate was another factor in the settling of Ormond Beach. In 1873, the Corbin Lock Company of New Britain, Connecticut, sent representatives to Florida to establish a suitable health resort for its employees threatened with tuberculosis, which was then prevalent. They chose a tract on the west side of the Halifax and 12 families came and called the place New Britain. The name was changed to Ormond in 1880 when the community incorporated.

In the late 1800s, the establishment of the **Ormond Hotel**, the completion of a bridge over the river, and an extension of the Flagler East Coast Railroad brought millionaires with names like Vanderbilt, Astor and Gould. Some, such as John D. Rockefeller, Sr, built homes here. Rockefeller found the place suited his health and spent more than 20 winters here until he died in 1937 at age 97. His home, **The Casements**, and the old Ormond Hotel are now historic landmarks. The hotel is now facing the threat of demolition.

Besides their money and their names, the wealthy who visited Ormond Beach brought something else at the turn of the century – the automobile. Like Daytona and New Smyrna Beach, Ormond Beach

Sunday drives on Daytona Beach were even popular back around 1920.

had its share of wide, hard ocean sand. It was ideal for driving your brand new gas buggie and seeing how fast you could go on a flat, smooth surface.

A "measured mile" was created and speed tests were run. Soon new vehicles built specifically for speed were raced and tested by men with names like Chevrolet, Olds, Duryea, Ford, Oldfields, Winton and others. Records were broken beginning with the first recorded 57 miles per hour by R.E. Olds and Alexander Winton in 1902, and continuing until Sir Malcolm Campbell's 5-miles-a-minute record of 276.82 mph in 1935.

To celebrate these historic achievements, the Birthplace of Speed Association holds an annual Antique Car Meet every Thanksgiving. The Turkey Rod Run, featuring antique cars, is also held during this period. During the day, sprints are held on the beach for old-time gas-eaters. There's also a **Flea Market** where antique car hobbyists can buy, sell, and swap parts to fit their treasured vehicles, some of them are worth up to $100,000 to a collector.

At Ormond Beach, motorists have a choice of routes north: You can pick up US 1 or A1A, or double back to I-95. A1A will take you through **Flagler County** and some of the less-traveled communities on the coast, where development has been slower, kinder and more individualized.

A1A will also take you through **Flagler Beach**, **Beverly Beach**, **Painters Hill** and a couple of state parks (there are three in the county altogether), including **Washington Oaks Garden Park**, which hosts a wide variety of flowers and plants. More importantly, A1A feeds right into **Marineland of Florida**, one of the oldest and serenest attractions in the state and a home for all manner of ocean dwellers. This attraction features two huge **Oceanariums**, an electric eel pavilion and the **Aquarius Theatre**, with performing porpoises doing six shows a day. Visitors are encouraged to take photographs – there are even experts on hand to help you get the photo you want.

STREET IN ST. AUGUSTINE.

COPYRIGHTED 1882.

OLD ST AUGUSTINE

A dozen or so miles north, you can turn the clock back 400 years at an archaeologist's delight called **St Augustine**.

Like many Florida cities, St Augustine lays claim to a title – The Nation's Oldest City. The rationale is this: St Augustine was the first permanent settlement by Europeans in what is now the continental US Jamestown, Virginia, was established 42 years later. St Augustine was 55 years old by the time the first Pilgrims came to New England.

Tourists rule today. The city likes to show off its wrinkles and years, so consequently there are a half-dozen ways to take the look you want. In addition to usual car, bus and foot tours, St Augustine also offers leisurely horse-drawn carriage rides to historic points of interest. Most carriage drivers offer a bit of narration on the city's history and key sites. Their drivers provide a flavorful report about all points past and passed,

and occasionally stop to allow riders to inspect on foot. There is also a sightseeing train that motors down the narrow one-way streets. Finally, there are *Victory II* cruises along the waterfront on a 75-minute tour of the city's edge and **Matanzas Bay**.

Throughout the city, bits of history beg for your attention. What better place to start than **The Fountain of Youth** itself, a memorial park on the site believed to be where Ponce de León first set foot on his fruitless, thirsty search for a magic elixir. Past a stone arch and a modest sign that advertises the fountain, you will find a natural spring bubbling in a coquina shelter presumably of Spanish design. Many visitors like to take a taste, just to see what all the legend's about and can buy a whole bottle of the stuff at a gift shop. But don't be disappointed if you come away without feeling younger.

Railway man Flagler's first compound of hotels, at the corner of Cordova and King, included the Alcazar, now the **Lightner Museum and City Hall com-**

Left, this 1882 postcard shows that St Augustine has changed very little in the past century.

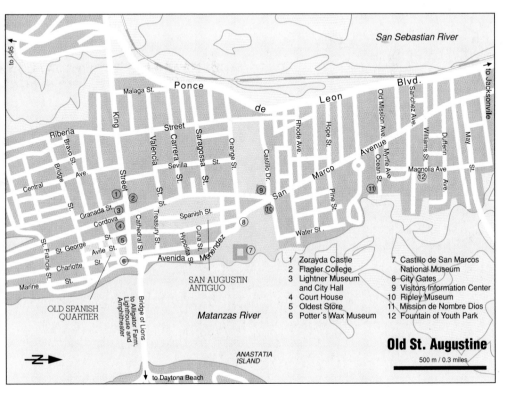

1 Zorayda Castle
2 Flagler College
3 Lightner Museum and City Hall
4 Court House
5 Oldest Store
6 Potter's Wax Museum
7 Castillo de San Marcos National Museum
8 City Gates
9 Visitors Information Center
10 Ripley Museum
11 Mission de Nombre Dios
12 Fountain of Youth Park

Old St. Augustine

500 m / 0.3 miles

plex, and the Ponce de León, now home of **Flagler College**. In its heyday the latter hotel had more than 400 rooms. Each boasted a fireplace with inlaid marble and rotundas with caryatid and gargoyles.

The city's founder, Pedro Menendez de Avilés, celebrated the New World's first mass where he landed near present day Ocean Avenue. A 208-foot stainless steel cross on the grounds of **Nombre de Dios** marks the consecrated site.

The oldest house in the oldest city: A capsule history of the city can be seen in the restored Oldest House on narrow **St Francis Street**. It is a visual history lesson, complete with antique furniture, thick coquina walls, a secluded Spanish patio and costumed guides who will answer all your questions. The house's construction is a combination of Spanish, British and American architectural influences. The building's ground floor (from the Spanish period) is of coquina that was quarried on **Anastasia Island** across the **Bridge of Lions** on Matanzas Bay. The second story, added by the English, is of wood. Archaeological research indicates this house has been occupied since the early 1600s. The current building rose, phoenix-like, upon the ashes of an earlier, cruder structure of palm thatch and wood.

No visit to St Augustine is complete without stopping to fantasize at the massive masonry fortress that dominates the Bay, **Castillo de San Marcos**, and its outpost, **Fort Matanzas**, 14 miles south. Built between 1672 and 1695 by the Spanish, it is a huge symmetrical fort surrounded by a moat. The impregnable fortress was never occupied, though it was threatened and besieged five times by outside marauders.

The National Park Service has even reconstructed the **Cubo Line**, a defensive earthwork which ringed the northern side of St Augustine and encompassed the town's historic **City Gate**. The city's **St Augustine Fiesta** is a mixture of waterfront shops and restaurants, including **Potter's Wax Museum**. In the **Spanish Quarter** there are history exhibits and craftspeople at work

Fringed surreys set the mood for a tour of historic St Augustine.

204

recreating aspects of early colonial life.

Alligators and actors: One of the most intriguing places to visit, at 4 Artillery Lane, is the **Oldest Store**, an authentic turn-of-the-century general store; its more than 100,000 items will take you back to the time of high-buttoned shoes and lace-up corsets. **Potter's Wax Museum** has more than 170 famous people from all eras and ages, and **Ripley's Believe It or Not Museum** is full of odd and slightly dusty artifacts from more than 198 countries.

The **St Augustine Alligator Farm** on A1A is another of the city's "oldests." Opened in 1893, it makes the plausible claim to be "the world's original alligator attraction." The farm features the usual performances of gator-wrestling on the hour and affords leisurely looks at the strong-jawed reptiles.

Back in the historical vein, the **Spanish Quarter** on St George Street is an intriguing reconstruction of a typical 18th-century Spanish colonial village, providing a glimpse of what life was like here in bygone days. Automobiles are prohibited from the narrow brick streets which are lined with quaint old shops and homes.

Further south at the corner of Granada and King streets is **Zorayda Castle**. This imposing building is a replica of The Alhambra, in Granada, Spain. Its gaudy trappings recall the pomp and gilt favored by ancient Moorish kings.

After all that looking, walking, riding, strolling and standing, you may want to just sit and enjoy "Cross and Sword," the story of the founding of St Augustine. This drama is acted out in a natural amphitheatre carved out of a hillside near the town's coquina pits. Written by Pulitzer Prize-winner Paul Green, the pageant is staged daily except Sundays from mid-June through to Labor Day.

For all its fascinating wrinkles, condominiums have begun to encroach upon this ancient city. One *New York Times* writer wryly commented that one day "100 years hence, some entrepreneur will claim that the city possesses 'America's Oldest Condominium'."

Ghosts appear to stroll the streets of America's oldest city.

JACKSONVILLE

Our trip northward continues through more beach communities whose history reaches back to the earliest days of Florida's development. When we reach the **St Johns River**, one of the few rivers in the US to flow northward, we are carried inland toward **Fort Caroline**, located about 5 miles from the mouth of the river. This sanctuary was established by Huguenots (French Protestants) in 1562. Like its cousin forts at St Augustine, Caroline saw warfare, sorties and massacres. Early French and Spanish colonists were a militant lot who treated one another's forces as pirates and marauders. They felt no remorse about killing men, women and children.

Today, the original site of Fort Caroline no longer exists. Its meadow-like plain and part of the bluff on which it sat overlooking the St Johns River washed away after the river channel was dredged deeper in 1880. To help visitors visualize the original scene, the fort's walls have been reconstructed on the river plain, according to 16th-century sketches by Jacques le Moyne, the colony's artist and mapmaker.

Jacksonville Beach has a 1,200-foot fishing pier that lances out into the Atlantic, and a **Flag Pavilion** that houses flags of all 50 states. **Mayport Naval Station**, home of giant US aircraft carriers, has at least one Navy ship open for public tours on weekends. The Mayport naval base also offers the old **St Johns Lighthouse**, a historical thorn that rises at the foot of Palmer Street inside the base's security fence. The Navy considers it a hazard to planes and would like it torn down, but it still stands as a landmark listed in the National Register of Historical Places.

Visitors to Jacksonville Beach can even go ghost-hunting. The 100-year-old **King House** in Mayport is said to play host to the restless spirits of some of its old seafaring residents.

Jacksonville, a bit farther inland on the St Johns River, is the largest city in

French artist Le Moyne drew this picture of Fort Caroline in 1564.

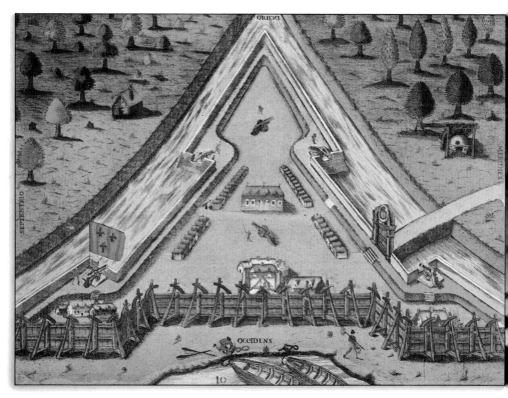

land area in the US covering 841 square miles with a population of over 600,000. It also boasts one of the tallest office buildings in Florida – the 37-story, 535-foot **Independent Life Insurance Company Building**.

The city spans both banks of the St Johns, and, as the local Chamber of Commerce is likely to point out, Jacksonville, unlike most of Florida, has seasons – all four of them. That's because the city is north of Florida's tropical zone. The seasons are mild, but noticeable. The city boasts more than 2,600 hotels and motels, and more than 2,400 restaurants that can, at any given time, seat 185,000 people. For football fans, Jacksonville has the 70,000-seat **Gator Bowl**.

The largest city in the US: Surveyors laid out the town site in 1822 at a long-used river cattle crossing called Cow Ford by the British and Wacca Pilatka by the Indians. The city continued to grow, despite a 1901 fire that burned down 2,400 buildings – half the town – and left 10,000 homeless.

Jacksonville prospered as the gateway to Florida's first tourist region – the St Johns River, described in "The Panhandle" chapter. One famous resident of that era immortalized the state in classical music. Composer Frederick Delius lived in a run-down orange grove on the St Johns. He was enthralled by the impromptu music of black farm laborers. When he returned to his native England, Delius incorporated those rhythms into musical compositions like *Florida Suite*. You can visit his restored cottage at **Jacksonville University**.

Jacksonville Port is one of the Southeast's busiest. Among unexpected sights here are the rainbow colors of thousands of bright imported cars arriving from Japan, or the slow, patient decay of an old tugboat rich in its rotting colors, bobbing serenly in some backwater cove.

There is also a **Seaboard Coast Line Locomotive** on view, sitting in the parking lot of the **Prime Osborn Convention Center**. This 1919 steam engine remains as a third tribute to the railroading era.

Work at Jacksonville's docks continues through the night.

Jacksonville Zoo is one of the South's finest, featuring some 225 species of animal life and one of the best collections of Southern waterfowl. Also on the north side of Jacksonville is the **Anheuser Busch Brewery**, on Busch Drive at I-95.

In the southern portion of Jacksonville, there is the **Alexander Brest Planetarium**, for star-gazers, and **Treaty Oak**, for nature-gazers. The oak in **Jessie Ball du Pont Park** is said to be 800 years old. According to local legend, the tree was an important meeting place for Indians and white settlers during peace negotiations. This 66-foot oak is thought to be the oldest tree on Florida's East Coast. It has a diameter of 5½ feet and a limb span of 180 feet and is still growing on Prudential Drive at South Main Street.

Jacksonville's **Friendship Fountain** is also one of the world's largest and tallest objects, spraying water higher than a 10-story building. At night it's lit in a rainbow of colors.

Under eight flags: Finally, as you head towards the Georgia border, A1A crosses the Intracoastal Waterway onto **Amelia Island**, 32 miles northeast of Jacksonville. Its southern end belongs to the 900-acre **Amelia Island Plantation** resort and the northern end to **Fernandina Beach**.

The island is rich in history – it's the only US location to have been under eight flags: French, Spanish, British, American Patriots, Green Cross of Florida (more patriots), Mexican, Confederate and US. Still, the island survived intact.

The city of Fernandina Beach recently restored 30 blocks of its **Old Town** core. Called **Centre Street**, the houses and buildings here date back to the 1850s and have a Victorian look about them. Their lacy "gingerbread" balustrades take you back to those times – Tiffany windows, gables, turrets and "leaning architecture" mark an era of handcraftsmanship. Noteworthy structures include **Baily House, Tabby House, Villa las Palmas**, and **Fairbank's Folly**.

During the 1870s and 1880s, Fernandina was a major East Coast shipping port and among the richest cities in Florida. It was also a terminal on the first cross state railroad to Cedar Key on the west coast. Today, its old **Depot** serves as the **Chamber of Commerce**.

The entire area, especially along the coast and the St Johns River, became the state's first resort destination. Rich northerners came to this area to vacation. Carnegies, Rockefellers, Bakers, Goodyears, Fergusons, Morgans and Pulitzers have been and still are regular visitors here.

On the northern tip of the island is **Fort Clinch**, located at the entrance to the **Fernandina Beach Harbor**. Though never finished, it saw action in the Civil War and was used for training in the Spanish-American War. On the first weekend of every month, state park rangers reenact the fort's 1864 occupation in dress, action and speech.

Amelia Island Plantation has three golf courses, trails for biking, jogging, horseback riding and on-site transportation. There are even ponds where only children under 12 may fish.

The important celebration is the annual Isle of Eight Flags Shrimp Festival. Shrimping is a major industry for Amelia Island, because it sits out in the Atlantic on one of Florida's barrier reefs. The shrimp festival, held on the first weekend in May, includes sidewalk art shows, craftshows, folk music and more boiled, fried, peeled and gumboed shrimp than you can possibly imagine.

While walking around Amelia Island, particularly along her beaches, you might notice the unusual quality of the sand. You're walking on bits and pieces of the Appalachian Mountains. The fine white sand is quartz – crushed bits that have traveled slowly southward along the coast, washed by the sea from the eroding Appalachians to the beaches of Amelia Island, where they rest as tiny fragments.

It is here where your trip up the East Coast ends. Just the other side of **Fort Clinch** is **Cumberland Sound**, and beyond that, **Cumberland Island**, visible from the ramparts of Fort Clinch. It is now a national seashore region.

A last dip in the cool Atlantic.

NORTH FLORIDA

In the midst of a seemingly endless swath of North Florida pine forest, a billboard needs only three words to tell the contemporary story of this largely undiscovered and undeveloped region.

"Florida's Last Frontier," proclaims the sign, put there by a real-estate man anxious to sell lots to modern "pioneers."

If the billboard gives the impression that the northern reaches of the Sunshine State are a little old-fashioned and move at a slower pace than the rest of Florida, perhaps it is correct. And if the sign means that some of the state's last hidden treasures – unsullied beaches, meandering rivers and inland wilderness – await discovery here, that is also true.

But if the billboard implies a place without a past, a clean slate ready for the first chalkings of civilization, then it is woefully misleading. For it was these piney woods that attracted Florida's first Spanish settlers, that resounded with the musketry of both international and civil warfare, that helped some men amass fabulous wealth but seldom allowed them to keep it.

No, this area is not one that lacks a past. If anything, it has too many pasts. Pensacola, for example, is now a thriving metropolis, but the city has been the booty of five different nations. There were places like Magnolia and Saint Joseph and New Port, once prosperous communities with fancy hotels and sedate mansions, now wiped off the face of the earth by fire or rain or disease. Madison's Southern charm and Gainesville's air of academia have roots dating back before the Civil War. Indeed, the heritage of this entire region is written in overnight success, in booms of lumber and cotton and citrus, followed by busts so total that little remains of the heady glory days.

And what of North Florida today, this last frontier? It is a land of contrasts, cosmopolitan in its big cities of Pensacola and Tallahasee, but overwhelmingly rural in the Panhandle that stretches between them. Like the rest of the state, it has its frenetic seaside communities. But there are fewer of them than elsewhere, and many more stretches of pristine beach, white and powdery as sugar, without a hint of a high-rise building.

THE PANHANDLE

At the western gateway to the state – more than 600 miles from the crowds and condominiums of fast-paced Miami – rests **Pensacola**, a coastal city that is a mixture of Old South charm, Spanish heritage and Navy bravado.

In many ways, it is the forgotten city of Florida. Tucked away in the far west corner of the state, Pensacola long has been shunned by snow-weary tourists migrating south on the interstate. Likewise, the state's more cosmopolitan residents have tended to ignore the city, tossing it off as South Alabama "Cracker Country."

If that weren't enough, the history books have all but ignored the city's claim to fame as the oldest settlement in America. Instead, the East Coast's St Augustine, the oldest *continuous* settlement, has garnered the glory and the tourists.

But never mind that others seem to have forgotten. Pensacola has not. The city has remembered its past and begun promoting its future in tourism. And well it might. There's no question it has the beaches, miles and miles of undeveloped coast where sand dunes – not condominiums – spiral high above blue seas. The northern tourist may not have discovered Pensacola's Santa Rosa Island yet, but Mississippians and Alabamans did long ago.

Pensacola also has history on its side. For the vacationer seeking more than sun, the city boasts dozens of blocks of history preserved in two districts near downtown, in museums, old battlesites and forts. And it isn't just in museum pieces that the city's history lives. It walks streets with names like Intendencia, Zaragoza and Cervantes, that somehow have survived in a grits-for-breakfast town. And it moves in the wind at St Michael's Cemetery, where tombstones bearing Spanish inscriptions date back to the 1700s.

Pensacola is the largest city in the Panhandle, with a metropolitan area population of more than 300,000. It offers good seafood restaurants, lively downtown, greyhound racing year round and stock-car racing during the summer tourist season. It is a city that moves at the pace of a slow southern drawl. But it is also a city of nightlife, with entertainment ranging from goodtime jazz to the more flashy pleasures of the famous **Trader Jon's**, where sailors from the nearby Naval Air Station drink and party surrounded by memorabilia of Navy history and famous pilots who came to Trader Jon's before them.

Make no mistake, Pensacola is a melting pot. It is a ragtag mixture of Spanish, French, British, American, Confederate and Navy influences that has been stirred for four centuries.

For the record, Pensacola was settled in 1559, six years before St Augustine. But alas, Don Tristan de Luna and the 1,500 colonists who ventured with him into Florida abandoned the settlement two years later, fed up with hurricanes, Creek Indians and each other.

So it was not until 1752 that Pensacola was established as a permanent settlement, though the Spaniards had tried again in 1698 and 1722. Since its founding, Pensacola has flown the flags of five countries in Plaza Ferdinand VII, a downtown park named for the one-time king of Spain. You might say Pensacola became a volleyball, tossed back and forth between countries so many times that its government changed 17 times in 300 years.

Springtime in Seville: Each year in May, the city remembers its checkered history with the Fiesta of Five Flags, a celebration complete with parades, art shows, exhibits and contests, capped by a local citizens' re-enactment of de Luna's landing in 1559. The fiesta is a good time to visit Pensacola, not only because of the pageantry, but also because May brings beach weather to the Panhandle. The bulk of the festival takes place in the **Seville Square** area, where the colony was established in 1752 and, under order of King Ferdinand VI, named "Panzacola." The name, later modified, is said to be of Indian origin, meaning "long-haired people."

Today, the original square near Pensacola Bay is the centerpiece of a 37-block section of restored homes, specialty shops and old-time eateries that is Pensacola's crowning achievement in historic preservation. Several museums trace the city's history and booms. The square is a pleasant place to spend an afternoon roaming on foot.

Most vaunted of the area's several restored houses (all open for touring daily) is, of course, "the Oldest House." Many Florida cities have one. This structure, also known as the **Lavalle House,** is part of the **Pensacola Historic Village**, which features three museums, including the **T.T. Wentworth Jr Museum**, once the city hall. The exact construction date of Lavalle House is unknown, but historians consider it typical of the French Creole cottages of the 18th century. Much sturdier than modern homes, its wood frame has brick nogging in all the walls to which plaster was directly applied.

Other old houses have been turned into stores specializing in antiques or handmade quilts, or quaint restaurants serving deli sandwiches, wine and cheese or gourmet ice cream. The **Pensacola Art Center**, housed in an old jail, is in their midst.

Seville Quarter, *the* nightspot in town, is located on the fringe of the Seville Square area in a restored 19th-century building. The most famous inhabitant is **Rosie O'Grady's Goodtime Emporium**, a jazz joint where the bartenders sing and dance as well as serve.

The atmosphere is beer-and-peanuts casual. Also in the Quarter are a disco, an easy-listening lounge featuring fruit drinks, an outside courtyard bar, an oyster bar and an aviators' pub as well as a restaurant.

"A vast, howling wilderness": Although most of the houses now in Seville Square's preservation district were built in post-Civil War days, the area has a history that began with the Revolutionary War. Then, the square was part of a British stockade. The English also occupied **Fort George**, the ruins of which still stand on Palafox Street. The British lost Pensacola in 1781 after a Spanish military leader named Bernardo de Galvez successfully commanded a month-long siege upon the fort. The victory not only returned the province to the Spaniards, but cut off British access to America and buoyed the hopes of colonists fighting for independence further north.

Four decades later, when the Americans – led by Andrew Jackson – marched into Pensacola to claim Florida as their own, the Spaniards may have pondered the wisdom of that assistance. Jackson, the first territorial governor of Florida, stomped about the city, struggling to convince the Spaniards to clean up streets and forts he found "filthy and disgusting." His prim wife Rachel was shocked by the vice she saw, and urged dancers and gamblers to "make the Sabbath the market day for thy soul."

"Oh, how shall I make you sensible of what a heathen land I am in?" she moaned in a letter to friends. "I feel as if I were in a vast, howling wilderness, far from my friends of the Lord."

The Jacksons stayed two months in Pensacola. Then they packed up and went home, leaving the job of governing the "heathen" city to a subordinate who later embezzled the town treasury.

The humiliation of Geronimo: Seville Square isn't the only area of Pensacola where a hundred tales of the past lie buried, waiting to be found. Across the bay, **Fort Pickens**, a pentagonal-star stronghold with a bastion at each corner, took five years to build and accom-

Aftermath of a 1906 hurricane that hit Pensacola Harbor.

modated as many as 600 men in battle. Here the ghosts of the Civil War mingle with that of a proud Indian chief.

In the opening days of the War Between the States, Fort Pickens on Santa Rosa Island went to war against **Fort Barrancas** on the mainland, just a few miles away. It was American against American, Rebel versus Yankee. Some historians believe the first shots of the tragic national conflict may have actually been fired here, not at Fort Sumter in South Carolina. In the end, the Union soldiers, manning the gunneries at Fort Pickens, triumphed over the Confederates at Barrancas, and the city of Pensacola fell into Union hands.

Both forts can be toured, and guides are available to answer questions. Pickens has 160 campsites. A mile and a half east, the **Dune Nature Trail** winds through spectacular sand ridges, towering slash pine and live oak laden with reindeer moss. Barrancas, built by the Spaniards and later fortified by the English, is located on the grounds of the Naval Air Station.

Although neither fort saw much action after the Civil War, Fort Pickens remained in the limelight through the 1880s. For two years, the fort was jail to Geronimo, the proud Apache chief who refused to give in to the white man. Soldiers chained Geronimo to the massive walls of the garrison from 1886 to 1888. On Sunday afternoons, it is said, Geronimo had to face the jeers of prosperous Pensacola residents, who came to Pickens to ogle the chief.

That was in the days of Pensacola's lumber boom, when the city was chopping and exporting trees with wild abandon. Without thinking of the day when the timber would be gone, the residents built big houses and made big money. Today, dozens of houses from that era still stand in a 50-block area called the **North Hill Preservation District**, near downtown. Thanks to preservationists who set out to save the decaying neighborhood, many of the homes have been restored, and others are in the process of being refurbished. They were built in Classic Revival, Queen Anne or Span-

Pensacola-based Blue Angels taxi for a take-off into the heavens.

ish Mission style. Visitors must content themselves with the view from outside, as most are private residences.

The same boom that produced the elaborate houses also brought the railroad to the the city through the work of a local man, W.D. Chipley. After linking Pensacola to eastern Florida by rail, Chipley turned to another job: promoting Pensacola. He dubbed the city "the Naples of Florida" and assured northerners that in "winter and summer, its healthfulness is marvelous, except during epidemics."

But a bust usually follows a boom. One day the trees were gone. The foreign ships left Pensacola's ports. And the ship-building at the Pensacola Navy Yard shut down. Without the Navy and a new-fangled contraption called the airplane, Pensacola might have turned into a ghost town. Instead, it became home to America's first **Naval Air Station** in 1914. Today, it is billed as the world's largest, the "Annapolis of the Air." All Navy training for land and sea is headquartered at the base. The Navy

is the city's biggest employer with 9,000 civilians on its payroll in addition to the 10,000 sailors stationed on base.

Blue Angels and bell bottoms: Located on the west side of town at **Sherman Field**, near Warrington, visitors will find the headquarters of the famous precision-flying team, the Blue Angels, who wing their way through two local shows each year. Fort Barrancas and the **National Museum of Aviation** are also on the base. Exhibits include 40 full-size aircraft, a Space Age Skylab module, and memorabilia from the exploits of "Pappy" Boyington and the Black Sheep Squadron.

From the base, it is just a jaunt across the bay to Pensacola's most natural attraction – its pristine beaches. On **Santa Rosa Island** off the coast of the city, the sand and sea are protected as part of the **Gulf Islands National Seashore**, and development is limited. From Pensacola Beach west to Fort Pickens, there's nothing but sand, scrub live oak and sea oaks for miles. Visitors can stop at park sites and unload for a day in the sun, or

Daredevil maneuvers by the Angels.

a picnic. There are also campsites for overnight stays and nature trails for exploring the area.

In the other direction on State Route 399, the resort city of Pensacola Beach mimics Miami along a crescent of natural coast packed with high-rise hotels. Further east, Route 399 again becomes a strip of concrete bordered only by sand and sea.

Pensacola is *the* military town in the Panhandle, but the US Air Force also has two bases to the east – **Eglin** and **Tyndall**. Eglin is the largest American air base in the world. It has an aircraft museum that is open daily.

Eglin also boasts the world's largest environmental test chamber, the **McKinley Climatic Laboratory**. Here, snow can be produced and tropical monsoons and jungle or desert climes simulated. It is not usually open to the public.

The smaller base at Tyndall lies east of Panama City, providing basic and advanced flight training for Air Force personnel. Tyndall opened on the morning that the US entered World War II and counted actor Clark Gable, a gunnery student, among its first graduates.

Forests, falls and caverns: the inland Panhandle: Interstate 10, a four-lane, limited-access superhighway, exits Pensacola and crosses the center of the Panhandle, putting motorists in Tallahassee in less than four hours. Most of the landscape is small farms and the ever-present pine tree, but there are places worth seeing on either side of the expressway.

The largest of Florida's four state forests is located northeast of Pensacola. **Blackwater River State Forest** is a 183,000-acre woodland with hiking, camping, boating and fishing. The **Red Ground Trail**, once a major trading corridor for the Indians, is now a popular hiking path, and an environmental center where visitors can learn about indigenous plants and animals.

East of Blackwater on US Highway 331 near the Florida-Alabama border is the state's highest point – 345 feet above sea level, but remember that most of Florida is as flat as a flyswatter. Follow **Pigs poke...**

the arrow to a crumbling church on **Britton Hill**.

Although Florida is full of rivers, the lack of much vertical contour in the land has contributed to its lack of waterfalls. So rare is the sight that the state has created a 154 acre recreation area in the pastoral surroundings of the 80-foot **Falling Waters**, just south of Chipley on State Road 77A.

An entirely different atmosphere oozes from the eerie surface of the **Dead Lakes**, a recreation area 4 miles north of Wewahitchka on State Road 71, you'll find a forest of barren cypress, oak and pine drowned by the natural overflow of the Chipola River.

Midway along the interstate to Tallahassee is the **Florida Caverns State Park**, north of Marianna. It is a labyrinth of limestone made by hard-shelled sea creatures centuries before the Ice Age, when all of Florida was submerged. The floor and ceiling are decorated by crystalline projections, some honed by the years into formations resembling animals, birds, fruit, flowers and human beings. One configuration even looks like a huge pipe organ. Chambers include the Waterfall Room, Cathedral Room and beautiful Wedding Room.

East of Marianna is **Torreya State Park**, now a retreat for campers and and anglers but once, according to local legend, the home of Adam and Eve. Local folks say this was the site of the biblical Garden of Eden, citing as evidence the nearby Apalachicola River and the rare tree from which the park takes its name.

The torreya tree also is known as gopher wood, which is said to be the substance Noah used to build his biblical ark. The tree grows naturally only on the banks of the Apalachicola, which is said to be the world's only "four-headed" river system – the one described in the Bible as being near the site of the downfall of Adam and Eve.

From Bagdad to Sumatra: Highway signs along the busy interstate point the way to small towns like Bagdad and Two Egg. Unfortunately, the names are

...and a granny plows, in Panhandle countryside.

more exotic than the places themselves.

Bagdad was once a prosperous lumber port where a company of the same name operated. Like the fabled Asian city, Florida's Bagdad lies between two rivers on a grassy peninsula.

Also in the same area, on US 90, is **Milton**, once known as Hard Scrabble and Scratch Ankle. Those names were warnings of its many briars, which caused painful ankles among those who had to scrabble their way through town. Most were smugglers trying to avoid the payment of tariffs at the official import-export station in Pensacola. On the last Thursday in March residents recall this bit of 1800s memorabilia at the Scratch Ankle Festival.

Closer to Tallahassee, visitors may see signs directing them to **Sumatra** and **Sopchoppy**. Sumatra owes its name to a variety of tobacco once cultivated in the area, a strain similar to that grown on the island of Sumatra in the Indonesian archipelago. Sopchoppy's name came from the Indian words for "long" and "twisted," certainly a precise description of the nearby Sopchoppy River.

Sand dunes and fishermen: the Panhandle coastline: If you have time on your hands and a yen for magnificent scenery, the route to take from Pensacola is State 399 east along Santa Rosa Island, later picking up US 98. Driving pleasure isn't the only plus here. The route passes through territory chock full of untrammeled vacation spots that might cause you to stop for a day or for the rest of your vacation.

Beyond the condominiums and hotels of **Pensacola Beach**, you can revel in miles of billowing sand dunes topped by miniature magnolias. This stretch is the beginning of the **Miracle Strip**, a sweep of beach from Pensacola to Panama City largely undiscovered by tourists. It's also part of the **Gulf Islands National Seashore**, which stretches 150 miles westward from Pensacola to Gulfport, Mississippi. The strip's promoters claim the sands are the whitest in the world. On a sunny day, with the wind rippling patterns across miles of empty beach, it becomes hard to argue with them.

Communities along here ebb and wane from small to smaller. They include a bevy of beaches: Oriole, Woodlawn, Navarre, Grayton, Seagrove.

Fort Walton Beach is the first big coastal city you run into after you swing back to US 98. Its proximity to the military bases lends it a honky-tonk air. The town is filled with swaggering young recruits whose patronage has resulted in a strip of tacky bars, amusement parks and miniature golf courses. But the small military paychecks have also kept the beach attractions relatively inexpensive.

Fort Walton earned its slapdash military look early, as the site of the garrison after which it was named. The fort served as a safe haven during the Seminole Wars against the Indians. Its sands are rich in remnants from its early days as a home for the Pensacola, Apalachicola and Apalachee tribes.

Next on US 98 is **Destin**. Named for a sea captain, it calls itself the "World's Luckiest Fishing Village." The waters here change color, from pale green to

A sensuous sand sculpture graces a Florida beach.

cobalt blue, where Choctawhatchee Bay merges with the Gulf of Mexico. Its fishing reputation stems from its proximity to De Soto Canyon where marlin and sailfish test their strength and cunning against fishermen. Once a quiet resort, towering condominiums now mar its beauty.

You can trade in those high-rises for a look at a gracious old Southern mansion that compliments the land just a mile north of Highway 98 in **Point Washington**. The white-columned home was built of heart-pine and cypress before the turn of the century by a local lumber baron. Located on Choctawhatchee Bay, it became a social center in the Panhandle. It has been restored and refurnished with antiques, among them a 200-year-old French grandfather clock and a 17th-century cherry bed. It is open to visitors.

Continue back to US 98, then turn off on the secondary road, State 283, that leads to State Road 30A. Near **Seagrove Beach**, you can park your car and hike through sand-dune valleys to the crystal

Gulf waters and blinding beach sands. Pick a warm day in February or March, and you will have complete privacy. Only a few dune buggy tracks and bird-claw prints blemish the sands at this time of year.

After an afternoon of solitude, more gregarious travelers may wish to continue back to US 98 and venture east to **Panama City Beach**, another stretch of garish "Goony Golf" courses and souvenir emporiums. This southern Coney Island is quiet in the winter when frosty winds make the Panhandle cooler than peninsular parts of Florida. But in the summertime it comes to life.

The Redneck Riviera: So many Southerners from Georgia and Alabama own summer retreats or standing reservations at hotels along the Miracle Mile, Panama City Beach has become the heart of what even the locals call the "Redneck Riviera." Here, country music saloons and a **Christian Music Hall** shaped like Noah's Ark mingle with **Magic World Amusement Park, Castle Dracula Wax Museum, Shipwreck**

Sand dune ramble on the Miracle Strip.

Shirts and other gaudy attractions. You can fly in a helicopter, ride on a dune buggy, surf on a sailboard or slide down water flumes. Penny arcades provide the latest in Japanese electronic wizardy. Round off your visit at the **Jungleland Zoo and Volcano, Snake-a-Torium,** or **Gulf World Aquarium**.

In spite of the clutter, it's advisable to spend a night here rather than vacationing in **Panama City**, on the mainland across St Andrews Bay, where fumes from the local paper mill are best avoided. The name may conjure up images of Latin architecture and Spanish revelry, but don't look for any. The founder merely noticed the fledgling community was on a direct line between Chicago and the real Panama City in the Canal Zone, so he borrowed the name. On the city's eastern outskirts is Tyndall Air Base.

Several parks with more breathable air are within driving distance of Panama City. At the **Washington County Kennel Club**, greyhounds chase mechanical rabbits to the cheers of hopeful bettors. The club's season is from May to September.

The beachy atmosphere tapers off somewhat after Panama City as the coastline becomes more rugged. The towns here are more compact and their night life less effervescent, but their region is rich in both nature and history.

The first community of any size is **Port St Joe**. It's the kind of slow-moving place where the local disco shares its dance floor with a bowling alley. Today's sleepy pace belies a tempestuous yesteryear that saw the town spurt into existence almost overnight in the 1820s, only to be wiped out repeatedly by disease and other calamities. Port St Joe earned recognition as the site of Florida's first constitutional convention in 1838 and 1839. A museum now marks the spot.

Port St Joe was originally known as Saint Joseph, but the pious name belied the freewheeling character of the community, once considered the "richest and wickedest city in the Southeast." In those days, the town jumped to the **Stilts and sails near the Miracle Mile.**

rhythm of a major cotton-shipping port replete with wharves, warehouses, casinos, racetracks and sprawling mansions. That ended when yellow fever ravaged the town, killing three-quarters of the population within a year. A woodland fire did further damage, and a tidal wave administered the final blow, literally burying the city in sand.

Detour south then west on State 30E to sample the otherwordly magnificence of the **Cape San Blas** shoreline. Sunset is a particularly moody time to sit on the sand dunes and gaze out over the sullen Gulf of Mexico. But be sure to take insect repellent.

Southeast of Port St Joe is **St Vincent Island**, a 13,000-acre wildlife preserve of stunning beauty. St Vincent is for those who enjoy sand between their toes. And wildlife enthusiasts will find nirvana here. A plethora of native and transplanted animals, including sambar deer from India and loggerhead turtles, mingle with white-tailed deer and wild turkeys. Once a private hunting preserve, it is now owned by the federal government. The preserve can be reached only by boat.

Apalachicola Bay – oysters, ice and pink gold: About 25 miles east of Port St Joe is the old cotton port of **Apalachicola**, now a city whose name is synonymous with oysters. Apalachicola Bay provides Florida with 90 percent of its annual oyster harvest, from its vast acres of meticulously tended beds.

Here you can watch "farmers" harvest oysters by hand in waters close to shore. They use tongs – two crossed shovels joined at the lower end of the handles – to pincer their prey, which is cultivated in carefully selected water, neither too salty nor too fresh. Befriend an oyster farmer and he may teach you the technique.

Oyster shucking is another art. Scrape them from the half-shell, then eat them the way the natives do at the "raw bars."

Although the city's reputation revolves around oysters, mouth-watering mollusks are not Apalachicola's only contribution to mankind. One of the city's early physicians made the world

Apalachicola blue crabs.

more bearable by giving us manmade ice, refrigeration and air-conditioning.

While struggling to control malaria in the region in the late 1840s, Dr John Gorrie succeeded in building a machine that kept his patients' rooms cool. Gorrie did get a patent for the machine, but did not get credit for his work until long after his death in 1851. Now, a museum in his honor in Apalachicola displays a replica of the first ice machine. The original is in the Smithsonian Institution in Washington, DC. A statue of Dr Gorrie stands in the Statuary Hall of Fame in the US Capitol.

You'll make use of another memorial to the good doctor when you leave Apalachicola, taking the Gorrie Bridge east over Apalachicola Bay. Here you cross into the Eastern time zone (you've been in Central), so set your watch ahead an hour. At the end of the Gorrie Bridge, across the toll bridge to the right, is **St George Island**, where a state park with more than 9 miles of undeveloped beach boasts mountains of sand.

Another remnant of a long-gone boom era is **Carrabelle**, about 30 miles east along the coast. Once a prominent lumber port, it is now a tiny town with an economy based on commercial fishing. In fact, business from the vacation crowd is only a sideline along most of the waterfront in the eastern Panhandle. The seafood industry brings in the big bucks. From dozens of small ports as you drive down US 98, you will see shrimp boats sally forth into the Gulf of Mexico for days or weeks at sea, dropping their nets into the isolated sandy haunts of the delectable crustacean known in these parts as "Pink Gold."

Buying the vote with mullet: The most exciting of the inshore catches here may be mullet. Fishermen use long, narrow skiffs in their search, the better to pole shallow bayous often favored by mullet. Paying out nets in a half-circle, the mullet fishermen wait until a school blunders into the mesh, then close the circle around the frantic fish, and pull the net in by hand. Numerous seaside industries in the Panhandle and other parts of Florida process and smoke mullet for export throughout the world.

Decades of back-slapping office seekers have made mullet the main course of the Panhandle political dinner. Candidates in other areas ply their potential constituents with any of a hundred vote-getting menus, but in North Florida, deep-fried mullet is the way to win votes. Politicians usually serve it with cole slaw or baked beans, grits and hush puppies – made from a batter of cornmeal mixed with eggs.

Beyond Carrabelle, the coastal drive dribbles away into even smaller settlements. A right turn on State 370 leads to more beaches, as well as that increasingly predominant denizen of the Florida coastline, the stilt house. The road deadends at **Alligator Point**.

Swing back to US 98, and take another detour at **Spring Creek**, off State Route 367. This is the first of the innumerable sleepy fishing villages dominating the Big Bend area of Florida, where the Panhandle arcs into the state's peninsula.

Necessity is one reason why commercial fishing looms so large in the economies of places like Apalachicola, Carrabelle and Spring Creek. Dense swamp and forest to the north make living from the land impossible. Indeed, Carrabelle lies near one of the most deserted areas of the state, **Tate's Hell Swamp**. Ironically, only 50 miles or so north is Torreya State Park, the place thought by some to have been the Garden of Eden.

An unusual place with an unusual name, Tate's Hell sprawls over most of Franklin County. Its inhospitable interior, a breeding ground for the deadly water moccasin, may have been a bog as long ago as 100 centuries, according to fossil discoveries. The swamp is owned by a lumber company that has identified trees deep within its recesses as more than 600 years old.

The strange name of this eerie enclave emanated from the legend of Old Man Tate, a hunter who vanished into its tangled depths almost a century ago. According to local lore, he entered the swamp in search of a panther that had been killing his livestock. It took him a week to find his way out, a terrifying ordeal during which he was fatally bitten by a snake. A Will McClean folk song tells the rest of the story:

When Tate was discovered, these words he did tell:
'My name is Old Tate boys, and
I've just been to hell!'
These few spoken words were the last that he said;
His spirit it left him, Old Tate he was dead.

That, at least, is the legend. Skeptics say Tate probably disappeared in the swamp, and that imaginative storytellers invented the rest of the tale. Invention or not, it resulted in a colorful name which also describes some pretty forbidding territory.

The swamp bleeds into another vast domain with remote nooks and crannies of its own, the **Apalachicola National Forest**. It covers parts of four counties, and extends to the fringes of Tallahassee Municipal Airport. The largest of the three national forests in Florida, the Apalachicola preserve has numerous recreational facilities.

The adventurous may wish to challenge the preserve's **Bradwell Bay Wilderness**. Though not actually a bay in the traditional sense, the low elevation of the Bradwell Bay terrain has left parts of it submerged and choked with underbrush. Federal law prohibits modern forestry techniques here, part of a national wilderness program designed to keep certain isolated regions in a natural state. Would-be explorers are welcome but forewarned of the formidable hiking conditions.

The lower end of the **Ochlockonee River** meanders through the Apalachicola National Forest, providing canoeists with pristine rowing through pine and cypress woodlands rife with wildlife. A canoe trail begins 20 miles west of Tallahasee and continues downriver for 67 miles to Ochlockonee River State Park, on US 319 south of Sopchoppy between Carrabelle and Spring Creek. The upper Ochlockonee River pours into Lake Talquin west of Tallahassee, 73 miles after commencing near Thomasville, Georgia.

Tasty catch.

TALLAHASSEE

The major city nestled among the Panhandle's vast pine forests is **Tallahassee**, a secluded jewel of old mansions and modern office buildings founded in 1823 for one purpose only – to be the capital of Florida.

In those days, the southern peninsula remained a daunting jungle. Settlement centered on the northern tier, when Pensacola and St Augustine were the largest communities. Each wanted to be the seat of territorial government, so explorers set out from the two rival cities to find a mutually acceptable site for the new legislative headquarters. They met near present-day Tallahassee and opted for its rolling landscape, largely because of the glittering cascades that graced the area's most prominent hillside. With three log cabins to house the territory's lawmakers, the city retained the name given it by Indians, meaning "old town" or "old fields."

Left, Goodwood Plantation, Tallahassee.

Tallahassee has undergone many changes since its rustic inception but one thing remains the same – it's still a government town. The skyline is dominated by the high-rise capitol soaring 22 stories above a steep hill that once boasted a shimmering waterfall. Of those employed in the city, almost half work for local, state or federal government.

But don't let visions of boring bureaucrats and their ponderous edicts frighten you from Tallahassee. A capital city's bureaucratic exterior conceals one of the best-kept secrets in Florida. A friendly community, Tallahassee has done an excellent job of preserving its landmarks, its natural beauty and a small-town flavor that belies its burgeoning growth rate.

All this adds up to a city of 170,000 people who live amid a pleasing blend of old and new. It is a city rich in Old South townhouses and plantation mansions that have been restored to their former grandeur. Some homes line streets rimmed by squat dark oaks dripping with gray moss; streets that explode in flowery beauty each spring when the dogwoods and azaleas are in full bloom.

An elevator ride to the 22nd floor observation deck of the skyscraping **Florida State Capitol** will give you an eagle's-eye view of the city and surrounding countryside, awash in a sea of trees. Houses and businesses are hidden beneath a green carpet that stretches in all directions.

To find out what's behind and under all that green, visit the **Museum of Florida History** in the R.A. Gray Building, two blocks west of the capitol. Open every day but Christmas, its exhibits outline the geographic development of the state. On display are artifacts of Florida's various inhabitants through the state's 10,000-year, eventful history.

While Tallahassee isn't a place often spotlighted by American history texts, it has occasionally bordered on national stardom. In the 1530s, Spanish explorer Hernando de Soto came to this area in search of the gold that he never found. Today, visitors can see where his troops

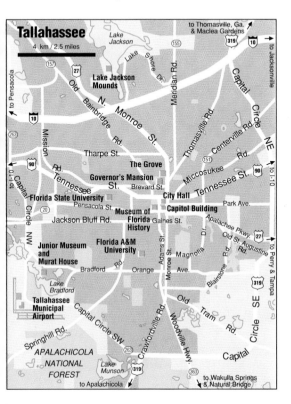

spent their first winter in the New World on the shores of Lake Jackson. On the banks of this lake, De Soto and his troops reportedly celebrated the first Christmas mass in what would become the continental United States.

Today the lake is renowned as one of the best bass fishing spots in the country. It is dotted by small fishing camps where accommodations, boats and fishing gear can be rented. On the western perimeter of the lake sits a small state park which preserves hallowed Indian burial mounds.

After De Soto's visit, Europeans neglected Tallahassee for two centuries, except for a Spanish mission west of the lake and infrequent sojourns by settlers from St Augustine to trade with the Apalachee Indians. When Florida became an American possession, Tallahassee was more noted for the people it attracted than for events that occurred there. The US Congress awarded part of its hilly countryside to the Marquis de Lafayette in return for the nobleman's service during the Revolutionary War.

And Napoleon's nephew, Prince Achille Murat, had a townhouse in Tallahassee. It was on a picnic in the city that Murat met his future wife, a grand niece of George Washington. Tallahassee today is blessed with a wealth of restored homes built by prominent citizens during the years immediately before and after the Civil War. The most outstanding of these residences is **The Grove**, completed in 1836 by the fifth territorial governor, Richard Keith Call. Located next to the ornate governor's mansion on North Adams Street, it is only one of a dozen such homesites within the city limits. The Grove, the Governor's Mansion and other residences can be seen on guided tours, arranged through any of the major hotels.

When Civil War engulfed the nation, Tallahassee lawmakers met to renounce the statehood they had achieved only 16 years before. Although the State's role in that bloody conflict was mainly to supply men and food for battles raging further north, a force of Union troops tried to occupy the capital city toward

Tallahassee lassies.

the end of the war. Tallahassee's leaders dispatched a rag-tag coalition of Confederate troops, militia, old men and teens to stop the invading Yankees.

With their naval support stranded miles to the south, the Union troops were already in trouble when the Confederates surprised them at **Natural Bridge**, several miles southeast of Tallahassee where the St Marks River vanishes underground for a short time. The Confederates inflicted heavy casualties on the union soldiers and beat them back, keeping Tallahassee the only uncaptured rebel capital east of the Mississippi. Federal troops returned in a few weeks, however, when the war ended. At a celebration of the Natural Bridge victory, word reached Tallahassee of the Confederacy's surrender.

A later version of Tallahassee's original Civil War capitol is being restored at the foot of its high-rise successor. The Natural Bridge battlefield today is a state-maintained historic site 10 miles southeast of town.

Tallahassee's white-collar work force

The South wins one at the Battle of Natural Bridge reenactment.

makes it a fairly well-to-do community. But the real wealth sparkles north of town on a dozen former plantations that now serve as exclusive hunting preserves. A case in point is the **Horseshoe Plantation**, an estate which has entertained the likes of Bing Crosby and the Duke of Windsor on its deer and quail-hunting grounds. It was once sold for $21 million – one of the largest land transactions in Leon County history.

These former plantations privately cater to the super rich. The lone exception is **Killearn**, now a state park near the city limits on US 319 North. Its original owner, Alfred Maclay, fashioned a fantastic garden of camellias, azaleas, palmettos and other native and exotic plants around a tiny lake. **Maclay Gardens State Park** also offers swimming, picnicking and guided tours.

Killearn Country Club, now a residential community and a state park, is host for an annual PGA golf tournament. For gamblers, there's a jai alai fronton 45 minutes west of the city via Interstate 10. East on the interstate is the

local greyhound track, the Jefferson County Kennel Club.

Most of Tallahassee kicks back quietly in the evenings – unless you venture into the bars along Tennessee Street flanking **Florida State University**, which rambles across a rolling campus of shady canopy trees, historic old buildings and flashy new ones. It numbers movie stars Burt Reynolds and Faye Dunaway among its alumni. If you are in Tallahassee in the fall, try to get a ticket to watch its well-known Seminole football team.

Tallahassee retained its rural Southern flavor longer than many other Florida communities of its size. The **Junior Museum** near the Municipal Airport pays homage to its not-so-distant past. Nature trails wind through the museum grounds, which also include a working 1880 farm depicting Florida pioneer life. Also exhibited are the restored home of Prince Murat, a one-room schoolhouse, and a grist mill.

The real Black Lagoon: To explore the pristine countryside around Tallahassee, head south on State Route 363. Turn east at Woodville and continue 6 miles to see the memorial to the soldiers who fought at the Battle of Natural Bridge. Backtrack to Route 363 and proceed south until you reach State Route 267. Head west here to **Wakulla Springs,** where a small admission fee will enable you to gaze upon the source of a river.

The park encompasses 4,000 acres of virgin hardwood and pine forest donated to nature lovers by the late Edward Ball, a key figure in 20th-century Florida politics who married into the Du Pont family fortune. Boat rides will take you upriver where alligators laze on the shores and anhinga "snake birds" dry their wings on twisted cypress branches. Hollywood filmed *The Creature from the Black Lagoon* here in the 1950s.

"Topless" oysters?: You can swim in the refreshing spring waters and dig in for a longer stay at the gracious lodge, with its rare Spanish tiles adorning the Moorish-style doorways. Note the ceiling beams in the lobby. They were etched with Aztec and Toltec Indian designs by a German immigrant reputed to have once painted castles for Kaiser Wilhelm.

Return to Route 363 and head south until the road ends in **St Marks**. This river port boasts several fishing camps that specialize in both freshwater and Gulf of Mexico angling. Another drawing card is **Posey's**, "Home of the Topless Oyster," most prominent of the many oyster bars that line the coast. Posey's is open only during prime oyster season, September to April.

An hour's drive east of St Marks along US 98 is **Perry**, a major crossroads for traffic headed into the south and central parts of the state. US 19, the most direct link between Tallahassee and the heavily populated Tampa Bay area 250 miles distant, also passes through Perry (although Interstates 10 and 75 carry travelers a little faster). Perry, a community of 8,000, bills itself as the "Tree Capital of the South." Logging is a bulwark of the economy throughout the northern part of the state and Perry is the hub of a forest kingdom that begins at the edge of the Gulf and extends several counties inland.

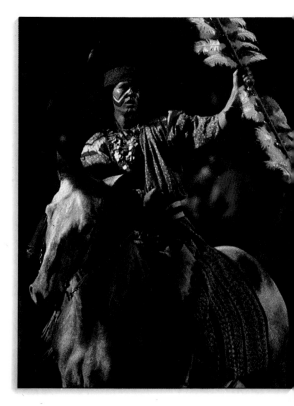

A Florida State Seminole rides team mascot "Renegade."

INTO THE PAN

South beyond Perry, US 19 inches further inland, bypassing a string of remote seaside hamlets along a shoreline so wild and overgrown it has been nicknamed the Hidden Coast. It provides a glorious lull in the state's helter-skelter development, but to investigate most of the villages requires driving down paved secondary roads that dangle from US 19, then backtracking to the main road before heading for the next hamlet – unless you wish to commit your fate to the rutted unmarked logging trails that link some of the communities.

This is the boondocks, and the names of the towns sound like it: Suwannee, Horseshoe Beach, Jug Island, Fish Creek. Keaton Beach, near the northern end of this strip, offers overnight accommodations and is joined to Perry and **Steinhatchee** by State Road 361. Steinhatchee, on the river of the same name, is one of the most popular desti-

Below, the courthouse in Monticello.

nations. It is renowned for its small seafood restaurants, which excel at dishing up the delights of Mother Ocean.

You won't find "square grouper" on any menus. But it's a popular catch all along the Hidden Coast, particularly in Dixie County. Fishing officially reigns second only to the timber industry in the area's economy. Unofficially, "square grouper" – the local lingo for bales of marijuana – has been injecting millions of unaccounted-for dollars into the sparsely populated region for the past decade. The difficulty of patrolling this desolate stretch of coastline has turned this part of Florida into a paradise for modern-day pirates smuggling grass from Colombia and Jamaica.

It's virtually impossible to reach much of the Hidden Coast by car, particularly the northern reaches toward Tallahassee. There are few towns, and fewer roads. One section of the upper coast is so secluded, rumors persist that it conceals a volcano.

In the land of Dixie: Should you wish to eschew this isolated coast upon leaving Tallahassee, and instead head off across the rolling, wooded fields that massage the landscape between the capital and Jacksonville, 168 miles to the east, stop and listen before making your choice of routes. If you can faintly hear a banjo player picking the opening notes of "Dixie," allow yourself to be lured off Interstate 10 into a few side trips from scenic US 90.

First stop is **Monticello**. The county courthouse in the town's main square is modeled after Thomas Jefferson's Virginia home – after which this community is named. More than 100 historic buildings crowd the compact town, including the restored **Monticello Opera House,** built in 1890. Other points of interest include old Southern homes that hark back to Monticello's heyday as a commercial center for surrounding cotton plantations. The Mexican boll weevil ended that era and the monied grandeur that King Cotton bought.

Monticello, like Tallahassee, claimed Prince Murat as a resident. Visitors to his cotton plantation reported that Murat was a chef of unpredictable taste, serving up such questionable delicacies as fancy sheep ears, buzzard meat and alligator tail. The latter is enjoying a revival on present-day Florida menus.

If you are a connoisseur of architecture, plan your tour to coincide with the annual spring Tour of Homes. This is the only time most of the privately owned mansions are open for public viewing.

Thirty miles east on US 90, more Southern charm can be sampled in **Madison**. The **Wardlaw-Smith House**, a white mansion that looks like it must belong to a latter-day Rhett Butler, occupies an entire block on Madison's main street. An impressive example of pre-Civil War architecture, it has been listed on the National Register of Historic Places.

A park commemorating the Confederacy is the city's centerpiece. **Confederate Memorial Park** on US 90 is built on the site of a former "blockhouse" which protected townsfolk during the Seminole Indian Wars.

"Way down upon the Peedee River"?: US 90 eventually bridges the dark and twisting waters of the **Suwannee River** of "Old Folks at Home" fame. Actually, composer Stephen Foster never laid eyes upon the river he immortalized. Foster lived in Pittsburgh. He picked the "S'wanee," as he spelled it, because it seemed to be a Southern-sounding name that fit the musical syllables following "Way down upon the..." His alternative? The Peedee River. It just didn't have the same ring.

Despite Foster's flimsy connection to Florida, a **Stephen Foster Folk Culture Center** has sprung up around his fame in **White Springs**, where State Road 136 joins US 41 east of Live Oak. Rides on a motorized riverboat called the *Belle of the Suwannee*, a carillon with 93 bells that ring out a medley of Foster favorites including "Oh, Susannah" and "Camptown Races," are among the attractions.

Better yet, White Springs rolls out the Florida Folk Festival every May on the banks of the Suwannee. You'll see baptisms in the river, eat black-eyed peas and collard greens, and hear the likes of well-known Florida storyteller Thelma

Boltin and folk singers Will McClean and Gamble Rogers.

Early this century, White Springs boasted a fashionable warm-water spa. The springs were reputed to be a cure-all for the ills of man, and people flocked here to drink and bathe. The resort had several hotels, a skating rink and theaters. All that remains today is an abandoned shell of the huge pool that once retained the healing waters.

The Suwannee rises in Georgia's Okefenokee Swamp and meanders back and forth across the middle of Florida, finally pouring into the briny Gulf of Mexico at the Hidden Coast town that shares its name, Suwannee. With its copper waters and untamed wilderness of cypress trees, the river is popular not only with songwriters, but with canoeists, divers and swimmers as well.

Four state parks lie near the banks of the Suwannee and its chief tributary, the Santa Fe, while private campgrounds and boat landings average one for every 5 miles of curving river. **Suwannee River State Park**, off US 90, 20 miles

The endangered manatee still lurks in Florida rivers.

east of Madison, offers boating, fishing and camping. **Ichetucknee Springs**, 4 miles northwest of Fort White, is equipped for picnicking, swimming and scuba diving; **O'Leno**, 20 miles south of Lake City, has campsites, electricity and water hook-ups, nature trails and fishing; and **Manatee Springs**, west of Chiefland, also offers full services.

Nine state parks in all pepper the upper tier of Florida. Most are on rivers, lakes or springs that can best be enjoyed in a canoe. Exploring these slow-paced creeks via canoe is not dangerous, but rangers advise that someone in the craft have prior paddling experience. Canoe rental outlets abound and often retrieve clients at predetermined spots downstream. A less expensive alternative is "tubing" – dropping yourself in an inner tube and floating downstream with the churning current.

On the **Santa Fe River**, the Suwannee's picturesque tributary, cave diving is a popular pursuit. At places like gorgeous **Ginnie Springs** and **Peacock Springs** and elsewhere along the river, diving equipment and lessons are available. Enthusiasts rave about the wonders of labyrinthine underwater caves, but emphasize that divers need proper training before attempting the hazardous sport. Florida newspapers often recount sad stories of divers who didn't surface. As many as 12 divers die in caves each year.

Alligator Town, USA: The next major point of interest on US 90 after leaving the Suwannee valley is **Lake City**, one of many Florida cities owing their existence to the big highways. The nearby juncture of Interstates 10 and 75 has put Lake City on the map as a truckers' haven, in a way that US 90 never did in the days before huge expressways. Once known as Alligator – after the nickname of Indian Chief Halpeter-Tustennuggee – the city recently became the home of **Alligator Town, USA**. One of Florida's umpteen "Gator Farms," this attraction is built on the reputation of the late Ross Allen, founder of the well-known Reptile Institute at Silver Springs.

Lake City is the gateway to the

Suwannee River cruising.

Osceola National Forest and all the outdoor pleasures that implies. The forest surrounds the site of Florida's other (besides Natural Bridge) important Civil War battle – **Ocean Pond**, near Olustee. Every February, more than 500 people from all over the United States dramatically re-enact the 1864 Confederate victory here in full blue-and-gray regalia.

Beyond the national forest, US 90 continues through another string of small towns before reaching Jacksonville (*see* "East Coast") and crossing the **St Johns River**, a wide channel that marks the eastern boundary of the region covered in this section. The renowned French marine explorer, Jacques Cousteau, filmed a television special about the endangered manatees of the St Johns. The river courses backwards – that is, south to north. Below Jacksonville, it passes through the last of the enclaves that fell victim to the boom-and-bust cycle of North Florida. Today strung out along US 17, these settlements saw sudden wealth vanish as industry and immigrants moved further south.

Here, steamboats and citrus brought the early wealth. In the middle and late 19th century, the steamboats cruised the St Johns, ferrying wintering northerners to fine hotels and hunting clubs at places like Mandarin, Enterprise, Palatka and Green Cove Springs. The paddle-wheelers followed the same routes blazed centuries earlier on the river by French and Spanish explorers. Citrus fruits, meanwhile, provided a stable income for growers in the area. Among famous residents was the author of *Uncle Tom's Cabin*, Harriet Beecher Stowe, whose home in Mandarin has succumbed to fire.

All that was before railroads put the steamboats out of business, a series of freezes killed the local citrus industry, and tourists and oranges headed south.

Now some old residences of the wealthy have been restored, mainly in **Green Cove Springs**. **Palatka** has traded in its reputation as a center of hostelries to become the "Bass Fishing Capital of the World."

The Palatka area also boasts its own Sasquatch or yeti-type creature. In miniscule **Bardin**, northwest of the town, residents talk of a hairy half-ape, half-man creature, about 7 feet tall, that stalks the woods around the village. They call it the Booger.

From Palatka, it's a pleasant drive west on State Route 20 through rural communities to **Gainesville,** home of the **University of Florida**, the state's largest center of learning. It dates back to 1854, when Florida achieved statehood and received a federal grant to establish two seminaries. East Florida Seminary later became the University of Florida, while West Florida Seminary was the precursor to Florida State University in Tallahassee.

The university area abounds with the restaurants, discos and taverns that are part and parcel of higher education today. Those seeking intellectual stimulation can try the school's art gallery, which presents regular showings by faculty members and students, and the popular **Hippodrome** for theatrical performances.

The home of author Marjorie Kinnan Rawlings is in **Cross Creek**, southeast of Gainesville on State 325. This setting provided the inspiration for her Pulitzer Prize-winning *The Yearling*. She migrated in 1928 from her native New York, wrote of her experiences among country folk, and is buried a few miles away at **Island Grove**.

West of Cross Creek is **Micanopy**, another 19th-century vacation spot and citrus center that fell on hard times and is now being restored.

Further west, off US 41, is **Payne's Prairie**, a vast sea of grass. It once encompassed a large lake that served as an Indian homesite as far back as 7000 BC. A herd of buffalo once hunted to extinction here has been replaced with a new herd allowed to roam this state preserve. Guided tours are available.

One of Florida's many illustrious sinkholes can be toured on the northwestern outskirts of Gainesville. **The Devil's Millhopper** is particularly remarkable. It covers 5 acres, drops 100 feet, and is overgrown with exotic subtropical rainforest, including giant ferns and a splendid waterfall.

Cross Creek crossing.

THE EVERGLADES

If our founding forefathers' foresight had inspired them to preserve natural treasures when they drew up the Constitution, they might have roped off Florida's northern boundary and declared the entire state a national park. Fortunately, latter day leaders stepped in before all was lost to the plow and bulldozer. In 1947 they established **Everglades National Park** encompassing 1.4 million acres, or most of Florida's southern tip – an area larger than the state of Delaware.

Unlike the Grand Canyon, Niagara Falls, Yellowstone and other national jewels, the Everglades does not overwhelm the casual visitor with majestic vistas. On the contrary, the seas of sawgrass that stretch in all directions, embellished only by island hammocks of hardwood trees, sparse stands of cypress and slash pines and clumps of mangroves, may strike many as boring.

But don't let this dull facade deter you from dipping down the Florida peninsula to the Everglades. It's just a clever disguise that cloaks a fascinating blend of earthy and watery environments, tropical and temperate species of plant and animal life and a laboratory where Nature experiments with her cycles of life and death.

Everglades National Park actually represents only a fraction of a slow-flowing river called *Pa-hay-okee* – "the grassy waters" – by Indians. An English surveyor dubbed it the "River Glades," but later English maps corrupted "river" to "ever" and the present name that seems so perfect came into common use during the 19th century.

To find the source of this "River of Grass," look north to the lakes of Central Florida's Kissimmee Valley which feed the mighty Lake Okeechobee, which in turn supplies the Everglades.

The beauty of the Everglades must be sampled slowly. Treat it like you would a bottle of good wine. Inhale its fragrance, sip its essence, swirl it on your

Preceding pages: the sun rises on an Everglades morning. Left, a fisherman wades into the Glades with net and pole.

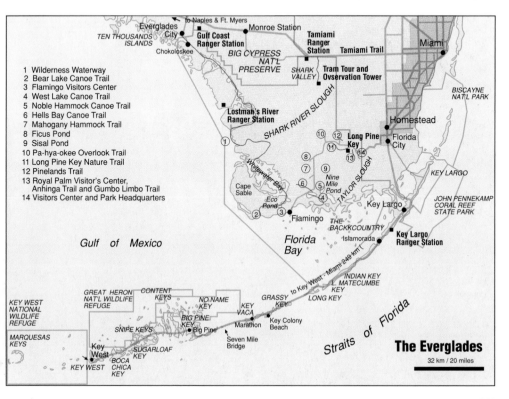

1 Wilderness Waterway
2 Bear Lake Canoe Trail
3 Flamingo Visitors Center
4 West Lake Canoe Trail
5 Noble Hammock Canoe Trail
6 Hells Bay Canoe Trail
7 Mahogany Hammock Trail
8 Ficus Pond
9 Sisal Pond
10 Pa-hya-okee Overlook Trail
11 Long Pine Key Nature Trail
12 Pinelands Trail
13 Royal Palm Visitor's Center, Anhinga Trail and Gumbo Limbo Trail
14 Visitors Center and Park Headquarters

The Everglades

32 km / 20 miles

palate, eye its color and texture. That's the only way to appreciate the subtleties of its splendors.

Fire and rain: The Glades flow for 200 miles, bulging up to 70 miles in width, at an average depth of only 6 inches that rise and fall during rainy and dry seasons. It oozes down a gradual incline in Florida's surface that drops only 15 feet over hundreds of miles. Above-ground waters move southwest to the Gulf of Mexico and, underground, they seep through porous limestone foundations east to the Atlantic Coastal Ridge that stretches from Fort Lauderdale to Long Pine Key. Its fresh water finally mixes with salt seas.

The Everglades is unique: Nearly 300 varieties of birds, 600 kinds of fish and countless mammals call it home. It even has 45 indigenous species of plants found nowhere else. Geologists and geographers say there is nothing quite like the Everglades anywhere else in the world. Unfortunately, there may soon be nothing at all like it in the world.

Some experts believe it is only a matter of a few decades before man's assault on South Florida irreversibly alters the fragile environment of the Everglades. Dikes and 1,500 miles of canals carved out of the landscape by man crisscross the once free-flowing river and impede its normal fluctuations in water levels. In fact, the Army Corps of Engineers has reversed these natural cycles, opening watergates and flooding fields in winter when The Glades should be dry, and curbing the flow in summer when South Florida should be submerged in water from torrential thunderstorms. The rich marl or muck built up from hundreds of centuries of rotting sawgrass has been plowed and seeded and has sprouted into sugar cane and vegetable farms, further upsetting the delicate ecological balance of the region. And populous cities of the Gold Coast and lower West Coast have plugged into its aquifer like leeches, draining precious reserves for their washing machines, swimming pools and toilets. The Glades is so dry during some springtimes that fires regularly

A bruising airboat cruise on the "River of Grass."

rage out of control, consuming sawgrass and hardwoods and robbing wildlife of its traditional habitats.

Shark Valley area park ranger Bill Wise warns that the Everglades may cease to exist within 20 years. "It's such a fragile environment. There's got to be water and there's got to be cycles and right now man has screwed up the water levels and screwed up the cycles. The park tries to exist on what water we get after the people in town get it."

Man's mistakes: Wise likened the Everglades environment to a tapestry in which every thread depends upon another for its survival. "If the water levels continually stay low, everything's going to die. If you don't have naturally fluctuating water levels, you won't have periphyton (algae) matter that little critters feed on. So the little critters will die and the bigger critters that depend on them for survival have nothing to eat. The food chain collapses."

The Everglades evolved during 6 million years or so of shifting sea action and limestone build up. But it has come to the brink of extinction in less than a century. Its chief enemy, man, first infiltrated its hammocks about 2,000 years ago with the arrival of early Indians. But the Calusas more often than not lived in harmony with The Glades.

The first white man to roam the Everglades appears to have been Hernando Escalante de Fontaneda, a Spaniard who washed up in the Keys after a shipwreck and lived among Indians for 17 years. He penned a vivid account of how the Calusas, Tequestas and Mayaimis lived throughout The Glades and South Florida. But it wasn't until the 1880s that man began efforts to drain what was simply considered useless swampland. Governor Napoleon Bonaparte Broward threw the government into the efforts and, by 1909, the Miami Canal that connects Lake Okeechobee to Miami became the main conduit in a network of waterways through the Everglades. The hurricanes of 1926 and 1928 that dumped Lake Okeechobee onto the heads of thousands of South Florida settlers sparked the involvement of the Army Corps of Engineers. It promptly ringed the lake, the core of the Everglades, with Hoover Dike in 1930.

Ironically, another 1947 hurricane that flooded Dade County dramatized the chaos caused by the uncontrolled dike and canal construction in the Everglades. It led to creation of the predecessor of the present-day South Florida Water Management District that has come to be known as Swiftmud. Meanwhile, efforts by the Audubon Society (to control the ruthless slaughter of birds for plumes), the Florida Federation of Women's Clubs and the Tropical Everglades National Park Commission culminated in dedication of the area as a National Park by Harry S. Truman in 1947. After realizing the Everglades system also depended on the survival of surrounding systems, the adjacent Big Cypress National Preserve was established in 1974.

A glades glossary: The Everglades possesses a variety of ecosystems essential to its maintenance. Among them:

• **Hardwood Hammock**, a big "island" likened by ranger Wise to a castle with a moat around it. These high and dry mounds of dead plant matter provide ground for the growth of cabbage palms, strangler figs, West Indian mahogany, gumbo limbo trees and satin leaf hardwoods. During high-water seasons, bob-cats, deer, otters, raccoons and opossums find refuge here.

• **Heads**, smaller shallower islands where the cocoplum, red bay, sweet bay and magnolia wax myrtle grow. They do not have the limestone mound base of the hardwood hammocks.

• **Willows**, the light green tails of vegetation that fill the deep water surrounding some hammocks. They are the home of the Everglades' most renowned inhabitant, the alligator. Seen from above, willows look like doughnuts with the nucleus of water in the middle called a solution hole or gator hole. Here, alligators soak, feed once every few weeks, and sink down out of the sun.

• **Saw grass prairie**, that fabled expanse of thin spiny-edged vegetation that seems to dominate the Everglades.

• **Fresh water sloughs** (pronounced

"slews"), channels of fresh water, like the major one in the Shark River Valley, that act as reservoirs and supply routes. They help plants and animals survive during the dry season.

• **Pinelands**, found in elevated areas of bare limestone outcroppings. Fire is necessary to their existence, because it cleans out competing vegetation.

• **Cypress eco-systems**, which contain bald and stunted varieties of this cousin of California's redwoods. Dripping with Spanish moss, they give The Glades its swampy reputation.

• **Coastal prairies**, containing salt-tolerant plants like cactus, yucca and prickly pear. A home to marsh rabbits.

• **Mangrove estuary** rims the southwest edge of The Glades, acting as a coastal barrier against high storm surges. The leaf provides food for microscopic animals, that are, in turn, eaten by larger animals.

For a crash course in identifying these critical features of the Everglades, and your best introduction to the "River of Grass," begin your expedition at the **Visitor Center** at the national park's main entrance on State Road 9336, also known as Ingraham Highway.

Beating the bugs while seeing the sights: The National Park Service had the presence of mind to lay a single paved road into the heart of the Everglades and attach side roads to trails and boardwalks. But that is as far as the park service has gone in tampering with nature for the convenience of man. So, pack a pint of insect repellent. Cutter's, or better yet army issue repellent, is advisable. Mosquitoes, deer flies and other biting bugs, obnoxious to man can be vicious, particularly during the wet summer season.

The Visitor Center sells repellent and provides maps, brochures and displays to help you fully appreciate your visit; it also has a brief film worth viewing.

Ingraham Highway is the only road into, and out of, Everglades National Park. It is about 38 miles to its southwest deadend at **Flamingo.** But even if you are wedded to your car, make sure you detour to at least a few of the other visitor centers, trails and observation decks along the way.

The **Royal Palm Visitor Center**, the first stop just 2 miles from the park entrance, has an easy trail through a typical hardwood hammock, named for the gumbo limbo tree, a common sight along the path. Here, you will find ferns, air plants and a cool, rain forest-type-environment. Carefully examine tree limbs for the dazzling *Liguus* snail found only on these hammocks and in Cuba and Hispaniola. There's also the **Anhinga Trail** boardwalk into a willow head at the tip of **Taylor Slough**. Yes, the lumps you see in the water are the eyes of live alligators.

Long Pine Key features a 7-mile nature trail that winds through a typical pinelands ecosystem. There are also campgrounds and picnic areas. You will drive over **Rock Reef Pass**, all of 3 feet above sea level to **Pa-hay-okee Overlook**, an observation tower in a hardwood hammock edged with cypress stands and a fresh water slough. There are about 100 species of grass in the Everglades and most can be observed from the boardwalk, although you may

A purple gallinule peeks out from his marshy glade surroundings.

find it impossible to distinguish between beard-grass, coinwort, marsh fleabane, love-vine, creeping Charlie and ludwigia. Saw grass, ironically, is not a true grass, but a sedge.

Mahogany Hammock Trail winds under some of the largest mahogany trees in the continental United States. Rare paurotis palms, 12 to 30 feet high, flank **Paurotis Pond** and its plethora of wildlife. The **Nine Mile Pond** sits in freshwater marl prairie and a mangrove estuary.

Paddlers are faced with a choice further down the road. **The Noble Hammock Canoe Trail**, named after a legendary Everglades bootlegger, traverses a 2½ mile loop through mangrove clusters. **The Hell's Bay Trail**, as its name implies, is for prepared and experienced canoers. It leads 5 miles deep into uncharted parts of the Everglades referred to as the backcountry and can take an entire day to paddle. Consult with rangers for other interesting routes.

The **West Lake** footpath wriggles through sawgrass and cattails. Pink shrimp feed and reproduce among the mangroves in places like this before maturing and migrating to the Gulf of Mexico. After passing **Mrazek Pond,** a popular perch for various migratory birds, and **Coot Bay Pond**, Ingraham Highway four-lanes and then circles back onto itself at Flamingo. From here, further exploration requires good feet.

Winging it in Flamingo: Once an isolated fishing village accessible only by boat, **Flamingo** now exists mainly as an isolated colony catering to tourism in Everglades National Park. There are 235 motor campsites, 60 tent plots, and, for the less hardy and traditional, 120 motel rooms at the Flamingo Inn. During the high winter and spring book a room well in advance.

Check with the ranger station or Inn office for a schedule of activities. If you have brought your own boat or hiking gear, be sure to file float or walk plans with the ranger station before disappearing into the backcountry. Even skilled sportsmen and locals have been known to vanish into the maze of man-

The great blue heron, one of many wonders native to the Everglades.

groves, rivers and bays – for good. Otherwise, you can rent a boat or whatever equipment you need. You can even move into a fully-equipped houseboat and cruise the waterways in comfort.

The **Flamingo Marina** is the southern terminus of the 100-mile **Wilderness Waterway** which begins way up at the Everglades City end of the park. It proceeds south through such alluring niches as **Chokoloskee Island**, the **Lopez River**, **Sunday Bay**, **Alligator Bay**, **Big Lostman's Bay**, **Cabbage Island**, the **Wood River**, and the **Shark River**. At **Canepatch** you will find wild sugar cane growing among wild limes, banana and papaya, evidence of Calusa and Seminole Indian settlements that survived until 1928. **Shark River** is one of the park's most popular fishing areas, featuring 45 species, including snook, redfish, sea trout, the silvery tarpon, grouper and snapper. **Gunboat Island** was named for its shape. Enormous **Whitewater Bay** pours into **Buttonwood Canal** which takes you to the Flamingo Marina. Plan on most of a

day's trip if you have a motorboat, at least seven days by canoe.

Of course, Flamingo offers shorter cruises and walks. Tour boats will take you to the white sand shores of **Cape Sable**, the southernmost point in the continental US. Or you can boat around the clusters of keys in **Florida Bay**. The park boundaries extend to the **Intracoastal Waterway** just a few miles north of the Florida Keys. Primitive camping is permitted on **North Nest Key**, the **Rabbit Keys** and **North Sandy Keys**.

Ask directions to the **Eco-pond**, a short walk from the Flamingo Inn. Ibis, herons, osprey and egrets hang out here. Most notable are the scarlet roseate spoonbills, thought to have inspired the village's name when early settlers mistook them for flamingos.

Good, but easy, hiking trails near Flamingo include the **Snake Bight** through tropical hardwoods to a boardwalk over Florida Bay; **Rowdy Bend**, under Spanish moss and brilliant red bromeliads; **Christian Point**, past giant wild pine bromeliads attached to the trees; and

An Everglades National Park ranger in a slushy shortcut through the swamp.

Bear Lake, formed by fill from the **Homestead Canal**.

In Shark Valley, over the Loop Road: There is another wheeled way of penetrating Everglades National Park, but you must drive all the way back to Homestead and north on US 27, then west on **Tamiami Trail**, nearly 50 miles, to get there. The **Shark Valley** entrance station is across the street from the **Miccosukee Village and Culture Center**. In the summer, most of this freshwater slough is underwater. But in the winter, the park operates a tram ride through the sawgrass prairie teeming with wildlife and up to an observation tower. Alligators congregate in willows at the foot of the tower. Ask a ranger to imitate their bellow and you will see dozens of them glide out from the brush. Alligators make a variety of sounds. A hiss is warning that they are annoyed and you should stay out of their way.

You can also walk or bike the tram route. The **Otter Cave Hammock Nature Trail** has a pamphlet to guide you. Tread softly and you may see otters munching on live frogs' legs in the trough beside the road. The splashes are probably garfish. They pile up as thick as cordwood here in the dry months.

Proceeding west from the Shark Valley entrance on US 41, you will pass through more Miccosukee territory. This is your chance to board an airboat piloted by an Indian. They operate north of the park boundaries.

The Tamiami Trail eventually forks. Bear left through **Pinecrest** to the **Everglades Nature Center**. You are on what is known as the "**Loop Road**." It eventually begins to deteriorate. The interesting dwellings along its perimeter house a colorful, but unsociable, assortment of characters. Many of them were born here and have made their living off The Glades, sometimes in defiance of park regulations. Some traditionally hunted and fished. They lived in an uneasy truce with park rangers. An early game warden was shot and killed by poachers hunting birds for their prized plumes in 1905. Current residents do not resort to such measures, but chide

Seminole Indians once used dugout canoes to navigate through the Everglades.

rangers about government attempts to drive them out.

Waist deep in the Big Cypress: The north fork makes for a faster ride into the Big Cypress National Preserve to **Everglades City** off State Road 29. This town is the water gateway to the **Ten Thousand Islands** and marine estuary parts of Everglades National Park. Guided boat trips originate at the Gulf Coast ranger station here. During the summer season, sunset cruises take passengers into upper **Chokoloskee Bay** to observe the spectacle of as many as 20,000 birds returning to roost. Guides can be hired for fishing trips.

About 4 miles east of Everglades City is the village of **Ochopee**, the site of the nation's smallest post office, it measures 8 feet 4 inches by 7 feet 3 inches.

The **Big Cypress National Preserve** is closer to the traditional image of a swamp than the Everglades. It consists of sandy islands of slash pine, marshes and large stands of dwarf cypress sprouting from knee-deep water and muck. Giant bald cypress trees that once distinguished the area were nearly wiped out by loggers for use in the manufacture of pickle barrels, boat hulls and coffins. The few that remain may be as much as 700 years old.

A ridge riddled with hammocks and cypress trees separates The Glades from the **Big Cypress Swamp**. It fills its own 2,400-square-mile basin of which 570,000 acres have been declared a national preserve. Hike into its heart and you may see the paw marks of the extremely rare Florida panther in the wet marl, or a black bear munching cabbage palmetto. Watch for the endangered Everglades swallow-tail kite. Another of its prized creatures, also in decline, is the stately wood stork, victimized by man's intrusion into this environment. This area was once home to about 2 million wading birds, but plume hunters drastically reduced their numbers to only a few hundred thousand by late last century. Laws enacted to protect fowl helped them rebound to near that number, but the flocks began diminishing again as man exercised more control over area water levels. By the middle of

the 1970s, only about 200,000 wading birds had survived.

The decline was particularly dramatic among wood storks, which stand at an average height of 3½ feet and fly on a wingspan of nearly 6 feet. About 50,000 wood storks in the 1930s have dwindled to about 10,000 at present.

One of the best spots to observe the survivors is at the fascinating Corkscrew on State Road 846. The storks valiantly fight for the survival of their species, nursing eggs in more than 1,000 nests in the trees overhead. Stand on the swamp boardwalk and look up at the awesome canopy of nests and giant birds squawking as they glide through the air in search of food for their young.

Corkscrew is a rewarding trip in all respects. Rescued from woodsmen by concerned citizens and the National Audobon Society in 1954, it now encompasses 11,000 acres. You will travel along a boardwalk into the largest stand of virgin bald cypress in existence in the US. You will experience the various ecosystems common to the Everglades and Big Cypress Swamp – pine flatwoods, wet prairie, willows, hardwood hammock and marsh. You will be able to meditate over lettuce lakes where adult alligators and their young lie low, where black racer snakes slither and rare birds like the purple gallinule walk.

Take your time strolling the mile-long boardwalk. And don't ignore small delights like the tree frogs, the Caroline anole and Southeastern five-lined skink lizards.

Not far from Corkscrew Swamp, **Janes Scenic Drive** off State Road 837, near an old logging railroad, zigzags into the magnificent **Fakahatchee Strand**, the only known forest of royal palms and cypress combined in the world and the largest concentration of native orchids in North America. About 44 species have been identified, including the catopsis which grows nowhere else.

Returning to State Road 837, proceed South to US 41. To the west lie the mellow resorts of Marco Island and Naples. Straight ahead is the Everglades Visitor Center of Everglades City. To the East is the wild life of Miami.

A damp trail in Big Cypress Swamp.

Bird
Observation Area

In keeping with the many idiosyncrasies that set Florida apart from other states in the country, its southern boundary doesn't just come to an abrupt end at some invisible line penciled in by cartographers. Instead, it trickles gently away in a splash of coral and limestone islands. They stretch 180 miles from Miami's Biscayne Bay to the Dry Tortugas, just 86 miles north of Havana, across seas shaded with implausible hues of blues and greens. Forty-three of the islands hang like freshly-washed linen on a clothesline: the 113-mile-long US Highway 1, "The Overseas Highway," stretching over 43 bridges along the way.

Some early American inadvertently anglicized the Spanish word *cayo* (for "little island"), and each splotch of land has been known as a "key" ever since. From the scuba culture of Key Largo to the Bohemian counterculture of Key West, each island maintains its own distinct identity.

Even the people are different from one key to the next. Disillusioned Gold Coasters populate the upper islands, while natives of the lower Keys proudly call themselves Conchs. It's a rare day in a Monroe County Commission meeting when residents of the northern Keys, "middle" dwellers and Conchs agree on any issue of concern to all Florida Keys.

As different as Keys residents may be from one another, though, they are even more different from Florida mainlanders. Out here in the islands, it's just not normal to get wrapped up in a hustle-bustle lifestyle, or even to be on time for appointments. Prices, too, differ from those of the mainland. Food, gasoline and accommodations cost progressively more the further down the Key chain you get. A day in Key West can be as expensive as one in Honolulu or New York.

Unless you have access to a boat or seaplane, an automobile is the best way to putter through the Keys. Because there is only the one major highway, not even the most wayward driver could get lost. To make things even easier, the Keys have their own navigational system. Most hotels, restaurants and businesses simply tell customers the number of the nearest green mile marker (MM) flanking Highway 1. The entrance to John Pennekamp Coral Reef State Park, for instance, is about a half-mile beyond MM 102 – that is, it's 102½ miles from Key West, which is MM0.

Mañanaland, Margaritaville, the American Riviera – the Keys have been called many things. Whatever the appellation, they are a place to take off your watch and kick back. Get up early and watch the sun rise over the Atlantic Ocean. At night, stroll to the other side of your island to catch the sun set into the Gulf of Mexico. Conchs will tell you that's the only way to tell time.

CRUISING THROUGH THE KEYS

Preceding pages: birds of a feather; underwater exploration. **Left**, deck decorations on a Keys' sailboat.

There are two ways to drive to the Keys from mainland Florida. The slower but more scenic one is to follow US 1 south of Homestead, then take a left at the fork in the road just past Florida City, the southern terminus of the Florida turnpike. A column of tall Australian pines graces the path to the $1 Card Sound toll bridge. On either side of the bridge, clumps of red and black mangroves impersonate solid islands.

The bridge ends on north Key Largo. A right on State Road 905 leads through hammocks of Jamaica dogwood, loblolly, feathery lysiloma and mahogany until the road runs directly back into US 1. A left on 905 eventually strands you at the tip of the key.

Beyond, boaters can continue to about 25 keys inside the **Biscayne National Monument**. Information on cruising the islands can be obtained at monument headquarters on **Convoy Point**, or at the ranger station on **Elliott Key**, a few miles north of Key Largo.

But take care: the many shipwrecks found here, some dating back to the 16th century, demonstrate just how hazardous boating can be in the Keys. This area was once the haunt of pirates, and boaters should be on the lookout for the ghost of the nefarious Black Caesar. He plundered around the turn of the 19th century and gave his name to the passage located between Elliott and Old Rhodes Keys.

The toll bridge and the scenic detour can be avoided by simply bypassing the fork south of Florida City. It's a straight shot to the Keys down US 1, over Jewfish Creek and a sliver of two-lane road known as "Death Alley" until it was widened slightly. Signs still advise drivers to be patient, because a passing zone is only minutes ahead.

A series of bridges spans **Barnes Sound** and **Lake Surprise**, the latter named by road crews who were startled to find it covering their construction site after a long weekend. A pipeline snaking past parts of the US is the Keys' only source of fresh water – other than natural rainwater. (A desalinization plant is in mothballs.) The mud mounds on the power poles are osprey nests.

When the highway curves right, you've entered the Keys. The road may appear to be a tacky strip lined with seedy storefronts, billboards and gas stations. That's exactly what it is. Stifle the disappointment. Like the Everglades, the Keys do not dazzle the casual tourist whose vacations are spent behind the windshield. Park the car. Get on a bicycle or boat. Suck in the sweet, clean air. Gape at the immense canopy of sky and the mounds of whipped cloud. Can you see the curve of the earth in the distance, where the sea turns from aqua to azure? Put on a mask, snorkel and fins. Rent a rod and reel. You'll soon be overcome by Keys Disease.

Diving Into Key Largo: Humphrey Bogart, Lauren Bacall and Edward G. Robinson confronted a killer hurricane here in the movie *Key Largo*. All that

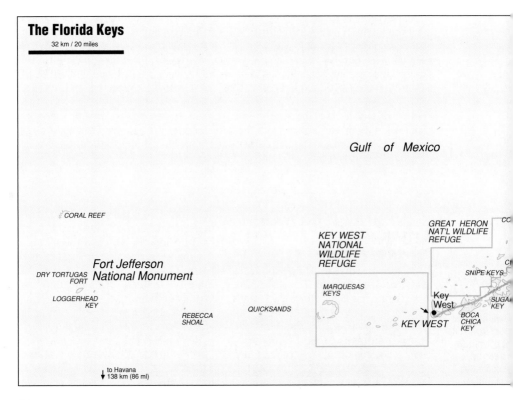

The Florida Keys

32 km / 20 miles

Gulf   of   Mexico

CORAL REEF

Fort Jefferson
DRY TORTUGAS *National Monument*
FORT

LOGGERHEAD
KEY

REBECCA
SHOAL

QUICKSANDS

KEY WEST
NATIONAL
WILDLIFE
REFUGE

MARQUESAS
KEYS

GREAT HERON
NAT'L WILDLIFE
REFUGE

SNIPE KEYS

Key
West

KEY WEST

SUGA
KEY

BOCA
CHICA
KEY

to Havana
138 km (86 ml)

remains of those nostalgic days is the **Caribbean Club Bar** near MM 104. A few minutes of that movie may or may not have been filmed inside. Some locals contend the filming actually took place in another bar – which has since burned down – near the present Caribbean Club. They also say only about 3 minutes of the film footage were actually shot in Key Largo, because the pampered Hollywood stars and crew fled the island's mosquitoes and biting sand fleas appropriately known as "no-see-ums." Nevertheless, with its coquina veneer, black-and-white blow-ups from the movie, and rowdy reputation, the Caribbean Club takes visitors a step back into the past.

Modern man has curbed Key Largo's insect problem, but progress still moves slowly here. Key Largo did not get its first movie theater until 1980. There's a smattering of civilization – supermarkets, gift shops, a Kentucky Fried Chicken, even a K-mart discount store.

The conch is queen of the Keys. (Key West High School even calls its football team the "Fighting Conchs.") Inside its shell – a familiar coffee-table ornament – the stalk-eyed blob is not among God's handsomest creations. But if you can put the conch's looks out of your mind, conch fritters, chowder or salad make a tasty meal with a spicy kick.

The Key West Cookie Lady can be seen strolling the streets, calling out, "Get your Key West Cookies! They're warm and chewy!" And they are.

For a close-up look at queen or horse-shoe conchs in their natural habitat, go sightseeing at Key Largo's main attraction: North America's only living coral reef. Many of the dive shops that clutter US 1 offer crash courses cranking out certified scuba-divers in a few days. They also conduct dive trips daily and rent all equipment.

The **John Pennekamp Coral Reef State Park** in mid-key provides some cheaper alternatives. Concessioners Randy and Mary Pegram offer snorkeling and glass-bottom boat rides, as well as scuba trips.

The first underwater park in the United

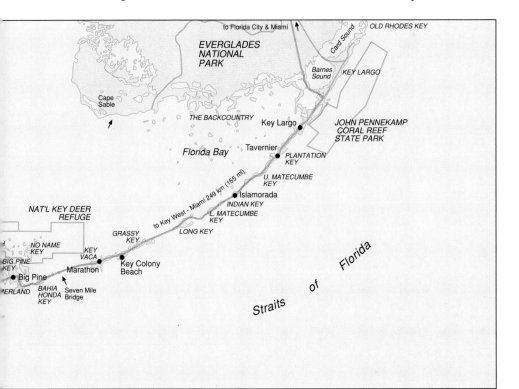

States, Pennekamp encompasses 78 square miles of living reef. The watery jungle harbors 40 types of coral and 450 species of fish.

Visitors to Pennekamp Park have never failed to astound Mike Bowman, the Pegrams' general manager, with questions about whether they can drive their cars out to the reef, and whether the reef has picnic tables and toilet facilities. Bowman directs purveyors of such questions toward the *Discovery*. This boat glides 6 miles out to sea several times a day. When it slows down at Molasses Reef, passengers are permitted to descend below deck to ogle the marine life through viewing windows. Sea fans brush the outer glass as a live technicolor show unfolds. Parrot fish gnaw at the coral, and curious barracudas bare their teeth.

A smaller, faster ship, *El Capitan*, carries bolder visitors one step beyond on daily snorkeling trips. No previous experience is necessary, although it helps to know how to swim. Trained divers outfit and educate the uninitiated.

Snorkelers can rub snouts with triggerfish and swim among schools of tang. But park rules strictly prohibit the collection of coral and advise against touching or standing on it. Boats must anchor well away from live coral, for the slightest touch can kill this living tissue.

The reef was seriously damaged in the '30s and '40s, as people ruthlessly harvested coral with dynamite and crowbars to stock souvenir shop shelves. Concerned marine scientists and conservationists pushed legislation that led to creation of the park in 1960. It was named for a *Miami Herald* reporter whose stories fired public interest in preserving offshore reef areas.

The Key Largo Dry Rocks, 5 miles from the barge at North Sound Creek, shelter **Christ of the Deep**. This replica of Guido Galletti's Christ of the Abyss (in the Mediterranean Sea off Genoa, Italy) is in a natural valley surrounded by coral reef in 21 feet of water.

Key Largo is the site of the world's first underwater resort, Jewel's Undersea Lodge, at MM 103, where guests

Diving after dark, Pennekamp.

actually swim to, and sleep overnight in, an underwater hotel.

Take a left turn at the Burger King, then follow the signs to the **Pilot House Restaurant**, a favorite among locals for seafood and homemade Key lime pie. The tiny limes that grow throughout the Keys make a tangy dessert.

Fishing the Matecumbe Keys: Highway 1 continues spectacularly through **Rock Harbor** to **Tavernier**, once the site of a huge 18th-century wrecking fleet that cruised the reefs each day claiming salvage from grounded ships. Another sign of civilization, Coral Shores School on the right side of the road on **Plantation Key**, serves as a combination elementary school and high school for most of the upper islands.

Across Snake Creek is **Windley Key**, which offers many reasonably priced motels. The realization that vast seas completely surround these small tufts of land finally sinks in as you cross the bridge over Whale Harbor to **Upper Matecumbe Key**. Polished, armed-to-the-teeth fishing vessels on either side of the harbor trumpet the area's focus on the sport fishing trade. If you have plenty of money and a hankering to haul home a huge sailfish or to battle a bonefish, put down roots here for a few days.

The action revolves around **Islamorada**, a town that considers itself the world's sport fishing capital. The alluring name – Spanish for "Purple Isle" – was left behind by an explorer who saw legions of violet *Janthina janthina* sea snails clinging to the shores here.

The best accommodations big money can buy are at the **Cheeca Lodge** at MM 82. Its main building features enormous rooms with beds which are big enough to accommodate three. Hurricane Donna leveled the first inn on the site in 1960, but its good beach – a rarity in the Keys – attracted A&P heiress "Cheechee" Twitchell to rebuild the lodge. Nearby Holiday Isle Resort – MM 84.5 – is a popular hangout for locals and visitors. The lodge offers villas for large groups and a par 3 golf course that has a green pond and more sand than grass.

The way fishing enthusiasts talk, you

Sloppy Joe's Bar.

would think blue marlin and world record tarpon virtually jump onto your hook. Oldtimers like Jimmy Wood, who has fished these waters since 1925, swears that's the way it used to be.

"It used to be a paradise," Wood said. "You could go back out here anywheres and catch fish in these channels. The 'back country' was just loaded with fish." He complained that the Army Corps of Engineers tampered with Florida's natural irrigation and severely reduced the numbers of fish, particularly in the back country – the Gulf fringes of the Everglades. "You can still catch a good bit of fish on the ocean side, and some back there, but it ain't what it used to be," Wood said.

Still, the fishermen come. Baseball legend Ted Williams, once a Key West resident, still returns regularly to fly fish. So does President George Bush. Chartering a boat and guide for a day costs $200 to $500. And if you snare the big one, mounting costs are particularly high. Party boats, which take larger groups out, are a far less expensive way to experience the fun of fishing.

After sweating through a hard day on the ocean, hungry fishing captains and crews patronize the area's many excellent restaurants and lively bars. You can listen or tell fish stories at the popular **Harbor Bar** behind the marina at Whale Harbor. **The Green Turtle**, **Ziggy's Conch Inn**, **Marker 88** and **Manny and Isa's**, which features Cuban cuisine, are favorite dinner spots. The **Coral Grill's** bargain seafood buffet is popular with visitors, but not with locals.

For a respite from fish-lined walls and menus, there's **Erik's**, just to the right as you come off the bridge onto Windley Key at MM 85.5. A native of Denmark, Erik Jorgensen personally prepares each of his gourmet meals, as he has for many distinguished guests. The restaurant is on a houseboat, but that's where the nautical theme ends. Inside, the decor is contemporary ski lodge with fireplaces and a cathedral ceiling. Peruvian llama skins, Brazilian cowhides and the Viking god Thor adorn the walls. Befriend Erik and he may join

Below, holing out at Cheeca. Right, mounting a big Keys' catch.

you for a toast with *akvavit*, the pungent national drink of the Danes.

After dinner, area bars offering live entertainment and plenty of local color include the **Whale Harbor Inn** located at MM 83.5 and **Holleman's Sunset Inn**, MM 82.3.

If you prefer to pet fish instead of catch them, Kenny McKinney's 40-year-old landmark, **Theater of the Sea**, features daily doings in a natural coral grotto. Islamorada town proper has a **Spanish Mission House** with an art gallery and a monument to the Labor Day hurricane of 1935.

Nearly 600 people died in that disaster. Jimmy Wood lost most of his family, including his 18-month-old sister, who was crushed to death by flying debris as he was holding her in his arms. Jimmy managed to cling to life until he could be shipped to a mainland hospital. The barometer at one point dipped to 26.35 the lowest pressure ever recorded in the Western Hemisphere.

Weird and wondrous hikes: More bridges lead to **Lower Matecumbe Key**, an embarkation point for "must" trips to Indian and Lignumvitae Keys. Accessible only by boat, a 26-passenger ferry is available daily except Tuesdays and Wednesdays.

Indian Key affords no hint of its remarkable landscape and history to passing boats. Those wise enough to dock and test its trails will find traces of early Calusa Indians, believed to have massacred 400 Frenchmen here in 1770. Jacob Housman later transformed the island into a busy port and home for about 50 residents. In 1836, he declared it the first seat of Dade County.

Scoop up a handful of dirt and you may find shards of ancient pottery that date from his colony. The foundations of Housman's town and its water cisterns have been overgrown by lush tropical foliage. All were destroyed, along with the importance of Indian Key, on August 7, 1840. An attack by Chief Chekika and 100 braves flattened the buildings and left seven people dead. Housman escaped, but was buried on this island later. His grave, emptied by vandals, can be seen on the trail.

In addition to the historic sites, the tropical foliage makes for a weird and wondrous hike. An observation tower brings you up to the level of the towering century plants that look like something out of a science-fiction movie. In May, petite white butterflies migrate here from South America. It's like walking through an enchanted tropical blizzard.

Back under the Overseas Highway bridge, off the northeast tip of Lower Matecumbe, lies **Lignumvitae Key**, named for a rock-hard tree found here. For a small fee, Ranger Jeanne Parks and her crew take visitors along several trails. They point out the gumbo-limbos, commonly called the "tourist tree" because of its peeling red skin, and large stands of lignumvitae, the "wood of life" considered a kind of medicinal fountain of youth by the Spanish. They will warn you to steer clear of poisonwood, nearly identical to lignumvitae, which was given its name for a good reason. All kinds of mangroves grow here: the familiar, low-lying red with its stilt-like root system slurping up sea water and separating out the salt; the more massive black mangrove with aerial roots that shoot vertically from the soil; and white mangroves, commonly called buttonwoods, which have rounded leaves and are used for charcoal. Despite the names, all mangroves have green leaves.

Birds from bobolinks to belted kingfishers thrive on the island, but its most magnetic feature is a mysterious 3,000-foot wall of hand-stacked stone. No one knows who built it, when or why.

Zane Grey Territory: From the Matecumbes, US 1 wends its way across increasingly breathtaking waterscapes to **Long Key** where an excellent state recreation area offers good campsites and a swimmable beach. The park has an observation tower, boardwalk and the Golden Orb Weaver Nature Trail – named after the large but harmless spiders that spin sturdy, ornate webs in the trees. Author Zane Grey retreated from his wild western novels to fish in the serenity of this island. A creek that leads to Long Key Blight now bears his name.

Long Key is so far from the madding

crowd that cable television has only recently caught up with it, and about 200 full-time residents still get only fuzzy black-and-white pictures on their sets. The Sea World marine park chain that has branches in Orlando, Cleveland and San Diego established a **Shark Institute** here next door to the lovely **Lime Tree Bay Resort**. The facility is not open to the public, but many of the menacing lemon, tiger, bull, hammerhead and sawfish sharks on view at Sea World in Central Florida are graduates of the institute. The sharks were caught within a 5-mile radius of Long Key.

The most famous graduate of a training academy that made the next island, **Grassy Key**, prominent was the dolphin Flipper of the television series. **Hawk's Cay Resort**, which has held a Four-Star rating, is one of four places in The Keys where guests can, for a fee, swim with resident dolphins. Grassy Key lies at the other end of Long Key Viaduct. The bridge skirts miniscule **Duck** and **Conch Keys** en route.

By now, the names and characteristics of each key begin to blur. There's **Key Colony Beach** and **Crawl Key**. You begin to feel as though you have finally left civilization behind. Then the metropolis of **Marathon** on **Vaca Key** leaps out to spoil that thought.

Not quite Seven Mile Bridge: With a colossal population of 7,000, Marathon boasts no less than three shopping centers. It masquerades as a resort town, but comes across as an urban hamlet plastered together by blue-collar workers lonely for Pennsylvania.

Knight's Key is the gateway to one of the nation's first great engineering marvels, the **Seven Mile Bridge**. The span, actually 110 feet short of 7 miles, is laser straight except for a bend at **Pigeon Key**. It was the crowning achievement of Henry Morrison Flagler's 8-year battle against nature and the elements while building his Overseas Railroad. About 700 men were killed on the job, which reached its conclusion when Flagler, then 82, rode the first train into Key West on January 22, 1912 – that city's biggest celebration

Peculiar plant life on Indian Key.

to date. By rail and steamer, the round-trip fare from Miami to Havana, Cuba, via Key West was $24.

The 1935 hurricane put the railroad out of commission. The state replaced it with a road using Flagler's bridges and foundations. One old mileage marker found on Big Pine Key has been roped off by road crews because of its historical value. The present Seven Mile Bridge, a hair-raisingly narrow structure, was replaced by a shorter, modern bridge.

The magnificent ride over the Gulf of Mexico and Atlantic runs aground again in the vicinity of **Ohio Key**, which developers now have renamed Sunshine Key. Continue to **Bahia Honda**, where the rickety old bridge that parallels the new one provides a glimpse into the past. The recreation area here has campsites, which should be reserved well in advance, and one of the best beaches in the Keys.

A big island with little deer: Bahia Honda, Spanish for "Deep Bay," marks the eastern boundary of the **National Key Deer Refuge**. Bridges across more blips of land lead to **Big Pine Key**, an island second in size only to Key Largo in the chain. This is the heart of deer country, as the signs warn. Follow these markers to the headquarters of the refuge on Watson Boulevard. Freshwater ponds and groves of Caribbean pines, nestled in the fossil coral and oölitic limestone that compose Big Pine, make you feel like you are back on the mainland. This key is so different from the others in the chain, some geologists believe it is part of the Appalachian Ridge forced up during some tumultuous period in the earth's infancy.

The star attraction here is a colony of diminutive deer, a subspecies of the Virginia white-tail. The animals grow to heights of about 30 inches, up to 38 inches in length. Hunters and developers reduced the population to less than 50 by 1947, but efforts by the refuge have boosted numbers back to nearly 300.

About two-thirds of the deer live on Big Pine and No Name Key, although a few have been spotted on 14 neighboring islands. Rangers say the best times to

Proffering snacks is discouraged, but hard to resist on No Name Key.

262

see Key Deer is early morning or late afternoon. But you can see them any time of the day if you are patient and quietly cruise the back roads. Resist the temptation to feed Key Deer or any wildlife. Animals can lose their fear of humans if hand-fed, which eventually makes them more vulnerable.

Overnight camping is prohibited on Big Pine, and housing subdivisions criss-cross the refuge land. But near the end of State Road 94, **Pine Woods Nature Trail** leads through the hardwood Watson Hammock. South of the trail is an old rock quarry, the Blue Hole, brimming with fresh water. Here, alligators lurk and Key Deer drink.

An aquatic showcase: Before leaving Big Pine, avid snorkelers and divers should consider a boat trip to **Looe Key Reef**, considered one of the world's most sensational aquatic showcases.

Further down the Overseas Highway, the **Torch Keys** are named for their flammable trees. **Summerland** offers some scenic side roads and **Cudjoe Key** some modern campsites for large trail-ers. **Sugar Loaf Key**, named for an Indian midden that looked like loaves of old-fashioned sugar, has a tall wooden tower, one of a pair built during World War I as boarding houses for bats. A local businessman imported bats in the hope they would swallow the island's mosquito problem – but once released from the tower, they never returned. The seas and keys to the north of Sugar Loaf are part of the **Great White Heron National Wildlife Refuge**.

The **Saddlebunch Keys** are little more than a series of mangrove outcroppings. **Big Coppit**, **Rockland** and **East Rockland** house the servicemen of the US Naval Air Station on **Boca Chica**, "Little Mouth" Key. **Stock Island**, once a center for cattle and pigpens, serves as a suburb to Key West and home of the **Tennessee Williams Fine Arts Center**.

Before crossing the next bridge, prepare yourself for the short hop into another, very different, world. You have literally reached the end of the road. Some even call it the end of the world. This is **Key West**.

Camping at Long Key.

CURIOUS KEY WEST

Key West was a town where you had to pick and choose. It was always a favorite of pirates.

—Thomas McGuane in
Ninety-two in the Shade

The gateway to Key West is as prosaic as any in Florida. US 1 deposits automobiles into a twisted intersection that forks into North and South Roosevelt boulevards. The latter road rims the Atlantic Ocean, which washes the shore on the left, and passes pungent salt flats of bygone industry on the right, finally dribbling into an oblivion of cement block-houses. North Roosevelt runs smack into Searstown and the modern rubble of any resort city – Holiday Inn, Days Inn, Burger King and company.

But the character of the town inevitably changes, slowly at first, then suddenly. Tacky neon storefronts begin to alternate with dignified old homes bur-
ied under fragrant pink blooms of frangipani. Legions of cats scramble along narrow alleys that cry out to be explored. The American flavor of fast-food emporiums and clean white houses evaporates in an ambience that's not quite Bahamian, not quite Cuban, not quite nautical… just very Key West.

Eventually you wind up on Duval Street, which bisects Old Town. Here, bars, shops and homes – some restored, some still crumbling – merge in a collage of discordant color that somehow suits this city. The people who blend into this bizarre landscape are as incongruous as the colors. Among them are long-haired survivors of the hippie era, impeccably groomed gay couples, leather-faced fishermen, and jet-setters in color-coordinated tennis ensembles. Only in Key West could so much so different seem so right.

Island of Bones: The uniqueness of Key West derives in large part from its history as a haven for transients from the ends of the earth. Its proximity to the US mainland and the West Indies has intro-

Revelers toast the setting sun…

duced many cultural influences, but its relative isolation from both has left it to develop in its own special way.

Somehow, the Calusa Indians managed to get to this speck 100 miles from the Florida peninsula, 90 miles from Cuba, 66 miles north of the Tropic of Cancer. Traces of even earlier inhabitants have occasionally been uncovered. Journalist-historian Wright Langley once stumbled upon some human bones on US Navy property, reviving tales that a cannibalistic tribe had inhabited Key West – though most historians laugh off the stories.

But mid-18th century Spanish explorers said they found this place buried in human bones, a tale that may have led to its Spanish name of *Caya Hueso*, "Island of Bones." The name eventually was anglicized into Key West, although a handful of keys lie further west.

In addition to the Calusas, who had good reason for developing a hostile streak toward Europeans, equally savage pirates made the Keys a risky place to settle. In fact, a young Spanish cavalryman – granted Key West by his governor in 1815 – gladly sold it six years later for just $2,000 to an Alabama businessman, John Simonton. The US government stepped in by 1822, after Simonton split his holdings with John Whitehead, Pardon C. Greene and John Fleming. Commodore David Porter added the first naval presence and systematically wiped out piracy. Construction of a naval base and lighthouse and incorporation of the city of Key West followed.

Cuban migrants brought cigar-making along with their rich culture, and Key West brands eventually became more prized than those from Havana.

Sponge fishermen also prospered. But the Key West economy was built on wrecking. Treacherous reefs, sand bars and unpredictable weather turned the surrounding waters into an "elephants' graveyard" for ships laden with treasures from the Caribbean, South America and Europe.

Lawmakers attempted to bring order to the ensuing plunder as Key West

...on Mallory Pier.

became a center of salvage operations. Licensed boat captains posted a watch: when the words "Wreck ashore!" ripped through the town's balmy air, the race to the floundering boat was on. The first ship to arrive at the wreck was legally entitled to strip it – after rescuing any remaining passengers. The trade became so lucrative, and sinkings so frequent, that the courts eventually wised up to under-handed schemes. Cargo ship captains were conspiring with wrecking crews to deliberately waste their vessels, then split the booty.

Meanwhile, the US government poured millions into the economy. Fort Zachary Taylor's position was substantially strengthened with the addition of the Martello Towers and Fort Jefferson in the Dry Tortugas.

All this activity combined to boost population to 18,000 by 1888, making Key West Florida's largest city. It also became the richest city per capita in the United States, a distinction that lasted through the turn of the century. Completion of the Overseas Railroad in 1912

added another dimension to the booming economy – tourism.

Yet by 1930, Key West faced collapse. The stock market crash of 1929, coupled with the closing of the US Naval station and disease in the sponge beds, began a decline that climaxed with the destruction of the railroad in the 1935 hurricane. Labor troubles forced cigar makers to Tampa. The population declined. But the "Bubbas" – long-time residents who compose the core of Key West's native-born Conch population – stayed and put the pieces back together.

A Little White House, cat houses and Cuban coffee: World War II provided a catalyst when the Navy reclaimed its island facilities. President Harry S. Truman established his "Little White House" on the base. The Cuban Missile Crisis and Bay of Pigs invasion during John F. Kennedy's presidency brought another brief wave of military money. But the Navy left for good in 1974. Only a branch of the Boca Chica Air Station remains. The Navy deeded most of its

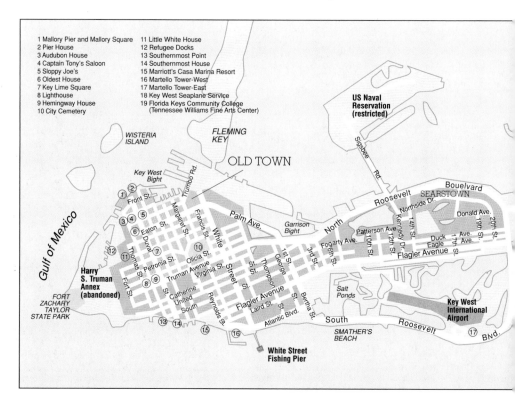

1 Mallory Pier and Mallory Square
2 Pier House
3 Audubon House
4 Captain Tony's Saloon
5 Sloppy Joe's
6 Oldest House
7 Key Lime Square
8 Lighthouse
9 Hemingway House
10 City Cemetery
11 Little White House
12 Refugee Docks
13 Southernmost Point
14 Southernmost House
15 Marriott's Casa Marina Resort
16 Martello Tower-West
17 Martello Tower-East
18 Key West Seaplane Service
19 Florida Keys Community College
(Tennessee Williams Fine Arts Center)

property to the city government, which plans to convert it into a tourist facility. Tourism, shrimping and (from the looks of things) restoration now appear to be Key West's major businesses.

To follow a concise blueprint for experiencing Key West would be tantamount to replaying a completed chess match – interesting but unsatisfying. You'll want to pay homage at the Hemingway House, ride the Conch Train, and sip a margarita at Sloppy Joe's; but don't allow some pre-packaged itinerary to prevent you from straying into conversation with a crusty old Conch at the Half Shell Raw Bar. Don't rush off to make a dinner reservation if you find yourself slipping into song with a banjo player and accordionist at Mallory Pier. You are more likely to find the real Key West if you follow your adventurous inclinations instead of a tour guide.

First, you'll need a base. The island has the usual range of accommodations and then some. Many restored homes have opened their doors as guest houses,

Ernest Hemingway with son, Bumpy, at play in Key West, 1928.

where you can watch Key West go by as you sip morning tea from a gingerbread balcony. The Spanish Renaissance-style Marriott's Casa Marina on Reynolds Street is another of Flagler's many monuments to luxury, also restored and catering to a new generation of big spenders under the Marriott banner. **The Pier House**, located at the northern tip of Duval Street, provides a more contemporary setting with two-story loft suites and balconies that overlook a private beach where topless sunbathing is permitted. It is centrally located and a magnet for many interesting personalities, once a favorite spot of Tennessee Williams.

After you settle in, there are two good introductions to the scene. The venerable **Conch Train** and its newer clone, the **Old Town Trolley**, both comb the streets on 1½-hour tours. These remarkable tours are very different from standard tram trips. Guides point out the city's warts as well as its treasures, from a "cat house where we've never seen any cats" to rookeries where winos con-

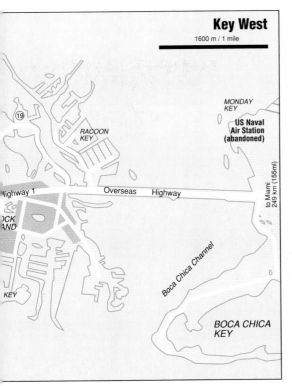

Key West

1600 m / 1 mile

(19)

MONDAY KEY

RACCOON KEY

US Naval Air Station (abandoned)

Highway 1

Overseas   Highway

to Miami 249 km (155ml)

CK AND

Boca Chica Channel

KEY

BOCA CHICA KEY

gregate and deposit empty "Cuban Coffee" bottles in the gutter.

The other prerequisite for venturing out into the streets is the **"Key West Picture Show,"** an award-winning, 40-minute film that captures the city's charm precisely by satirizing 1950s-style travelogues. The film features the late Reverend Furlow Weed and his wife playing the blues on horse conchs. Local saloon keeper and city mayor Captain Tony appears before the camera to explain one popular local pastime: "The closer to the equator, the greater the sex drive." The movie unreels at various intervals at the Conch General Store at Mallory Market.

Hemingway brawled here: Quench your thirst afterward at **Captain Tony's Saloon**, 428 Greene Street. The interior, wallpapered in business cards and newspaper clippings, will take you back to the days when the legendary Ernest Hemingway relaxed here with a drink or a fist fight after a hard day at the typewriter or fishing rod. This was the original Sloppy Joe's. Captain Tony

Tarracino took over and added his own colorful presence. Considered the oldest bar in the state, it was used as a set piece in the recent movie "Kill Castro."

The current **Sloppy Joe's** is only a few steps away at the corner of Greene and Duval. Hemingway also patronized this establishment, as the writing on its facade unblushingly announces, when it was called the Midget Bar. Old photos and memorabilia inside recall the great writer's presence. The moth-eaten fish, mounted on the walls may or may not have been caught by him. Claims that certain artifacts belonged to Hemingway are as rampant and hard to substantiate in Key West as stories about where George Washington slept in Washington, DC. Parachutes, which definitely have no Hemingway tie-in, hang from the ceiling and give the interior an Arabian tent aura. At night the music is loud: the crowd here likes it that way.

You may as well make it a Hemingway day after the bar stops. Pay a visit to his home, now called the **Hemingway House**, on the corner of Whitehead and

The prim Pool House study where "Papa" Hemingway wrote.

Olivia streets. He bought the Spanish colonial in 1931 and lived and worked there for about 10 years before moving to Cuba. In the second-floor study of the pool house out back, he wrote classics like *For Whom the Bell Tolls, A Farewell to Arms* and *The Snows of Kilimanjaro.*

Key West's popularity with creative geniuses pre-dates and post-dates Hemingway's presence. Pulitzer Prize-winning playwright Tennessee Williams, author of *The Glass Menagerie, A Streetcar Named Desire* and *Cat on a Hot Tin Roof,* lived here for 34 years until his death in 1983. He kept a low profile at a home near Duncan and Leon Streets. Thomas McGuane, James Leo Herlihy, Gore Vidal and Carson McCullers all spent time inhaling the creative airs that apparently waft through the streets of Key West.

Today's generation most readily associates the city with the Bahamian-flavored ballads of pop star Jimmy Buffet and his Coral Reefer Band. After years of frequent visits, he now has a permanent Key West address and oper-ates a café on Duval Street. He is presently involved in efforts to save Florida's dwindling race of manatees.

John James Audubon usually heads the lists of painters associated with Key West. In actuality, the naturalist-artist spent only a few weeks here while studying and sketching Florida's countless species of birds. That tenuous connection with the city didn't stop entrepreneurs from renovating and reopening as "Audubon House" the place where he spent those weeks. The building has been standing at Greene and Whitehead since 1830. It showcases period furnishings, including Chippendale antiques, most of them hauled off sinking ships by wreckers.

Conch House ramble: Conchs are not only shellfish and people. They are also houses. Fortunately for Florida, Key Westers have indulged in an infatuation for restoring vintage homes, a hobby that has transformed the island into a live-in architectural museum.

There is no strict definition of a Conch House. Anything that looks like it be-

Below, Captain Tony and friend. Right, playwright Tennessee Williams with novelist pal James Herlihy.

longs in Key West qualifies, particularly if it has gingerbread railings and expansive verandas. The styles recall Early American in New England, British Colonial in the Bahamas, the Spanish and French homes of New Orleans – often all in the same structure. Most are at least 100 years old.

Conch Houses were built in the 19th century, usually by ship's carpenters who had never designed homes before. Some of the best samples can be seen in the heart of Old Town. Start on Caroline Street where several of the old mansions have been modified into office suites. The **Captain George Carey House** at 410 is typical of Bahamian styles as is the building at 310. The **George A.T. Roberts House** at 313, with its blazing red poinciana, spacious double veranda and gingerbread trim, exemplifies Conch architecture. A building's history can also put it into the Conch House category. The notorious **Red Door Inn** at the corner of William Street has become a legend because of the prostitution, drinking, gambling, even murder that occurred behind its red doors.

Wind up your ramble with a look at the colorful homes on Whitehead Street.

Gingerbread buffs should make it a point to take in a two-story house on Duval Street next to **La Terraza De Marti Restaurant** (which locals call "La-Te-Da"). Gingerbread is the ornamental wooden grillwork that became popular fence and veranda art in the Gay Nineties. The gingerbread here – bottles, hearts and spades – reputedly served as a surreptitious sign to sailors and other fun-seekers that they would find wine, women and gambling inside.

A circus at Sunset: Inanimate objects like homes and saloons get their real color here from the characters who people them. The Conchs, native-born, are low-key and unpretentious. Freshwater Conchs are usually a bit more flashy, but have lived here long enough to earn "bubba" status. Hippies here still paint their homes with garish colors and pretend the '60s never ended. Transients find no more road to hitchhike down **Conch House corner.**

and stay awhile. Gays dress exquisitely and run many of the shops and restaurants. The total population is just 28,000, according to the state (32,000 according to the mayor), yet Key West seems to encompass more races, cultures and lifestyles than many metropolises.

For watching this wonderful world and mingling with it, there's no better place than Sunset – with a Capital S. The sun doesn't just set here. On the contrary, the shiny orange orb gets an extraordinary send-off every evening from an astonishing assortment of jugglers, fire-eaters, acrobats, para-sailors, bongo players, cookie peddlers, peg-legged pirates, even ordinary people.

The spectacle begins at the **Mallory Pier** shortly before the sun drops. The miniature Mardi Gras occasionally upstages even the main attraction. But a sunset that teases the sky with a pink streak before torching it aflame in reds and oranges, can elicit standing ovations from the assemblage.

Conservative visitors and families may wish to exercise discretion when attending Sunset, however. It's that time of day when the people here get mellow – some drink wine, some smoke pot. With its proximity to South America, Jamaica and Mexico, Florida is the major port of entry into the US for marijuana and other illegal narcotics. State narcotics agents have their hands full trying to police the vast coastline; some of the biggest drug busts in US history have been made in Florida.

Key West is still vulnerable to clever smugglers who float drugs past the law in many ingenious ways. Bales of marijuana sometimes literally wash up on the shores of the Florida Keys. Locals call it "square grouper." Once word gets out that a load has been dropped in the ocean, boats and beaches fill up with potential rescuers like in the wrecking days of old. A catch of "square grouper" can bring in infinitely more money than the edible kind.

Toasts to the sun and moon: If you wish to toast the setting sun, you can do so aboard the very houseboat patronized by the cast of the '60s television series

Lounging on Pier House beach.

"Surfside 6." Anchored at Mallory Pier, the house-boat has a large, autographed blow-up of the stars inside.

Some folks fan out from Mallory Pier to other parts of town after the sun takes its nightly plunge into the sea. Key West restaurants usually have an exotic atmosphere, but their food rarely rates the expensive prices. **The Bagatelle**, **Poor Richard's Buttery**, **The White Elephant**, "**La-Te-Da**" and **Lazy Afternoon** (the names are subject to occasional changes) feed you in elegantly rejuvenated old homes and buildings, sometimes under ceiling fans or in garden settings. **Claire** on Duval Street provides diners with a box of Crayolas with which they can create their own designs on the paper tablecloth. For the money, the food at **The Pier House** is as good as any, and its seaside setting is very romantic.

In very informal surroundings, the **Half Shell Raw Bar** on the dock at the foot of Margaret Street lustily advises you to "Eat It Raw" and features oysters and other fresh, reasonably priced seafood. The delights of Cuba – *picadillo* (a ground beef dish), black bean soup, and *cafe con leche* (coffee with milk) can be sampled at **La Cacique** on Duval.

Bars, other than Captain Tony's and Sloppy Joe's, include **The Bull & Whistle** (right out of a Schlitz Malt commercial); **Fitzgerald's**, a straight disco; and **Delmonico's**, primarily gay. **The Monster** on Front Street is a multilevel, indoor-outdoor extravaganza that carries a membership charge and warns those who enter that it caters to a gay clientele. (Again, the names and clientele may change.)

Grunt Bone Alley and the City Cemetery: The tourist who deems it his duty to race through a sightseeing quota will find no lack of attractions in Key West. **Mallory Square** is a standard starting point. It is the spot around which the city grew, and lately the spot around which its renaissance has revolved. You can stock up on brochures and tips at the **Hospitality House**, once a ticket office for passenger and freight services in the late 19th century. **Waterfront House**, circa 1850,

The late Iguana Man walked his pets on Duval Street.

and **Harbor House**, 1892, are also here.

A decade ago, much of Old Town, and most of Mallory Square and Duval Street barely stood. Locals had abandoned the decaying gambling halls, bawdy houses and tenements for modern concrete block structures (CBs) on the fringes of the island. Now a new infusion of entrepreneurial money has restored its charm and driven out some of its undesirable elements. You can spend days exploring **Pirates' Alley, Key Lime Square** and **Grunt Bone Alley**. You can wash clothes at the **Margaret Truman Launderette**.

For the record, popular attractions scattered around the city include the Martello Towers, part of the 19th-century effort to fortify the southern boundary of the United States. The East Martello Tower houses the **Key West Art and Historical Society Museum**. Nearby, **Fort Zachary Taylor** looms over the southwest tip of the island, another mid-1800s edifice destined to become an attraction. The **Oldest House** attracts its share of visitors to 322 Duval Street, while the **Lighthouse** at Truman and Thomas avenues dates to 1846 and houses a military museum.

The **Southernmost Point** at the end of Duval Street has lost its title to a spot on the Big Island of Hawaii. But it is still 375 miles south of Cairo, Egypt, and 755 miles south of Los Angeles. Chinese immigrant Jim Kee began selling shiny sea shells here in the late '30s, and his descendants continue to do so. Nearby is none other than the opulent, privately owned **Southernmost House**.

Even the **City Cemetery** bordered by Francis, Angela and Olivia streets has fascinating sights. Among them are a monument to men who died aboard the *USS Maine* in Havana in 1898, and a statue of a Key Deer that marks the grave of a beloved pet. The cemetery has been the center of a controversy because of the local custom of recycling the graves. There's so little space, Key Westers for the past 60 years have shoveled up old skeletons and reburied them deeper to make room for newcomers. Officials estimate that up to 100,000

A candid epitaph at City Cemetery.

bodies may be buried in just 15,000 spaces in the Solares Hill section of the cemetery.

The abandoned **US Naval Base**, best visited aboard the Conch Train or Trolley, encompasses President Harry Truman's Little White House, President Kennedy's Bay of Pigs Invasion command post, and Key West's newest tourist attraction – the refugee landing docks. Many of the 125,000 Cubans who fled their country in 1980 on anything that could float landed here. Hundreds of rotting refugee boats line the docks in a bureaucratic limbo created by US immigration laws during the illegal boatlift.

Shoppers looking for souvenirs representative of the city can try **Key West Hand Print Fabrics**, 201 Simonton Street. There, Cuban workers apply acrylic paint in tropical patterns to the cloth, which you can buy as raw fabric or ready-made fashions from the racks. A block away, the **Key West Fragrance Factory** sells smells made on the premises.

Purists may find it all a bit too touristy, too commercial. But even the locals take the new look in stride as just another of the many phases in the city's unorthodox history. Whether shopping, sightseeing, sipping, supping, sunbathing, snorkeling or simply slumming, you'll find an alternative way of doing it in Key West.

The farther Keys: The Overseas Highway ends in Key West, but Florida doesn't. The breathtaking, cobalt blue seas to the west embrace islands even more surprising than Key West. Getting to them is in itself an adventure. Several seaplanes operating out of the lower keys provide beautiful bird's-eye trips.

Pilot Russ Sprague, who operates out of **Key West Seaplane Service** at Murray's Marina on Stock Island, takes passengers slow and low over the waters for a good look at the **Quicksands** – shifting sandbars that create gorgeous patterns in the surf. Nearby are a ring of islands called the **Marquesas**, considered the only atoll in the Atlantic Ocean (although Russ says they are technically in the Gulf of Mexico). You'll see **Rebecca Shoal**, where a rusty ship manned by one or two people marks the spot of treasure hunter Mel Fisher's claim to tens of millions of dollars in gold and silver, lying below in the hull of the Spanish ship *Nuestra Señora de Atocha,* which sank here in 1622.

The most impressive sight lies at the end of the 35-minute flight in the **Tortugas**, 68 miles from Key West. From the air, it looks like a piece of the Lost City of Atlantis is rising straight out of the sea. The hexagonal fortress is the "Gibraltar of the Gulf" – **Fort Jefferson**. As your plane drops closer for splashdown, you can see that the fort actually covers most of the 16-acre **Garden Key**.

Construction commenced in 1846 and continued for 30 years without completion. Federal troops occupied the fort in 1861 to keep it from falling into Confederate hands during the Civil War, but it saw little action then or at any other time. After the war, it served as a prison. Inmates included four men linked to the assassination of Abraham Lin-

The mascot of the Bull and Whistle Bar leaves via the wall.

coln. The most famous was an innocent victim of that crime, Dr Samuel A. Mudd. Obeying his physician's code, he set the broken leg of John Wilkes Booth, unaware that Booth had injured it after shooting Lincoln. Mudd was convicted of conspiracy and sentenced to a life of hard labor at Fort Jefferson. During a yellow fever epidemic that struck the Tortugas in 1867, he worked tirelessly to aid the stricken, earning an early pardon two years later.

The fort is now a national monument. You can roam the ramparts and wonder what it must have been like to be imprisoned behind its 50-foot-high walls, cut off from the world by a moat as well as an ocean.

Outside, you'll find primitive camping facilities and a secluded sand beach. Take a picnic lunch and bathing suit. The snorkeling is excellent. Though victimized by indiscriminate hunting, the huge turtles – loggerheads and hawkbills – after which Ponce de León named the Tortugas, can still be seen cruising the waters. Further west is Loggerhead Key, the end of Florida, with a 130-year-old lighthouse that is still in use.

Sooties, frigates and terns: Plan your trip to the Tortugas for April or early May, if possible, for another educational experience – if you don't mind sharing the island with armies of bird watchers wielding cameras.

East of Fort Jefferson is **Bush Key** where, for some inexplicable reason known only to Mother Nature, thousands of sooty terns come each year from the Caribbean, the west central Atlantic Ocean and as far away as West Africa. They zero in on Bush Key each spring to lay eggs in depressions in the warm sand. The parents take turns shading their single egg from the sun. Juvenile sooties fly 9,000 miles to West Africa, but manage to find their way back to tiny Bush Key when they are 4 years old. Other spectacular species that can be observed on Bush Key are brown noddy terns and the monstrous but graceful frigate birds which have wingspans of nearly 7 feet.

Below, airstrip on Garden Key. Following pages: Fort Jefferson floats in the Dry Tortugas.

P.de S.Ioan navidad.

P.bo ã Fueo baxo.

Sinus Morguel.

Rio de flores

Phondor de Medavo.

LA
FLORID

Lacus &
Sarro

Sinus Ioãnis Ponce.

Golfo Mexicano

Rio Canotes.

Rio Pacis.

Aquatio

Arena Arena

CALOS

Infulæ dictæ Testudines

Calos.

Cauarias

Scopuli dicti Martires

Baya honda

Mariel in

Portus Matancas

Cauana

Portus principt.

Hauana

S.

CVBA INSVLA

Xaqua.

Guanaguarico

S.Trinitatis

Albay hamo

C.d.Cruz

Atalia.

Seuilla

Inf.Pinnorum

N

C.Cateche.

Jardines scopuli nauigantibus formidabiles

Merida.

Inf.Mulierum

Seu

IAMAICA

Orista

Cuspis anata

Comaiaqua. Aquia

Hoc loco prima disens

Sorrochos.   R. Sorrochas.

arracou.

Iucayonoque sii

Oathkagua

LVCAYA

Mocoſſou.

Prom: Canaueral.

P. de Sant Hellenæ.

La Emperadada

Bahama.

C. de Canareal

Canalis Bahamæ versus Septemtrionem semper fluit.

Bimini.

Ciguateo Guanima

Hæc Maris pars plena est Inſulis, ſcopulis, breuibus et puluinis valde inſidioſis.

Carybdis magna.

Guanahaiy

Quibeniaca

Inſula Arenarum Iumeto

Samana.

Portus patris

Maya guana

Hinagua

Cyſpis Mayaci

Portus Conceptionis

Inſ. S. Tome.

Porralyſcon Barac̃a

P. Nicolai

Guanique

Mons Chriſti.

Natiuita

Mos Carniata

Cibao

obi.

Valles paradiſi Xaragua

Portus Regius

Iſabella

Cap franco.

Hanc Inſulam ſecunda N et Hiſpaniol

HAYTI SIVE SPAÑIOLA

Lago ſal.

Caymiti.

Guanaba.

Port plati

C. Capris

Banco mõs

La Yaguana

Lago dolce

C. Samana

Rio de luna

Caput de- ceptionis

SCIA Catana RA

Yaguina

G.

S. Iulian

Rio d'Ozana.

Aſua.

S. Dominici

Riod'Achina

Yguey

Zachei

S.

uay

ormica- rum

Rio d'Or.ama

S. Catelina.

Saona.

THE LURE OF LOST TREASURE

The Coins were relics of the annual currents of trade that once pulsed through the great Portobello fair, the port of Cartagena, and the entrepôt of Havana. Here were the surrogates for the hopes, lusts, fears and savings of private persons, the risks taken by long-dead merchants, and the once-coveted revenues of half-forgotten kings. Yes, here was death – the dissolution of men's hopes, the fatal decline of empire, the passing of an epoch. But the coins also spoke of life: the culture and commerce of colonial Spain. And we were privileged, as we sat among the heaps of coins, to touch all this.

—Eugene Lyon in
The Search for the Atocha

A uniformed guard, shotgun propped on hip, stood in front of the two-story Key West Conch House. Guests checked in on the ground floor, where they received a name tag and clearance to proceed to the second floor. A room at the top of the stairs contained more guards and displays of what looked like museum pieces – broken bowls, pottery shards, old cannon balls, muskets. Most people then gravitated to an adjoining room. There, jaws fell to chests the way the unhinged mouths of puppets would.

Amid the guards were several long cases lined with electric blue material. Inside, absorbing the glint of spotlights until it glowed richly, was *gold*. Bars, chains, plates, coins, ingots, bullion and solid chunks of pure gold. Not ounces, but pounds of gold. In one squat case alone was $10 million worth of long, thick gold chains. The total value of the treasure in those two rooms well exceeded $20 million.

"Here, feel it," a man said. He plopped a lump of yellow rock into a visitor's hand. An armed guard trained his eyes on the exchange. "You're holding a quarter million dollars."

The visitor needed two hands to hold it. It was more than a heavy piece of precious

metal, more than a king's ransom. Here was something that had the most romantic of histories, something that had lain on the bottom of the sea for nearly 400 years. Indeed, it and all the treasure on display had been recovered from the worm-eaten, barnacle-encrusted hulls of two legendary Spanish galleons that sank in 1622 – the *Nuestra Señora de Atocha* and the *Santa Margarita*.

The exhibit was a routine affair in Key West held at the offices of Treasure Salvors, Inc. Company founder Mel Fisher has be-

come as much of a legend here as the fabulous treasures he has found. A strong, imposing figure, he bears no resemblance to those comic book characters who follow "x-marks-the-spot" maps to buried treasure chests. Fisher has made treasure-hunting a legitimate business. And he's helped make Florida a magnet for other dreamers hoping to find their fortune at the bottom of the sea or buried under a rock on an island.

Doubloons and pieces of eight: During the 16th and 17th centuries, Spanish ships listed with loads of gold, silver, precious commodities and other goods from their New World colonies in South America and the

Preceding pages: "X" marks the spot. Left, treasure hunting king Mel Fisher brandishes gold chain and an ancient kris from the *Atocha*. Right, a diver brings up more booty.

West Indies. These galleons plied routes that skirted Florida's southern coasts and keys. They made prime targets for marauding bands of pirates who darted from behind mangrove islands in swift, small ships, butchered passengers and crew, and made off with anything of value. Sometimes the buccaneers stashed the loot in island hideaways where it remains undiscovered today. Just as deadly as pirates were the forces of nature – violent thunderstorms, tricky currents, jagged reefs and sea-shaking hurricanes which put many a vessel on the bottom of the sea.

Two powerful war galleons, the *Atocha* and *Santa Margarita*, left Havana on September 4, 1622, in a Spanish fleet brimming

with consignments of royal and private treasure. A hurricane devastated the fleet in the Straits of Florida the next day. The violent storm shredded eight ships, killing 550 people and swallowing a fortune in gold, silver, indigo, copper and tobacco. The *Atocha* and *Margarita* were among the missing vessels.

Legends grew around the ships and their immense treasures, as usually happens. But no one seriously investigated the story or pursued the ships until Mel Fisher vowed to find them in the mid-1960s. It took the kind of man who was ready to devote a life to scouring vast, trackless seas in search of a dream. Encouraged by successful efforts in

recovering doubloons and pieces of eight from the wreck of a 1715 Spanish Plate Fleet off the coast of Vero Beach, Fisher began his new quest in the Keys.

The story of his search for the *Atocha* has all the ingredients of a best-selling novel. There was a false start off Islamorada; suspenseful hunts through yellowing, old documents in archives in Spain; and years of cruising treacherous seas. Fisher's own son and daughter-in-law, as well as a crew member's son, were killed in boating accidents. And still he raced to beat other treasure hunters to the *Atocha* and to find it before he went broke. Tragedy and intrigue at last climaxed in triumph in June 1971.

Fisher demonstrated he had indeed found the *Atocha* with his typical flare for the dramatic. A silver bar he found in the wreck, with the number 4584 carved on it, had been listed on a 17th-century manifest which documented items loaded on the *Atocha* in Havana Harbor. All that remained was to weigh his bar and see if it matched the weight of the one listed on the manifest – 63.6 pounds. Before an excited crowd of newsmen, photographers and friends in Key West, Fisher adjusted a scale to 63.6 pounds. Then he put silver bar number 4584 on the scale. The balance beam hesitated for a moment and stopped in the middle. The weights matched.

Uncontrolled treasure-hunting?: Since then, Fisher's Treasure Salvors, Inc. has settled into comfortable Conch House quarters at 425 Caroline Street where visitors can buy T-shirts and books. Fisher has been the subject of a *National Geographic* magazine article and television special, as well as numerous newspaper stories. His crew have since turned up the *Santa Margarita*, which has added another $20 million to the $8 million in treasure recovered from the *Atocha*. Still, Fisher searches for the mother lode of the wrecks that he believes may yield as much as a half-billion dollars.

Treasure Salvors occasionally shows off its finds in exhibits for potential investors. There's an emerald ring valued at $40,000, an exquisite rosary with coral beads, a gold chain carrying a baroque cross of chased gold, and a finely-etched, mint-condition gold plate valued at a half-million dollars.

It remains uncertain how much money Fisher, his employees and investors will reap from all this. The US government and State of Florida have both battled in court for the right to the treasure. So far, Fisher has won and the riches remain in his hands. But legal challenges continue to arise. Florida officials and state archaeologists argue that an uncontrolled treasure-hunting industry here could damage other wrecks and the historical value of their cargoes. Fisher's attorneys contend that the US and State governments are merely trying to cash in on their client's good fortune.

Fisher's exploits have indeed helped make Florida a mecca for treasure hunters. Competitors discovered another old galleon off the coast of Brevard County in 1980 just 1,000 feet from shore and in only 15 feet of water. It's believed to contain 20,000 to 50,000 silver coins. Further south, near Elliott Key in Biscayne National Monument, a diver stumbled upon a Spanish-era wreck while spearfishing – and surfaced with old cutlasses and pottery instead of dinner.

Further afield, Florida-based Burt Webber, an old foe of Fisher's, discovered the sunken hull of the *Concepcion* off the coast of the Dominican Republic after a 15-year search. His operation, Seaquest International, has so far salvaged about $40 million in booty. Doubloon Salvage has been working wrecks near Fort Pierce thought to be more of the 1715 Spanish Plate Fleet, and Soul Treasures of Florida has been exploring the potentially lucrative waters around St Augustine Harbor.

Men like Fisher and Webber have turned treasure-hunting into businesses, utilizing sophisticated equipment and investing hundreds of thousands of dollars in searches. But the simple man who goes out to the woods or beaches with pick, shovel and some sketchy information is more common.

"Pirate tree markings": St Petersburg's L. Frank Hudson claims to be the authority on treasure along Florida's West Coast, although in his various publications he never admits to unearthing any pirate chests. In his *Lost Treasure of Florida's Gulf Coast*, he diagrams "pirate tree markings" and advises amateur hunters to keep their shovels sharp. He also obligingly provides the general locations of dozens of "treasures," some of which he says may be worth as much as $200 million.

Among some of the choice spots identified

by Hudson are Naples Beach, where gold doubloons and silver pieces of eight have washed ashore after high tides or storms; Cockroach Island in lower Tampa Bay; Indian Rocks Beach and Ross Island near St Petersburg's archaeologically rich Weedon Island. Cara Pelau Island near the mouth of Charlotte Harbor reputedly served as headquarters – and therefore personal bank vault – for José Gaspar, one of the most famous of Florida pirates despite claims by modern historians that he is a fictional character. There is, in fact, some doubt whether the West Coast ever attracted many pirates because Spanish shipping lanes were near the Keys and the southeast coast of the state –

where most real treasures have been discovered to date.

Yet neither the doubts nor the unlikelihood of striking it rich deter the determined. Many can be seen solemnly scouring Florida's beaches, waving metal detectors around like divining rods, listening intently for the "bleep" in their headphones, while keeping sand scoops and sifters poised in their belts. After all, it was a $15 metal detector that led a Brevard County man, Kip Wagner, to a cache of 1715 Spanish Plate Fleet coins a number of years ago. Now his Real Eight Salvage Company has dredged up about $6 million worth.

<u>Left</u> and <u>right</u>, samples of old *Atocha* gold.

THE BASEBALL BOYS

Flashback. Shea Stadium, New York, 1967. Mets vs. Pirates. First Inning. Woodie Fryman, a 27-year-old pitcher with greased-back hair, is on the mound for the Pirates. First batter, Ron Hunt, leads off for New York with a high chopper. The ball bounces over Fryman and catches in the web of the shortstop's glove. He gets off a hurried throw, but Hunt beats it to first base. On the next pitch, Hunt is nailed dead trying to steal second. Fryman goes on to retire the next 26 batters in a row. But his perfect game has been lost by a bad bounce and a tough call. Woodie Fryman will never forget it. "I remember every out. If it had been the last batter of the game, he would have been called out. But that's been a while ago. I don't throw like I used to."

Spring, West Palm Beach, 1981. Ol' Number 35 is a junk-baller heading into what could be his final season in the majors 14 years after throwing a near perfect game. The fastball is shot, but the mind is keen and the desire is as strong as ever. Woodie Fryman gives it as much at the end as he did when he came out of a semi-pro league in Kentucky way back in 1966.

He had no high school education when the Pirates expressed interest in him. He was playing slow-pitch softball three nights a week and milking cows and shoveling manure 12 hours a day. On Sundays, he chucked fastballs in the Bluegrass League. It was his last shot, so he accepted Pittsburgh's offer of $500 a month, shoved the money in an envelope and mailed it back home to his wife on the family farm. If he didn't make it, he'd be home in time for the harvest.

"I made the club," says Woodie, leaning up against the bullpen fence in a red, white and blue Montreal Expos uniform. "And 15 years later, here I am."

The Expos like to call him their "Old Goat." But there are plenty of innings left in Woodie Fryman. He's still a 10-year-old kid in a 40-year-old body who threw like a 30-year-old All-Star just the previous season.

It is noon and the Old Goat is blowing Spring Training bubbles. Perfect, tight pink Bazooka balls. Veteran bubbles. It is another priceless day at the ballpark. And Woodie is happier – as they say back in Ewing, Kentucky – than a pig in mud. He is with Freddie Norman, a 38-year-old reliever who has traveled the same road. Fryman subconsciously blows a bubble, pops it and leans into Norman, squeezing his leg like he would a brother's.

At 7.30 every morning, Fryman and Norman are the first to arrive at the Expos' training camp. A janitor is sweeping out the locker room when they arrive. Practice starts at 10.30. The two men sink into the warm waters of a whirlpool and spend an hour just getting the old bones loosened up.

"It takes us old guys longer to get going," says Fryman.

The old and the new: The scene occurred during the first exhibition series of the 1981 season. Norman Rockwell could have painted it. Two veterans reaching the end of the road in the lazy spring rays at West Palm Beach Stadium. In the outfield, some rookies were in the first of what could be 20 more springs. In the bullpen, the old pitchers were already past the point of no return.

Norman and Fryman spent the first three innings the way two Little Leaguers would, ribbing, teasing and laughing at elementary school humor. But they were being watched. A bovine boy in braces from Boynton Beach waddled over.

"Boy," the kid said, nervously grabbing at the chain-link fence. "I hope they foul one off over here."

Fryman looked over his shoulder and tried to look mean. "Now why would you want that to happen," he said in his syrupy Kentucky drawl.

"So I could get a baseball," the fat kid said.

Fryman got up and walked to where a few scarred baseballs sat against the rubber on a clay mound. Looking around to see if anyone was watching, Fryman tossed the ball over his shoulder.

"Gee, thanks, mister," said the kid. The Old Goat grinned, the way a cat does after eating the canary. The kid stuck the ball in his front pocket and waddled away.

"You think the kid's got enough baseballs?" said Norman, pointing to two baseball size lumps in the youngster's back pockets.

Norman just shook his head. After all, it's only Spring Training. Fryman watched his little friend join a group of 25 kids chasing foul balls. He looked over at the dugout where Bill Gullickson, 22, and David Palmer, 23, were waiting to take his job. The oldtimer sat in the sun for maybe the last spring, waiting to come on in relief.

"We communicate good, me and the young kids on the club," Fryman said. "I guess they figure if a guy who is 40 years old can give it his all, day after day, they can too. Just getting the opportunity to be around these young kids all the time makes me feel young. Heck, I'm old enough to be one of their fathers."

Peanuts, popcorn and mediocre hot dogs: Careers are reborn every spring in Florida. A renaissance takes place that puts young and old on common ground. Everybody becomes a kid again.

Baseball is bursting out all over the state. Aspiring umpires squat, wave their hands and scream "Safe!" at a training school in Daytona Beach. Wrinkled, but eager, octogenarians take the field in St Petersburg's Kids and Kubs league where the minimum age of the baseballers is 75 years. And the pros shake off winter rust at baseball parks throughout Florida.

The grass is green. The air is fresh off the sea. The sounds of the ballpark make sweet music – an American rhapsody. "Get your peanuts. Peanuts here! Hey Popcorn. Ice Cream. Get your ICE cream!" Two senior citizens shade themselves. Two college students take off their shirts and order a couple of beers. A game ends with professional players doing a springtime version of windsprints – windtrots. The fundamentals are reviewed. Home run hitters practice bunting. Pitchers practice base running. Fungo after fungo is hit into the outfield. Million-dollar All-Stars shag half-heartedly. Such absurdity. Such casual ambience.

A hot dog is essential in appreciating all this. It may be Florida, but the dogs are as mediocre here as they are in Shea Stadium or Fenway Park. A hot dog gives you something to do between innings. It's either eat, or

fall asleep in the mid-afternoon sun.

That's Spring Training. A sedate season that, like the regular 162-game schedule, is stretched out too long. Why? Because it's a tradition, that's why.

"I don't need all of spring training to get in shape," Stan Musial once said. "All I need is about 10 days to get the blisters on my hands and have the blisters turn to callouses."

Pitchers and catchers are the first to report, because it does take them longer. The Johnny Benches and Tom Seavers. Grown men playing catch for two weeks. Living the American Dream that little kids on the other side of the fence wish for. Playing baseball for a living. It sure beats work.

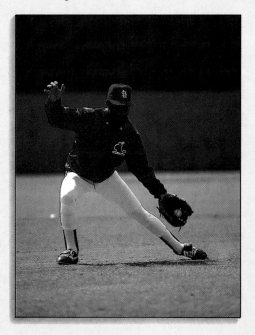

Nightlife in the Grapefruit League: Like polar bears awakening from a winter hibernation, members of baseball's 26 major league teams arrive in Florida every February. Batterymates punch the clock. Stiff pitching arms are loosened slowly, giving all the muscles and tensions time to stretch and strengthen themselves. Catcher's hands burn at the first pop of a 96-mile-per-hour fastball. First red, then black and blue, they harden. A few people with nothing better to do come by for a look. Other veterans start to filter in.

Spring Training is a 2-month joy ride that warms up the National Pastime. Nothing counts. You can throw away the records, batting averages and poor performances. But you can't forget them. Especially if they carry through to the regular season.

Baseball fans who travel 1,500 miles won't let you forget it. Even though it's March, they think it's late October and the pennant is on the line. Baseball players make too much money not to take every game seriously. Soft focus euphoria is a sharp contrast to a $20-million-dollar contract. Hard-core baseball fans want more for their money. They want to see Dave Winfield hit home runs from the first day of spring training until the last day of the World Series. The Grapefruit League is just supposed to be a dress rehearsal. But fans want to see victories.

This is absurd, of course. Spring training was not meant to be a pressurized microcosm of the regular season.

"Spring training," Ernie Banks once said, "is a chance to be a boy again."

But boys will be boys. It's also a time for baseball players to enjoy the same things college students and vacationers experience during the annual Spring migration to Florida. Rules were made to be broken.

Back in the '50s when the New York Yankees used to train in St Petersburg, Don "Perfect Game" Larsen crashed his car into a lamp post after a night on the town. Casey Stengel, Larsen's boss, told reporters that there would be no fines for breaking team regulations.

"Anyone who can find something to do in St Petersburg at five in the morning deserves a medal, not a fine," said Stengel.

The Yankees now train in Fort Lauderdale. There is no problem finding trouble in Fort Lauderdale at five in the morning – or five in the evening. They don't call it "Fort Liquordale" for nothing.

There has been talk that the Yankees' spring training site may move to Ocala, a horse-breeding town in the state's heartland where team owner George Steinbrenner owns stables. Steinbrenner believes there are too many distractions in Fort Lauderdale. No way to corral his superstars.

This problem is not isolated to the Yankees. In Tampa, the Cincinnati Reds face the same dilemma every year from groupies trying to find their way into player's rooms at the International Inn. "The fellows are pretty sweet," said Lynn Allman, marketing director for the Reds. It's the girls the Reds have to worry about. Girls will be girls.

Pass the suntan oil and play ball!: Most of the US is still scraping ice off their rearview windows and shoveling snow off their driveways when Spring Training's first pitch is thrown. Sooty snow pollutes the streets. Trees are barren, shivering in 20-degree northwesterly gusts.

Ice hockey and basketball seasons are in full swing. Sturdy logs are on the roaring fires in New England. Snowmobiles are run-

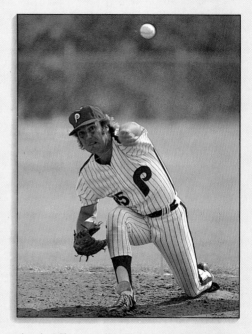

ning in Minneapolis. The heat is turned right up in Chicago.

In Florida, they're passing the suntan oil and playing golf and tennis. The skies are their azure clearest. Diamond days. Egrets circle in the sky. Royal palms sway lazily in cool tropical breezes. The temperature seems locked in the 70s.

In Orlando, Disney World bulges with vacationers in Mickey Mouse ears. In Sarasota, sailboats float luxuriously on a pastel blue bay. On Fort Lauderdale Beach, a Frisbee skims across the sand.

Northerners dream weave. The first glimpse of Reggie Jackson. A Louisville

Left, St Louis Cardinal Ozie Smith fields a baseball during practice in St Petersburg, Fla. **Right**, Steve Carlton fires a spring training strike in Clearwater.

slugger poking out of a bat rack. Hot, buttered popcorn. Linseed oil on a new Wilson glove and fresh cut, fertilized grass. A salt breeze. Coppertone. The first sip of beer in the top of the first inning. J.R. Richard's first comeback pitch. Pete Rose's first headfirst slide. Steve Garvey's first Ultra Brite smile.

If you're a real hard core baseball junkie, you know that Tinker Field is in Orlando, where the Minnesota Twins train. Joker Marchant is not a playing card but where the Detroit Tigers train, out in a Lakeland Orange Grove. Chain-o-Lakes Field? Winter Haven, of course, the winter haven of the Boston Red Sox. The Red Sox are not to be mistaken for the White Sox from Chicago.

It is difficult to say what is more representative of Spring Training – laid-back Dunedin or the strip on Fort Lauderdale Beach. Both are scenes from postcards.

As Roger Kahn, who covered the Brooklyn Dodgers for the *New York Times*, wrote in *The Boys of Summer*:

You see young players around camp and the retirement village around camp. You see some 21-year-old kid who maybe will make it – and maybe he won't – but he tries hard because he doesn't want to go back to Pittsfield. And then, you see the old lady on a tricycle going to get her blood checked. The contrast is so great it's the stuff of poetry.

Windy City fans know that Payne Park is in Sarasota the way Canadians know that the Toronto Blue Jays call Grant Field in Dunedin their spring home.

Each geographic area is a magnet for each city's baseball team. Philadelphians take their vacations in Clearwater. Yankee fans go to Fort Lauderdale, Mets fans to St Petersburg. Both the Expos and the Braves share accommodations at West Palm Beach Stadium, French Canadians and Crackers.

Even the Los Angeles Dodgers, blessed with their own glorious spring weather, make a traditional pilgrimage to Vero Beach to train.

Catching autographs: There is nothing cuter than a 4-year-old boy walking shyly up to a superstar with pen and program in hand. But one little 4-year-old quickly becomes 100 little 4-year-olds. This is when ball players decide that they have to get back to the hotel or they have an appointment to keep.

"If we sign one, we have to sign them all," lamented one ballplayer. "We would be here all day. So if we can't sign them all, we sometimes won't sign any."

Autograph hounds refuse to take no for an answer, though. They come in all sizes and shapes, in baby carriages and wheelchairs. They want everything signed from pennants, caps and plaster casts, to school notebooks and parts of the body.

There's something about getting a baseball player's autograph that dates back to the childhood rush of getting close enough to touch and talk to someone who never before seemed real.

During the regular season, it is almost impossible to get an autograph. Players are too wound up and inaccessible. But in these miniature ballparks, they seem as much a part of the total picture as the fans do.

Author Pat Jordan wrote: "Spring training is like a big summer picnic, where everyone's playing softball and eating barbeque. It's like a big country fair with people all around the ballpark."

Brightly colored signs plaster the outfield at Jack Russell Stadium in Clearwater. The football stadium dominates the backdrop outside the left-field fence at Al Lopez Stadium in Tampa. Cessnas descend on an executive landing strip while bucolic baseball fans absorb a shimmering of Yankee pinstripes in Fort Lauderdale. But every stadium has an outfield wall that is a billboard for local commerce. The local hangouts like Caponga's Dugout Restaurant in Clearwater and Malio's Le Club in Tampa. The national Madison Avenue campaigns like Panasonic's Reggie-vision on the right field wall in Lauderdale.

Bring on the bucks: Spring Training is big business. For 6 weeks, Florida is in the national spotlight. Gobs of money are spent. Television crews and news organizations from around the country and the world are dispatched. Hotels fill up. Rates change. Prices become "seasonal." Restaurants require reservations.

"The dollar figure must be enormous," said Tony Mercer, manager of tourism and conventions for the Fort Lauderdale Chamber of Commerce. "It would probably boggle your mind."

In South Florida, Spring Training adds an estimated $30 million a year to Fort Lauderdale's coffers, $20 million to West Palm Beach and $15 million to Pompano, where the Texas Rangers train.

John Lomelo, the mayor of Sunrise, a Fort Lauderdale suburb, has made several unsuccessful efforts to lure the Houston Astros from Cocoa Beach.

"We figured out that Spring Training would mean about $15 million more to our area," said Lomelo. "And that's a conservative figure."

The Galt Ocean Mile in Fort Lauderdale rents blocks of rooms to the Yankees. That's 80 rooms at a total cost of $4,000 each day. The Sheraton Hotel in West Palm Beach houses both the Expos and Braves for an added $75,000.

Each team also rents city ball parks. The Yankees' contract with Fort Lauderdale guarantees the city 10 percent of gross ticket sales and 10 percent of all billboard advertising plus 30 percent of all concessionaire profits. The city of Pompano made $28,000 from the Texas Rangers above the many benefits to local businesses.

"And believe me," said one Pompano Beach official, "the Texans that come here every spring aren't blue-collar workers. They spend big money."

Baseball is on the rise again after a decade of decline, and Florida is more than happy to help it on its way.

Left, Atlanta Braves' skipper Ted Turner (left) and Yankees' owner George Steinbrenner (right) exchange pre-season pleasantries in Florida.
Right, Los Angeles Dodger pitching sensation Fernando Valenzuela meditates before screwballing a batter.

SPEED!

On a February day in 1959, they held a race at Daytona International Speedway. Three days later, they named a winner.

Since then, headlines in newspapers worldwide have chronicled racing in Florida, but no story ever approached that first race at Daytona International in significance. It was *the* contest that took stock cars out of the proverbial backwoods and brought them a following that previously had been reserved for open cockpit vehicles raced at Indianapolis and on Formula One circuits.

a candidate to become the molder and emperor of a racing dynasty. When he took an interest in the speed contests constantly being conducted on the old beach course, he was just another of countless men who showed up to work on their cars and floor their accelerators to see who could make them go fastest. But France envisioned better things for his new automotive avocation.

First, he organized a sanctioning body. After much haggling with his compatriots, France called it the National Association for

Not that stock car racing was new to Daytona Beach. Years before anybody could even envision an oval of asphalt there, drivers came to race on a course laid out on the hard-packed sands of its beach.

It is legend now how William H.G. "Bill" France, seeking his fortune in the South, arrived in Daytona penniless and went to work for a few dollars a week pumping gas. France was young and ambitious, but hardly

Left, Indy-style and rubber-burning speed vehicles glide through a banked curve at Daytona. **Above**, the famous 1959 dead-heat finish photo at the first 500.

Stock Car Auto Racing – an abbreviated title that spells out a tidy word, NASCAR. Soon, France and NASCAR were the recognized rulers of the stocks. France also dreamed of building a showplace of speed in his adopted hometown. Stock cars then had many tracks to race on, but most were little quarter-and-half-milers laid out in the clearings of hill country in Appalachia, where stock car racing was born. There it was a hobby for speed demons who made their livings outrunning "revenuers" in hot pursuit of their loads of moonshine.

If the popular open-wheel cars could have a 2½-mile showplace like Indianapolis, France wondered, why couldn't stock cars have a similar showplace? Thus inspired, he opened Daytona International Speedway in 1959. The "D" shape of the speedway and the ultra-high banking in its turns – both a departure from Indianapolis' "pure" oval shape with little banking – was built for blazing speed. But could the cars and drivers handle such blazing speed?

The photo finish: A huge mixture of racing fans and the curious came to that first 500-mile race on this daring new course. They left enthralled.

The lowest margin of victory ever registered at Indianapolis was 5 seconds – a huge gap between two fast-moving cars. When

the decision over to a camera at the start-finish line that had snapped a picture of the two cars as they crossed. That picture became one of the most celebrated in all of auto racing. A print still hangs today in the press box at Daytona International.

From "Thunder Road" to Daytona Beach: If the fans, the drivers and writers couldn't decide who won, neither could the officials. It took them three days to award the victory to Lee Petty. Because of Petty's high standing in the stock car racing community, the choice proved popular.

It was big news at the time, but it really doesn't matter anymore who won. What mattered were the lasting repercussions that

the first Daytona 500 ended, the margin was not seconds, tenths of seconds, or one-hundredths of seconds. It was nothing.

Lee Petty, the most popular of the old-time stock car racers, and Johnny Beauchamp battled for the lead all day. They fought down to the final laps. More than three decades later, drivers at Daytona talk intelligently about the moves necessary to win races when facing heavy competition late in the race. But in that first race they were experimenting, gaining knowledge for future use.

Petty and Beauchamp finished side-by-side. Nobody in the stands knew who won. Neither driver was even sure. Officials turned

first Daytona event had on auto racing.

Stock car racing, born in the hill country, had been born again. This time, the blessed event made news beyond the hills. It proved that these cars and drivers could handle the tremendous speeds (Petty averaged 135.52 miles per hour) necessary on such a track. And, yes, they could put on a good show that would lure spectators.

France had his Dixie version of the Indianapolis 500. The stock car boys had themselves a showcase where their successes and failures would be recorded. And the nation had developed an interest in the doings of those rednecks down south.

Good 'ole Southern boys, whether they raced for fun or to escape confiscation of illicit cargo and jail, always had considered themselves to be among the world's best drivers. Now, Yankee urbanites who judged such things on factors other than the ability to handle a car over treacherous mountain roads were tending to agree.

That patch of land in suburban Daytona Beach has since become the second most famous racecourse in the nation, next to Indianapolis. Officials at the Daytona 500 never release attendance figures, but estimates are that between 100,000 and 130,000 fans jam the speedway each February to see its premier race.

ondary to the use of drugs or alcohol. Most of the people who travel in cars and campers from the Carolinas, Tennessee, Virginia, Alabama, Georgia and other states don't come to Daytona just to party.

The shrewd "D"-shaped design of the speedway enables the drivers to reach great speeds down the long, back straightaway and through the steeply banked tri-oval that allows them to negotiate curves without slowing down. It also makes the racecourse more compact. Race cars rarely disappear completely from the view of spectators who want to watch every maneuver. From everywhere but ground level in the infield, the cars can be seen through all four turns, down the tri-oval

Unlike Indianapolis fans, those here are hard-core speed voyeurs. They come to cheer the most popular stars. Hardly a soul goes out of the gates at the end of the race without knowing who has won and without being able to describe in detail the race's most dramatic moments.

The crowd packs the infield, but there is no area like Indianapolis' infamous "snakepit" where the action on the race course is sec-

Left and **above**, it's the pits – by day and night – as skilled mechanics work fast to keep their sensitive charges tuned during the 12 grueling hours of Sebring.

that curves slightly in front of the main grandstand, and down the backstretch.

Of drafts, slingshots and fistfights: Junior Johnson, whose moonshining past was chronicled in a movie called *The Last Great American Hero*, is a successful car owner now. But he was still a champion driver in the early 1960s when he discovered that two cars in tandem could circle the racecourse much faster than one traveling alone.

Johnson is a slow-talking North Carolinian who once described his exit from a race by simply saying "blowed a tar." He is also a mechanical genius who will go down in stock car lore for discovering "drafting" at

Daytona – a technique now commonplace at any high-speed track.

When one car gets behind another, the lead car cuts down wind resistance, and the trailing car uses this absence of friction to accelerate beyond its normal speed. "Drafts" at Daytona and similar tracks may include up to 20 cars – many which otherwise would be well off the pace.

This drafting theory spawned the "slingshot," a force which enables a driver to leave his vacuum and pass the lead car with a sudden burst of power. Lee Petty and Johnny Beauchamp, without knowing it, played with that "slingshot" on that dead-heat day in 1959.

ing out of the fourth turn and into the tri-oval, they bump again. Both cars go into an incredible series of spins.

It looks as if Petty might skid across the finish line and become the first man ever to win the Daytona 500 sideways. But his car stops short. Meanwhile, Pearson engages his clutch to keep his engine running while the car is spinning. He pokes down the grassy area next to the pit row and wobbles across the finish line at the school-zone speed of about 15mph.

• 1979 – On the last lap, victory awaits Cale Yarborough or Donnie Allison. They are far in front. But neither finishes. Yarborough tries to pass going into the third

The "stock car finish": Those early drivers also pioneered the "stock car finish." Only in stock cars can so many drivers race within inches of each other, either side-by-side or back-to-front. In an open-wheel racer like those at Indy, such crowding would cause a huge disaster.

Nothing has matched that first year photo finish, but subsequent Daytona 500s have had their moments. Consider these:

• 1976 – Richard Petty is in a duel similar to that waged by his father 17 years earlier. The competition, again, is Pearson, and the two enter the last lap nose-to-tail. Between the third and fourth turns, they bump. Com-

turn. Allison runs him into the grass. The two cars collide and self-destruct.

Halfway down the backstretch, Richard Petty sees the yellow caution lights suddenly flash on the track, but in his earpiece hears a radio message from his pit crew – "Go, go, go!" – and he easily outruns four-time Indianapolis 500 winner A.J. Foyt to win the sixth of his Daytona 500 championships.

As Petty takes his slowdown lap and goes through the third turn again, he sees a strange sight. "Donnie was out of his car and Cale was headed thataway," he said later. The pair traded the track for their fists. But Yarborough became outnumbered when Donnie's brother

Bobby showed up. While watching films of that last lap in the press box later, Petty said, "The heck with this, I want to see the fight."

Today's stock car drivers are judged by what they do at Daytona. "This is the race to win," said Petty. "This is the one everybody shoots for."

Indeed, Daytona is the end of racing's greasy rainbow for an aspiring stock car driver. As many as 80 drivers often enter the Daytona 500. Half never make the 40-car starting lineup determined by two 125-mile qualifying races. Most who do are never heard from again because of the forbidding expense and challenge of going against the nation's premier stock car drivers. But, ultimately, the stars spring from obscure tracks in Hialeah, Tampa, Jacksonville, Bradenton, Fort Myers and Pensacola.

More speed, on land and sea: For all its stock car glory, Daytona is also famous for international racing. Snaking through that renowned oval track is a road course that each February brings together big names in worldwide racing. Stars such as Brian Redman, Jacky Ickx and Mario Andretti gather for the 24 Hours of Daytona.

The 24 Hours, the only round-the-clock race in North America, is a test of driving skill and endurance. Only the 24 Hours of Le Mans is better known on the endurance circuit. There's also sports car racing in July and November at Daytona, and the nation's biggest motorcycle road race which is held in early March.

Not long after the participants in the 24 Hours leave Florida, they return for the famous 12 Hours of Sebring in mid-March. In the days of racing prototypes, when red Ferraris and blue Porsches dueled for the manufacturers' points championship, Sebring was unsurpassed in popularity.

Even though the prototypes are gone, Sebring remains a major stop for sports car drivers after the world endurance points championship, a grueling test for man and machine. The course is laid out in steamy Central Florida over the old Sebring Airport runways and taxiways. In some places, the concrete is crumbled so badly that racing can be treacherous.

Left, Gators snap in the stretch as Hawaiians punch at their tail at Daytona. **Right**, a hydroplane spits saltwater as it speeds past Miami.

The drivers relish the rugged conditions. "If the course was in real good shape, then it wouldn't be Sebring," said one. "That's what makes this race so unique and makes winning it so much more enjoyable."

For the 35,000 or so spectators who converge on this small Florida town each March, the 12 Hours is a good excuse to throw a party. The land surrounding the course turns into a huge campground the Friday eve of the race. During the competition it looks like a giant cook-out. Fans often get rowdy in some sections of the infield as drugs and alcohol take effect.

Cigarettes and hydroplanes: The other speed sport popular and particularly suited to wa-

tery Florida is boat racing. Every kind of craft from speed boats to cigarette boats to hydroplanes churn through its bays, lakes, rivers and seas in quest of aquatic supremacy.

The sport's focal point is Miami Marine Stadium on the Rickenbacker Causeway spanning Biscayne Bay. Limited inboards, outboards and offshore power-boats also ply Miami's waters in major events each year.

The limited drivers buzz around St Petersburg's Lake Maggiore every February on a course considered to be one of the sport's fastest. Speed records fall frequently. Smaller races are run in Stuart and Cocoa and on Lake Alfred.

The players: It is a mecca for the "player," this peninsula dotted with 32 establishments – race tracks and frontons – engaged in the business of pari-mutuel gambling. The games and the people attracted to them vary as radically as the regions of the state in which they flourish. Nineteen greyhound tracks and nine jai-alai frontons operate, from Pensacola to Key West. Thoroughbred racing, centered in the Miami area, is conducted virtually year-round at four locations. Harness racing thrives here during the winter

his profession or status in life away from the track, approaches his specialty with unbending dedication. Few places rival Florida for providing sport in unmatched surroundings. Ask a dedicated player his concept of the ideal environment in which to gamble and he will probably say Florida in winter time. These are people generally a step out of synch with the mainstream, the more casual patrons of pari-mutuel establishments.

This second type comprises the bulk of fans – vacationers or residents betting more

months, quarter horse racing during the summer. Combined, they attract more than 16 million people in an average year who wager about $1.6 billion. In addition to regular performances at all establishments that pour $104 million into state coffers, additional dates benefit a cornucopia of charitable causes, scholarship funds and cultural movements throughout Florida. More than $600,000 a year is donated to the State Board of Regents Scholarship Fund and almost $2 million to the State School Fund.

Generally, pari-mutuel sports attract two types of fans with distinctly dissimilar approaches. The serious player, no matter what

for fun than for profit while having lunch or dinner and drinks in a plush clubhouse dining room, sunning themselves on a lawn, or off in a corner handicapping the next event on the program.

The horses: Thoroughbred racing dominates the pari-mutuel industry in Florida. It is, after all, known throughout the world as the "Sport of Kings." It has tradition, glamor, aura and heroes – equine and human.

Miami has been a winter mecca for the nation's best horses and horsemen for more than a half-century. The area blossomed as a training and racing center with the establishment of Hialeah Park. In its "Golden

Age," Hialeah was also the winter capital of the nation's socially elite. Droves of splendidly dressed Kennedys, Vanderbilts, Whitneys and others who wintered in Palm Beach arrived daily by train. Sports and entertainment figures, statesmen and European aristocracy joined the Palm Beach socialites in the Hialeah clubhouse, where they watched competition among the finest thoroughbred horses in the world. It was a gentle, idyllic time. Hialeah Park, possibly the most breathtaking racecourse in North America, became the place to be and be seen. It became as much an institution as a race track.

Those days still have a strange, ghostly hold over the track. If anything, the grounds

pines; its classic Mediterranean architecture and its expansive, lushly landscaped grounds – draws thousands of tourists even when there is no racing. The management maintains an aviary and aquarium on the grounds. During the racing season, breakfast is served at track-side while thoroughbreds are put through their morning work routine. There may be no better way for one who loves horses to spend a winter morning in Florida.

Hialeah remains the Grande Dame of thoroughbred racing in Florida, unique in the respect that she may be history's only racetrack to have acquired gender, since she is usually referred to in feminine terms. But she is no longer dominant. She has recently faced

have gained increased beauty with maturity. The graceful architecture and walking ring were patterned after Longchamps, the most stately of French race courses. Like a refined, dignified European lady, the lines of age have chiseled a certain regal distinction into her image.

Today, the magnificence of Hialeah – its flamingos, the largest domestic flock in the world; towering royal palms and delicate coconut palms; gently swaying Australian

Left, the famous finish line at Miami's renowned racetrack. **Above**, speeding steeds streak into a tight stretch run during a Florida night race.

the threat of closing and has passed the limelight on to Gulfstream Park.

Gulfstream is north of Miami Beach, minutes from the Atlantic and amidst cliffs of snow-white, high-rise condominium complexes. The track is beautifully appointed, not in the graceful European style of Hialeah, but in a more modern, comfortable and pleasing orchid-dominated decor all its own.

Together, Gulfstream and Hialeah compose the proving grounds for the best 3-year-old thoroughbreds in the nation, those bound later in the spring for the Kentucky Derby, Preakness and Belmont Stakes – racing's Triple Crown sweepstakes.

The Florida Derby at Gulfstream and the Flamingo Stakes at Hialeah bring promising young horses into major competition in preparation for the Kentucky Derby. Events leading up to those races, Hialeah's Bahamas Stakes and Gulfstream's Fountain of Youth Stakes, are also regarded nationally as important events. In a routine winter season every important thoroughbred in training east of the Mississippi is likely to be stabled at Hialeah or Gulfstream or shipped to one or the other to race from one of the many nearby training centers.

Hialeah and Gulfstream operate on 100 afternoons each year. The remainder of the season occurs at Calder Race Course in North Downs began to assert itself. Steinbrenner established the Tampa Bay Derby in 1981 as another race for Kentucky Derby aspirants.

South Florida is also the focal point of the nation's harness racing between October and April. The opening of Pompano Park in Pompano Beach about 20 years ago served as the catalyst for what was to become an annual southern migration of name harness horsemen to Florida. Virtually all of the sport's superstars ship their stables to Pompano for winter racing. They also prepare young horses being developed for the next summer's stakes races in the north.

Pompano is the only harness track in the world where fans have the opportunity to

Miami, a more utilitarian track that has become the backbone of the thoroughbred racing in the state since it opened in 1980.

Calder is weatherproof, a necessity in Florida's rainy summer season. Its sand-covered tartan racing surface remains fast no matter how much water falls on it.

Only one other track in the state is the scene of thoroughbred racing. Tampa Bay Downs, known until 1980 as Florida Downs, has long lived in the shadow of its better known neighbors to the south. But under the leadership of New York Yankees owner George Steinbrenner, who acquired controller interest in the track at Oldsmar, Tampa Bay watch famous jockeys such as Stanley Dancer, Billy Haughton and Del Insko – all members of the sport's Hall of Fame.

When harness horsemen move to northern racetracks for the summer season, Pompano Park changes. The atmosphere becomes decidedly Western. The sport is quarter horse racing. Quarter horse racing is native to the West, most notably Southern California. Pompano's is the the only pari-mutuel race meeting in the Eastern United States. The track draws stables from Texas, Oklahoma, Louisiana and Western locales as well as a large population of Florida-bred horses. Quarter horses run faster even than thoroughbreds over a short stretch in an equine version of drag racing. The season lasts from June to early August.

The dogs: Men have been racing horses throughout history. The same is true of greyhounds. Archaeologists claim the breed was domesticated more than 7,000 years ago and records date the earliest greyhound races to 2500 BC. Cleopatra fancied greyhounds, a trait she shared with most Egyptian royalty. In England, coursing reached its greatest popularity during the reign of Queen Elizabeth I, who inspired the slogan "Sport of Queens."

The modern version of greyhound racing is believed to have evolved from a coursing

Emeryville, California, in 1919. Tracks soon opened at Tulsa, Oklahoma; East St Louis and Chicago, Illinois; Erlanger, Kentucky; Hialeah and St Petersburg, Florida.

The Hialeah track closed long ago. But St Petersburg's Derby Lane is still one of the most attractive facilities of its kind. Greyhound racing is now prominent everywhere in Florida. Annual paid attendance statewide approaches 8 million people (who wager almost $953 million).

Derby Lane remains the largest Florida operation, but the Miami area tracks – Hollywood Greyhound Track, Biscayne Kennel Club and the Flagler Kennel Club – are close behind. At the opposite end of the spectrum,

meet held in 1904 near Hot Springs, North Dakota. Owen Patrick Smith of the Hot Springs Chamber of Commerce was so smitten by the sport that he left his job as an engineer to promote greyhound meetings. In search of a method to alleviate pressure from humane groups which opposed the use of live hares in coursing, Smith developed the artificial lure still in use today. Smith demonstrated his imitation rabbit successfully at

Left, "Greyhounds on parade" in an old postcard look at a Miami track. <u>Above</u>, modern hounds chase "Rusty" the mechanical rabbit around and around the oval.

the track at Key West averages only about 534 fans per performance.

Florida's greyhound racing industry is without peer. The state is, by far, the most important greyhound area in the nation if for no reason other than sheer volume. All major metropolitan areas here have at least one track nearby and the sport even flourishes in tiny resort areas like Bonita Springs, near Fort Myers and Monticello, site of the Jefferson County Kennel Club. The Hollywood International Classic, considered the sport's version of the Super Bowl, is held each year in March at the height of the South Florida tourist season.

Since greyhounds do not run at the crack of a whip from a jockey, an alternative method is used to motivate them to sprint around the track to the cheers of bettors. Owen Smith's artificial rabbit lure, affectionately called "Rusty," rides on a rail along the inside of greyhound tracks. A race begins when the lure whips past the starting gate as an official calls, "He-e-e-re comes Rusty!" The paddocks open and the hounds sprint after their mechanical quarry. Unfortunately, it's the genuine rabbit smell of Rusty that sends the dogs into their running frenzy. To the dismay of fans and humane society officials, trainers occasionally have been discovered using live rabbits to drill their dogs.

nomenon refined through the centuries at religious festivals in the Basque provinces of Spain and France. The game remains an important aspect of Basque life in Europe, but is now played in seven nations and in the Portuguese territory of Macau.

Florida dominates the jai-alai industry in the US, although frontons also operate in Connecticut and Las Vegas. There are nine frontons here – the largest in Miami, the second largest in Dania, a suburb of Fort Lauderdale. But jai-alai also flourishes in smaller communities like Ocala, Fort Pierce and Volusia.

Jai-alai is tremendously popular with occasional visitors to Florida, since the game is

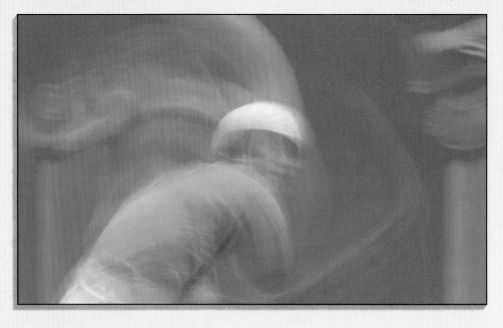

The pelotari: As if three breeds of race horses and one of dogs did not present sufficient opportunities to gamble, Florida is also one of the few states in the nation where you can wager on human beings – provided they are playing the ancient Basque game called jai-alai, which means joyous festival.

The wagering concepts common to other pari-mutuel sports hold for jai-alai. Win, place, show, quiniela, perfecta, trifecta – all apply to these helmeted men with baskets attached to their hands who play a huge version of handball on an oversize court. The game originated as simple handball and evolved into this inflated, super-fast phe-

rarely played in their home cities. But a crash course in the game's language helps. Jai-alai's vernacular is a blend of Spanish and Basque. The player is a *pelotari*; the ball, virgin rubber layered with nylon thread and covered with two layers of goatskin, is called a *pelota*. The basket-like device used to catch the speeding *pelota* is the *cesta*. It is secured to the wrist by a string known as a *cinta*. Each *pelotari* wears a red sash as part of the uniform called a *faja* and a helmet, the *casco*.

Above, a *pelotari* unwinds in Miami. **Right**, detail from an Ocala Jai-Alai billboard by the side of the highway.

An appalling, unearthly report followed instantly, such as can be compared to nothing whatever, not even to the roar of thunder or the blast of volcanic explosions! No words can convey the slightest idea of the terrific sound! An immense spout of fire shot up from the bowels of the earth as from a crater...

At the moment when that pyramid of fire rose to a prodigious height into the air the glare of the flame lit up the whole of Florida; and for a moment day superseded night over a vast expanse of the country. This immense canopy of fire was perceived at a distance of 100 miles out at sea and more than one ship's captain entered in his log the appearance of this gigantic meteor.

The discharge of the Columbiad *was accompanied by an earthquake. Florida was shaken to its very depths.*

> —Jules Verne in *From the Earth to the Moon*, 1863.

Thus did visionary author Jules Verne describe the launch of a mid-19th century space shuttle. With uncanny prescience, he named today's spacecraft and identified its launch site more than a century before the actual event occurred. Indeed, Verne's spirit may well have been at the Kennedy Space Center on April 12, 1981, almost 118 years after his vivid launch.

That morning, a blast of light burned the eyes, as if a photographer had just snapped your picture with a flash gun. The *Columbia's* flash outshone the rising sun. Then, smoke bathed the horizon. Suddenly, incredibly, an enormous flying machine eased up out of its self-made cloud, hesitated, and accelerated atop a tail of angelic white smoke.

It was then you heard the rumble – faint at first, but rapidly building to a solid roar that astonished Florida's flatlands with its tremble and rippled through nearby human bodies. It turned into a staccato jackhammer beat as a vapor column vanished above. The sound finally faded away, but the quickened beat of

hearts left earthlings in a state of exhilaration long after the *Columbia* ripped itself from the earth's gravity. Florida was indeed "shaken to its very depths."

Seeing, hearing and feeling the launch of a vehicle bound for the future from the Kennedy Space Center is the highlight of a trip to Florida for many people. Even memories of a hot pink sun melting into the Gulf of Mexico at dusk recede when the countdown reaches "t minus one second."

Unlike many of Florida's fanciful attrac-

tions, which bend nature and technology into mediums aimed at making people believe they are somewhere they aren't, the Kennedy Space Center is real. It is functioning technology in the midst of a natural wonderland, transporting human beings into the vacuums of a place far more mysterious than the plastic paradise of Walt Disney World or the manicured veldts of Busch Garden's Dark Continent.

Of course, seating aboard its space shuttles is still limited to trained astronauts and scientists. But viewing the start of a voyage into space, and wandering among the "ancient" rocket graveyards of Cape Canaveral,

Preceding pages: the space shuttle poised on its pad. **Left**, the first shuttle launch. **Right**, Navy Capt. Robert Crippen, commander of two shuttle flights, floats in space.

at least propels one's brain waves into the ozone, if nothing else.

Sharing a subtropical wilderness: The Space Center sprawls across the ecological Eden of the Merritt Island National Wildlife Refuge and Canaveral National Seashore, 220 square miles of primitive swamp, savanna, hammock, marsh and windswept beaches. Flocks of egrets, ibis, herons and ducks appear unruffled about sharing this kingdom with monstrous birds that occasionally rocket past them with deafening roars. (According to one study, some of the local birds have indeed lost their hearing.) More than 280 species of avifauna have been observed in the refuge, including endangered or threat-

the refuge offers the Oak Hammock hiking trail. There are also two wildlife driving tours, one along Max Hoeck Creek and the other along Black Point.

Only about 7 percent of the 140,000 acres owned by the National Aeronautics and Space Administration (NASA) has sprouted launch pads, industrial complexes, base-support facilities and roads. Most of the miles of grassy scrub, palmetto and brackish waters remain much as they must have looked when Europeans first set foot in the New World.

"We protect not only the wildlife but the habitats it needs to survive. We have demonstrated that high technology, natural landscapes and wildlife can co-exist success-

ened marvels like the Southern bald eagle, the brown pelican and the rare Arctic peregrine falcon.

Other inhabitants include about 200 affectionate but imperiled West Indian manatees or "sea cows" and about 5,000 alligators, many of which can be seen lolling on the banks of canals that run along the main roads of the Space Center. Guides warn against wearing white tennis shoes while venturing near bodies of water because the local gators have become addicted to tourist-tossed treats, particularly marshmallows. Colored footwear is suggested for those wishing to take in a little flora and fauna with their technology:

fully," says Space Center Director Richard G. Smith.

It is fitting that America's first explorers – men who walked on lands that would become the continental United States – first stepped off their ships not far from this cape, which has served as the port of embarkation for ships carrying the first explorers to walk on the moon.

Ponce de León first sighted the sandy cape that juts into the Atlantic Ocean in 1513 and named it *Corrientes*, a Spanish reference to its turbulent currents. The name did not last. A word used by the Ais Indians who peopled the wilderness, persevered instead. *Canave-*

ral, meaning canebearer, is thought to have appeared on maps of the cape after 1520, following a battle in which a slave-ship captain named Francisco Gordillo lost many of his men to laser-sharp Ais arrows made from canes or reeds. Except for a brief identity crisis in the 1960s when it became Cape Kennedy, it has been Canaveral ever since.

It has also remained wilderness through most of its existence. Few, with the exception of the Ais Indians, have braved its mosquito-infested brush. The Ais left behind their burial mounds and shell middens, which today stand side-by-side with the bunkers and block-houses of the space program.

Breakfast in Florida, dinner on the moon:

created NASA nine months later. On May 5, 1961, it put the first American, Alan Shepard, into space in a Mercury capsule atop a Redstone rocket.

NASA originally established its offices and laboratories on the cape itself, but in 1964 shifted most operations west across the Banana River to Merritt Island. The two-man Gemini missions followed. Scientists, engineers, technicians – and their money – flooding in. Contractors followed, putting up housing developments faster than NASA could send up rockets.Employment peaked at about 26,000 in 1968.

By then, NASA was shooting three men into space at a crack as part of its Apollo

Missiles began flights to the heavens from Cape Canaveral about 1947. The War Department chose the site that year because it provided miles of uninhabited buffer zone to catch stray projectiles, as well as offshore islands for tracking stations. The first satellite launched by the United States, *Explorer I*, left Cape Canaveral on January 31, 1958, in a belated attempt to match the feat of the Soviet Union's *Sputnik*. The government

program. That culminated in Neil Armstrong's historic football on the Moon on July 20, 1969. The kind of monstrous Saturn V rocket that took man to the Moon lies on display in front of the Vehicle Assembly Building (VAB).

Enter Kennedy Space Center's Spaceport USA from State Road 405, which runs into NASA Parkway. Whether you enter here through Gate 3, or take State Road 3 from the Cocoa Beach area through Gate 2, just follow the signs to Spaceport USA. A row of rockets pointing starward identifies the Visitors' Center on the south side of the parkway. Facilities include a Gallery of Space Flight

Left, from footsteps in Florida sand to imprints in moondust: astronaut James B. Irwin of *Apollo 15* salutes in 1971. **Above**, the lunar module *Intrepid* during a 1969 mission by *Apollo 12*.

which traces the chronology of the space program's achievements.

Spaceport USA includes a huge IMAX movie. "The Dream Is Alive," shown on a 5½ story-high screen. There's a nominal charge for the film, and another for a guided tour.

A tour of the launch site: Drivers are not permitted to tour the grounds of Kennedy Space Center unescorted. The best way to see the Saturn, the VAB and other sites is aboard one of the inexpensive, NASA-sanctioned bus tours.

The boarding station for these buses, which take you on a 2-hour tour of the premises, is here at Spaceport USA. Enthusiastic guides provide a lively, running commentary, an-

Apollo Moon missions, Skylabs and the space shuttles left the earth; and past the rusting remnants of abandoned complexes. Guides take visitors through the Astronaut Training Building, where a recreated Launch Control Center, and the Lunar Excursion Model (LEM) used for the Apollo XI moon mission, are on display.

The space program reborn: With the end of the Apollo program in the mid-'70s, NASA's activities at Kennedy Space Center wound down. Rows of "astro-bars" closed as NASA laid off aerospace workers, who left Florida and took their severance checks with them. Interest in the space program flagged.

All that changed dramatically, probably

swering questions which range from how astronauts use the bathroom to how they eat.

Barring schedule changes because of launches or other activity, the buses usually stop at the imposing Vehicle Assembly Building. At 525 feet tall, 716 feet long and 588 feet wide, the VAB is one of the world's largest buildings with a total volume of 129.5 million cubic feet. The entire Empire State Building in New York, if chopped into sections, could be stored inside the VAB.

The buses take you past the monstrous crawler-transporter that carries spaceships to the launch pads at a snail's speed. They continue by Complex 39, from which the

permanently, on April 12, 1981. Early that morning, more than a million people lined the banks of the Indian and Banana rivers to experience the beginning of a new era in space – the launch of the space shuttle *Columbia*. In its maiden voyage, *Columbia* became the first vehicle to be shot into orbit on the spine of a rocket and return to earth under its own power by landing like an airplane. The space-craft was flown from its landing site in California back to Florida aboard a Boeing 747, and it may make more than 100 similar flights.

More than 5,000 newsmen from around the world gathered to witness that momentous launch. Even veteran launch-goers admitted the shuttle lift-off was the most spectacular and satisfying they had ever observed. The whir of the shutters of thousands of cameras and the whoops of spectators were smothered by the earthquaking sound of that launch, which has reverberated throughout Florida's Space Coast. Employment at Kennedy has steadied at 13,000. The astronauts are back, and with them legions of new space fans.

Since the first historic mission, NASA's ambitious space shuttle program has successfully carried out numerous tests and experiments with each successive launch. *Columbia* flew four additional missions. It was

that the Spaceport USA expects to host more than 3 million visitors a year, which could make it second only to Walt Disney World among the state's attractions.

Viewing space-age drama: Information about shuttle launches is available by calling 1-800-432-2153 after you get to Florida. Or write NASA well in advance of a scheduled launch and ask for a car pass. This will get you through the gate on a launch day and allow you to park your car and carcass along the Indian River only about 5 miles from the pad. A good set of binoculars or a camera with a 500- or 1,000-mm telephoto lens can aid in viewing, although the naked eye will provide an equally inspiring sight.

followed by *Challenger* which carried the first women astronaut, Sally K. Ride, into space during the seventh shuttle flight. It was the first shuttle to lift-off and land at Kennedy Space Center, making it the site of the world's first operational spaceport.

The routine flights should make it easy for visitors to plan a trip around a shuttle mission. Interest has already grown so rapidly

Left, Saturn and her rings as seen by *Voyager 1* in its 1980 flight past the planet. **Above**, Mother Earth, swaddled in clouds, as seen by the awestruck and moonbound crewmembers inside *Apollo 10*.

Failing those options, you can park anywhere outside the Space Center where you see cars and recreational vehicles gathering for a glimpse of a launch. There are choice spots along US Highway 1 in Titusville and along State Road 402 north of Complex 39. If you approach the area from Orlando, take the Bee-Line Expressway until it turns into the Bennett Causeway, another choice viewing spot. Jetty Park, at the end of the causeway near Cape Canaveral city, and beaches north to Ponce's Inlet, afford a view of the rising rockets.

Kennedy Space Center has made Florida the closest place to the stars – on earth.

TRAVEL TIPS

Getting There

314 By Air
314 By Sea
315 By Rail
315 By Road

Travel Essentials

315 Passports & Visas
315 Money Matters
315 Health
316 Emergency Numbers
316 What to Wear
316 Customs

Getting Acquainted

317 Time Zones
317 Climate
320 Holidays
320 Tipping

Communications

321 Media
321 Postal Services
321 Telegrams & Telex
321 Telephone

Getting Around

321 Driving in Florida
322 Public Transport
322 Private Transport
322 Hitchhiking

Where to Stay

322 Accommodation
329 Camping

Food Digest

330 What to Eat

Things to Do

331 Tours & Attractions
336 National Forests
336 National Parks &
     Preserves
337 National Seashores
337 Fairs & Livestock
     Shows
338 A Birdwatcher's Extra

Culture Plus

339 Music & Theater
340 Arts & Crafts Shows
342 Special Events

Shopping

348 What to Buy
348 Speciality Shopping

Sports

349 Fishing
350 Hunting
350 Golf Tournaments
351 Tennis
351 Water Sports
351 Racing
352 Football
353 Running
353 Rodeo
354 Pari-Mutuels
354 Miscellaneous Events

Further Reading

355 Historical/Political/
     Cultural
358 Guides, References,
     Special Interest
360 Photographic
360 The Space Program &
     Cape Canaveral
361 Fiction & Writers of
     Fiction
361 Music

Useful Addresses

362 Airlines
362 Chambers of Com-
     merce
366 Daily Newspapers

368 Art/Photo Credits

369 Index

GETTING THERE

BY AIR

Most major US carriers serve Florida, but since deregulation of the airways and the air traffic controllers' strike, routes and schedules have been in a constant state of flux. Visitors, therefore, are advised to consult a travel agent or their favorite airline before choosing a flight. A variety of discount fares and "package deals" which can significantly cut round-trip rates to and from Florida are also available.

Generally, however, domestic carriers with regular commuter services to **Miami International Airport** are American, Pan Am, United, Continental, TWA, Delta, Northwest, Braniff, Piedmont and Western.

US Air, American, Continental, Delta, Pan Am, Northwest, Piedmont, TWA and United serve **Tampa International Airport**.

Northwest, US Air, Continental, Delta, American, Pan Am, Ozark, TWA and United fly to **Orlando International Airport**.

Fort Lauderdale-Hollywood is served by Continental, United, TWA, Delta, Pan Am, Northwest, Ozark and Western.

Delta and Pan Am are the two airlines which have regular flights to Jacksonville.

In addition, many international airline companies serve Florida; most land at Miami International Airport. They include Air Panama, Cayman Airways, Lacsa, Iberia, Aeroperu, Lan Chile, Air France, British Airways, KLM-Royal Dutch Airlines, Air Jamaica, BWIA, Dominica, Mexico, Aerolines Argentinas and Air Canada. Air Canada also flies to Tampa International and Orlando airports. Air Canada, CP Air, Eastern Provincial, Nordair and Western offer connecting flights, usually through Montreal, to major destinations in Florida. Jacksonville has direct routes to Spain and from London and Orlando has direct service to Belgium.

Florida is a good jumping-off point for direct flights to many exotic destinations. Most Caribbean ports can be reached on short, direct flights from Miami International. You will also find occasional non-stop service to foreign destinations such as Mexico City, Acapulco, Rio de Janeiro, Buenos Aires, Paris and Amsterdam.

Piedmont is the major intra-Florida carrier, although a number of smaller air commuter, charter and taxi lines serve out-lying communities. They come and go, so it's wise to check with a nearby travel bureau. Also, major carriers frequently serve smaller cities with competitive fares.

Florida has a total of 32 airports serving commuters and general aviation. Tampa International, opened in 1971 and expanded in 1982, has been rated the best airport in the United States by the 82,000-member Airline Passengers Association. However, the new Orlando Jetport may steal some of Tampa's luster. Long walks to terminals and slow moving lines at customs' checkpoints have marred Miami International's image.

BY SEA

CRUISE SHIP

You can travel or leave Florida by cruise ship. You can also book one of many ships while in the state for cruises to a variety of exotic ports, particularly South American and Caribbean destinations.

There are seven major cruise ship ports in Florida, with **Miami** and **Port Everglades** leading with the most sailings. Minor ports include **St Petersburg**, **Madeira Beach**, **Treasure Island** and **Port Manatee**. The packages vary tremendously, with cruises that can last from one day to more than two weeks, and cruise-ship sizes also varying, as well as destination ports of call.

The best suggestion is to check with your local tourist agencies or cruise agents for the various choices available to you, for the places you plan on visiting in Florida. All cruise ports offer free parking facilities for those who are driving to their cruise departures, and some offer van or mini-bus accommodations from nearby hotels.

Although Florida offers year-round cruise departures into either the Atlantic, Caribbean or Gulf of Mexico, there are also seasonal – warm weather – cruises. Again, for a complete view of choices, check with a travel agency or look at the travel ads in any Sunday newspaper.

Innumerable cruise operators in most major coastal cities offer short strips and dinner cruises on Florida's waterways and rivers. Check local literature for schedules and rates.

YACHT

Finally, you can come to Florida or cruise around it in your own vessel. Most marinas offer slips and facilities for waterway transients. The **Intracoastal Waterway** parallels the east and west coasts of the state. Write to the Dept of Natural Resources, Crown Bldg, Tallahassee 32304, for a copy of *Florida Boating*.

BY RAIL

Amtrak offers slow, but leisurely, service to Florida from America's Midwest, Northeast and South – and connecting service from points west – to many Florida cities. Amtrak stations are located at Jacksonville, Kissimmee, Lakeland, Ocala, Orlando, Sanford, Sebring, Winter Haven, Winter Park, Tampa, Delray Beach, Deerfield Beach, Fort Lauderdale, Hollywood, Miami and West Palm Beach. For those who want to take their car along, Amtrak offers Auto Train ferry-type service from Lorton, Virginia (near Washington, DC), to Sanford, near Orlando. For information on all rail service to Florida, call Amtrak's toll-free number: 1-800-872-7245.

BY ROAD

Greyhound provides service to Florida and throughout the state. (For information contact individual city Greyhound telephone listings.) Smaller operators with Florida routes include North Star Lines, Gulf Transportation Co., ABC Coach Lines, Jefferson Lines, Inc., Orange Belt Stages, Southeastern Stages, Bluebird, Iowa Coaches, Inc., and Illini-Swallow Lines Inc.

Gray Line offers a variety of sightseeing tours which are within Florida, while Greyhound, Trailways and Gulf Coast Motor Lines also have special travel services between Florida cities.

Many bus terminals, however, tend to be in "problem areas" of town, so exercise caution when traveling to and from stations and when venturing from the terminal on solitary walks.

Travel Essentials

PASSPORTS & VISAS

For foreign visitors to Florida, a passport, a passport-size photograph, a visitor's visa, evidence that you intend to leave the United States after your visit is over, and (depending upon your country of origin) an international vaccination certificate will help smooth your entry into the United States and Florida at government customs booths. Canadian citizens and British subjects residing in Canada and Bermuda are normally exempted from these requirements when arriving from countries in the Western Hemisphere. Citizens of Mexico bearing Form 1-136 and coming from Canada or Mexico are also normally

exempted from passport and visa requirements.

Obtain visas by mail, or by personal application at the US Embassy or consulate nearest your home. Evidence of intent to leave the United States may be in the form of a return ticket or any other documentation satisfactory to the embassy or consulate issuing the visa.

Vaccination certificate requirements vary, but proof of immunization against smallpox or cholera may be necessary.

MONEY MATTERS

Visitors to Florida may encounter problems exchanging foreign currency; the use of American dollar traveler's checks is advised. An increasing number of statewide banking corporations and community banks in Florida, including the Barnett, Southeast and Sun Bank chains, offer foreign exchange services, but this practice is not universal. Banks generally close on Saturday afternoons and Sundays. The increase in the number of foreign visitors has led some department store chains to offer foreign-currency exchange services.

HEALTH

SUNBURN

An early overdose of sun can ruin, in a few short hours, a vacation that involved months of planning and saving. One of the most common sights in Florida is that of the over-baked tourist, red as a beet, painfully trying to sit or walk without rubbing against anything. If you are set on getting a suntan, do so gradually. Begin with a sunscreen, containing PABA and marked with its numerical level of safeguard, and work up to less protective tanning lotions. The glare from Florida's azure seas and white sands increases the sun's intensity. Don't neglect to apply sunscreen on overcast days; the sun's ultraviolet rays still penetrate the cloud cover and the shade can lull you into staying outside too long.

INSECTS

People aren't the only living creatures attracted to sun and sand. Insects also prefer Florida's climate. Be prepared to itch, scratch, burn and curse while trying to swat or stomp on a variety of pests.

Entomologists call them bibinoid flies, but to Floridians they are simply known as **love bugs** – because you will usually find them "flying united" right into your hair, face or car's windshield.

Love bugs don't bite. They are too busy mating. But they can cause trouble during their May and September appearances in various parts of the state. In moist or wooded hammock areas, black clouds of love bugs occasionally hang over interstates and highways, slowing down traffic as they clog radiators and splatter windshields.

Florida is even more infamous for its swarms of **mosquitoes** that can take the joy out of watching summer sunsets. Most big cities have effective mosquito control programs that have effectively curtailed the pest's activities. But pack a bottle of Cutter's or even army-issue insect repellent when venturing into backwoods areas like the Everglades.

You should also tread carefully in the outdoors, particularly when barefoot. Grassy fields are prime locations for mounds of **fire ants**. These tiny red ants inflict a painful, burning sting and leave a reddish weal that turns into a chickenpox-like blister. The blister can become infected if scratched. Some persons are allergic to the sting of a fire ant, and can suffer chest constriction, wheezing, nausea or dizziness that requires prompt medical attention.

Visitors new to tropical or subtropical regions may be startled during their first confrontation with the local **cockroaches**. Often called palmetto bugs, they grow to sizes unheard of in colder climates, usually resembling miniature armored patrol cars as they dart under the carpet or disappear into cracks in the wall. They will eat book bindings, clothing, paper, garbage and virtually anything else, but they steer clear of people. Pest control services and regular house cleaning will aid in control, but rarely eradicate roaches.

Sand flies, appropriately called "no-see-ums" by the locals, are another nemesis of the sunset beachgoers. They are what you feel – but can't see – gnawing at your legs as you sink your toes into the sand. Insect repellent can help.

RED TIDE

This form of "sea sickness" is caused by a microscopic organism called *gymnodinium brevis* (or "Jim Brevis"), always present in Gulf Coast waters in small quantities. It becomes deadly to fish and other marine life when its numbers multiply suddenly, for reasons still unknown to scientists even today. The coastal waters turn a brownish red color and thousands of dead fish wash ashore. After a few hours in the hot sun, they make beaches unbearable with their foul odor.

EMERGENCY PHONE NUMBERS

Telephone numbers for police, fire and ambulance in Florida are as numerous as the numbers of cities. The best policy in case of emergency is to dial the operator "0," state the nature of the emergency and clearly give your name and address. Better yet, telephone books in each city always list emergency numbers on a detachable yellow page near the front. An increasing number of Florida emergency numbers have begun using "911" as an all-purpose emergency number for fire and police and rescue ambulances.

WHAT TO WEAR

Light-colored, lightweight clothing is the norm in Florida. Most attractions permit shorts, swimsuits and sportswear, attire commonly seen even on city streets. Only posh Palm Beach has dared to differ from the laid-back Florida lifestyle by outlawing topless jogging – for both men and women.

There is little need for formal wear, except at the most sophisticated resorts (again, like those in Palm Beach). A sports coat with an open-neck sports shirt is the rule, rather than the exception, for men; and cocktail dresses or pants ensembles are acceptable in most instances for women. A light raincoat or umbrella may prove handy, particularly during the summer. A sweater or jacket should be packed in case of cold spells during the winter.

CUSTOMS

Residents of other countries visiting Florida have non-resident customs status. All articles brought into the United States, including gifts for other persons, must be declared to US Customs at the time you enter. Articles should be listed on the customs declaration form you receive while on board your plane or ship.

IMPORT REGULATIONS

No limit on the amount of money – American or foreign, cash traveler's checks, money orders or negotiable instruments in bearer form – that you may bring into or take out of the United States. But you must file a report with US Customs at the time you arrive or depart for amounts exceeding $5,000 or the foreign currency equivalent.

Non-residents may bring into the United States, free of duty and internal revenue tax, not more than one quart (0.946 liters) of alcoholic beverages for personal use. Excess quantities are subject to duty and tax; Florida permits a tax exemption for up to one gallon. Foreign visitors may also bring in not more than 200 cigarettes (one carton), 100 cigars, or 3 pounds of smoking tobacco, or proportionate amounts of each. An additional quantity of 100 cigars may be brought in under gift exemption.

Special forms or declarations are also required to bring in firearms, prescription drugs, illegal drugs, food, animals, plants and alcoholic beverages. Some of those items are forbidden, or normally require a period of quarantine.

IMPORTING AUTOMOBILES

A non-resident may import an automobile free of duty for personal use and for the transportation of family and guests. The vehicle must be imported at the time of arrival. However, there is no time limit on the period that the vehicle may remain in the United States.

Motorists from countries which have ratified the Convention on Road Traffic of 1949 may drive in the United States for one year with their national license plates on their cars, but an International Distinguishing Sign must be displayed on the car to indicate the motorist's country of origin. Motorists from more than 120 countries with valid national driving licenses may drive in Florida.

LIQUOR LAWS

The legal drinking age in Florida is 21, except for active military personnel. Liquor is sold by the bottle at all retail stores; low taxes here keep prices lower than in many northern states. Retail stores may not sell liquor on Sundays until after 1pm. Public intoxication is not considered a criminal offense without an accompanying violation such as disorderly conduct, although police may detain intoxicated persons in jail for several hours.

GETTING ACQUAINTED

TIME ZONES

Most of Florida runs on Eastern Standard Time. The exception is the western Panhandle – west of the Apalachicola River – which is in the Central Standard Time zone, an hour earlier than the rest of the state. Set your clocks and watches an hour ahead for Daylight Savings Time, which begins in May and ends in October.

CLIMATE

In her book *Cross Creek*, Marjorie Rawlings said that Florida seasons "move in and out like nuns in soft clothing, making no rustle in their passing."

Indeed, it is hard to tell spring from summer. And lacking the brilliant colors of a northern autumn, fall slips into winter without notice. Temperatures do drop in winter. Sometimes they even plunge, surprising tourists who brought their bikinis and little else. But snow and ice are so rare that a touch of either can cripple even northernmost Florida cities.

TEMPERATURE RANGES

January traditionally ranks as the coolest month, as the chart on page 318 indicates. Nighttime lows range from a low average of 41° in Tallahassee in the Panhandle to 66° in balmy Key West. Occasional temperatures below those have brought frost and threatened Florida's fruit and vegetable crops.

Afternoon highs in January climb as high as an average of 76° in Key West and 61° in nippy Apalachicola on the northern Gulf coast. Due to the relatively mild winters, many South Florida homes are not equipped with heating systems, and erratic winter weather in recent years – including in 1977 the first snow flurries in Miami's recorded history – has caught residents quite unprepared.

In sharp contrast, June through September can get quite hot; a condition that is complicated by high humidity. Sea breezes along the coast and clockwork-like daily thunder showers can cool off Florida cities to temperatures more bearable than some northern cities in summer.

Average daytime highs during the dog days range from 86° to 91° with little variation from northern to southern regions. At night, temperatures "cool off" to between 70° and 80°, which usually necessitates the use of an air-conditioner for comfortable sleeping conditions.

RAINFALL

Florida's hottest months are also the rainiest. But the thunderstorms occur with such regularity each day that you can virtually set your watch by them. They also bring a welcome relief from the day's heat. Southern parts of the state get rain almost daily during June and July. The Everglades soak up nearly 9 inches on average each June.

In contrast with other parts of the United States, there is little precipitation during November and December – only 2 inches on average statewide.

Florida wears its nickname "The Sunshine State" so well the *St Petersburg Evening Independent* since 1910 has given its daily edition away free the day after any sunless day. The newspaper has only given away an average of 3.7 editions each year, and during one **Guiness Book of World Records** stretch, the newspaper's rooftop sun meter was activated 765 days in a row.

LIGHTNING

One of nature's most frightening – and one of Florida's most dangerous – phenomena is lightning. Unofficially dubbed the "lightning capital of the country," Florida records an average of 11 deaths and 25 injuries from lightning each year. Fort Myers averages 100 lightning-packed days per year, Tampa has 90 and Miami 76.

Florida's dubious distinction has been attributed to the hot wet air close to the ground and unstable atmospheric conditions that exist mainly from May until September. The air near the ground gets hot, rises, then begins to cool. Droplets of water form menacing dark clouds. The air moves up and down so rapidly that it splits the water droplets in the clouds, causing an electrical spark to shoot out. The spark jumps from cloud to cloud or cloud to ground, passing through the air so quickly that a thunderclap occurs.

Lasting 1/1000th of a second, a bolt of lightning carries 30,000°F in a 1-inch channel and delivers a shock of 6,000 to 10,000 amps that can paralyze bodily functions. Nevertheless, two-thirds of those people hit by lightning in Florida have somehow survived.

The only way to avoid lightning is to take cover when you see dark clouds and bolts begin to approach. If you are riding in a car, stay inside it until the storm passes. If you are at home, in a shopping center or inside any building, don't attempt to "make a run for it." Many lightning victims have been killed when entering or leaving their automobiles. Boaters should head for the nearest place they can tie up and evacuate the boat.

If the lightning doesn't get you, waves churned up during the violent storms may.

TORNADOES

Florida's comparatively small **tornadoes** usually cause less damage and death than the awesome twisters that can develop in the Midwest and Northern United States. The many trailer parks that proliferate throughout the state are the most vulnerable.

HURRICANES

Much more damaging and definitely more dangerous is a weather phenomenon more common to Florida and other Gulf Coast states – the **hurricane**.

Seasonal: Hurricane season usually runs from June through October, although Hurricane Alice in

Average Monthly Temperatures*							
Month	Northwest Division	Northern Central	North Central Division	South Central Division	Southwest & Everglades Division	Lower East Coast	Florida Keys
Jan	52.7	55.7	59.7	61.9	64.7	66.6	70.7
Feb	54.7	57.5	60.9	63.1	65.6	67.2	71.6
Mar	60.2	62.7	65.6	67.2	69.1	70.5	74.6
Apr	67.9	69.5	71.3	72.3	73.2	74.4	78.1
May	73.7	75.5	75.5	76.9	77.1	77.3	80.9
Jun	79.8	80.0	80.3	80.4	80.5	83.2	83.5
Jul	81.1	81.4	81.5	82.7	82.0	81.8	84.6
Aug	81.1	81.4	81.7	81.9	82.4	82.2	84.7
Sep	77.0	79.0	80.0	80.5	81.5	81.1	83.2
Oct	69.5	71.5	73.8	75.0	76.9	77.3	79.6
Nov	59.4	62.6	65.9	67.7	70.5	71.8	75.1
Dec	53.6	56.7	60.8	63.0	65.9	67.7	71.5
Yr	67.7	69.4	71.5	72.6	74.1	74.9	78.2
Temperature, Degrees Fahrenheit							

Average Monthly Rainfall*							
Month	Northwest Division	Northern Central	North Central Division	South Central Division	Southwest & Everglades Division	Lower East Coast	Florida Keys
Jan	3.97	2.89	2.38	2.15	1.79	2.13	1.67
Feb	4.30	3.62	3.11	2.71	1.91	2.04	1.85
Mar	5.68	4.17	4.01	3.28	2.65	2.22	1.56
Apr	4.36	3.00	2.79	2.84	2.35	3.26	2.17
May	3.68	3.27	3.17	4.10	4.29	5.66	2.51
Jun	5.77	5.97	7.05	8.68	8.90	8.53	4.55
Jul	7.93	7.71	8.32	8.48	8.58	6.48	4.11
Aug	7.03	7.27	7.77	7.57	7.72	6.36	4.47
Sep	6.87	6.95	6.90	7.35	9.17	8.76	7.34
Oct	2.96	3.99	3.75	3.85	4.75	8.61	5.57
Nov	3.09	2.12	1.76	1.76	1.46	2.58	2.67
Dec	4.22	2.78	2.20	1.83	1.40	1.85	1.52
Yr	59.90	53.77	53.25	54.65	55.02	58.54	39.99
*Based on National Climatic Center records							

1955 formed off Florida's southeast coast in the month of January, an extremely unusual occurrence. The number of hurricanes that forms in a given year has ranged from as few as 2 to as many as 20, but most never swing into Florida. Still, the National Hurricane Center in Miami tracks each of the massive storms carefully with sophisticated radar detection equipment, satellites and reconnaisance planes – ready to issue evacuation orders if a hurricane appears headed for land or if resulting winds, rain and high waters threaten Florida or other coastal states.

Damage: Rarely a year goes by that some Caribbean or Gulf Coastal area from Florida to Mexico is not pounded by a hurricane or its side effects. 1992's Hurricane Andrew caused massive destruction, but the death toll was low. In 1979, Hurricane David killed about 900 in the Dominican Republic, 16 in the United States and an estimated 1,100 more people throughout the Caribbean. The most intense storm of the decade, the "Labor Day Hurricane of 1935" belted the Florida Keys, destroying Henry Flagler's Overseas Railroad with winds estimated at up to 250 miles per hour.

Formation: A hurricane forms when winds rushes toward a low-pressure area and takes on a distinctive swirling motion. It begins as a tropical depression, and is classified a hurricane when winds reach 74 miles per hour. The size of storms can range from 60 miles in diameter to monsters more than 1,000 miles wide. Their patterns and routes remain difficult to predict. Hurricanes thought to be on the wane have reformed into bigger storms. Others move out to sea away from land areas only to double back and come ashore.

Duration: The average life of a hurricane is 8 to 10 days. It begins to lose its punch and organization when it strays too far inland or over colder northern waters where tropical wind patterns are no longer able to feed it. Florida's eastern and southeastern seaboards are most vulnerable to hurricanes in August and early September, but patterns traditionally shift to the Caribbean later in September and in October, endangering the Keys, the West Coast and Panhandle.

Christening: Once named only for women, a practice thought to have begun when World War II servicemen in the Pacific named storms after their girlfriends, the National Weather Service adopted an equal rights policy in 1979 when it began alternating male names for every other hurricane.

Precautionary Measures: Florida residents are well versed on precautions that should be taken when a hurricane approaches. Newspapers and magazines publish special sections on the subject at the beginning of each season. Most coastal communities publish evacuation plans and routes. Many locals have adopted the hobby of tracking the path of each storm on special charts – available in newspapers, from radio and television stations, and even printed on the sides of grocery bags.

Needless to say, a tourist caught in Florida during an impending hurricane should drop plans to work on suntans or visit tourist attractions and follow National Weather Service advisories, television directives and common sense in riding the storm out.

HURRICANE DEVELOPMENTS

Tropical disturbance: This phase in a hurricane's development has no strong winds. But it may feature a weak counter-clockwise circulation of wind. Disturbances of this sort are common throughout the tropics in summer months.

Tropical depression: A small low pressure system develops and the counter-clockwise rotation of air increases to speeds under 39 miles per hour.

Tropical storm: By now, the low pressure system has developed winds ranging from 39 to 73 miles per hour and can be accompanied by heavy rains.

Hurricane: The low pressure system has intensified to the point where strong winds of more than 74 miles per hour rotate in a counter-clockwise direction around an area of calm called the "eye." Storm tides may rise as much as 15 feet above normal and can surge as much as 6 feet in minutes.

STORM ADVISORIES

Hurricane watch: This signal means that the National Hurricane Center in Miami has determined a hurricane may threaten your immediate area within 24 hours. It is time to begin taking final precautions against a direct hit. Stay tuned to radio or television for the latest storm information.

Watch Precautions:
• Check car battery, water and oil and make sure your gas tank is full.
• Make sure you have new batteries for your radio and flashlight.
• Gather containers for storing out clean drinking water. Fill drug prescriptions and make certain you have special medications like insulin on hand.
• Arrange for the safety of pets, because they will not be permitted into public shelters at all.
• Put together a survival kit consisting of non-perishable food (including a manual can opener), water (half a gallon per person per day), eating and cooking utensils, personal toilet articles and sanitary needs (like diapers and toothpaste), bedding (or sleeping bags), changes of clothing, portable cooler and ice, and a first aid kit.

HURRICANE WARNING

This is issued when the storm has reached winds of at least 74 miles per hour and high water and storm surges are expected in a specific area within 24 hours. Warnings will identify specific coastal areas where these conditions may occur. Be prepared to evacuate your home or hotel, even if the weather does not appear threatening when the warning is issued.

• Clear your yard of loose objects, lawn furniture, garbage cans, bicycles and any other objects which will harm you when they are hurled about during the hurricane.

• Secure your boat. Remember that most draw or swing bridges will be closed to boat traffic after an evacuation order is issued.

• Protect windows and take down awnings to secure your home. Also shut off gas valves, pull main electrical power switches, turn off main water pipes, open a window slightly, take all important papers with you and leave your swimming pool full and super chlorinated.

• Complete the assembly of materials needed to take to a shelter or that you will need if you stay home.

• Prepare to evacuate if and when ordered. Most of Florida's coastal communities now have put together detailed evacuation procedure plans. Evacuation route signs are located along highways in many of these areas. Consult your local civil defense or hurricane emergency officials for details.

If your area does not have an evacuation plan, check the elevation of your property above mean sea level, study the storm surge history of your area and plan an evacuation route. Tornadoes may also be spawned by hurricanes, so follow news bulletins closely and be prepared to take immediate shelter. If your home is above or away from areas threatened by high tides, remain where you are so you do not inhibit evacuation of people from those areas.

During the storm: Stay indoors and do not travel once the hurricane begins buffeting your area. When the eye passes over you, there will be a temporary lull in wind and rain that may last up to half an hour or more. Do not mistake this for an end of the storm, although you may take the opportunity to make emergency repairs. Prepare for resumption of the storm, possibly with even greater force, from the opposite direction. Wait for word from the proper authorities before venturing out of your home.

If ordered to evacuate: Follow instructions and designated routes as quickly as possible. Take blankets, a flashlight, extra clothing, medications, dietary foods (if needed), infant necessities and lightweight folding chairs. Leave behind alcoholic beverages, pets, weapons or extra food.

The storm surge: Ninety percent of all hurricane-related deaths are directly a result of the storm surge. It occurs when a massive dome of water that can be up to 50 miles wide sweeps across the coastline near an area where the eye comes ashore. It is caused by an extreme drop in barometric pressure and the force of high winds pushing on open waters. The hammering effect of breaking waves and the surge act like a giant steamroller crushing everything in their path.

After the storm passes: Drive with caution when ordered to return home. Debris may fill some streets and cause hazardous conditions. Roads in coastal areas may collapse if soil has been washed from beneath them. Avoid sightseeing as you may be mistaken for a looter. Steer clear of downed or dangling utility wires.

Seek medical attention if necessary at designated Red Cross disaster centers or hospitals. Stay tuned to radio stations about emergency medical, food, housing and other forms of assistance.

Re-enter your home with caution and make temporary repairs necessary to correct safety hazards and to minimize further damage. Open windows and doors to air out and dry the house and in case of gas leaks. Exercise caution when dealing with matches or fires. Report broken sewer or water mains to local utility departments.

Above all, do not take a hurricane lightly by inviting friends over for a "hurricane party." The deadly forces of wind, rain and tides that accompany a hurricane are no causes for celebration.

HOLIDAYS

During some of the holidays listed below, some or all state, local and federal agencies may be closed. Local banks and businesses may also stop operations during some of these holidays.

New Year's Day: January 1
Martin Luther King Jr.'s Birthday: January 15
Abraham Lincoln's Birthday: February 12
Robert E. Lee's Birthday: Third Monday in February
Shrove Tuesday or **Mardis Gras** (in some counties only, mainly in the Panhandle)
Good Friday
Memorial Day for Veterans of all Wars: Last Monday in May
Independence Day: July 4
Labor Day: First Monday in September
General Election Day: First Tuesday after the first Monday in November of even-numbered years
Veterans' Day: November 11
Thanksgiving Day: Fourth Thursday in November
Christmas Day: December 25

TIPPING

Service personnel expect tips in Florida. The accepted rate for baggage handlers in airports is about 50 cents per bag. For others, like taxi drivers and waitresses, 15 to 20 percent is the going rate depending on the level and quality of service rendered. Sometimes tips are included in restaurant bills when dining in groups. Generally, tipping is not required in cafeterias where you serve yourself, unless your tray is carried to your table for you.

Moderate hotel tipping may range from 35 to 50 cents per bag or suitcase handled by bellboys or porters. A doorman should be tipped if he holds your car or performs other services. It is not necessary to tip chambermaids unless you stay several days. Florida hotels generally do not add a service charge to cover gratuities.

COMMUNICATIONS

GETTING AROUND

MEDIA

Newspapers: Award-winning daily newspapers roll off the presses in every area of the state. Color photography and artwork fill the newspapers; highly sophisticated, extremely expensive equipment are used to allow presentation of color photographs just hours after a news event occurs. There are more than 125 weeklies; including the Spanish-language *El Imparcial* and *El Noticiero*. The *Miami Herald* also has a Spanish-language section.

Television: All major Florida cities have stations affiliated with major national networks, local stations and a vast offering of cable television hookups. Local newspapers provide daily and weekly information about television and radio programs.

POSTAL SERVICES

Post office hours vary in central, big-city branches and smaller cities and towns. Hotel or motel personnel will answer questions about hours of the post office nearest you. If you do not know where you will be staying in any particular town, you can receive mail simply by having it addressed to your name, care of General Delivery at the main post office in that town. But you must pick up such mail personally. Check with postal officials about current charges and the variety of mail delivery services available.

TELEGRAMS & TELEX

Western Union and International Telephone and Telegraph (ITT) will take telegram and telex messages by phone. You can check the local phone directory or you can call local information for the toll-free numbers of their offices.

TELEPHONE

Public telephones are located in hotel lobbies, drugstores, restaurants, garages, roadside kiosks, convenience stores and other locations throughout the state. The cost of making a local call is 25 cents at all pay telephones throughout the state. Long distance call rates decrease after 5pm, decrease further after 11pm, and are lower on weekends and holidays.

DRIVING IN FLORIDA

The automobile is the most popular means of getting to Florida. More than 20 million visitors enter the state by car annually, about twice as many as those entering by plane. One of the reasons for the reliance on the automobile is that it is practically a necessity to have a car once you arrive. Bus, train and taxi services within Florida are quite irregular, unreliable and slow to cover the state's vast distances.

Another reason for car-hopping is the excellence of interstate highway systems leading into Florida and within the state. The main north-south arteries which bring in droves of tourists from Ohio, New York, Michigan, Pennsylvania and other Northwest, Midwest and Southeastern states are Interstates 75 and 95. The latter thoroughfare ribbons its way down Florida's East Coast. Interstate 75 parallels the West Coast to Naples where bits and pieces are still under construction. Spurs from both interstates connect major cities with the expressway. The major expressway for travelers coming from the West is Interstate 10, which enters Florida near Pensacola, intersects Interstate 75 near Lake City and ends by melting into I-95 in Jacksonville.

The Florida Turnpike begins its southwest slash through the state's midsection from I-75 near Wildwood and peters out at Florida City south of Miami. Your toll depends on how much of the turnpike you use. The only other limited-access superhighway, Interstate 4, is Florida's "Fantasy Highway." This highway links Tampa to Daytona Beach with exits at Disney World, Circus World, Sea World, Stars Hall of Fame and other Central Florida attractions.

For easy driving, you can obtain excellent road maps by writing: Florida Dept of Commerce, Collins Bldg, Tallahassee 32304. Virtually all service stations also sell Florida maps, as well as detailed maps of the cities in which they are located. Another advantage of driving into Florida are the state's Welcome Stations which dispense information and free orange juice. The main station is located on Interstate 75 near Jennings. Others are at Havana on US 27; Pensacola on US 90; near Yulee on US 17; at the junction of US 1, 301 and 23 at Hilliard; and on County Road 688 off Interstate 275 near the St Petersburg-Clearwater International Airport.

PUBLIC TRANSPORT

Taxis are available in major tourism centers of the state, rare in smaller cities. They tend to be expensive, particularly for long rides. There is also an extra charge for each 1³/₅ minutes that the cab waits for you.

PRIVATE TRANSPORT

Visitors wishing to rent or lease an automobile after arriving in Florida will find offices of all US firms – including Hertz, Avis, Budget and National – in most Florida tourism centers, at international airports and even some smaller airports. Shop around for the best rates and features. Often, smaller local rental firms outside the airports offer less expensive, more desirable conditions than the large national companies. But be sure to check insurance coverage provisions with them before signing anything.

Most automobile rental agencies require you to be at least 21 years old (sometimes 25), and to hold a valid driver's license and a major credit card, before permitting you to rent one of their cars. Some will take cash deposit, sometimes as high as $500, in lieu of a credit card. Foreign travelers may need to produce an international driver's license or a license from their own country. Liability is not automatically included in the terms of your lease, so advertised rates usually do not include additional fees for insurance. You should also check with your airline, bus or rail agent or travel agent for special package deals that provide rental cars at reduced rates.

Drivers must abide by Florida traffic laws. For a copy of "Florida Driver Information," write to the following address: Division of Tourism, Direct Mail Section, 107 W. Gaines St, Tallahassee 32304.

HITCHHIKING

Hitchhiking is not advised and may prove to be hazardous in Florida. Picking up hitchhiking strangers is also potentially dangerous. Florida newspapers regularly recount stories of robbery, rape and even murder that began with an extended thumb.

If you choose to drive, you should also learn what areas of cities to avoid before starting out. Miami's Liberty City has most notoriously been the scene of criminal incidents involving motorists unfamiliar with the city. Ask questions of your rental clerk at the airport when you arrive or check with tourism offices before taking a drive.

WHERE TO STAY

ALACHUA

Overnight Inn: Rt. 1 Box 225, I-75 and US 441 (32615). Tel: 904/462-3251. 48 rooms; near the expressway; restaurant; lounge.
Sundance Inn: I-4 & Hwy 436 (32714). Tel: 305/862-8200. 150 rooms; near the expressway; in a suburban area; most major credit cards accepted; restaurant; lounge; non-smoking rooms; meeting facilities; 24-hour food service; swimming-pool; children's playground; golf and tennis nearby; pets allowed.

APOKA

Silver Palms Motel: 429 E. Main St (32703). Tel: 305/886-2092. 15 rooms; downtown; most major credit cards accepted; restaurant nearby.

BIG PINE KEY

Parmer Place Cottages: Barry Ave, Gulfside, MM 28.5, Little Torch Key (33043). Tel: 305/872-2157. 10 rooms; resort area; waterfront; fishing; watersports; pets allowed.

BOCA RATON

Boca Raton Motel: 1801 N. Federal Hwy (33432). Tel: 305/395-7500. 50 rooms; downtown; most major credit cards accepted; restaurant; lounge; handicapped facilities; meeting facilities; swimming-pool; golf and tennis nearby.
Shore Edge Motel: 425 N. Ocean Blvd (33432). Tel: 305/395-4491. 16 rooms; on the beach; downtown; swimming-pool; restaurant nearby; tennis nearby.
The Bridge Hotel: 999 E. Camino Real (33432). Tel: 305/368-9500. 121 rooms; on the beach; restaurant; lounge; handicapped facilities; swimming-pool; golf and tennis nearby; exercise gym; fishing.

BONITA SPRINGS

Shangri La Natural Hygiene Institute: 27580 Old 41 Road (33959). Tel: 813/992-3811. 53 rooms; resort area; suburban area; most major credit cards accepted; restaurant; handicapped facilities; swimming-pool; tennis; golf nearby.

BOYNTON BEACH

Golden Sands Inn: 520 S.E. 21 Ave (33435). Tel: 305/732-6075. 24 rooms; resort area; downtown; most major credit cards accepted; room service; the following facilities nearby: golf; fishing; marina; beach.

BRADENTON

Dumas Motel Court: 1526 14th St W. (34205). Tel: 813/746-3051. 23 rooms; downtown; most major credit cards accepted; the following facilities nearby: golf; tennis; restaurant.

CAPTIVA ISLAND

South Seas Plantation: P.O. Box 194, S. Seas Plantation Road (33924). Tel: 813/472-5111. 600 rooms; on the beach; resort area; most major credit cards accepted; restaurant; lounge; room service; handicapped facilities; meeting facilities; shuttle services; swimming-pool; children's playground; marina; fishing; golf; tennis; watersports.

CEDAR KEY

The Island Place: First and "C" streets (32625). Tel: 904/543-5307. 21 rooms; on the beach; downtown; resort area; waterfront; swimming-pool; jacuzzi; sauna.

CHATTAHOOCHEE

Morgan Motel: E. US 90 (32324). Tel: 904/663-4336. 22 rooms; downtown; most major credit cards accepted; restaurant; fishing; pets allowed.
The Sportsman's Inn: 516 W. Washington, W. Hwy 90 (32324). Tel: 904/663-2352. 26 rooms (18 rms, 5 kitchenettes, 3 suites); watersports; fishing; handicapped facilities.

CLEARWATER

New Ranch Motel: 2275 Gulf to Bay Blvd (34625). Tel: 813/799-0512. 21 rooms; downtown; near the expressway; swimming-pool; handicapped facilities; language interpreters: latin; golf nearby; fishing.

CLEARWATER BEACH

Best Western Gulfview Inn: 504 S. Gulfview Blvd (34630). Tel: 813/441-1722. 65 rooms; resort area; most major credit cards accepted; swimming-pool; fishing; restaurant nearby.
Best Western Sea Wake Inn: 691 S. Gulfview Blvd (34630). Tel: 813/443-7652. 110 rooms (50 eff.); on the beach; restaurant; lounge; swimming-pool; fishing.
Clearwater Beach Hotel: 500 Mandalay Ave (34630). Tel: 813/441-2425. 96 rooms (90 eff.); on the beach; resort area; most major credit cards accepted; restaurant; room service; lounge; non-smoking rooms; swimming-pool; tennis nearby; handicapped facilities; shuttle services, meeting facilities; foreign language interpreters: French; pets allowed.
Clearwater Travelodge: 711 Cleveland St (34615). Tel: 813/446-9183. 48 rooms; downtown; swimming-pool; golf and tennis nearby; handicapped facilities; foreign language interpreters: Polish.
Flamingo Motel Apartments and Cottages: 450 N. Gulfview Blvd (34630). Tel: 813/441-8019. 35 rooms; resort area; on the beach; swimming-pool; tennis nearby; children's playground; exercise gym; spa; watersports.
Sheraton Sand Key Resort: 1160 Gulf Blvd (34630). Tel: 813/595-1611. 390 rooms; on the beach; resort area; swimming-pool; golf nearby; tennis; restaurant; lounge; children's playground; foreign language interpreters: German; currency exchange.
Spy Glass Motel: 215 S. Gulfview Blvd (34630). Tel: 813/446-8317. 64 rooms (56 apts); on the beach; swimming-pool; golf and tennis nearby.

CLEWISTON

Clewiston Inn Hotel: US 27 and Royal Palm (33440). Tel: 813/983-8151. 60 rooms (4 eff., 4 apts); downtown; restaurant; lounge; golf and tennis nearby; marina (service); shuttle services; pets allowed.

COCOA

Econo Lodge: 3220 N. Cocoa Blvd (32926). Tel: 305/632-4561. 112 rooms; near the expressway; restaurant; lounge; swimming-pool; golf nearby.

COCOA BEACH

Cocoa Beach Oceanside Inn: 1 Hendry Ave (32931). Tel: 305/784-3126. 40 rooms; on the beach; fishing; swimming-pool; restaurant; handicapped facilities; shuttle services; golf and tennis nearby.
Crossway Inn and Tennis Resort: 3901 N. Atlantic Ave (32931). Tel: 305/783-2221. 94 rooms; on the beach; resort area; most major credit cards accepted; restaurant; lounge; meeting facilities; in-room safe; swimming-pool; tennis; golf nearby; foreign language interpreters: French.
Econo Lodge Beachside: 5500 N. Atlantic Ave (32931). Tel: 305/784-2550. 100 rooms (10 eff.); resort area; most major credit cards accepted; swimming-pool; handicapped facilities; in-room safe; non-smoking rooms; pets allowed; golf and tennis nearby; fishing.

CORAL GABLES

David William Apartment Hotel: 700 Biltmore Way (33134). Tel: 305/445-7821. 85 rooms (55 eff., 18 apts); near airport; restaurant; lounge; swimming-pool; exercise gym; golf and tennis nearby; foreign language interpreters: Spanish, French.

Hotel Place Saint Michel: 162 Alcazar (33134). Tel: 305/444-1666. 28 rooms; near airport; downtown; expressway; waterfront; most major credit cards accepted; restaurant; room service; lounge; in-room safe; golf and tennis nearby; handicapped facilities; meeting facilities; foreign language interpreters: French, Spanish.

DAYTONA BEACH

Americano Beach Lodge: 1260 N. Atlantic Ave (32018). Tel: 904/255-7431. 199 rms (81 eff.); on the beach; resort area; restaurant; lounge; swimming-pool; golf and tennis nearby; children's playground; handicapped facilities; foreign language interpreters: French, German, Spanish; currency exchange; shuttle services.

Casa Blanca Motel: 2125 S. Atlantic Ave (32018). Tel: 904/252-1558. 22 rooms; on the beach; swimming-pool; golf and tennis nearby; shuttle services; foreign language interpreters: French, German.

Daytona Inn at Seabreeze: 730 N. Atlantic Ave (32018). Tel: 904/255-5491. 98 rooms (36 eff., 16 apts); on the beach; swimming-pool; golf and tennis nearby; children's playground; in-room safe.

Tropical Manor Motel: 2237 S. Atlantic Ave (32018). Tel: 904/252-4920. 36 rooms (8 eff., 26 apts); on the beach; most major credit cards accepted; swimming-pool; children's playground; fishing; the following facilities nearby: restaurant; golf; tennis.

DAYTONA BEACH SHORES

Best Western Aku Tiki Inn: 225 S. Atlantic Ave (32018). Tel: 904/252-9631. 132 rooms (62 eff.); on the beach; restaurant; lounge; swimming-pool; fishing; golf and tennis nearby; foreign language interpreters: French.

El Caribe Motel: 2125 S. Atlantic Ave (32018). Tel: 904/252-1558. 102 rooms (30 apts, 72 eff.); on the beach; swimming-pool; golf and tennis nearby; foreign language interpreters: French, German; shuttle services.

Sun Viking Lodge: 2411 S. Atlantic (32018). Tel: 904/252-6252. 91 rooms (21 rms, 48 eff., 22 suites); on the beach; most major credit cards accepted; restaurant; swimming-pool; exercise gym; fishing; golf and tennis nearby; handicapped facilities; meeting facilities; non-smoking rooms; in-room safe.

FORT LAUDERDALE

Bahia Cabana Motel: 3001 Harbor Drive (33316). Tel: 305/524-1555. 76 rooms (45 rms, 9 apts, 22 eff.); on the beach; resort area; most major credit cards accepted; lounge; in-room safe; swimming-pool; marina; fishing; golf and tennis nearby.

Gold Coast Apartment Hotel: 545 N. Atlantic Blvd,

A1A (33304). Tel: 305/564-4361. 39 rooms (24 eff., 7 apts, 8 rms); waterfront; most major credit cards accepted; swimming-pool; the following facilities nearby: restaurant; golf; tennis.

Howard Johnson Motor Lodge: 700 N. Atlantic Blvd (33304). Tel: 305/563-2451. 144 rooms; resort area; on the beach; 24-hour food service; swimming-pool; lounge; shuttle services; foreign language interpreters: Spanish.

Irelands Inn: 2220 N. Atlantic Blvd (33305). Tel: 305/565-6661. 83 rooms (including eff., apts); on the beach; resort area; most major credit cards accepted; restaurant; lounge; room service; in-room safe; meeting facilities; swimming-pool; tennis nearby.

Moby Dick Motel: 3100 Windamar St (33304). Tel: 305/565-0306. 8 rooms (7 eff., 9 rms, 3-1 brm apts); on the beach; most major credit cards accepted; golf nearby; swimming-pool (heated).

FORT MYERS

Cottage Court Apartment Motel: 3079 Cleveland Ave (33901). Tel: 813/332-0301. 27 rooms (13 eff., 13-1 brm apts, 1-2 brm apt); downtown; restaurant nearby; golf nearby.

Ramada Inn: 2220 W. First St (33901). Tel: 813/332-4888. 179 rooms; downtown; waterfront; restaurant; lounge; swimming-pool; handicapped facilities; shuttle services; exercise gym; fishing; golf and tennis nearby.

Ta Ki Ki Motel: 2631 First St (33916). Tel: 813/334-2135. 22 rooms; waterfront; swimming-pool; fishing.

GAINESVILLE

Apartment Inn: 4401 S.W. 13th St (32608). Tel: 904/371-3811. 35 rooms; suburban area; most major credit cards accepted; restaurant; shuttle services; pets allowed.

GULFPORT

Pine Grove Cottages: 5139 S. Tangerine Ave (33707). Tel: 813/321-7263. 10 cottages. Resort area; near the following facilities: airport, expressway, downtown, beach, golf, marina, tennis. Pets allowed.

HOLMES BEACH

White Sands Motel Apartments: 6504 Gulf Drive (34217). Tel: 813/778-2577. 14 apartments; near airport; on the beach; resort area; waterfront; fishing; swimming-pool; golf and tennis nearby; foreign language interpreters: French.

JASPER

Scottish Inn: Rt. 3, Box 136, I-75 and S.R. 6 (32052). Tel: 904/792-1234. 57 rooms; near the expressway; golf nearby; swimming-pool.

JENNINGS

Holiday Inn: I-75 and S. R. 143 (32053). Tel: 904/938-3501. 120 rooms; near the expressway; restaurant; swimming-pool; golf; tennis; handicapped facilities; children's playground.

KISSIMMEE

Days Lodge: 5820 W. Irlo Bronson Hwy (32741). Tel: 305/396-7900. 615 suites; near the expressway; resort area; most major credit cards accepted; restaurant; swimming-pool; in-room safe; non-smoking rooms; children's playground; golf nearby; pets allowed; shuttle services.

Florida Vacations Villas: 2770 Poinciana Blvd (32741). Tel: 305/396-6010. 18 rooms; resort area; golf nearby; swimming-pools (2); tennis.

Regency Inn: 8660 W. US 192 (32741). Tel: 305/396-4500. 230 rooms; resort area; most major credit cards accepted; restaurant; rooms service; in-room safe; lounge; swimming-pool; fishing; tennis; golf nearby; foreign language interpreters: Spanish.

Sheraton Lakeside Inn: 7711 W. US 192 (32741). Tel: 305/828-8250. 650 rooms; resort area; most major credit cards accepted; restaurant; room service; lounge; swimming-pool; handicapped facilities; children's playground; fishing; golf nearby; tennis.

LAUDERDALE BY THE SEA

Sea Cloud Resort Motel: 4546 El Mar Drive (33308). Tel: 305/772-2450. 16 rooms; on the beach; most major credit cards accepted; foreign language interpreters: Spanish; the following facilities nearby: restaurant; golf; tennis.

Windjammer Resort and Beach Club: 4244 El Mar Drive (33308). Tel: 305/776-4232. 33 rooms; on the beach; most major credit cards accepted; swimming-pools (2); fishing; foreign language interpreters: French; the following facilities nearby: restaurant; golf; tennis.

MARIANNA

Robin Hood Inn: 1308 E. Lafayette St (32446-3532). Tel: 904/482-8076. 25 rooms (5 eff., 5 apts); near the expressway; suburban area; restaurant; 24-hour food service; swimming-pool; handicapped facilities; children's playground; pets allowed; most major credit cards accepted; fishing; watersports.

Rio Vista Motel: 1046 S. Harbor City Blvd (32901). Tel: 305/727-2818. 28 rooms; downtown; near airport; waterfront; most major credit cards accepted; fishing; the following facilities nearby golf; tennis; restaurant.

MIAMI

Airport Lakes Holiday Inn: 1101 N.W. 57th Ave (33126). Tel: 305/266-0000. 269 rooms; near airport; expressway; waterfront; restaurant; lounge; 24-hour food service; swimming-pool; shuttle services; exercise gym; fishing; golf and tennis nearby; watersports; handicapped facilities; foreign language interpreters: Spanish, French, German, Greek.

Best Western Miami Airport Inn: P.O. Box 592417, N.W. LeJeune Road, 2 blocks south of terminal exit (33159). Tel: 305/871-2345. 200 rooms; near airport; restaurant; lounge; 24-hour food service; swimming-pool; golf and tennis nearby; shuttle services; currency exchange; pets allowed.

Biscayne Bay Marriott Hotel and Marina: 1633 N. Bayshore Drive (33132). Tel: 305/374-3900. 757 rooms; downtown; waterfront; most major credit cards accepted; restaurant; room service; lounge; swimming-pool; marina; fishing; handicapped facilities; meeting facilities; foreign language interpreters: Spanish; non-smoking rooms; pets allowed.

Carl's El Padre Motel: 5950 Biscayne Blvd (33137). Tel: 305/754-2092. 10 rooms; downtown; beach (15 minutes); foreign language interpreters: German.

Silver Sands Motel: 301 Ocean Drive (33149). Tel: 305/361-5441. 56 rooms (51 eff., 7 apts); resort area; on the beach; restaurant; lounge; in-room safe; swimming-pool; tennis; watersports; golf nearby; children's playground; foreign language interpreters: German, Spanish.

The New Airliner Hotel: 4155 N.W. 24th St (33142). Tel: 305/871-2611. 112 rooms (8 eff.); near airport; restaurant; swimming-pool; foreign language interpreters: Spanish; shuttle services.

MIAMI BEACH

Bel Aire Hotel: 6515 Collins Ave (33141). Tel: 305/866-6511. 111 rooms (8 eff., 2 apts); on the beach; resort area; most major credit cards accepted; restaurant; lounge; swimming-pool; golf and tennis nearby; watersports; foreign language interpreters: French, Italian, Spanish.

Doral Hotel on the Beach: 4833 Collins Ave (33140). Tel: 305/532-3600. 420 rooms; on the beach; resort area; restaurant; lounge; 24-hour food service; swimming-pool; exercise gym; handicapped facilities; children's playground; marina; watersports; tennis; golf nearby; foreign language interpreters: Spanish, French, Portugese, German.

Eden Roc Hotel: 4525 Collins Ave (33140). Tel: 305/531-0000. 350 rooms; near airport; on the beach; resort area; most major credit cards accepted; restaurant; room service; lounge; swimming-pools (2); health club; marina; tennis and golf nearby; handicapped facilities; meeting facilities; foreign language interpreters: French, German, Spanish.

Golden Strand Ocean Villa Resort: 17901 Collins Ave (33160). Tel: 305/931-7000. 152 rooms; resort area; on the beach; restaurant; lounge; swimming-pool; golf; tennis nearby; currency exchange; foreign language interpreters: French, German, Spanish.

Hawaiian Isle Beach Resort: 17601 Collins Ave (33160). Tel: 305/932-2121. 110 rooms (40 eff.);

on the beach; resort area; most major credit cards accepted; currency exchange; in-room safe; restaurant; room service; lounge; swimming-pool; children's playground; exercise gym; spa; fishing; tennis; golf nearby.

Hilyard Motel: 9541 Collins Ave (33154). Tel: 305/866-7351. 30 rooms (27 apts); on the beach; resort area; most major credit cards accepted; currency exchange; swimming-pool; the following facilities nearby: restaurant; golf; tennis.

Netherland Hotel: 1330 Ocean Drive (33139). Tel: 305/534-4791. 64 rooms; resort area; on the beach; meeting facilities; restaurant nearby; swimming-pool; foreign language interpreters: Spanish, Yiddish, German, Portugese, French, Hebrew.

Ocean Roc Resort Motel: 19505 Collins Ave (33160). Tel: 305/931-7600. 100 rooms (25 eff.); resort area; on the beach; most major credit cards accepted; restaurant; lounge; swimming-pool; golf and tennis nearby; foreign language interpreters: Spanish, French, German, Polish; shuttle services.

Pan American Ocean Hotel, A Radisson Resort: 17875 Collins Ave (33160). Tel: 305/932-1100. 146 rooms; on the beach; restaurant; lounge; swimming-pool; tennis; fishing; watersports.

NAPLES

Fairways Motel: 103 Palm River Blvd (33942). Tel: 813/597-8181. 32 rooms (12-1 brm apts, 8 eff., 12 rms); resort area; most major credit cards accepted; swimming-pool; health club; handicapped facilities; children's playground; foreign language interpreters: German, Spanish; the following facilities nearby: restaurant; golf; tennis.

Naples Beach Hotel and Golf Club: 851 N. Gulf Shore Blvd (33940). Tel: 813/261-2222. 308 rooms (54 eff., 51 apts); resort area; on the beach; most major credit cards accepted; restaurant; lounge; room service; in-room safe; swimming-pool; handicapped facilities; meeting facilities; foreign language interpreters: Spanish, French, German; golf; tennis; fishing; watersports.

Quality Inn Gulfcoast: 2555 N. Tamiami Trl. (33940). Tel: 813/261-6046. 120 rooms; downtown; near airport; expressway; restaurant; lounge; swimming-pool; golf and tennis nearby; foreign language interpreters: Japanese; fishing; shuttle services (Nov–May).

Vanderbilt Beach Motel: 9225 N. Gulf Shore Drive (33963). Tel: 813-597-3144. 50 rooms (20 eff., 20 apts); on the beach; swimming-pool; tennis; fishing; golf nearby; handicapped facilities.

NEPTUNE BEACH

Travelers Best Western: 1401 Atlantic Blvd (32233). Tel: 904/249-3852. 133 rooms; resort area; most major credit cards accepted; restaurant; lounge; swimming-pool; handicapped facilities; golf nearby; pets allowed.

NEW PORT RICHEY

Holiday Inn: 5015 US Hwy 19 (34652). Tel: 813/849-8551. 135 rooms; downtown; waterfront; restaurant; lounge; swimming-pool; fishing; golf and tennis nearby; handicapped facilities.

NEW SMYRNA BEACH

Cedar Creek Resort: 855 Ladyfish Ave (32069). Tel: 904/428-5844. 8 rooms (2-brm condos); resort area; fishing.

NOKOMIS

Wishing Well Beach to Bay: 221 Casey Key Road (34275). Tel: 813/488-5011. 17 rooms (8 effs., 5 apts); on the beach; near the expressway; marina; fishing; golf and tennis nearby.

ORLANDO

Gateway Inn: 7050 Kirkman Road (32819). Tel: 305/351-2000. 354 rooms; resort area; restaurant; lounge; swimming-pool; shuttle services; children's playground; handicapped facilities; golf and tennis nearby; pets allowed; foreign language interpreters: French, German, Spanish.

Harley Hotel of Orlando: 151 E. Washington St (32801). Tel: 305/841-3220. 297 rooms; downtown; most major credit cards accepted; restaurant; lounge; meeting facilities; non-smoking rooms; room service; swimming-pool; shuttle services; foreign language interpreters: Spanish; handicapped facilities; exercise gym; tennis nearby.

Howard Johnson Motor Lodge: 2014 W. Colonial Drive (32804). Tel: 305/841-8600. 110 rooms; downtown; most major credit cards accepted; restaurant; lounge; swimming-pool; meeting facilities; handicapped facilities; golf and tennis nearby; pets allowed.

Howard Vernon Motel: 600 W. Colonial Drive (32804). Tel: 305/422-7162. 24 rooms; downtown; foreign language interpreters: Chinese, Japanese.

Quality Inn University: 11731 E. Colonial Drive (32817). Tel: 305/273-1500. 122 rooms (1 apt); resort area; restaurant; lounge; swimming-pool; golf and tennis nearby; foreign language interpreters: Spanish.

Sheraton World: 10100 International Drive (32821). Tel: 305/352-1100. 793 rooms; resort area; near the expressway; restaurant; lounge; swimming-pool; handicapped facilities; exercise gym; tennis; golf nearby; children's playground; foreign language interpreters: Spanish, German, French; pets allowed.

ORMOND BEACH

Ivanhoe Beach Lodge: 205 S. Atlantic Ave (32074). Tel: 904/672-6711. 147 rooms (70 apts); on the beach; resort area; most major credit cards accepted;

restaurant; lounge; swimming-pool; children's play-ground; in-room safe; meeting facilities; shuttle services; golf and tennis nearby.

Makai Motel: 707 S. Atlantic Ave (32074). Tel: 904/677-8060. 110 rooms (59 eff., 3 apts); resort area; on the beach; most credit cards accepted; swimming-pool; meeting facilities; fishing; the following facilities nearby: restaurant; golf; tennis. Pets allowed.

PALM BEACH

Beachcomber Apartment Motel: 3024 S. Ocean Blvd (33480). Tel: 305/585-4648. 50 rooms; near airport; on the beach; waterfront; most major credit cards accepted; swimming-pool (salt water); the following facilities nearby: restaurant; golf; fishing.

Colony Hotel: 155 Hammon Ave (33480). Tel: 305/655-5430. 100 rooms; resort area; restaurant; lounge; swimming-pool; golf and tennis nearby; handicapped facilities; pets allowed.

Howard Johnson Motor Lodge: 2870 S. County Road (33480). Tel: 305/582-2581. 100 rooms; resort area; waterfront; most major credit cards accepted; restaurant; lounge; non-smoking rooms; room service; swimming-pool; handicapped facilities; golf and tennis nearby; foreign language interpreters: Spanish.

Palm Beach Hawaiian: 3550 S. Ocean Blvd (33480). Tel: 305/582-5631. 58 rooms; on the beach; resort area; most major credit cards accepted; restaurant; lounge; swimming-pool; in-room safe; golf and tennis nearby.

PALM BEACH GARDENS

Holiday Inn Palm Beach: 4431 PGA Blvd (33410). Tel: 305/622-2260. 282 rooms (6 eff.); resort area; near the expressway; restaurant; tennis; swimming-pool; golf nearby; handicapped facilities; pets allowed.

PANAMA CITY

Best Western Bayside: 711 W. Beach Drive (32401). Tel: 904/763-4622. 97 rooms; downtown; waterfront (Bay); restaurant; lounge; swimming-pool; fishing; watersports.

PANAMA CITY BEACH

Pier 99 Motor Inn: 9900 Beach Blvd (32407). Tel: 904/234-6657. 100 rooms (33 eff.); on the beach; lounge; swimming-pool; restaurant; watersports; golf nearby.

RIVIERA BEACH

Rutledge Resort Motel: 3730 Ocean Drive (33404). Tel: 305/848-6621. 60 rooms; on the beach; near airport; resort area; restaurant; lounge; swimming-pool; fishing; golf and tennis nearby; watersports.

SANFORD

Holiday Inn of Sanford: 530 N. Palmetto Ave (32771). Tel: 305/323-1910. 100 rooms; downtown; waterfront; restaurant; lounge; swimming-pool; handicapped facilities; marina; fishing; golf and tennis nearby.

SANIBEL ISLAND

Blue Dolphin Beach Cottages: 4227 W. Gulf Drive (33957). Tel: 813/472-1600. 9 rooms; resort area; on the beach; fishing; golf and tennis nearby; pets allowed (small).

Gallery Motel: 541 E. Gulf Drive (33957). Tel: 813/472-1400. 31 rooms; on the beach; resort area; swimming-pool; golf and tennis nearby; fishing; shelling charters available.

Island Inn: 3111 W. Gulf Drive (33957). Tel: 813/472-1561. 56 rooms (29 eff., 7 ctgs); on the beach; resort area; most major credit cards accepted; restaurant; room service; in-room safe; swimming-pool; fishing; tennis; golf nearby; handicapped facilities; meeting facilities.

Song of the Sea: 863 E. Gulf Drive (33957). Tel: 813/472-2220. 30 rooms (22 eff., 8 apts); on the beach; resort area; swimming-pool (with spa); golf and tennis nearby (complimentary).

The Castaways: 6460 Sanibel Captiva Road (33957). Tel: 813/472-1252. 20 rooms; resort area; waterfront; most major credit cards accepted; restaurant; swimming-pool; children's playground; fishing.

SARASOTA

Coquina on the Beach: 1008 Ben Franklin Drive (34236). Tel: 813/388-2141. 33 eff.; on the beach; resort area; most major credit cards accepted; swimming-pool; children's playground; fishing; watersports; the following facilities nearby: restaurant; golf; tennis.

Galaxy Motel: 1716 N. Tamiami Trl. (34234). Tel: 813/953-5568. 14 rms (1 apt); near airport; expressway; most major credit cards accepted; room service; children's playground; the following facilities nearby: restaurant; golf; tennis.

Surf View Motel: 1121 Ben Franklin Drive (34236). Tel: 813/388-1818. 27 rooms; resort area; on the beach; swimming-pool; children's playground; shuttle services (airport).

ST AUGUSTINE

Holiday Inn Downtown: 1300 Ponce de León Blvd (32084). Tel: 904/824-3383. 122 rooms; downtown; restaurant; lounge; swimming-pool; handicapped facilities.

Howard Johnson Motor Lodge: I-95 and St Road 16 (32084). Tel: 904/829-5686. 64 rooms; near the expressway; most major credit cards accepted: restaurant; swimming-pool; children's playground; handi-

capped facilities; non-smoking rooms; pets allowed.
Monson Motor Lodge: 32 Avenida Menendez (32084).
Tel: 904/829-2277. 50 rooms; downtown; near airport; waterfront; lounge; swimming-pool; restaurant; shuttle services; tennis nearby; dinner theatre.

ST AUGUSTINE BEACH

La Fiesta Motor Lodge: 3050 S. Hwy A1A (32084).
Tel: 904/471-2220. 37 rooms; on the beach; resort area; most major credit cards accepted; restaurant; swimming-pool; children's playground.

ST PETERSBURG

Avalon Hotel: 443 N. Fourth Ave (33731). Tel: 813/822-4783. 34 rooms; downtown; shuttle services; the following services nearby restaurant; golf; tennis.
Bay Crest Hotel: 161 N. Second Ave (33701). Tel: 813/822-4243. 34 rooms; downtown.
Gordon Hotel: 526 N. Fifth Ave (33701). Tel: 813/821-7710. 30 rooms; downtown.
Huntington Hotel: 226 N. Fourth Ave (33701). Tel: 813/898-4416. 105 rooms; downtown; restaurant; tennis and golf nearby.
Ponce de León Hotel: Central Ave and Beach Drive (33701). Tel: 813/822-4139. 85 rooms; downtown; restaurant; lounge.

ST PETERSBURG BEACH

Breckenridge Resort Hotel: 5700 Gulf Blvd (33706).
Tel: 813/360-1833. 200 rooms (196 eff., 4 apts); resort area; on the beach; most major credit cards accepted; restaurant; lounge; room service; in-room safe; swimming-pool; golf nearby; tennis; foreign language interpreters: French, Spanish; handicapped facilities; meeting facilities.
Colonial Gateway Inn: 6300 Gulf Blvd (33706). Tel: 813/367-2711. 200 rooms (132 eff.); on the beach; resort area; restaurant; lounge; meeting facilities; golf and tennis nearby; currency exchange.
Registry Don CeSar Beach Resort: 3400 Gulf Blvd (33706). Tel: 813/360-1881. 277 rooms; on the beach; resort area; most major credit cards accepted; restaurant; lounge; room service; 24-hour food service; children's playground; marina; fishing; watersports; exercise gym; spa; swimming-pool; tennis; golf nearby; shuttle services; currency exchange; foreign language interpreters: French, Spanish, German; handicapped facilities; meeting facilities; non-smoking rooms.
Sandpiper Resort Hotel: 6000 Gulf Blvd (33706). Tel: 813/360-2731. 159 rooms; on the beach; currency exchange; restaurant; lounge; swimming-pool; exercise gym; golf nearby; tennis nearby; watersports.

SUN CITY

Sun City Center Inn: 1335 Rickenbacker Drive (33570). Tel: 813/634-3331. 100 rooms; resort area; restaurant; lounge; swimming-pool; golf and tennis nearby; pets allowed.

SUNNYSIDE

Howell Cottages, A Family Place, A Church Retreat: 22026 W. Alt 98 (32461). Tel: 904/234-3247. 30 cottages (2 assembly buildings); resort area; meeting facilities; swimming-pool; restaurant nearby; golf nearby.

TALLAHASSEE

Skyline Motor Lodge: 2400 W. Tennessee St (32304). Tel: 904/576-2157. 40 rooms; near airport; swimming-pool.

TAMPA

Admiral Benbow Inn: 1200 N. Westshore Blvd (33607). Tel: 813/879-1750. 238 rooms; near airport; restaurant; lounge; swimming-pool; exercise gym; golf and tennis nearby; handicapped facilities; pets allowed; shuttle services.
Bay Harbor Inn: 7700 Courtney Campbell Cswy (33607). Tel: 813/885-2541. 261 rooms, on the beach; most major credit cards accepted; currency exchange; restaurant; lounge; room service; meeting facilities; handicapped facilities; shuttle services; swimming-pool; tennis; golf nearby.
Best Western By Busch Gardens: 1701 E. Busch Blvd (33612). Tel: 813/933-7681. 45 rooms; resort area; near the expressway; swimming-pool; golf and tennis nearby.
Star Motel: 10809 E. US 92 (33610). Tel: 813/626-2302. 27 rooms; near the expressway; suburban area; swimming-pool; most major credit cards accepted.
8 Inn: 4530 East Columbus Drive (33605). Tel: 813/621-4661. 48 rooms; near the expressway; near airport; downtown (2 minutes).

TREASURE ISLAND

Bilmar Beach Resort Hotel: 10650 Gulf Blvd, P.O. Box 9548 (33706). Tel: 813/360-5531. 172 rooms (106 eff.); on the beach; resort area; most major credit cards accepted; restaurant; lounge; room service; in-room safe; swimming-pool; meeting facilities; fishing; golf and tennis nearby; foreign language interpreters: German.
Commodore Adult Waterfront Apartments: 11760 S. Capri Cir. (33706). Tel: 813/367-3100. 20 apartments; resort area; waterfront; marina; fishing; golf and tennis nearby; swimming-pool.
El Rey Apartment Motel: 240 108th Ave (33706). Tel: 813/363-9832. 18 apartments; on the beach; swimming-pool; fishing; golf and tennis nearby.

Sands of Treasure Island: 11800 Gulf Blvd (33706). Tel: 813/367-1969. 34 rooms (11 effs., 23 apts); on the beach; golf and tennis nearby; children's playground.

VENICE

Best Western Sandbar Hotel: 811 N. Esplanade (34285). Tel: 813/488-2251. 44 rooms; resort area; on the beach; most major credit cards accepted; restaurant; swimming-pool; fishing; golf and tennis nearby; foreign language interpreters: German.

VERO BEACH

Aquarius Resort Motel: 1526 Ocean Drive (32963). Tel: 305/231-5218. 22 rooms (20 apts); on the beach; swimming-pool; fishing; watersports.

Days Inn: 8800 20th St (32966). Tel: 305/562-9991. 174 rooms (5 eff.); near the expressway; restaurant; swimming-pool; golf and tennis nearby; children's playground.

WEST PALM BEACH

Holiday Inn: 6255 W. Okeechobee Road (33409). Tel: 305/686-6000. 154 rooms; near the expressway; lounge; restaurant; 24-hour food service; swimming-pool; tennis nearby; handicapped facilities; children's playground; pets allowed.

Parkview Motor Lodge: 4710 S. Dixie Hwy (33405). Tel: 305/833-4644. 28 rooms; suburban area; near airport; most major credit cards accepted; restaurant nearby; tennis nearby.

Sheraton Inn West Palm Beach: 1901 Palm Beach Lakes Blvd (33409). Tel: 305/689-6100. 160 rooms; near airport; restaurant; lounge; swimming-pool; exercise gym; golf and tennis nearby; handicapped facilities; children's playground; shuttle services.

WINTER HAVEN

Quality Inn Townhouse: 975 Cypress Gardens Blvd (33880). Tel: 813/294-4104. 24 rooms; resort area; swimming-pool; handicapped facilities; golf nearby.

WINTER PARK

The Langford Resort Hotel: 235 E. New England Ave (32789). Tel: 305/644-3400. 213 rooms; downtown; resort area; suburban area; most major credit cards accepted; lounge; restaurant; room service; handicapped facilities; meeting facilities; foreign language interpreters: French, Spanish; fishing; swimming-pool; health club; golf and tennis nearby; pets allowed (small).

CAMPING

FACILITIES

100,000 campsites at nearly 700 campgrounds sprinkled throughout Florida provide an ample choice of outdoors accommodations for the mobile traveler – from primitive areas marked off for tents and sleeping bags to elaborate facilities with utility hook-ups for home-on-wheels recreational vehicles (RVs), restaurants, heated pools, mini-golf courses and planned activities. There are even campgrounds that cater to nudists. Most state parks and forests offer at least primitive camping facilities. (*For details see Parks listings under "Things to Do."*) But since state and national facilities usually offer the best rates in some of the best settings, reserve your space well in advance of your arrival to avoid disappointment. Most of these public camping facilities are booked solid during the busy late winter and early spring seasons.

PRIVATE CAMPGROUNDS

Private campgrounds have blossomed around many of the popular public and commercial attractions and usually have vacancies. Central Florida now appears to have the major share of these facilities (to accommodate the droves of people that descend on Walt Disney World each year). Within The World itself, Walt Disney offers 825 campsites at Fort Wilderness Resort. It's not even necessary to bring a tent or trailer, because upon arrival you can rent Fleetwood Travel Trailers complete with air-conditioning, carpeting, color TV, AM/FM radio, cookware and even linen. They sleep up to six people. The camping resort is located admist 650 acres of woods and winding streams on Bay Lake. River Country and Pioneer Hall are a short walk or tram ride from your campsite. For more information and reservations, write: Walt Disney World Central Reservations, P.O. Box 78, Lake Buena Vista, Florida 32830. Or phone 305/824-8000, preferably between 5pm and 11pm in the Eastern Time zone. Information about special group rates can be obtained by writing: Fort Wilderness Resort, P.O. Box 40, Lake Buena Vista, Florida 32830.

Information: To obtain information about the numerous other private campgrounds near Disney World or in other parts of the state, write to the **Florida Campground Association**, 1638 N. Plaza Drive, Tallahassee, Florida 32308-5323. The association publishes an annual *Florida Camping Directory and Map* that it will send you free of charge. The directory lists hundreds of campgrounds representing nearly 50,000 campsites in Florida divided by regions and with details about amenities. You can phone many of the parks for reservations via toll-free numbers listed in the brochure.

The association estimates that about 5 million people camped in Florida in 1987. About 3.9 million of those campers came from other states and another 100,000 from foreign countries. According to the association, one out of every 10 Florida tourists camps out.

CAMPING REGULATIONS AT PUBLIC FACILITIES

State parks rent sites for a small fee for periods up to 14 days. Fees are slightly higher in the Florida Keys. Reservations are accepted up to 60 days in advance of check-in and can only be made by calling the park where you plan to camp. The base fee covers a maximum of 4 people and a maximum of 8 people may stay at any site. At least one person 18 years or older, or a married person, must be present in each group. There is a small additional charge for extra cars and for electricity. Only Florida residents may obtain an annual camping permit (effective January 1 of each year). Only pets on handheld leashes are allowed in state park picnic areas. No pets are allowed in the campgrounds or on public beaches. For further information about camping at state parks, write: Florida Dept of Natural Resources, Bureau of Education and Information, Rm 616, Marjory Stoneman Douglas Bldg, 3900 Commonwealth Blvd, Tallahassee, Florida 32399-3000. Tel: 904/488-7326.

FOOD DIGEST

WHAT TO EAT

The unique and familiar fruits and vegetables that thrive in this temperate climate flavor Florida cuisine, even though most recipes are seasoned with a dash of the fare common to homelands thousands of miles away. You'll savor Key lime pie and Greek baklava, stone crab claws and Cuban sandwiches, Ruskin tomatoes and Plant City strawberries, Mandarin oranges and Dade County sapodillas.

Florida's most famous dessert, **Key lime pie**, originated in Key West where you'll find small, yellow-colored limes that apparently immigrated from Haiti and other Caribbean countries. This sweet resembles lemon meringue, but has a more tart taste. True Key lime pie is yellow but ome Florida restaurants substitute ordinary green limes, or even artificially-flavored filling.

Prime **strawberry** season is March and April. Whole berries lightly dusted with sugar, or straw-

berry shortcake buried in real whipped cream are the most popular ways of eating these Plant City specialities.

At breakfast, Florida is one of the few places in the country where you can walk into your backyard and pick a fresh **grapefruit** or **orange** from a tree. Most restaurants feature freshly-squeezed juice. Production runs mainly from September until early August. The most important Florida varieties are **Valencia**, **Hamlin** and **Pineapple**, with the **Lue Gim Gong's** hybrid and the **Parson Brown** variety of lesser importance.

Grapefruits, introduced to Florida by the Frenchman Phillippe Odet about 1823, are tastier when full of seeds. The state produces more than 70 percent of the world's grapefruit crop. The **Duncan** grapefruit remains the most popular.

Another item you may encounter at a Florida breakfast is a tradition throughout the southeastern US. It tastes and looks like its name – **grits**. Grits are whole kernels of white corn, ground into a coarsely-granulated dry form. Some Floridians prefer their grits with milk and sugar, but the most common way to eat them is hot with melted butter on top. Grits are served as a side dish with eggs, instead of "home fries," common in other parts of the country. Many Florida restaurants will offer you a choice of grits or home fries with your breakfast.

Cornbread and **biscuits** are other special culinary masterpieces that bespeak Florida's Old South influences. But when the main dish is fish, the side dish is **hush puppies**. Resembling little croquettes, hush puppies are fashioned from fine white cornmeal, salt, baking soda or baking powder, eggs and finely chopped raw onion. They are fried in deep fat until piping hot and golden brown. Hush puppies can turn a plain piece of fish into a feast.

Needless to say, seafood tops the list of Florida food favorites. But even though you may see the ocean or the gulf right outside the window next to your table, beware of restaurants that try to pass off frozen varieties from other parts of the United States (or even from other countries) as fresh Florida seafood. The better restaurants will usually list their fresh offerings or "catches of the day" on the menu, but when in doubt, ask. Often you will find that dockside hole-in-the-wall cafés offer better fish than fancier, high-priced spots, so don't judge a restaurant's seafood by its appearance.

SEAFOOD SPECIALITIES

Among popular Florida seafood specialities are: **Stone crab claws:** The tender meat of the claw, dipped in butter, is considered by many *aficionados* to be the nectar of the sea and even better than lobster. Crabbers use long-handled pole with wire hooks on the end to coax these crabs from rocks near beaches, then break off the large claw and return the crab to the water, according to Florida laws. You will only find frozen claws, or no stone crab at all on Florida menus during the closed season that occurs from May 15 to October 15.

Mullet: Plentiful in open waters and saltwater inlets, this fish may be fried or broiled. Even more popular is smoked mullet found in many specialty restaurants.

Shrimp: There are almost as many recipes for shrimp as there are shrimp. Eat 'em boiled and peeled, dipped in sauce, deep fried as a main dish, broiled, baked, in casseroles, on shish-kebabs, and etcetera. Most come from the Gulf of Mexico. Allow about 1½ pounds for each ¾ pounds of eating after cooking. Be sure not to overcook them.

Oysters: These too may be prepared in a variety of ways, but Floridians prefer no preparation at all. Raw oysters, fresh from the shell after it has been pried open, can make a meal in itself for oyster fanatics. Local experts believe oysters taken during cooler months are juicier and more delicious than summer shellfish. The closed season runs from June to September and oysters must be at least 3 inches long to be legally removed from Florida waters.

Pompano: A paper bag is a prime ingredient for a favorite dish with this fish. Called pompano paillote, the recipe calls for baking the fish after it's been covered with a sauce and tucked into a paper bag.

Catfish: This freshwater fish, rare on northern US menus, is very tasty when fried crispy and is increasingly becoming regular fare on Florida seafood menus.

Spotted sea trout: Found in coastal waters, this fish is usually served with almonds in a dish that can be fried or broiled.

Spiny lobster (crawfish): Arguments will never end about whether it's as good or better than its cold water relative in Maine. It differs in that it does not have meaty claws, so you must be content with digging into its tail. Off season for the lobster is April 1 until July 25. Most restaurants advertise it merely as lobster, so check with your waiter or waitress as to whether they serve the Florida or Maine variety.

Grouper: The Red Snapper and Mahi-mahi of Florida. It is a staple in seafood restaurants and stores. Steer away from broiling it, a cooking technique that tends to dry it out too much. You will also encounter grouper fingers and grouper filet.

Depending on where you are in Florida, you will also want to sample regional foods and seafoods. In the Keys, for example, the natives eat and enjoy spicy conch chowder, salad and fritters. Conch has a rubbery texture, not unlike clams or squid, and is difficult to cook properly. Blue crabs are tiny, but are another Florida delicacy when broiled. Shallow bays and inland waterways are the breeding grounds for scallops. The small variety, found in bays, are more delicious than the tougher deep sea variety.

OTHER CUISINE

Diners who prefer meat to seafood will find reasonably-priced, choice cuts of beef. The state ranks among the nation's top 10 in numbers of beef cattle. You will feel right at home on the range in South Central sections of the state, particularly around Arcadia, Brighton (near Okeechobee) and Kissimmee. To ensure you're getting Florida beef, eat in those areas. Otherwise, Winn-Dixie and Public supermarkets across the state and many restaurants carry Florida beef.

For more exotic tastes, an increasing number of restaurants have begun serving alligator meat. It tastes similar to veal but the texture is more rubbery, like squid.

Florida-flavored side dishes include the usual range of southern favorites: fried eggplant, okra, collard greens, black-eyed peas, hogjaws, chicken pot pie. Start your meal with a heart of palm salad.

Naturally, the enormous influx of immigrants from around the nation and the globe has introduced the usual range of cuisines you'll find in other states. Particularly evident are the tastes of Greece, Cuba, the Caribbean, New York deli-culture, Italy, Czechoslovakia, Spain, France, Germany and, increasingly, the Orient.

THINGS TO DO

TOURS & ATTRACTIONS

Alligatorland Safari: Nine miles south of Kissimmee on US 192. Monkeys and alligators in a swamp setting reached by a long board walk. Open daily. Tel: 407/396-1012.

Adventure Island: 4545 Bougainvillea Ave, Tampa. East of Busch Gardens. Water-oriented theme park on 22 acres. High drive platforms, water flumes, wave-making machines, restaurant, gift shop. Open daily March–December 10am–10pm; June 8–September 9; until 6pm at other times. Tel: 813/977-6606 for more information and ticket prices.

African Safari in the Caribbean Gardens: At 1590 Goodlette Road off US 41, Naples 33940. No tours are provided so you have to go on a self-guided tour. "Circus Africa" wild animal shows are held at 11.30am, 2pm and 4pm daily from November 1–May 1. Lions, tigers, elephants, snakes, birds and even more wildlife. Authentic souvenirs of Africa, India and Florida are available. The safari is open 9.30am–5pm daily. For ticket prices and further information, tel: 813/262-4053.

Audubon House: 205 Whitehead St, Key West 33040. Restored home of US Navy pilot John H. Geiger. The naturalist-artist John James Audubon lived here for several weeks in 1832 while sketching area birds. His original Double Elephant folio of *Birds of America* is on display along with other period antiques. Open 9am–5pm daily. Closed noon–1pm for lunch. Tel: 305/294-2116.

Bellm's Cars and Music of Yesterday: 5500 N. Tamiami Trail (US 41), Sarasota 33580. More than 170 restored antique and classic cars and 1,200 music boxes from the Gay '90s and Roaring '20s. Also features a country store, livery stable, blacksmith shop, 250-piece antique arcade, high-wheeled bicycles and more. Open 8.30am–6.30pm Monday–Saturday; from 9.30am on Sundays. Tel: 813/355-6228 for more information and current ticket prices.

Busch Gardens "The Dark Continent": 3000 Busch Blvd, Tampa. An African theme park full of wild animals, birds, reptiles, rides, restaurants and carnival games built around the Anheuser-Busch Brewery. Themed lands include the Serengeti Plain where more than 500 heads of big game roam free and can be inspected by train, monorail or cable car; Morocco, with a bazaar full of shops, belly dancers, snake charmers and magicians; Stanleyville, with trained animal shows, a jungle ride, flume ride, looping Python thrill ride and more; Timbuktu, trained dolphin shows, a continual Oktoberfest in the Festaus, and more rides; the Old Swiss House Restaurant; Hospitality House, with free beer; and daily brewery tours. The list of daily shows and events is subject to change. Open 9.30am–6pm daily; until 10pm June–Labor Day. Tel: 813/971-8282.

Church Street Station: West Church St, Downtown Orlando 32801. A shopping and eating complex fashioned out of historic old buildings. Attractions include Rosie O'Gradys Good Time Emporium, Phineas Phogg's Balloon Works (weekly champagne flights over Central Florida), Apple Annie's Courtyard, Lili Marlene's Aviators' Pub and the Rosie O'Grady's Flying Circus. Open 11am–2am daily. Tel: 303/422-2434.

Conch Tour Train: Key West 33040. Stations located at 501 Front St, 3850 N. Roosevelt Blvd, and at the corner of Angela and Duval streets. A 14-mile, 1½-hour narrated tour through Key West, old and new, historic and contemporary. These tours are available from 9am–4pm daily. Tel: 305/294-5161.

Coral Castle: 28655 S. Federal Hwy, Homestead 33030. The unrequited love of an eccentric genius is reflected in this fairy tale mansion that conjures up images of Stonehenge in England. Includes rock furniture, a sundial and a 9-ton swinging gate. The late Edward Leedskalnin never revealed how he moved the massive coral rocks weighing up to 35 tons each. He claimed to know the secrets used to build the pyramids of Egypt. Open 9am–9pm daily. Tel: 305/284-6344.

Cypress Gardens: State Route 540, Winter Haven 33880. One of Florida's oldest and most venerable tourist attractions. Water skiers create pyramids and perform other amazing acrobatic feats, in Lake Eloise, a waterway flanked by acres of carefully-nurtured gardens. Magnificent moss-draped cypress giants live here. Cruise the Cypress River and lake in electric boats. View the Aquarama where Esther Williams filmed her underwater musical spectacles. Photograph southern belles who decorate the gardens in their old-fashioned hoop skirts. A recent $5.5 million project has created 13 theme areas, including the New Southern Crossroads, a Living Forest, South Sea Island waterfalls, a fern forest, English courtyard, Japanese Garden, aviary and rose garden. Restaurants, two marine stadiums. Open 8am–6pm daily. Water ski performances at 10am, noon, 2 and 4pm. Tel: 813/324-2111.

Edison Home: 2350 McGregor Blvd, Fort Myers 33901. The sprawling 14-acre estate of one of the world's greatest inventors. Home, guest house, gardens, laboratory and a museum with some of Thomas Alva Edison's personal light bulbs, gramophones, batteries, movie cameras and automobiles. Guided tours every 30 minutes. Souvenirs, refreshments. Open 9am–4pm Monday–Saturday; from 12.30pm Sunday. Closed at Christmas. For ticket prices and more information, tel: 813/334-3612.

Everglades Wonder Gardens: US 41, Bonita Spring 33923. The mammals, reptiles and birds of South Florida, including the rare Florida panther, endangered Everglades crocodiles, otters and alligators in their natural tropical setting. Continuous guided tours from 9am–5pm daily. Tel: 813/992-2591.

Fairchild Tropical Garden: 10901 Old Cutler Road, Miami 33156. A botanical garden with 83 acres of palms, cycads, a rain forest, vine pergola, sunken garden, palm glade, rare plant house. Hourly tram tours. Open 9.30am–4.30pm daily. Closed Christmas. Tel: 305/667-1651.

Flipper's Sea School: US 1, Grassy Key, Florida Keys. Dolphin shows. This is the training center for the star of television's "Flipper." Open 10am–5pm daily. Tel: 305/289-1121.

Florida Citrus Tower: US 27, Clermont 32711. Observation deck providing views of rolling citrus country and lakes. Carillon, large souvenir center, packing house, candy shop, restaurant, ice cream parlor. Open 8am–6pm daily. Tel: 904/394-2145.

Fountain of Youth: 155 Magnolia Ave, St Augustine. Built around Ponce de León's legendary search for a spring that would provide eternal youth. Sip from the fountain, see traces of ancient Indian burial mounds, gaze at a statue of the famed explorer, and tour a museum, Discovery Globe and planetarium. Open September–June 8am–5pm daily; June–Labor Day 8am–7.30 p.m. Closed Christmas. Planetarium shows hourly from 9am For admission charges and further information, tel: 904/829-3168.

Gatorland Zoo: Hwy 441 North, Kissimmee 32741. Feed thousands of alligators and crocodiles. See Florida wildlife and birds. Take a swampwalk. Free tram. Covered walks. Open 8am–7pm daily during summer; otherwise until 6 p.m. Tel: 305/855-5496.

Gold Coast Railroad Museum: 12450 Coral Reef Drive, Miami. Steam into Florida's past aboard replicas of early Florida railroading. Included is the *Ferdinand Magellan*, the only Pullman ever built specifically for US Presidents, used by Roosevelt, Truman, Eisenhower and Reagan. Open 10am–3pm Monday–Saturday; 10am–5pm Sunday. Train rides Saturday, Sunday and holidays. Tel: 305/253-0063.

Gulfarium: US 98, Okaloosa Island, Fort Walton Beach 32548. Fish and scuba diving exhibitions. Trained porpoise and sea lion shows. Reef tank. Open 9am–6pm daily in summer; until 4pm in winter. Tel: 904/244-5169.

Hemingway House and Museum: 907 Whitehead St (US 1), Key West 33040. A Spanish Colonial built in 1851. Ernest Hemingway purchased the building in 1931 and added a swimming pool. He lived here for about 10 years during a prolific writing period that included publication of *The Snows of Kilimanjaro, To Have and Have Not* and *Death in the Afternoon*. Open 9am–5pm daily. For further information and admission fees, Tel: 305/294-1575.

Homosassa Springs: US 19, Homosassa Springs 32647. Walk under water in "Nature's Giant Fish Bowl." Cruise through tropical jungle waterways, hike on nature trails. Daily alligator and hippopotamus feedings. Located on a 55-foot deep spring at the source of the Homosassa River. Coffee shop, gift shops, orchid collection. Open 9.30am–5.30pm daily. Tel: 904/628-2311.

Jacksonville Zoological Park: 86806 Zoo Road off Heckscher Drive. Hundreds of animals, picnic facilities, children's rides, safari train. On the Trout River. Open 9am–5.30pm daily. Closed holidays. Tel: 904/757-4463.

Jungle Queen Cruises: Located on State Route A1A, Fort Lauderdale Beach. Daily departures from Bahia Mar Yacht Center for 3-hour sightseeing cruises into the Everglades at 10am and 2pm. Evening cruises include barbeque and shrimp dinner at 7pm. Reservations are recommended. Tel: 305/462-5596.

Kennedy Space Center Tours and Air Force Space Museum: Kennedy Space Center 32899. Begin at Spaceport USA on NASA Causeway 6 miles east of US 1 near Titusville. Two-hour narrated bus tours with stops at the enormous Vehicle Assembly Building (VAB), Mission Control, the Astronaut Training Facility and abandoned launch sites. Thirty rockets and more at the Air Force Museum near the south gate. Hall of History and more exhibits at Visitors' Center. Carousel Cafeteria. Tour itinerary and schedule may vary depending on launch schedule. Open 8am daily. Closed on launch days. Tel: 407/452-2121.

King Henry's Feast: 8949 International Drive, Orlando 32819. Unique dinner theater, with 3-hour show of fun, frivolity, food and drink in "olde English" manner, with knights in armor and serving maidens. Continuous entertainment and guest participation. Showtimes 8pm Sunday–Thursday; 6pm & 8.30pm Friday & Saturday. Tel: 305/351-5161.

Lightner Museum: St Augustine. One of the South's largest exhibits of antiques, collectibles and mechanical musical instruments. The exhibits are displayed on three floors of the former Alcazar Hotel, built in 1888. Open daily 9am–5pm except Christmas. Tel: 904/824-2874.

Lion Country Safari: Drive over miles of jungle trails that feature more than 1,000 roaming animals. Keep car windows rolled up. Safari boat rides, Everglades express train ride, petting and feeding area for small animals. Reptile park, dinosaur park, hiking trail and more. Restaurants, gift shops. Open 9.30am–4.30 p.m. Tel: 305/793-1084

London Wax Museum: 5505 Gulf Blvd, St Petersburg Beach. More than 100 life-sized wax figures from England in appropriate settings. Historical figures, Chamber of Horrors. Open 9am–9pm Monday–Saturday; noon–9pm Sunday. Tel: 813/360-6985.

Marie Selby Botanical Gardens: 800 S. Palm Ave, Sarasota. Six acres of exotic plants. Greenhouse. Open 10am–5pm daily. Closed at Christmas. Tel: 813/366-5730.

Marineland: P.O. St Augustine 32084 on A1A south of St Augustine. An entire village built around the granddaddy of all marine attractions. Huge oceanariums on the Atlantic Ocean side provide constant salt water environments, housing porpoises, manatees, electric eels, sharks, dolphins, barracudas. Eleven exhibits. Aquarius Theater, newly-renovated and expanded. Shows at 9.30am, 11am, 12.30pm, 2pm, 3.30pm and 4.50pm. Restaurants, gift shops, motel. Park open 8am–6.30pm daily. St Augustine Chamber of Commerce, tel: 904/471-1111.

Metrozoo: 12400 S.W. 152 St Miami. Animals roam free over 295 acres. More than 3 miles of walkways, a monorail and petting zoo. Open daily 9.30am–4pm. Tel: 305/251-0400.

Miami Seaquarium: 4400 Rickenbacker Causeway, Key Biscayne 33149. Killer Whale and "Flipper" dolphin shows. Pet sea lions, shark feedings, huge "living sea" aquarium. Monorail ride. Open 9am–6.30pm daily. Shows on the half hour beginning at 10am Tel: 305/361-5703.

Mission of Nombre de Dios: San Marco Ave, St Augustine 32084. Believed to be the site of the first Christian mission in the nation started by Father Lopez de Mendoza Grajales about 1565. Prince of Peace Church, Shrine of Our Lady of La Leche, Mission Art Guild building. Illuminated, stainless steel cross marks site of the nation's first mass. Open 7am–8pm daily in summer; 8am–6pm daily in winter. Admission free, but donations requested. Tel: 904/824-2809.

Monkey Jungle: 14805 S.W. 216th St, Miami 33170. The place "where humans are caged and monkeys run free." Safe caged walkways. "Amazonian rain forest." Exotic monkeys, gorillas, baboons, orangutans. Continuous shows. Open 9.30am–5pm daily. Tel: 305/235-1611.

Museum of Science and Industry: 4801 E. Fowler Ave, Tampa 33605. Exhibits include the Gulf Coast Hurricane, a recreated 75 mph wind tunnel that you can lean into to sample Nature's seasonal fury. Also available are lots of hands-on exhibits and a working weather station. Open 10am–4.30pm daily. Tel: 813/985-5531.

Mystery Fun Houses: 5767 Major Blvd, Orlando, off I-4. Fifteen entertainment areas with magic floors, rolling barrels, laughing doors. Spectacular minature golf. Tel: 407/351-3355.

Ocean World: 1701 S.E. 17th St Causeway, Ft. Lauderdale. Porpoise shows, sharks, alligators and sea lions. Tour boat rides and a sky ride are available. Open 10am–6pm daily, but box office closes at 4.30 p.m. Continuous shows. Tel: 305/525-6611.

Oldest House Museum: 322 Duval St, Key West 33040. Built by sea captain Francis B. Atlington in 1829, it has been restored and refurnished with antiques, paintings, model ships and toys. Open 9am–5pm daily, except Wednesday. Tel: 305/294-9502.

Oldest House: 14 St Francis St, St Augustine 32084. First built in the early 18th century. Constructed of coquina from Anastasia Island. Full of antiques. Open 9am–5pm daily. Closed Christmas. Tel: 904/824-2872.

Oldest Store Museum: 4 Artillery Lane, St Augustine 32084. Modeled upon a turn-of-the-century general store. Thousands of antiques on sale and display. Open 9am–5pm Monday–Saturday; from noon Sunday. Closed Christmas. Tel: 904/829-9729.

Oldest Wooden Schoolhouse: 14 St George St, St Augustine 32804. Built by Spanish for use as a private home and later utilized as a school. Open 9am–5pm daily. Tel: 904/824-2896.

Orchid Jungle: 26715 S.W. 157th Ave, Homestead 33030. Tom Fennel Jr. operates family gardens that include about 250,000 plants. Most are in natural habitats. Potted plants are on display and are also for sale. Open 8.30am–5.30pm daily. Closed on Thanksgiving and Christmas. Tel: 305/247-4824.

Paddlewheel Queen: 2950 N.E. 32nd Ave, Fort Lauderdale. Three-hour sightseeing cruises on the Intracoastal Waterway beginning at 2pm daily. Dinner cruises are scheduled at 7.30pm on Tuesday, Thursday, Friday and Saturday. Reservations needed; Tel: 305/564-7659.

Parrot Jungle: 11000 S.W. 57 Ave, Miami 33156. Free-flying macaws, marching flamingos in natural settings. Bird shows. Six shows daily in amphitheater at 1½-hour intervals. Open 9.30am–5pm daily. Tel: 305/666-7834.

Potter's Wax Museum: 17 King St, St Augustine 32084. One of the oldest and largest in United States. More than 240 wax sculptures of famous personalities from history and legend in period settings that include authentic antiques. Open 9am–8pm daily during summer; until 5pm otherwise. Closed Christmas. Tel: 904/829-9056.

Ringling Museums: P.O. Box 1839, Sarasota 33578. Off US 41. The Venetian-Gothic Ringling residence, **Ca'd'zan,** built by circus king John Ringling for his wife Mable in 1925. Features colored glass windows; antiques, tapestries, marble floors. The estate also includes the Italian-style **Museum of Art** containing an impressive collection of Pierre Paul Rubens paintings, classical sculpture in a courtyard, contemporary collection and special exhibits. The adjoining **Asolo State Theater** presents annual repertory plays, films and operas. The interior was brought from Asolo, Italy, where it had served as a theater since 1798. The **Museum of the Circus** has antiques and memorabilia from Ringling's "Greatest Show on Earth." One price admission tickets. Open 9am–

7pm weekdays; until 5pm Saturday; 11am–6pm Sunday. Tel: 813/355-5101.

Ripley's Believe It or Not Museum: 19 San Marco Ave, St Augustine 32084. Unusual collection of oddities, curiosities and art objects collected by Robert L. Ripley during his world travels. Three floors stocked with thousands of exhibits. Open 9am–9pm daily during summer; 9am–6pm at other times. Tel: 904/824-1606.

St Augustine Alligator Farm: On A1A South, St Augustine 32084. Billed as "the world's original alligator attraction." Established in 1893. Alligators and crocodiles piled high. Florida wildlife shows are screened every hour, featuring reptiles. Gator wrestling. Open 9am–5.30pm daily. Tel: 904/824-3337.

St Augustine Sightseeing Trains: 3 Cordova St, St Augustine 32084. A 7-mile conducted tour of the nation's oldest city. Stop-off privileges at attractions. Regular tickets are good for a period of 24 hours. Tel: 904/829-6545.

Sarasota Jungle Gardens: 3701 Bayshore Road, off Myrtle Street, Sarasota. A 15-acre park containing more than 5,000 varieties of tropical plants – including orchids, flame vines and birds of paradise. Alligators, macaws, mynah birds, flamingos and swans share the grounds. Bird and reptile shows. Open 9am–5pm daily. Tel: 813/355-5305.

Sea World: 7007 Sea World Drive, Orlando 32821. World's largest marine life park starring Shamu the killer whale, dolphins, seals and other shows, marine exhibits and aquariums, water-ski show, Hawaiian and Japanese Villages. Walk through a tunnel surrounded by toothy creatures in **Shark Encounter**. More than 125 acres of attractions, stadiums, shops, restaurants. Also a 400-foot observation tower decorated as a giant Christmas tree in December. Deer park. Computerized indoor water fountain show. Open from 9am until dark daily. For more information and current admission charges, tel: 305/351-3600.

Silver Springs: State Road 40 Silver Springs 32688. Veteran attraction built around the source of the Silver River and the largest spring in the state. It flows at a rate of 587 gallons per day. Water is a constant 73.4° temperature. Swimming, picnicking, parks, glass-bottom boatrides, jungle cruise, reptile institute, antique car collection, deer park. The grounds abound with alligators, wild monkeys and waterfowl. One price admission. Restaurants, souvenir shops. Open 9am–6.30pm daily during summer; 9am–4.30pm rest of year. Tel: 904/236-2121.

Six Flags Atlantis: Bordering an 11-acre lake in Hollywood, Fort Lauderdale (at the intersection of I-95 and Stirling Road). Water theme park with wave-action pool, speed slides, rapids rides, diving platforms, coves and pools for children. Also live performances at a land amphitheater. Restaurants, games arcades and shops. Boats and rafts for rental. Open daily at 10am (closing hours vary with seasons). One admission price. Tel: 305/926-1000.

Snake-A-Torium: US 98, Panama City Beach, 32401. Watch venom extraction demonstrations called "snake-milking." Open from 9am until dusk daily. Tel: 904/234-3311.

Spaceport USA: TWS Kennedy Space Center 32899. Daily bus tours plus IMAX Theater showing Space Shuttle launches and space activity on screen 5½-stories high. Free parking, free kennels and free admission to Spaceport USA. Open 9am daily. First bus tour starts at 9.45am and operates continuously until 2 hours before dark. Tel: 305/452-2121.

Spongerama: 510 Dodecanese Blvd, Tarpon Springs 33589. Attraction revolving around the sponge-diving industry and Greek heritage. Sponge factory and museum. Displays, photographs. Film of sponge diving trip on the half-hour. Arts and crafts shops. Genuine sponges for sale. Tel: 813/942-3771.

Stephen Foster Center: US 41, White Springs 32096. Memorabilia, museum displays, dioramas, musical instruments, in memorial to the composer who immortalized the Swannee River. Also a 97-bell Deagan carillon in a 200-foot tall tower that plays medleys of Foster's music at regular intervals. Entertainers, gift shops and a restaurant. Park open 8am until sunset daily; museum and tower open 9am–5pm daily. Tel: 305/397-2733.

Theater of the Sea: US 1, Islamorada 33036. Dolphin shows, glass-bottom boat rides, shark pit. In coral grotto. Open 9am–4pm daily. Tel: 306/664-2431

Tiki Gardens: 19601 Gulf Blvd, Indian Shores 33535. Items from Hawaii, Polynesia and other South Seas places ornament a winding walk through gardens filled with colorful strutting peacocks and other exotic birds. Gift shops, Trader Frank's Restaurant. Open 9.30am–10.30pm daily. Tel: 813/595-2567.

Vizcaya Museum and Gardens: 3251 South Miami Ave, Miami 33129. Private palace of 50 rooms built by James Deering in 1914. Italian Renaissance architecture and formal gardens overlooking Biscayne Bay. Guided or self-guiding tours. Collection of European decorative arts. Gift shop and café. Sound and light shows at 8pm Friday and Saturday. Open 10am–5pm except Christmas. Ticket window closes at 4.30 p.m. Tel: 305/579-2708.

Voyager Sightseeing Train: Bahia Mar Yacht Basin, Fort Lauderdale. A highway train takes an 18-mile tour to points of interest in and around the city. Additional tours are run to Flamingo Gardens and Kapok Tree on Tuesday, Thursday and Saturday. Operates at 10am, noon, 2pm and 4pm daily. Tel: 305/463-0401.

Wakulla Springs and Lodge: Wakulla Springs 32305. Glass-bottom boat tours the crystal waters of the Wakulla River, a registered natural landmark. Jungle Boat tours. Swimming, picnicking, wildlife trails, souvenirs, accommodations. Open 9.30am–5pm daily in winter; until 5.30pm during summer months. Tel: 904/640-7011.

Walt Disney World: P.O. Box 10040, Lake Buena Vista 32830. (*See "Walt Disney World" in the Places section for detailed descriptions.*) Mickey Mouse's Vacation Kingdom opens at 9am daily. Closing times vary from 7pm during winter to midnight during summer and later on special holidays. Extended operating hours also during Christmas and New Year holidays. Write to: Box 78 for reservations. You can choose from several types of tickets and admissions packages at gate. The kingdom includes the River Country water-oriented theme park, Walt Disney World Village, Discovery Island and much more. For details, tel: 407/824-4321 or 407/824-4500.

Weeki Wachee Springs Mermaid Show: US 19 at Florida 50, Weeki Wachee 33512. Exotic bird show, wilderness river cruise, enchanted rain forest, nature trails and the unique underwater swimming show featuring beautiful mermaids who dance and perform music in the depths of the spring. The mermaids can be viewed through an underwater amphitheater. Open 9am until dusk daily. The spring is the source of the Weeki Wachee River. Climactic mermaids dive to a depth of 117½ feet. Thirty-minute shows at regular intervals. Tel: 904/596-2062.

Wet 'N' Wild: 6200 International Drive, Orlando 32809. Surf lagoon, whitewater slideways, crazy water playground, puddle jumper pool, *kamikaze* water slide, picnicking, boating, beach activities. Open 9am–9pm daily during summer; 10am–5pm the rest of the year. Tel: 305/351-1800.

Wild Waters: State Route 40, next to Silver Springs 32688. Water theme park with flume rides, wave pool, frisbee court, water fort, wet miniature golf, picnic areas. Open late March–early June, 10am–5 p.m; from the first week in June to the first week in September, 10am–8 p.m. Tel: 904/236-2121.

Zorayda Castle: 85 King St, St Augustine 32084. A huge architectural reproduction of the Alhambra, Spain's most famous castle in old Granada. Within the walls of this replica are displays of how the Moorish kings lived, entertained and ruled Spain. Treasures from around the world on display as well. Open 9am–5.30pm daily. Tel: 904/824-3097.

NATIONAL FORESTS

Apalachicola: Extending west from Tallahassee to the Apalachicola River, its 557,000 acres of pine hardwood forest, swamps, rivers, sinkholes and springs make it the largest of Florida's three national forests. Encompasses the Silver Lake Recreation Area with tent camping, trailer sites, swimming and picnicking for a small fee, south of Florida 20 on Florida 260. Hitchcock, Wright and Camel Lake areas also offer recreational facilities. Contact: Apalachicola Ranger Station, Sumatra Star Route, Box 9, Tallahassee 32304. Wilma Ranger Station is located 20 miles southwest of Hosford, Florida on Hwy 65.

Ocala: Situated east of the city of Ocala between the Oklawaha and St Johns River; the "Big Scrub" covers 366,000 acres of sand, longleaf and slash pine, cypress and hardwoods. Tubing, canoeing, and cave-diving are extremely popular at Juniper Springs, 24 miles east of Ocala on State Hwy 40. Write: Juniper Springs Recreation Area, Route 2, Box 701, Silver Springs, Florida 32688, or tel: 904/625-2520.

Alexander Springs Recreation Area, 16 miles north of Eustis, east of Florida 19. More tubing, swimming, camping and picnicking. Contact: Alexander Springs Recreation Area, P.O. Box 11, Altoona, Florida 32702. For general information on the park contact: Lake George Ranger District, Post Office Bldg, P.O. Box 1206, Ocala 32670. The Lake Bryant Ranger Station is 18 miles east of Ocala on Florida 40 and Pittman Ranger Station is 11 miles north of Eustis on State Road 19.

Osceola: East of Lake City on US Hwy 90, comprises 157,000 acres. Controlled hunting of deer, quail and dove is permitted; bass, bream and perch fishing is also popular. Ocean Pond, 15 miles east of Lake City and 3 miles north of US 90, has good swimming, fishing and camping. Contact Route 7, Box 95, Lake City, 32055. The Olustee Guard Station is 3 miles east of Olustee on US 90.

NATIONAL PARKS & PRESERVES

Everglades: Florida's only National Park, it covers most of Florida's southern tip. You can camp, fish, hunt, hike, boat, canoe and observe its wide range of fascinating wildlife concentrated over more than 1.4 million acres of pinelands, cypress forest, marshes and mangroves. (*See* "The Everglades" *in this book for further information*.) Boat tours into the park and the Ten Thousand Islands can be arranged, write to Everglades National Park Boat Tours, Box 119 Everglades City 33929; or tel: 813/695-2591. Reservations for the lodge or campsites can be made by writing to Everglades Park Catering, Flamingo Lodge, Flamingo 33030; or tel: 813/695-3101.

Big Cypress National Preserve: Established in 1974 on 570,000 acres, or about 40 percent of the Big Cypress Swamp; offers nature trails, camping, hunting, trapping and fishing. (*See* "The Everglades" *in the Places section*.) Or write to: S.R. Box 110, Ochopee, Florida 33943. Tel: 813/695-2000.

NATIONAL SEASHORES

Canaveral: More than 67,000 acres of dunes and beach due south of New Smyrna Beach to Cape Canaveral. Headquarters are 7 miles east of Titusville on Florida 402. Most portions accessible only by foot. Swimming, surfing and picnicking at Playalinda Beach, 12 miles east of Titusville on Florida 406 or at Apollo Park, 10 miles south of New Smyrna Beach on A1A. No camping. Contact: P.O. Box 6447, Titusville, Florida 33090. Tel: 407/867-0634.

Gulf Islands: 150 miles of pristine coastline stretching from Destin in the Panhandle to Gulfport, Mississippi. Encompasses the ruins of Fort Pickens in Pensacola Beach, where Indian warrior Geronimo was imprisoned. Beach, swimming, picnic and concession facilities at the Santa Rosa area on Florida 399. Also includes historic sites at the Naval Air Station. More recreational facilities at Perdido Key on Florida 292 and Okaloosa, east of Fort Walton Beach. Contact: Superintendant, P.O. Box 100, Gulf Breeze 32561.

FAIRS & LIVESTOCK SHOWS

JANUARY

Collier Co. Fair: 751 39th Ave N.E., Naples 33964. Tel: 813/263-2949.
South Florida Fair: Box 15915, West Palm Beach 33406. Tel: 407/793-0333.

FEBRUARY

De Soto Co. Fair: Box 970, Arcadia 33821. Tel: 813/494-3476.
Florida Citrus Festival: Box 9229, Winter Haven 33880. Tel: 813/293-3175.
Florida State Fair: Box 11766, Tampa 336080. Tel: 813/621-7821.
Highlands Co. Fair: P.O. Box 1981, Sebring 33871. Tel: 813/382-225.
Hillsborough Co. Fair & Strawberry Festival: Box 1869, Plant City 33566. Tel: 813/752-9194.
Kissimmee Valley Fair Livestock Show: Box 639, Kissimmee 32741. Tel: 305/846-6040.
Pasco Co. Fair: 1510 Hwy 52 West, Dade City 33525. Tel: 904/567-6678.
South Dade County Fair: Drawer 1390, Homestead 33030. Tel: 305/247-2234.
Southeastern Youth Fair: P.O. Box 940, Ocala 32678. Tel: 904/732-4143.
St Lucie Co. Fair: 4116 St Lucie Blvd, Fort Pierce 34946. Tel: 407/464-2910.

MARCH

Central Florida Fair: P.O. Box 2268, Orlando 32802. Tel: 407/295-3247.
Citrus Co. Fair: 3600 South Florida Ave, Inverness 32650. Tel: 904/726-2993.
Clay Co. Fair: P.O. Box 1066, Green Cove Springs 32042. Tel: 904/269-6355.
Dade Co. Youth Fair: 10901 Coral Way, Miami 33165. Tel: 305/223-7060.
Glades Co. Fair: P.O. Box 490, Moore Haven, 33471. Tel: 813/946-0440.
Hardee Co. Fair: P.O. Box 1831, Wauchula 33873. Tel: 813/773-2164.
Hendry Co. Fair: State Road 833, Clewiston 33440. Tel: 813/983-9422.
Indian River Co. Fair: 1840 25th St, Vero Beach 32960. Tel: 407/562-2028.
Martin Co. Fair: 2616 S.E. Dixie Hwy, Stuart 34996. Tel: 305/287-8988.
Pinellas Co. Fair: 7801 Park Blvd, Pinellas Park 34665. Tel: 813/541-6841.
Polk Co. Youth Fair: 1702 Hwy 17 South, Bartow 33830. Tel: 813/533-0765.
Putnam Co. Fair: 20 Yelvington Road, Suite 1, East Palatka 32031. Tel: 904/329-0318.
Sarasota Co. Fair: 3000 Ringling Blvd, Sarasota 33577. Tel: 813/365-0818.
Sumter Co. Fair: P.O. Box 655, Bushnell 33513. Tel: 904/793-2750.
Suwannee River Fair & Livestock Show: P.O. Box 219, Bronson 32621. Tel: 904/486-2165.
Tomato-Snook Festival: P.O. Box 2756, Bonita Springs 33959. Tel: 813/992-3982.

APRIL

Bradford Co. Fair: P.O. Box 576, Starke 32091. Tel: 904/964-5252.
Hernando Co. Fair: 6436 Broad St, Brooksville 34601. Tel: 904/796-4552.
Lake Co. Fair: P.O. Box 221, Eustis 32726. Tel: 904/357-7111.
Sugar Festival: 100 Berner Road, Clewiston 33440. Tel: 813/983-9101.

MAY

Desoto Watermelon Festival: P.O. Box 149, Arcadia 33821. Tel: 813/494-4033.
Flager Co. Fair – Bunnel: P.O. Box 308, Palm Coast 32010. Tel: 904/437-3122.

OCTOBER

Bay Co. Fair: P.O. Box 68, Panama City 32401. Tel: 904/769-2645
Columbia Co. Fair; P.O. Box 1376, Lake City 32056. Tel: 904/752-8822
Hamilton Co. Fair: P.O. Drawer K, Jasper 32052. Tel: 904/792-1276

Holmes Co. Fair: 306 E. Minnesota Ave, Bonifay 32425. Tel: 904/547-3394
Jackson Co. Fair: Route 7, Box 53, Marianna 32446. Tel: 904/482-5474
North Florida Fair: 441 Paul Russell Road, Tallahassee 32301. Tel: 904/877-3628
Northeast Florida Fair: P.O. Box B, Callahan 32011. Tel: 904/879-1029
Okaloosa Co. Fair: 1958 Lewis Turner Blvd, Fort Walton Beach 32548. Tel: 9004/862-0211
Pensacola Fair: P.O. Box 255, Pensacola 32592. Tel: 904/944-4500.
Suwannee Co. Fair: P.O. Box 266, Live Oak 32060. Tel: 904/362-7366
Walton Co. Fair: Route 8, Box 38, Defuniak Springs 32433. Tel: 904/892-2598

NOVEMBER

Alachua Co. Fair: P.O. Box 2566, Gainesville 32602. Tel: 904/372-1537
Brevard Co. Fair: P.O. Box 594, Cocoa 32926. Tel: 407/639-3976
Broward Co. Fair: 2201 Hayes St, Hollywood 33020. Tel: 305/923-3247
Florida Heritage Festival: 2000 S. Dixie Hwy, West Palm Beach 33401. Tel: 407/832-6397
Harvest: A County Fair: 101 W. Flagler St, Miami 33130. Tel: 305/375-1492
Volusia Co. Fair and Youth Show: Drawer X, Deland 32720. Tel: 904/734-9514

A BIRDWATCHER'S EXTRA

Visitors have always marveled at Florida's prolific bird population. Even master naturalist John James Audubon came here more than 100 years ago to sketch Florida's colorful fowl. The birds in our montage on pages 248–249 and the photographers who captured them are:

1   an osprey (Paul Zach)
2   a little blue heron (José Azel)
3   a snowy egret-detail (Ron Jett)
4   a purple gallinule (Paul Zach)
5   a snowy egret (José Azel)
6   American flamingos (Joe Viesti)
7   burrowing owl (Ron Jett)
8   a brown pelican (Tom Servais)

CULTURE PLUS

MUSIC & THEATER

Here is a guide to the various cultural activities one can expect during certain months of the year.

FEBRUARY

Asolo State Theater Season – Sarasota: The Asolo Theater (February–September) is known nationally and internationally as one of the most brilliant professional theaters in America. During its 7-month season, 7 or 8 of the world's best plays, ranging from classics to world premieres, will be performed in straight run and rotating repertory. (Director of Information, Asolo State Theater, Drawer E, Sarasota 33578. Tel: 813/355-2771.)

Bok Tower Gardens Moonlight Recital – Lake Wales: Held every full moon, these recitals are quite a special treat, featuring the music of the carillon – a different carillon every full moon. (Bok Tower Gardens, P.O. Box 3810, Lake Wales 33853. Tel: 813/676-1408.)

Miami Film Festival – Miami: At the beginning of February, you will find the Gusman Theater reverberating to the sounds of US and foreign films, lectures, seminars and jazz music. (Film Society of Miami Inc., 444 Brickell Ave, Suite 229, Miami 33131. Tel: 305/377-3456.)

MARCH

Bok Tower Gardens Easter Sunrise Service – Lake Wales: Easter Sunrise Service at the Bok Tower Gardens. (Bok Tower Gardens, P.O. Box 3810, Lake Wales 33853. Tel: 813/676-1408.)

Kissimmee Bluegrass Festival – Kissimmee: (Always second weekend in March) Bluegrass bands, performers and fans gather in the Silver Spurs Arena for 3 days of fun and music. (Semoran Management Corp., 1080 Woodcock Road, #210, Orlando 32803. Tel: 407/896-4461.)

APRIL

Bluegrass Camp-O-Ree – Live Oak: Blue grass music performed in the natural amphitheater on the banks of the Suwannee River at the Spirit of the Suwannee Park (Route 98, Live Oak 32060. Tel: 904/364-1683.)

Florida Jam – Pompano Beach: South Florida's largest 1-day country music event. Past entertainers include Hank Williams Jr., The Charlie Daniels Band, Alabama, The Oak Ridge Boys. (Fantasma Productions Inc., 2000 South Dixie Hwy, West Palm Beach 33401. Tel: 407/832-6397.)

Pensacola Jazz Festival – Pensacola: Held at Bartram Park, this jazz festival features nationally known musicians and locals playing a variety of jazz styles, along with an arts-and-crafts fair, food and parties. (Arts Council of Northwest Florida, P.O. Box 731, Pensacola 32594. Tel: 904/432-9906.)

MAY

Seminole Bluegrass, Folk and Art Festival – Seminole: Always held one week after Mother's Day. Features continuous bluegrass and folk music, and arts-and-crafts fair and children's games. (Seminole Junior Women's Club, 14053 80th Ave North, Seminole 34646. Tel: 813/391-2165.)

SunFest – West Palm Beach: Always held the first weekend in May, SunFest features "Florida's largest outdoor jazz festival" with past performers such as George Benson, Wynton Marsalis, Gato Barbieri and Spyro Gyra. There's also a juried art show, an international bazaar, professional power boat races, water ski shows, food festivals and more. (SunFest of Palm Beach County Inc., 319 Clematis St, Suite 209, West Palm Beach 33401. Tel: 407/659-5980.)

JUNE

Cross and Sword – St Augustine: (Always mid-June through August) Florida's official state play is an outdoor symphonic drama by Pulitzer Prize winner Paul Green. A 65-member cast re-enacts in song, dance, drama and comedy the founding of St Augustine in 1565, and the early years of the nation's oldest permanent city. (General Manager, Cross and Sword, Box 1965, St Augustine 32084. Tel: 904/471-1965.)

Hammocks Pop Music Festival – Miami: Held annually on the weekend before Fourth of July, with a symphony pop concert, family activities and a fireworks display among the highlights (PACE, P.O. Box 40, Miami 33168-0040. Tel: 305/681-1470.)

SEPTEMBER

Tampa's Jazzin' Jubilee – Tampa: A 4-day extravaganza featuring traditional jazz bands from around the world in cabaret-style performances throughout the city. (Tampa/Hillsborough Convention and Visitors' Bureau, 100 S. Ashley Drive, Suite 850, Tampa 33602. Tel: 1-800/826-8358.)

OCTOBER

Florida National Jazz Festival – Jacksonville: One of the largest outdoor jazz festivals in the US, drawing thousands of jazz fans to Metropolitan Park. (WJCT-TV, 100 Festival Park Ave, Jacksonville 32202. Tel: 904/353-7770.)

Sanibel Jazz On The Green – Sanibel Island: Held the second weekend of October (Saturday evening and Sunday afternoon event) featuring popular jazz entertainers in an open air concert. It also offers foods and wines and other speciality entertainment. (The Dunes Country Club, 949 Sandcastle Road, Sanibel Island 33957. Tel: 813/472-3355.)

DECEMBER

Bok Tower Gradens Christmas Eve Recital – Lake Wales: Each Christmas Eve, the story of Christmas is presented, alternating with Christmas carillon music. (Bok Tower Gardens, P.O. Box 3810, Lake Wales 33853. Tel: 813/676-1408.)

ARTS & CRAFTS SHOWS

In addition to music and drama, arts and crafts shows are also popular events which draw the crowds.

JANUARY

Lake Placid Art League Annual Show And Sale – Sebring: Usually held the third or fourth weekend in January at the Agri-Civic Center, with a strong flavor of regional arts and crafts on display and for sale. (Lake Placid Art League, P.O. Box 1467, Lake Placid 33852. Tel: 813/678-1452.)

Redland's Natural Arts and Crafts Festival – Miami: This annual event features artists and craftsmen from South Florida and is held in Redland Fruit and Spice Park. The park also offers nature walks, guided tours, a petting zoo and an international food bazaar and entertainment. (Metro-Dade County Park and Recreation Dept, 50 S.W. 32nd Road, Bldg #9, Miami 33129. Tel: 305/579-2676.)

FEBRUARY

Artists' Day – Miami: More than 200 artists display their works in the formal Italian gardens of Vizcaya, James Deering's palatial winter home built in 1916. (Vizcaya Museum & Gardens, 3251 S. Miami Ave, Miami 33129. Tel: 305/372-7955.)

Coconut Grove Arts Festival – Coconut Grove: More than 350 artists and craftsmen display and sell their works while performing artists entertain at one of the nation's top-rated outdoor art festivals. (Coconut Grove Association, Box 330757 Coconut Grove 33133. Tel: 305/447-0401.)

Mount Dora Art Festival – Mount Dora: Held on the sidewalks of Mount Dora, the event has become one of the most popular art festivals in Florida. Over 50,000 attend 2 days of exhibits shown in several categories. (Mount Dora Center for the Arts, 138 E. Fifth Ave, Mount Dora 32757. Tel: 904/383-0880.)

MARCH

Art In The Sun Festival – Pompano Beach: Several hundred artists throughout the United States and Canada display and sell their works. (Chamber of Commerce, 2200 E. Atlantic Blvd, Pompano Beach 33062. Tel: 305/941-2940.)

Delray Affair – Delray Beach: The Delray Affair is an annual sidewalk art festival which is held along Atlantic Avenue in downtown Delray Beach on the first weekend after Easter. Lots of food and entertainment to look forward to. (Greater Delray Chamber of Commerce, 64 S.E. Fifth Ave, Delray Beach 33483. Tel: 407/278-0424.)

Gasparilla Sidewalk Art Festival – Tampa: This outdoor 1-day art festival features more than $20,000 in prizes, and therefore draws some of the top artists in the country for a juried show. (Gasparilla Art Festival, 1211 N. Westshore Blvd, Tampa 33607. Tel: 813/873-2129.)

Great American Love Affair – Boynton Beach: On the first weekend of March and featuring more than 120 artists and craftsmen in a juried show. There is also food, music, dance exhibitions, theater performances and a business exposition. (City of Boynton Beach, P.O. Box 232, Boynton Beach 33425-0232. Tel: 407/738-7444.)

Islamorada's Annual Rain Barrel Arts Festival – Islamorada: On the third weekend of March, this event offers original works by more than 60 artists and craftsmen in categories such as ceramics, glass, jewelry, sculpture, photography and fine art. (The Rain Barrel, 86700 Overseas Hwy, Islamorada 33036. Tel: 305/852-3084.)

Mandarin Art Festival – Jacksonville: Every Easter weekend the Mandarin Community Club sponsors this juried art show as the club's chief fund-raiser. (Mandarin Community Club, 12380 Mandarin Road, Jacksonville 3223. Tel: 904/268-3411.)

Sidewalk Art Festival – Winter Park: (Always held on the third weekend in March.) The most prestigious festival of its kind in the Southeast, this sidewalk art display features a show and sale, concerts, strolling musicians and folk-song session. (Winter Park Art Festival, P.O. Box 597, Winter Park 32790.)

St Patrick's Day Arts and Crafts Show – Fort Pierce: Held every Saturday before St Patrick's Day, this arts-and-crafts show is a strong showcase for local and regional work. (Fort Pierce Community Center, 600 N. Indian River Drive, Fort Pierce 34982. Tel: 407/464-1777.)

APRIL

Tarpon Springs Arts & Crafts Festival – Tarpon Springs: Here, hundreds of artists display their work against the backdrop of Spanish moss-draped trees and beautiful Spring Bayou. (Greater Tarpon Springs Chamber of Commerce, 210 South Pinellas Ave, #120, Tarpon Springs 34689. Tel: 813/937-6109.)

JUNE

Summer Fest: Always on the last weekend of the month and featuring a 2-day arts-and-crafts festival along with top name musical entertainers. (Fantasma Productions Inc., 2000 Dixie Hwy, West Palm Beach 33401. Tel: 407/832-6397.)

JULY

Misccosukee Annual International Crafts And Music Festival – Miami: On the third weekend of the month, South Florida's ethnic communities join together at the Miccosukee Village for a cultural festival of food, music, arts and crafts, dancing and much more. (Lee Tiger and Associates, 22020 S.W. 100th Place, Miami 33190. Tel: 305/252-0791.)

SEPTEMBER

Keystone Heights Festival Of The Lake Art Show – Keystone Heights: Always held on the first weekend of the month, featuring all types of arts and crafts in a juried show. (Keystone Heights Junior Women's Club, P.O. Box 995, Keystone Heights 32656. Tel: 904/473-2682.)

Lake Wales Quilt Exhibition – Lake Wales: Featured are quilts by local residents, the local museum's quilt collection and other various handcrafts. (Lake Wales Museum and Cultural Center, The Depot, 325 South Scenic Hwy, Lake Wales 33853. Tel: 813/676-5443.)

Osceleo Art Festival – Kissimmee: Artists and craftsmen display their works on the shores of Lake Tohopikaliga. (Kissimmee-St Cloud Jaycees, 134 Japonica Drive, Orlando 32807. Tel: 407/277-1004.)

OCTOBER

Autumn Art Festival – Cocoa: This autumn festival is held on the first weekend of the month. (Autumn Art Festival, P.O. Box 1967, #Cocoa 32923-1967. Tel: 305/452-5256.)

Festival In The Park – Jasper: Always in the second week of October, on the last day of the Hamilton County Fair. (Hamilton County Chamber of Commerce, P.O. Drawer P, Jasper 32052. Tel: 904/792-1300.)

Lake Mary-Heathrow Festival Of The Arts – Heathrow: On the weekend prior to Halloween, this show features music, visual arts, dance, crafts and other entertainment. (The Centerra Group, 250 International Parkway, Suite 204, Heathrow 32746-4121. Tel: 407/333-1111.)

NOVEMBER

Art Harvest Show and Sale – Dunedin: A 2-day show involving about 200 artists and craftsmen. (Junior League of Clearwater-Dunedin, 129 N. Fort Harrison Ave, Clearwater 34615. Tel: 813/442-0223.)

Community Craft Show – Longwood: This local show is held on the Saturday right after Thanksgiving at the Longwood Recreation Center. (Chamber of Commerce, 2200 Virginia Ave, Fort Pierce 34982. Tel: 407/461-2700.)

Festival Of The Masters – Lake Buena Vista: (Always 2nd Weekend In November.) More than 200 award-winning artists display their work in oil paintings, water colors, drawings and graphics, mixed media, photographs, sculpture, ceramics and creative crafts. The outdoor festival take place along shores of Lake Buena Vista Lagoon. (Special Events, P.O. Box 10000, Lake Buena Vista 32830. Tel: 407/828-3425.)

Great Gulf Coast Arts Festivals – Pensacola: Pensacola's historic Seville Square comes alive with contemporary and traditional arts as 225 artists and craftsmen from across the nation compete for $4,000 in cash prizes. Also featured are performing arts, street entertainment and demonstrations of historic American crafts. (Arts Council of Northwest Florida, P.O. Box 731, Pensacola 32594. Tel: 904/432-9906.)

Halifax Art Festival – Ormond Beach: (Always first weekend in November.) This is an art show and sale. The event is sponsored by the Daytona Beach Museum of Arts and Sciences, and is held on the grounds of the stately Old Ormond Beach Hotel, a historic landmark. (Museum of Arts and Science, 1040 Museum Blvd, Daytona Beach 32014. Tel: 904/255-0285.)

Longwood Arts And Crafts Festival – Longwood: (Usually weekend before Thanksgiving.) The preservation district and in the fully restored Bradlee MacIntyre House. Original works in all media are featured. (Central Florida Society of Historic Preservation, Box 500, Longwood 32750. Tel: 305/260-3440.)

Lower Keys Art Fair – Big Pine Key: Held the last Sunday of November and designed to give local artists at the tip of the US a chance to draw a crowd and show off their talents. (Lower Keys Chamber of Commerce, P.O. Drawer 511, Big Pine Key 33043. Tel: 305/872-2411.)

Ringling Crafts Festival – Sarasota: (Always held on the weekend before Thanksgiving.) More than 150 craftsmen from 10 southeastern states will vie for $7,000 in prize money during this major showcase of contemporary American crafts display. The festival also features a Parisian Left Bank Lunch. (John and Mable Ringling Museum of Art, 5401 Bayshore Road, Sarasota 32242. Tel: 813/355-5101.)

South Miami Art Festival – South Miami: (Always first weekend In November.) Nearly 300 artists gather at this outdoor festival awarding 6,000 prizes. (South Miami-Kendall Chamber of Commerce, 6410 S.W. 80th St, Miami 33143. Tel: 305/661-1621.)

DECEMBER

Palm Harbor Arts, Crafts And Music Festival – Palm Harbor: The first Saturday and Sunday of every December sees the combination of booths, displays, artists and musicians out in full force at Palm Harbor. (Greater Palm Harbor Area Chamber of Commerce, 1000 US 19 North, Suite 300, Palm Harbor 34684. Tel: 813/784-4287.)

St Cloud Country Art Festival – St Cloud: Works ranging from wood carvings to watercolors are on display and sale at this show. (St Cloud Junior Women, P.O. Box 522, St Cloud 32770. Tel: 407/892-8200.)

Woodstock Arts and Crafts Festival – Sunrise: More than 200 exhibition booths, continuous musical entertainment, international cuisine, carnival rides and a visit by Santa for the kids. (Woodstock Arts and Crafts Festival, 11100 N.W. 26th Place, Sunrise 33322. Tel: 305/741-1426.)

SPECIAL EVENTS

Note: This list is provided courtesy of the Division of Tourism of the Florida Department of Commerce.

JANUARY

Art Deco Weekend – Miami Beach: Every year in January, the Miami Design Preservation League sponsors this event to celebrate Miami Beach's historic architecture. This is a street festival complete with Art Deco antique vendors, two stages of continuous 1930s big band music and tours through the increasingly popular Art Deco District. (Miami Design Preservation League, P.O. Bin L, Miami Beach 33119. Tel: 305/672-2014.)

Brooksville Raid Festival – Brooksville: Famous Florida Civil War battle "The Battle of Brooksville" is re-enacted. Fashions of that era, a parade, museum activities, a barbecue dinner, the Blue/Gray Ball and other events are featured. (Brooksville Raid Festival Inc., 101 East Dade Ave, Brooksville 34601. Tel: 904/796-2420.)

Epiphany Celebration – Tarpon Springs: (January 6.) Continuing ties between Florida's sponging village and the tradition and culture of the homeland are demonstrated in this colorful Old World observance honoring the baptism of Christ. Pageantry and elaborate finery give the celebration grace and dignity; symbolic ceremonies reflect its significance. (St Nicholas Greek Orthodox Church, Box 248, Tarpon Springs 34689. Tel: 813/937-3540.)

Snow Fest – Pensacola Beach: This event is held on the last Saturday of January with man-made snow shipped in for a giant snow slide. Other activities include a snowman-building contest, sandman-building contest and a variety of other games. (Sants Rosa Island Authority, P.O. Box 1208, Pensacola Beach 32561. Tel: 904/932-2259.)

FEBRUARY

Big Orange Festival – Miami: This month-long event has garnered much attention in the music industry as one of the country's top winter music festivals. A variety of jazz, country, classical, rock, Latin and bluegrass music is performed by local musicians and major national and international artists in over 30 free concerts. (The Orange Bowl Committee, P.O. Box 350748, Miami 33135. Tel: 305/642-1515.)

Cortez Fishing Festival – Cortez: On the third Saturday of the month, an arts-and-crafts show with a nautical theme dominates the activities that include net-making demonstrations, environmental exhibits and sea-food featuring catch from the area. (Cortez Fishing Festival, P.O. Box 33, Cortez 34215. Tel: 813/794-0280.)

Edison Pageant of Light – Fort Myers: (Held the week of Edison's Birthday, February 11.) Thomas Alva Edison lit up our lives, invented the phonograph and developed rubber from goldenrod, so each year in Fort Myers – his winter home for many years – he is honored with a festival including an honorary birthday party, a square dance, sports events, exhibits and the Grand Parade of Light. (Box 1311, Fort Myers 33902. Tel: 813/334-2550.)

Everglades City Fisherman's Seafood Festival – Everglades City: Delicious seafood, Seminole Indian displays, arts and crafts, conservation exhibits and other activities highlight this festival that pays homage to the lush Everglades. (P.O. Box 5029, Everglades City 33929. Tel: 813/695-2555.)

Flagler Anniversary Open House – Palm Beach: Since 1960, the Henry Morrison Flagler Museum has celebrated the anniversary of the restoration of Mr Flagler's private home, Whitehall, into a museum. Volunteer guides in full costume, an orchestra in the main hall, organ music in the music room, films of early Palm Beach and free refreshments are featured. (Henry Morrison Flagler Museum, Box 969, Palm Beach 33480. Tel: 305/655-2833.)

Florida Citrus Festival – Winter Haven: Florida's citrus industry is hailed with pageantry and lots of "fruity" festivities such as the Orange Squeeze-Off, Fresh Fruit Competition and the Florida Citrus Hall of Fame. (Florida Citrus Showcase, Box 9229, Winter Haven 33880. Tel: 813/293-3175.)

Florida Strawberry Festival – Plant City: The Winter Strawberry Capital of the World celebrates the strawberry season with a fair and festival. More than 250,000 attend the event held annually since 1936, and activities include a strawberry cookout, strawberry shortcake buffet, free nightly entertainment, grand parade and coronation of a Strawberry Queen. (Box 1869, Plant City, 33566. Tel: 813/752-9194.)

Gasparilla Pirate Invasion – Tampa: (Second Monday every February.) Since 1904, an authentic pirate ship has sailed into Tampa Bay manned with more than 500 fully-costumed pirates. These swashbucklers capture the keys to the city of Tampa and take over for a day of fun and festivity, including a spectacular parade through downtown Tampa. (Ye Mystic Krewe of Gasparilla, Box 1514, Tampa 33601. Tel: 813/228-7338.)

Menendez Day Celebration – St Augustine: Each year the birthday of the city's founder is commemorated with speeches, historical plays and a musical presentation at the base of the Menendez statue, a gift from the government of Spain. (Chamber of Commerce, P.O. Drawer O, St Augustine 32084. Tel: 904/829-5681.)

Miami International Boat Show – Miami Beach: This is the nation's largest public marine extravaganza, with more than 600 national and international exhibitors. (Miami International Boat Show, 2655 Le Juene Road, Coral Gables 33134. Tel: 305/448-7450.)

Palm Beach Seafood Festival – West Palm Beach: Live entertainment combined with fresh seafood indigenous to the shores of Palm Beach County are held on the second weekend of the month. (Fantasma Productions Inc., 2000 South Dixie Hwy, West Palm Beach 33401. Tel: 407/832-6397.)

People's Gasparilla – Tampa: For 4 days, the Franklin Street Mall in honor of the legendary pirate José Gaspar, offers activities appealing to all ages – children's parade, bluegrass festival, art show, street dance and coronation of the people's king and queen. (Krewe of Gasparilla, P.O. Box 1514, Tampa 33601. Tel: 813/228-7338.)

St Petersburg International Folk Fair – St Petersburg: More than 30 ethnic groups celebrate their cultural contributions with entertainment in native costumes and language, arts and crafts displays and food booths offering specialities from around the world. (2201 First Ave North, St Petersburg 33713. Tel: 813/327-7999).

Swamp Cabbage Festival – Labelle: (Last full weekend of the month.) Held near the northwestern fringe of the watery Everglades, it pays tribute to Florida's state tree, the cabbage palm, and its tender growth bud. The edible heart of the palm is chopped crossways and then prepared much like regular garden variety cabbage and is just one of the Cracker foods featured. Top-named country music performers, a parade and pioneer craft demonstrations round out scheduled festivities. (Swamp Cabbage Festival, P.O. Box 2021, Labelle 33935. Tel: 813/675-1717.)

Winter Equestrian Festival – Statewide: This series of six week-long hunter and jumper shows on the Florida winter horse-show circuit offers spectators the opportunity to enjoy Olympic and World Cup qualifying competitions. The Festival includes the Palm Beach Classic, West Palm Beach; the Palm Beach Masters, West Palm Beach; the Golden Hills International Charity Horse Show, Ocala; the Jack-Sun-Ville Classic, Jacksonville; the Delta Air Lines Internationale, Tampa; and the Michelob Suncoast Tournament of Champions, Tampa. Through March.

(Tully-Menard, Inc., 2207 S. Dale Mabry, Tampa 33609. Tel: 813/253-0447.)

Ybor City Fiesta Day – Ybor City: (Always held on the Saturday after the Gasparilla Invasion.) Be a "Latin for a Day" at Ybor City's celebration of its Spanish heritage. There is Latin music, dancing, costumes and art to enjoy, and the Fiesta Sopa de Garbanzo offers free bean soup, Cuban bread and cafe con leche. The Illuminated Night Parade winds its way through the picturesque community. (Ybor City Chamber of Comerce, 1800 E. Ninth Ave, Tampa 33605. Tel: 813/248-3712.)

MARCH

Animal Fair – Gainesville: Every year the Florida Museum of Natural History hosts Animal Fair, an event which gives the public a chance to learn about amphibians, reptiles and a host of furred and feathered creatures. There is also an animal nursery for hands-on experience with baby animals. (Florida Museum of Natural History, Museum Road, University of Florida, Gainesville 32611. Tel: 904/392-1721.)

Chalo Nitka Festival and Rodeo – Moore Haven: Chalo Nitka means "day of the bass" in Seminole language, and the festival features an 8-week bass fishing contest that culminates in the Seminole Indian program and rodeo. (Glades County Chamber of Commerce, Box 490, Moore Haven 33471. Tel: 813/946-0440.)

Conch Shell Blowing – Key West: The contest, held on the second Saturday of the month, features the finest in conch shell music. Contest is open to the public. (Old Island Restoration Foundation, P.O. Box 689, Key West 33041. Tel: 305/294-9501).

Festival of States – St Petersburg: More than 100 high school bands from throughout the nation, plus Florida's own, gather in the Funshine City to participate in one of the most dramatic and elaborate festivals held in the state. More than 200 events include national band marching, parade and field marching competition; out of state competition for the Mayor's and Governor's Cup, a series of concerts and sports tournaments; a fireworks display; and cornation of Mr and Miss Sungoddess. (Executive Vice President, Festival of States, Box 1731, St Petersburg 33731. Tel: 813/898-3654.)

Fun 'N' Sun Festival – Clearwater: A nighttime, illuminated parade highlights this annual affair, which includes activities ranging from skateboard competition to horseshoe tournaments. (Chamber of Commerce, 128 N. Osceola Ave, Clearwater 33515. Tel: 813/461-0011.)

Hatsume – Delray Beach: "Hatsume" (first bud of the new year) honors the horticultural exhibits at Delray Beach's Morikami Museum. The relationship between Japanese culture and Delray Beach began in the early 1900s when Japanese farmers settled the Yamato Colony, which produced much of the nation's winter vegetable crop. During Hatsume, exhibits and demonstrations by bonsai and other plant-related societies promote community interest in native and ornamental plants. (Curator, The Morikami Museum, 4000 Morikami Park Road, Delray Beach 33446. Tel: 305/499-0631.)

Highland Games – Dunedin: The competition features Scottish games of skill, such as tug of war, sheaf and hammer throw, the singing of highland tunes, and competition in drumming, dancing and piping. (Chamber of Commerce, 434 Main St, Dunedin 33528. Tel: 813/736-5066.)

Lehigh Spring Festival – Lehigh: This nostalgia-themed festival features a grand parade as the finale, which also includes a steak dinner, outdoor band concerts, hot air balloon lift-off and food and vegetable-growing contests. (Lehigh Corp., 201 East Joel Blvd, Leigh 33939. Tel: 813/369-2121.)

Manatee Heritage Week – Bradenton: Held the last full week of March. Features tours of the historical districts of Manatee County and historical houses. There is also a festival at the Manatee Village Historical Park displaying quilts, basketry, crafts and other items. (Manatee Historical Society, 1405 Fourth Ave W., Bradenton 34205. Tel: 813/749-7162.)

Medieval Fair – Sarasota: The atmosphere of a medieval city square is recreated annually at the Ringling Museum complex. (Ringling Museums, 5401 Bayshore Road, Sarasota 34243. Tel: 813/355-5101.)

Sanibel Island Shell Fair – Sanibel Island: Amateur and professional collectors gather at the fair to display their collection of shells from around the world. (Sanibel Island Chamber of Commerce, P.O. Box 166, Sanibel Island 33957. Tel: 813/472-1080.)

Spring Orchid Auction and Plant Sale – Sarasota: Thousands of choice plants at bargain prices, plant demonstrations and exhibits, and a plant auction highlights this festival event held at Selby Botanical Gardens. (811 S. Palm Ave, Sarasota 34243. Tel: 813/366-5730.)

APRIL

Black Gold Jubilee – Belle Glade: The rich black muck of the eastern Everglades yields much of the nation's winter supply of sugar, cane, corn and leaf vegetables. Residents of Belle Glade, in the heart of this vegetable producing region, celebrate their the harvest with a parade, arts and crafts show, raft races, fireworks and a barbecue dinner. (Black Gold Jubilee, 417 N.W. 16th St, Belle Glade 33430. Tel: 407/996-4404.)

Conch Republic Celebration – Key West: The anniversary of the Florida Keys "Secession" from the United States. This was the "island republic's" response when the US Board Patrol blocked off all traffic into and out of the island's only highway more than a decade ago. Annual events include the Conch Bed Race, the Key West Fishing Tournament, the Battle of the Tall Ships, windsurfing regatta, a dedication ceremony honoring the founding fathers

and more. (Conch Republic Celebration, P.O. Box 230, Key West 33041. Tel: 305/294-4440).

Indian River Festival – Titusville: (Last weekend.) Titusville, on Florida's Central East Coast, pays fun-filled tribute to the broad Indian River, which flows between the city and one of the most famous strips of land in the world – Cape Canaveral, site of Kennedy Space Center. The 5-day event will include an arts and crafts show, Deggler's Carnival, food booths, and several water activities, such as water ski shows, canoe racing and the Great Indian River Raft Race. (Chamber of Commerce, Box 880, Titusville 32780. Tel: 305/267-3036.)

May Day In The Park – Orlando: A day of family fun and fanfare, always celebrated on the closest Sunday to May Day (May 1). Food is provided by the local chefs'association and entertainment is by the local bands. (Orlando Science Center, 810 E. Rollins St, Orlando 32803-1291. Tel: 407/896-7151.)

Oceans Miami/Bounty Of The Sea Festival – Miami: This event is always held the weekend after Easter and features a nautical trade show and food festival. The trade show features state-of-the-art marine products and boats, while the seafood fest offers delicacies from the nearby deep, the Atlantic and the Gulf. (International Oceanographic Foundation, 3979 Rickenbacker Causeway, Miami 33149. Tel: 305/361-5786.)

Taste Of The Islands – Sanibel Island: Held the last Sunday in April, many of the top chefs from Sanibel and Captiva Islands offer their specialities for tasting. The event is sponsored by CROW (Care and Rehabiliatation of Wildlife). There is also an annual Waiter and Waitress Olympic. (Dunes Country Club, P.O. Box 166, Sanibel Island 33957. Tel: 813/472-1080.)

MAY

Chautauqua – Defuniak Springs: This Northwest Florida community hosts a celebration recapturing the cultural atmosphere of the early 1900s, when performers gathered and entertained in the Florida Chautauqua, the southern lyceum that was sister to the New York Chautauqua. (Walton County Chamber of Commerce, Box 29, De Funiak Springs 32433. Tel: 904/892-3191.)

Eight Flags Shrimp Festival – Fernandina Beach: One of the nation's oldest cities hosts this festival that salutes the history of Amelia Island and the birthplace of Florida's shrimping industry. Activities include a pirates landing, beard contest, sky diving contest, blessing of the fleet, an arts and crafts show, folk festival and booths specializing in fresh seafood. (Fernandina Beach Shrimp Festival, 1235 S. Tenth St, Suite 101, Fernandina Beach 32034. Tel: 904/261-7130.)

Fiesta De La Riba – St Petersburg: Held at the Salvador Dali Museum to celebrate the birthday of the surrealist painter, admission is free all day to the museum, which offers birthday cake and live entertainment. Children's activities include pinatas and other games and Spanish cuisine is also available. (Salvador Dali Museum, 1000 Third St South, St Petersburg 33710. Tel: 813/384-0027.)

Fiesta of Five Flags – Pensacola: A re-enactment of the 1559 landing of Don Tristan de Luna and his Spanish colonists is one of the highlights of this celebration that commemorates the city's turbulent history under the flags of five nations. Other events in the fiesta include a treasure hunt, festive parade and pageantry, art exhibitions, concerts and also water sports. (Fiesta of Five Flags Association, P.O. Box 1943, Pensacola 32589. Tel: 904/6512.)

Flying High Circus – Tallahassee: Florida State University's internationally known collegiate circus presents its annual Home Show on two consecutive weekends. Composed entirely of students, this "educated" circus features acts such as trick bicycle riding, tightrope walking, tumbling, adagio, intricate feats on the high trapeze and performances by the inevitable clowns. The circus has appeared throughout the nation and abroad. (Director, FSU Flying High Circus, Florida State University, Tallahassee 32306. Tel: 904/644-4874.)

Selby Gardens Orchid Festival – Sarasota: A weeklong celebration offering the garden's world-famous orchid displays, plus slide shows, lectures ans demonstrations on how to grow orchids. (Selby Botanical Gardens, 811 S. Palm Ave, Sarasota 34236. Tel: 813/366-5730.)

Up, Up and Away Airport Show – Orlando: Always held on the third weekend in May, the show is sponsored by the Greater Orlando Aviation Authority and the Orlando International Airport. This showcase highlights local merchants and the various facilities they offer. The highlight of the show is usually the airport art show. (Greater Orlando Aviation Authority, One Airport Blvd, Orlando 32827.)

JUNE

Kissimmee Boat-A-Cade – Kissimmee: The oldest and largest annual boat cruise in America, this 9-day event has been described by *Reader's Digest* as the "World's Greatest Outdoor Adventure." The caravan of boaters starts on Kissimmee's Lake Tohopekaliga and winds its way through many scenic areas of the state. Banquets, barbecues and other landlubber activities are some of the items which are scheduled at points along the Cade route. (Kissimmee Boat-A-Cade, Box 1855, Kissimmee 32742-1855. Tel: 305/847-2033.)

Lower Keys Food Fest And Craft Race – Sunshine Key: Held prior to Memorial Day weekend, this event combines ethnic foods and seafood festival with a water race for canoes, kayaks and homemade rafts. (Lower Keys Chamber of Commerce, P.O. Drawer 511, Big Pine Key 33043. Tel: 305/872-2411.)

Palm Beach Taste – West Palm Beach: A chance for central and south Florida to sample Palm Beach's finest foods and enjoy live jazz and folk music.

(Fantasma Productions Inc., 2000 S. Dixie Hwy, West Palm Beach 33401. Tel: 407/832-6397.)

Panhandle Watermelon Festival – Chipley: "Watermelon Time is Fun Time" is the slogan of this festival, and nothing could describe the harvest celebration better. Activities include a 10,000-meter run, pancake breakfast, parade, horse show, big melon contest and auction and, of course, watermelon eating and seed spitting competition. (Watermelon Festival Committee, P.O. Box 561, Chipley 32428. Tel: 904/638-1874.)

Pirate Days – Treasure Island: (Through July 4.) A pirate invasion and fireworks highlight this festival which is designed for family entertainment. Other activities include a sandcastle contest, canoe races and square dancing. (Treasure Island Recreation Dept, 120 108th Ave, Treasure Island 33706. Tel: 813/360-0811.)

Sea Turtle Watch – Jensen Beach: For decades visitors and residents have gathered during this period each year to observe the ancient sea turtles making their way from the cool Atlantic Ocean onto the beach, where they dig nests and deposit their eggs. Supervised outings offer spectators the opportunity to gain an unusual understanding of the mysteries of nature. (Chamber of Commerce, 1910 N.E. Commercial St, Jensen Beach 33457. Tel: 305/334-3444.)

Southwest Florida Wine Fair – Captiva Island: The wine fair is held the first weekend of June and offers seminars, panel discussions and tastings showcasing wines from all over the world. (Gravina Associates Inc., 4575 Via Royal, Suite 214, Fort Myers 33919. Tel: 813/275-5758.)

JULY

Hemingway Days Festival – Key West: Always held the week of Ernest Hemingway's birthday (July 21). The great writer spent all of the 1930s in Key West. This week-long festival is held to honor both the man and his works. Highlights include a short story contest, a billfish tournament, an arm-wrestling contest, a story-telling contest, the Papa Hemingway look-alike contest and a 1930s-theme party which is held at the Hemingway House. (Hemingway Days Festival, P.O. Drawer 4045, Key West 33041. Tel: 305/294-4440.)

AUGUST

Boca Festival Days – Boca Raton: A community celebration that includes the Boca Expo, an arts-and-crafts fair, barbership quarter singing, concerts, a sand castle building contest, a fishing tournament and more. (Community Redevelopment Agency, 201 W. Palmetto Park Road, Boca Raton 33432. Tel: 407/338-7070.)

Jaycees Bed Race – Port St Lucie: Sponsored by the local junior Chamber of Commerce, the community enjoys a watermelon-eating contest, pizza-eating contest, bikini contest and the culminating event: the annual jaycees bed race. (Port St Lucie Jaycees, 592 S.W. Duxbury Ave, Port St Lucie 34983. Tel: 407/878-8812.)

Wausau Fun Day and Possum Festival – Wausau: (First Saturday of the month.) This small Northwest Florida town annually stages a day-long, old-fashioned celebration that includes numerous fun contests like cornpone baking, greased-pole climbing and hog-calling. Plenty of gospel, country and bluegrass music, and a parade and possum auction round up the day's activities. (Wausau Community Development Club, Rt. 4, Box 734, Chipley 32428. Tel: 904/638-0250.)

SEPTEMBER

Anniversary of the Founding of St Augustine – St Augustine: (Celebrated on the Saturday nearest September 8.) 1565 landing of Don Pedro Menendez de Aviles, founder of St Augustine, is re-enacted each year. Costumed Spanish settlers join a priest for a Mass at the Mission of Nombre de Dios, approximately the same spot where the original colonists had stepped ashore. (Preservation Board, P.O. Box 1984, St Augustine 32085. Tel: 904/824-3355.)

Great American Raft Race – Port St Lucie: If it floats and can be propelled by humans, odds are it'll be racing on the north fork of the St Lucie River in the "anything-goes" celebration of paddle-power. Event is held annually. (Port St Lucie Exchange Club, P.O. Box 7341, Port St Lucie 34985. Tel: 407/464-1100.)

Oktoberfest – Orlando: Oktoberfest gets off to be early start in this celebration of German heritage, where oompah bands, street dancing and ethnic foods are just part of the fun. Held at Orlando's Church Street Station. (Fantasma Production Inc., 2000 S. Dixie Hwy, West Palm Beach 33401. Tel: 407/832-6397.)

Pioneer Days – Englewood: (Labor Day weekend.) Since 1955 this community has celebrated its roots with street dancing, a beard contest, country fair, clambake, sports tournaments, boat races, a shark fishing tournament and sand sculpting contest. (Englewood Jaycees, P.O. Box 464, Englewood 34295-0464. Tel: 813/474-9158.)

Seafood Festival – Pensacola: Pensacola salutes its bustling seafood industry with two weekends of festivities. Land and water activities offer entertainment both in town and on Pensacola Beach, including a blessing of the fleet, boat parade, water ski show, sandcastle building contest, and seafood cooking contests. (Fiesta of Five Flags, P.O. Box 1943, Pensacola 32589. Tel: 904/433-6512.)

OCTOBER

Baggy Bayou Mullet Festival – Niceville: Valparaiso – the humble fish, "mullet," is honored with a special celebration that features sports events, an arts and crafts show and beauty contest. There's plenty of food to eat, and freshly caught mullet is the main dish. (Boggy Bayou Mullet Council, Inc., P.O. Box 231, Niceville 32578. Tel: 904/678-1615.)

Brandon Balloon Festival – Tampa: Balloonists converge and traverse the treetops of the city in a colorful array of huge hot-air balloons. Spectators are treated to balloon rides, special events, a Halloween Ball and national and local entertainers. (Alessi Promotions, 106-A N. Albany, Tampa 33606. Tel: 813/251-4115.)

Fantasy Fest – Key West: This Halloween festival celebrates the city's unique lifestyle with costume parties, top-name recording artists in open concerts, the Old Town Street Fair, displays by mask-makers and the ultimate celebration – the Night Time Grand Parade, a grand and colorful procession of marching bands and more than 40 floats stretching all the way down Duval Street. (Fantasy Fest, P.O. Box 4045, Key West 33041. Tel: 305/294-4440.)

Guavaween Extravaganze – Tampa: Always held on the Saturday closest to Halloween, this spoof of traditional celebrations features a parade down Seventh Avenue by locals who come dressed to poke fun at the aspects of life in Tampa and Ybor City. The Mama Guava Stumble Parade floats are the zaniest around. (Ybor City Chamber of Commerce/Playmakers, P.O. Box 5055, Tampa 33675. Tel: 813/248-3712.)

Kissimmee Boating Jamboree – Kissimmee: Outdoorsmen enjoy this 3-day cruise beginning on Kissimmee's Lake Tohopekaliga. Landlubber activities are planned at different stop-points along the route. (Box 1855, Kissimmee 32742-1855. Tel: 407/847-2033.)

Maritime Festival – St Augustine: Highlight of this 2-day seafood festival is an offering of everything from stone crab and blue crab to mackerel and flounder. The festival also features waterfront events, games, art show, sail boat races and a costume ball. (St Augustine Chamber of Commerce, P.O. Drawer O, St Augustine 32085. Tel: 904/829-5681.)

Oktoberfest – Titusville: Held at Fox Lake Park with a 1-day celebration of German foods, wines, beverages, music and dance. (Titusville Chamber of Commerce, 2000 S. Washington Ave, Titusville 32780. Tel: 407/267-3036.)

Pioneer Day – Lake Wales: Pioneer Day activities emphasize three main areas; historic Lake Wales and its pioneers, music and entertainment, and old-fashioned "Cracker" foods and crafts. (Lake Wales Downtown Association, P.O. Box 2396, Lake Wales 33859-2396. Tel: 813/676-2317.)

Pioneer Day – Mayo: In City Park, this small community celebrates its founding with an arts-and-crafts show, a food festival, bluegrass music and more. (Pioneer Day Committee, P.O. Box 92, Mayo 32066. Tel: 904/294-2536.)

Quincyfest – Quincy: A local festival in this small north-Florida town features arts and crafts, a 5-km run, entertainment and friendly folks. (Main Street

Quincy, P.O. Box 1106, Quincy 32351. Tel: 904/627-2346.)

St Anne's Autumn Round-Up Pensacola: This is 3 days of the Old West in a reconstructed frontier town. There are staged shoot-outs, country/western and Dixieland music, can-can girls, square dancers, guest celebraties and food and drink. (St Anne's Catholic Church, 5200 Saufley Field Road, Pensacola 32506. Tel: 904/456-5966.)

NOVEMBER

Birthplace of Speed Antique Car Meet – Ormond Beach: (Weekend after Thanksgiving.) This historic setting dates back to 1902 and activities scheduled during the meet include a gaslight parade of horseless carriages, a costume contest, a re-enactment of early races on the hard-packed sand beach and an antique auto flea market. (Ormond Beach Jaycees, Box 67, Ormond Beach 32074.)

Chili Cook-Off – Pensacola Beach: Always held the weekend after Thanksgiving, this annual event features chili cooking competitions in various categories, plus arts, crafts, games and more. (Quietwater Beach Resort, 400 Quietwater Beach Road, Pensacola Beach 32561. Tel: 904/934-3777.)

Deerfest – Deerfield Beach: Carnival-style rides, games, arts and crafts and spreads of international cuisine. (Greater Deerfield Chamber of Commerce, 1601 E. Hillsborough Blvd, Deerfield Beach 33441. Tel: 305/427-1050.)

Fall Plant Fair – Sarasota: Thousands of plants for sale, a wide variety of exhibits and horticultural demonstrations. (Marie Selby Botanical Gardens, 811 S. Palm Ave, Sarasota 34243. Tel: 813/366-5700.)

Florida Seafood Festival – Apalachicola: The state's oldest seafood festival, held to honor the area's thriving seafood industry on Apalachicola Bay. Local merchants, fishermen and the chamber of commerce come together for a 2-day celebration. (Florida Seafood Festival Inc., P.O. Box 460, Apalachicola 32320. Tel: 904/653-8051.)

Florida State Air Fair – Kissimmee: Held at Kissimmee Municipal Airport, this 2-day event is highlighted by a thrilling stunt jet team. Food concessions are also plentiful. (Rotary Club, P.O. Box 2185, Kissimmee 32742-2185. Tel: 407/933-2173.)

Official Florida State Air Fair – Kissimmee: Proclaimed as the State of Florida's official air fair in 1976, this non-profit event is organized by the Kissimmee Rotary Club. Since its creation in 1965, the Air Fair has donated more than $250,000 in proceeds to charity. The US Navy Blue Angels and the US Air Force Thunderbirds headline the huge show on alternate years. (Rotary Club, P.O. Box 2185, Kissimmee 32742-2185. Tel: 407/933-2173).

Seafood Festival – Madeira Beach: John's Pass Village, with its driftwood-toned shops, galleries, docks and boardwalk, is the setting of a festive weekend of seafood feasting, arts and crafts shows and a variety of entertainment. (Madeira Beach Chamber of Commerce, 501 150th Ave, Madeira Beach 33708. Tel: 813/391-7373.)

The Harvest – Miami: There's as much to do as there is to see at the Harvest, a celebration of South Florida's heritage. Scheduled are folk music and dance, regional foods, historical exhibits and demonstrations of traditional crafts. (Metro-Dade Parks and Recreation Dept, 50 S.W. 32nd Road, Bldg #19, Miami 33129. Tel: 305/579-2676).

Umatilla Fall Festival and Christmas Parade – Umatilla: (Last Saturday of the month.) A gala Christmas parade is followed by an arts and crafts display along main street. (Chamber of Commerce, Box 300, Umatilla 32784. Tel: 904/669-3511.)

DECEMBER

Christmas Boat-a-Cade – Madeira Beach: (Sunday before Christmas.) Residents decorate their boats and cruise beautiful Boca Ciega Bay, near St Petersburg on Florida's West Coast. (Recreational Director, City of Madeira Beach, Box 8605, Madeira Beach 33708. Tel: 813/391-9951.)

Christmas in Lantana – Lantana: Thousands attend this free display featuring the World's Largest Decorated Christmas Tree and the World's Largest Minature Railroad Display – both in the Guiness Book of World Records. (Greater Lantana Chamber of Commerce, Box 3696, Lantana 33462. Tel: 305/585-8664.)

Florida Tournament of Bands – St Petersburg: An all-Florida marching band competition, sponsored by the Festival of States, presents bands competing for awards in inspection, parade and field show performances. (Festival of States Association, Box 1731, St Petersburg 33731. Tel: 813/898-3654.)

Harvest Fest – Miami: Held at Tropical Park in downtown Miami, this festival celebrates the pioneers of Florida with arts, crafts, food, historical re-enactments, an antique machinery exhibit, livestock show and more. (Metro-Dade Parks and Recreation Dept, 50 S.W. 32nd Road, Bldg #9, Miami 33129. Tel: 305/579-2676.)

Holiday Extravaganze – St Petersburg: Children flock to The Science Center to enjoy a day of craft-making, computer activities and a planetarium presentation. (The Science Center, 7701, 22nd Ave North, St Petersburg 33710. Tel: 813/384-0027).

King Mango Strut – Miami: A hilarious off-beat spoof of the annual Orange Bowl football game parade and every other serious parade. Spectators are required to bring along their zany senses of humor because everything under the sun is parodied – including the sun. (Friends of King Mango, 3800 Irvington Ave, Coconut Grove 33133. Tel: 305/441-0944.)

Orange Bowl Festival – Miami: What started in 1935 with a football game and parade has grown to include more than a dozen holiday activities. A tradition in the Sunshine State, the Orange Bowl festival is highlighted by the nationally-televised

New Year's Eve King Orange Jamboree Parade and the Orange Bowl Classic Football game on New Year's Night. Other festival activities include a fishing tournament, inter-collegiate sports events, fireworks pageant, Fiesta Hispanica and the Three Kings Day Parade through Miami's Little Havana district. Through to mid-January. (Orange Bowl Committee, Box 350748, Miami 33135. Tel: 305/642-1515.)

Ramble, A Gardening Festival – Miami: Annual plant sale, plus arts, crafts, food, games and entertainment running throughout the weekend. (Fairchild Tropical Garden, 10901 Old Cutler Road, Miami 33156. Tel: 305/667-1651.)

Ye Olde Musical Christmas Feaste – Captiva Island: Always the third Saturday of the month, the event features a six-course meal in traditional 16th- and 17th-century style. People come costumed in the attire of the period and there are Madrigal singers providing live entertainment. (South Seas Plantation Resort and Yacht Club, P.O. Box 194, Captiva Island 33924. Tel: 913/472-5111.)

SHOPPING

WHAT TO BUY

Traditional souvenirs: If you are into kitsch – plastic flamingo ashtrays with "Florida" embossed on the bottom, shell "sculptures," "canned sunshine," "fresh Florida air," orange wine or liqueur, Sunshine State keychains, spoons with the names of the state or city or beach or amusement park of your choice on the handle, and the like – you will find Florida a veritable treasure house. From roadside shacks to massive, futuristic malls, all carry a healthy supply of such traditional souvenirs. But don't be disappointed if your plastic walking orange or Silver Springs souvenir picture plate has a little sticker on the botton that says "Made in Taiwan."

Homegrown souvenirs: You can avoid the junk and return with real Florida souvenirs by simply looking for items made or grown in the state. One of the best souvenirs, whether you are shipping it home to friends or carrying it home in your car or on the plane, is a crate of Florida citrus. Choose from Hamlin, Valencia, Washington Navel, or Temple oranges, Dancy tangerines, Marsh seedless grapefruit, Key limes, Avon lemons, Tangelos, Thompson pink grapefruits, or even kumquats. The larger

shippers and packers usually provide better prices than the specialty stores. And all citrus outlets offer a variety of prices to fit your traveling budget.

Shells: Another popular souvenir that spells Florida is the seashell. Either pick them yourself right off the beach or buy them in bulk. The **Shell Factory** in Fort Myers has an enormous selection. You can buy individual shells, shell astrays and even toilet seats with shells set into the lid.

Art: Increasing numbers of artists have made Florida their home. Some of their paintings, sculptures or crafts have a Florida flavor or motifs that make them prized souvenirs or gifts. Check the "Arts & Crafts Shows" section in this Travel Tips for a listing of the dozens of art and crafts shows that are held in Florida annually. The largest and most prestigious occur in Winter Park, Coconut Grove and at the Ringling Museums in Sarasota.

Fashion: A number of clothing lines originated in Florida, including **Key West Hand Print Fabrics**, **Palm Beach** and **Lilly Pulitzer**. They tend toward sporty, cottony, colorful, summery styles. Bargains on clothing not necessarily made in Florida can be found in **Miami's Fashion District**.

Unique souvenirs: Use your ingenuity for finding other kinds of unique Florida souvenirs. Try Tampa's **Ybor City** for fine, handsome cigars, or **Tarpon Springs** for huge, highly-absorbent natural sponges hand-picked from the Anclote River. If your bank account is flush, you may wish to check out some of the yacht lots. **Gulfstar**, **Irwin**, and **Watkins** are among noted yacht companies based in Florida. They will customize one to your specifications, if you can afford it. If you have expensive taste, but favor dry land opulence, the stables of the Ocala area offer beautiful thoroughbred horses of all shapes and sizes. The number of national champions in horse races and horse shows that were born and bred around Ocala is increasing every year.

SPECIALITY SHOPPING

Worldwide merchandise: In addition to innumerable malls, themed shopping villages and roadside stands, Florida offers several shopping areas of note. One, Walt Disney World, has attempted to top them all with its **Walt Disney World Village**. Here you will find exactly what the name says – a world of shopping. In addition to the expected Walt Disney-oriented merchandise, you will find items from virtually every corner of the earth. Hand-crafted European chess boards and pieces, hand-carved African art, hand-blown English crystal, hand-polished sterling silver sets, even hand-cut leather puppets from the distant Indonesian island of Java. There is of course, Florida-oriented merchandize.

Shopping plazas: The state's "posh" shopping plazas include famed **Worth Avenue** in Palm Beach, where prices are rarely posted because most customers can't afford to buy anything; **St Armand's Circle** in Longboat Key near Sarasota, where prices are reasonable (when compared to Worth Avenue); St Petersburg's **Beach Drive**, where you can watch yachts slip into Tampa Bay while browsing; and **Bal Harbour**, north of Miami Beach, where **Saks Fifth Avenue** and **Neiman Marcus** are nestled among the coconut palms. Shopping districts more funky than posh include **Duval Street** in Key West's Old Town, Fort Lauderdale's **Las Olas Boulevard**, and Miami Beach's Art Deco **Lincoln Road Mall**.

Haute couture: Other points of shopping interest in the sprawling Miami area include the luxurious **Mayfair Mall** in Coconut Grove, which boasts three levels of haute couture boutiques; the **Omni International Hotel's** maze of equally haute couture boutiques; and Coral Gables' **Miracle Mile**.

Flea markets: Bargain hunters looking for an offbeat souvenir will find a bounty of flea markets here. St Petersburg has the **Wagon Wheel** and Webster has another that claims to be "*The World's Largest Flea Market.*" Restorers of antique cars, meanwhile, will want to visit car parts flea markets at Daytona and Ormond Beach.

Indian handicrafts: The best places to purchase genuine Seminole Indian handicrafts are at the Seminoles' reservation in Hollywood or the **Miccosukee Village** and **Cultural Center** on the Tamiami Trail in the Everglades.

SPORTS

FISHING

The Industry: Besides being one of the major sources of protein, eating enjoyment and a source of recreation, fishing is also a major commercial endeavor. Florida's commercial fleets stalk more than 60 kinds of food fish, including non-edible varieties for oil and fertilizer, a half-dozen kinds of shellfish and even sponges. Only the Game and Fresh Water Fish Commission can issue commercial fishing licenses. Fishermen who take non-game fish using nets, trap or trotlines with more than 25 hooks must possess a commercial license as well as regular sport fishing licenses. The Game and Fresh Water Fish Commission has strict rules on the use of wire traps, slat baskets, minnow seines, cast nets, shad haul nets, pound nets, gill nets and hoop nets. The total harvest from the sea continues to grow, totaling more than 175 million pounds of fish and shellfish annually.

Recreation: No license is needed for saltwater fishing for recreation and there is no closed season on any game fish. Florida's 8,000 miles of tidal coastline are home to more than 600 varieties of saltwater fish. Try a variety of methods for catching them: deep sea fishing, surf casting, bridge and pier fishing and tidal water fishing. Grouper, amberjack, marlin, pompano, sea trout, mackerel, red snapper, snook, redfish, sailfish, bonefish, kingfish and dolphin lurk in the deepest waters. In the late spring and summer, tarpon wait to challenge deep sea fishermen off Tampa Bay, Marathon, Boca Grande pass and Bahia Honda Channel. The Keys, the lower East Coast and upper Gulf regions are the homes of marlin.

Florida's 30,000 lakes and untold miles of rivers and streams also provide outstanding freshwater fishing. Non-resident freshwater fishing licenses are inexpensive and residents' licenses even cheaper. There has been growing pressure by conservation groups for the state to instigate a saltwater fishing license. For information about all fishing licenses, and about any limits on fish, salt or fresh, or any closed seasons on certain species, call the Florida Marine Patrol: 800/342-5367. Military personnel who live in Florida are not required to purchase fishing licenses, but must produce their military leave orders upon the order of wildlife officers. Residents fishing in the county in which they live with not more than three poles or lines are also not required to produce a license.

FISHING TOURNAMENTS

F**EBRUARY**: **B.A.S.S. Megabucks Tournament – Leesburg.** Elimination-round narrowing 250 anglers down to 10. Finalists start with an even score in the last 2 days of the tournament fishing 10 buoy-marked fishing holes. They rotate until each finalist has fished all 10 holes. (Bass Anglers Sportsmen Society, P.O. Box 17900, Montgomery, AL 36109. Tel: 205/272-9530.)

M**AY**–J**ULY**: **Tarpon Tides Tournament – Boca Grande.** It takes skill, strength and luck to hook and land these Florida favorites, especially for 3 months straight. Fishermen from all over the US compete for cash prizes in this tarpon tournament. (P.O. Box 715, Boca Grande 33921. Tel: 813/964-2232.)

M**AY**: **Key West Fishing Tournament – Key West.** Competition in nine divisions throughout the Lower Keys. (K.W.F.T. Inc., P.O. Box 2154, Key West 33041. Tel: 305/294-9286.)

JUNE: **Father's Day Dolphin Derby – Key Colony Beach.** Two-day event held on Father's Day weekend, with the whole family encouraged to fish for dolphin – not the "Flipper" variety but a food fish popular in the Gulf of Mexico. (WAVK-AM Radio, Marathon 33050. Tel: 305/743-4386.)

JUNE–JULY: **Pensacola International Billfish Tournament – Pensacola.** This is one of the largest billfish tournaments in the waters of the Gulf of Mexico, with cash and prize awards in excess of $150,000. (Pensacola Big Game Fishing Club, 1000 New Warrington Road, Pensacola 32506. Tel: 904/453-4638.)

JULY: **Tournament Fisherman's Championship – Jacksonville.** A 5-day fishing championship scheduled to offer $150,000 in an all-cash purse, held at the Harbor Club Marina on the Intracoastal Waterway. An awards ceremony and fish fry conclude the event. (T.F.C., 14535 Beach Blvd, Jacksonville 32550. Tel: 904/223-0644.)
Jacksonville Kingfish Tournament – Jacksonville. Tournament is held at Pablo Creek Marina, with $300,000 in cash and prizes. (Jacksonville Kingfish Tournament, P.O. Box 4, Atlantic Beach 32333. Tel: 904/241-7127.)
Boca Grande Club Invitational Tarpon Tournament – Boca Grande. Billed as "the world's richest tournament," cash awards total $180,000, with $100,000 going to the first-place winner, $50,000 to second place and $30,000 to third. (Boca Grande Club, 5000 Gasparilla Road, Boca Grande 33921. Tel: 813/964-2211.)
Hemingway Billfish Tournament – Key West. -of the Hemingway Days Festival, this tournament was established by Ernest Hemingway's brother, Leicester. The tournament consists of two categories, big game and "fun" fishing. More than $5,000 in cash and prizes awarded. (Hemingway Days Festival, P.O. Box 4045, Key West 33041. Tel: 305/294-4440.)

AUGUST: **Fishing And Diving Tournament – Deerfield Beach.** Always held the second weekend in August, this local event features fishing in Atlantic waters and diving competitions in local pools. (Greater Deerfield Beach Chamber of Commerce, 1601 East Hillsboro Blvd, Deerfield Beach 33441. Tel: 305/427-1050.)
Jaws Shark Tournament – Marco Island. Designed to promote the public's awareness of the 10,000 Islands and Everglades areas. Prizes are awarded for shark catches in the following three categories – men's division, women's division and children's division. There's also a massive cook-out after the tournament. (Port of The Islands, 25000 Tamiami Trail East, Naples 33961; Florida: 800/282-3011; nationwide: 800/237-4173.)

OCTOBER: **Redfish Tournament – Marco Island.** Held usually the second to last weekend in October, the focus is on one of Florida's favorite gamefish, the redfish, and on the plentiful fishing grounds around the 10,000 Islands and the Everglades. Special weekend activities also include live entertainment and open buffets at the Port of The Islands Resort. (Port of the Islands Resort, 25000 Tamiami Trail East, Naples 33971; Florida: 800/282-3011; nationwide: 800/237-4173.)

DECEMBER: **Bass Angler's Sportsman Society Top 100 Tournament – Clewiston.** For 4 days, 100 top bass fishermen compete with an amateur partner in this bass tournament on Lake Okeechobee. More than $380,000 in cash and prizes. (B.A.S.S., P.O. Box 17900, Montgomery, AL 36141. Tel: 205/272-9530.)

HUNTING

Game: Hunting enthusiasts will find a profusion of game in Florida's vast forests, swamps and grasslands. Deer, turkey, wild hogs, rabbits, bear, turtles, frogs, and birds, raccoon, possums and fox are popular game. Open seasons vary.
Licenses: There is a complex list of licensing options for residents and non-residents issued by County Tax Collectors and other authorized agents. Annual combination hunting-fishing licenses for residents cost $17.50. Non-residents must pay $50.50 for annual licenses or $15.50 for 10 consecutive days.
Bag Limits: The daily bag limit for a species changes frequently, depending on the annual review of state resources. For the latest information, contact the Florida Game and Fresh Water Fish Commission, 620 S. Meridian St, Tallahasee 32301.

GOLF TOURNAMENTS

MARCH: **Chris Collinsworth Scramble For Youth Golf Tournament – Titusville.** Held on the first weekend of April, this event always features Collinsworth and other celebrities in a tournament to benefit students by providing scholarships and youth athletic programs. (Titusville Chamber of Commerce, 2000 S. Washington Ave, Titusville 32780. Tel: 407/267-3036.)

APRIL: **Russell F. Sullivan Memorial Golf Tournament – Key West.** This was designed to raise funds for a scholarship to the Florida Keys Community College for regular, on-duty police officers to continue their education. (P.O. Box 2502, Key West 33040. Tel: 305/296-6981.)
Indian River Festival Golf Scramble – Titusville. Held at the LaCita Country Club, the golf scramble is open to the first 100 golfers and benefits everyone in the community through funds raised to support the Titusville Chamber of Commerce. (Titusville

Chamber of Commerce, 2000 S. Washington Ave, Titusville 32780. Tel: 407/267-3036.)

MAY: Florida Citrus Bowl Coaches Classic – Orlando. Held at the Grand Cypress Resort Golf Club, this is a benefit golf tournament for the Florida Citrus Bowl, featuring top football coaches and athletic directors from across the US. (Florida Citrus Bowl, 250 N. Orange Ave, Suite 300, Orlando 32801. Tel: 407/423-2476.)

JULY: Crazy American Golf Tournament – Key Biscayne. Open to all – amateurs, novices, locals, out-of-towners and anybody else, this is a tournament designed to be fun and to raise community awareness. (Metro-Dade County Parks and Recreation, 50 S.W. 32nd Road, Bldg #9, Miami 33129. Tel: 305/579-2676.)
Southern Amateur – Orlando. Normally held at the Grand Cypress Resort and Golf Club, with a roster of top US amateur golfers. (Southern Golf Association, P.O. Box G, Birmingham, AL 35253. Tel: 205/979-4653).

AUGUST: Atlanta Junior Grand Golf Championship – Destin. The Atlanta Juniors consist of approximately 140 players of which the highest point winners in each age category will participate in the Grand Championship. There will be a parent-junior event before the Grand Championship as well. (Sandestin, Emerald Coast Parkway, Destin 32541. Tel: 305/427-1050.)

Bartow Youth Classic – Bartow. A benefit for the Florida Sheriff's Youth Villa, and the tournament includes a welcome party and dance, a women's team championship, a fashion show and champagne lunch, an open golf tournament and more. (Bartow Chamber of Commerce, P.O. Box 956, Bartow 33830. Tel: 813/583-7125.)

DECEMBER: South Seas Golf Traditional – Captiva. Held to benefit the Big Brothers/Big Sisters Organization of Lee County, and always held the first weekend in December. (South Seas Plantation Resort and Yacht Harbor, P.O. Box 194, Captiva 33924. Tel: 813/472-5111.)

TENNIS

MARCH: Lipton International Players Championship – Miami. Held at the International Tennis Center on Key Biscayne, this 2-week festival features top players from throughout the world. (Metro-Dade County Parks and Recreation Dept, 50 S.W. 32nd Ave, Bldg #9, Miami 33129. Tel: 305/579-2676.)

APRIL: Dupont Tennis Classic – Orlando. Held at the Grand Cypress Resort Racquet Club, this week-long men's tournament always features a number of top names on the pro tennis circuit. (Grand Cypress Resort, 60 Grand Cypress Blvd, Orlando 32819. Tel: 407/239-4600.)

JUNE: Florida State Tennis Championship – Delray Beach. Visitors are invited to watch Florida's top-ranked players compete in this tournament sanctioned by the Florida Association. Held since 1950, it is played at Delray Beach Municipal Tennis Courts. (Chamber of Commerce, 64 S.E. Fifth Ave, Delray Beach 33444. Tel: 305/278-0424).

DECEMBER: Mission Inn Winter Open Tennis Tournament – Howey-in-the-Hills. Held the second weekend in December at the Mission Inn Golf and Tennis Resort. (Mission Inn Golf and Tennis Resort, P.O. Box 441, Howey-in-the-Hills 32737. Tel: 904/324-3103.)

WATER SPORTS

APRIL: Mount Dora Sailing Regatta – Mount Dora. Sponsored by The Mount Dora Yacht Club, the oldest inland yacht club in Florida, this event features more than 100 boats in 20 different classes. (Mount Dora Chamber of Commerce, Mount Dora 32757. Tel: 904/383-2165.)

MAY: Great Dock Canoe Race – Naples. In celebration of the beginning of Spring, the community holds a 3-mile canoe race starting at the dock at the Crayton Cove Restaurant. (Crayton Cove Restaurant, 840-B 12th Ave South, Naples 33940. Tel: 813/261-4191.)

JUNE: Safe Boating Week and Nautical Festival – Fort Myers. Combining boating safety with fun; boat exhibitions and demonstrations are held at various locations throughout Lee County. The week ends with the Nautical Festival, which includes a sailboat, canoe and catamaran race, overboard demonstrations, and the blessing of the fleet ceremony. (National Safe Boating Committee, 937 S.W. 54th Lane, Cape Coral 33914. Tel: 813/542-7123.)

AUGUST: World Cup Jet Ski Races – Islamorada. Held the last weekend of August, the top jet-skiers from US and abroad compete. (Holiday Isle, P.O. Box 588, Islamorada 33036. Tel: 305/664-2321.)

RACING

This section is divided into three parts, providing brief descriptions of the various events during particular months.

AUTO

FEBRUARY: Sun Bank 24 At Daytona – Daytona Beach. Exotic Sports cars compete in this IMSA and Camel GT endurance race. It is one of only two 24-

hour races in the world (the other being the LeMans in France) and is always held 2 weeks before the Daytona 500. (Daytona International Speedway, P.O. Drawer S, Daytona Beach 32015. Tel: 904/253-6711.)

FEBRUARY: **Busch Classic – Daytona Beach.** This is a 50-mile race (20 laps) for a $50,000 first prize. Only the drivers who win Busch Pole Awards during the previous NASCAR Winston Cup season are eligible. (Daytona International Speedway, P.O. Drawer S, Daytona Beach 32015. Tel: 904/253-6711.)

Daytona 500 – Daytona Beach. The most important and richest 500-mile stock car race in the world culminates 2 weeks of racing activity at Daytona International Speedway, (Drawer S, Daytona Beach 32015. Tel: 904/253-6711.)

MARCH: **Gatornationals – Gainesville.** One of the top races on the National Hot Rod Association circuit, this event attracts dragsters from all places across the nation. (National Hot Rod Association, P.O. Box 5555, Glendora, CA 91740-0750. Tel: 818/914-4761).

Twelve Hours of Sebring – Sebring. (Always third week of March.) Scheduled events include the classic 12 Hours of Sebring International Grand Prix of Endurance Race, the Automobile Hall of Fame induction ceremonies, a power boat regatta, parade and golf and tennis tournaments. (Chamber of Commerce, 309 S. Circle, Sebring 33870. Tel: 813/385-8448.)

APRIL: **Antique Motor Car Race – Panama City.** This race begins in Panama City, travels through Port St Joe and continues on to its conclusion in Apalachicola. From Model T Fords to StuDbakers, this race features a variety of cars from the past. (Miracle Strip Region AACA, State Road 5710 and Hwy 98, Panama City 32404. Tel: 904/871-4077.)

JULY: **Summer Speed Week – Daytona Beach.** Held at Daytona International Speedway, these holiday races attract top professional drivers. The Paul Revere 250 takes place midnight July 3 and the Firecracker 400, July 4. (Daytona International Speedway, Drawer S, Daytona Beach 32015. Tel: 904/253-6711.)

SEPTEMBER: **Labor Day Rod Run – Wakulla Springs.** Sponsored by the Tallahassee Streetrodders, the Labor Day Rod Run features an exhibition and races of customized automobiles. (Tallahassee Streetrodders, P.O. Box 532, Woodville 32363. Tel: 904/421-3938.)

MOTORCYCLE

MARCH: **Cycle Week – Daytona Beach.** This concentrated period of motorcycle racing includes road, motor-cross, supercross and enduro races in novice, amateur and expert classes. The Daytona 200, which concludes the week of racing, is one of the richest and most prestigious motorcycle races in the world. (Daytona International Speedway, Drawer S, Daytona Beach 32015. Tel: 904/253-6711.)

OCTOBER: **Daytona Pro-AM – Daytona Beach.** The event is a combination of amateur and professional motorcycle road racing, which are preparation for the prestigious Cycle Week races in March. (Daytona International Speedway, Drawer S, Daytona Beach 32015. Tel: 904/253-6711.)

BOAT

FEBRUARY: **Southland Sweepstake – St Petersburg.** The largest hydroplane regatta in the South, this event manages to draw 200 entries from the United States and other countries. (American Power Boat Association, Box 41065, St Petersburg 33473. Tel: 813/535-2006.)

Southern Ocean Racing Conference – St Petersburg. Racing yachts from almost every part of the world compete in this prestigious grand prix sailing event, comprised of 6 ocean races between Florida and the Bahamas. (SORC, 2087 Kansas Ave N.E., St Petersburg 33703. Tel: 813/522-3248.)

FOOTBALL

JANUARY 1: **Orange Bowl Football Classic – Miami.** (Always New Year's Night.) The champion of the Big Eight Conference meets a nationally ranked opponent in the Orange Bowl Stadium during this nationally televised event. (Orange Bowl Committee, 1501 N.W. Third St, Miami 33125. Tel: 305/642-1515.)

DECEMBER: **Gator Bowl – Jacksonville.** The River's City draws football fans to the Gator Bowl for competition between two nationally ranked collegiate teams. The Gator Bowl Regatta, December 4–5, attracts sailors to a 20-mile race. (Mazda Gator Bowl Association, 1801 Art Museum Drive, Suite 101, Jacksonville 32207. Tel: 904/396-1800.)

Hall of Fame Bowl – Tampa. Nationally televised collegiate post-season game, ranking in the top 10 of such bowl games. (Hall of Fame Bowl, 4511 N. Himes Ave, Suite 135, Tampa 33614. Tel: 813/874-2695.)

SPRING TRAINING

Atlanta Braves: Municipal Stadium, West Palm Beach. Tel: 407/863-6100.

Baltimore Orioles: Miami Stadium, Miami. Tel: 305/633-9857.

Boston Red Sox: Chain O' Lakes Park, Winter Haven. Tel: 813/293-3900.

Chicago White Sox: Ed Smith Stadium, Sarasota. Tel: 813/752-3388.

Cincinnati Reds: Plant City Stadium, Plant City. Tel: 813/953-7337.

Detroit Tigers: Marchant Stadium, Lakeland. Tel: 813/686-8075.

Houston Astros: Osceola County Stadium, Kissimmee. Tel: 407/933-5500.

Kansas City Royals: Boardwalk and Baseball, Haines City. Tel: 813/424-7115.

Los Angles Dodgers: Holman Stadium, Vero Beach. Tel: 407/569-4900.

Minnesota Twins: Tinker Field, Orlando. Tel: 407/849-6346.

Montreal Expos: Municipal Stadium, West Palm Beach. Tel: 407/684-6801.

New York Mets: St Lucie County Sports Complex, Port St Lucie. Tel: 407/879-7378.

New York Yankees: Ft. Lauderdale Stadium, Ft. Lauderdale. Tel: 305/776-1921.

Philadelphia Phillies: Jack Russell Stadium, Clearwater. Tel: 813/442-8496.

Pittsburgh Pirates: McKechnie Field, Bradenton. Tel: 813/747-3031.

St Louis Cardinals: AL Lang Field, St Petersburg. Tel: 813/896-4641.

Texas Rangers: Charlotte County Stadium, Port Charlotte. Tel: 813/625-9500.

Toronto Blue Jays: Grant Field, Dunedin. Tel: 813/733-0429.

RUNNING

JANUARY: Orange Bowl 10 km Race – Miami. Top national and international long-distance runners join more than 2,500 other competitiors in this race. Festivities after the race include awards, refreshments and entertainment. (Runner's international, Inc., c/o Orange Bowl Committee, P.O. Box 350748, Miami, Florida 33135. Tel: 305/642-5211.)

FEBRUARY: Gasparilla Distance Classic – Tampa. Tampa Bay's long distance classic consists of two running events: the Run for Fun, 5,000 meters; and the Distance Run, 15,000 meters. World class runners compete in the race, in which individuals of all ages may compete. The Classic, which also has gained national acclaim in four short years, will also include a pre-race clinic. (S.I. Amberg Public Relations, 4141 Bayshore Blvd, Suite 804, Tampa 33606. Tel: 813/833-2601.)

MARCH: Red Lobster 10K Classic – Orlando. Athletes from more than 22 countries meet for this 6.2-mile (10-km) race for one of the top race purses in the US (Red Lobster, 6770 Lake Ellenor Drive, Orlando 32809. Tel: 407/850-5272.)

Easter Weekend 5K Run – Destin. The course is through Sandestin, 16 kilometers east of Destin, and is part of a series of 5 kilometer races held each summer in the area. (Sandestin, Emerald Coast Parkway, Destin 32541. Tel: 904/267-8135.)

APRIL: St Cloud Spring Fling – St Cloud. Three days of outdoors activities, including a 10 kilometer race, a bass-fishing tournament, an offshore boat race and Sports Olympics are held on the St Cloud lakefront. (St Cloud Rotary Club, P.O. Box 711, St Cloud 32770. Tel: 407/892-9141.)

Eastern Beach Run – Daytona Beach. (Always held on Easter Sunday.) Organized 13 years ago for vacationing college students, this 4-mile (6.4-km) run has developed into a race of national reputation. Thousands of runners compete in several divisions on the wide hard-packed sands of Daytona Beach at low tide. (Recreation Dept, Box 551, Daytona Beach 32015. Tel: 904/252-6461.)

MAY: Running Festival – Pensacola. This 10,000-meter run is one of 20 races in a southeastern grand prix series. It attracts more than 2,500 runners, all out to improve their national standings. (Tourist Information Center, 803 N. Palafox St, Pensacola 32501. Tel: 904//433-3065.)

AUGUST: Elephant Walk Triathlon – Destin. The event includes a half-mile (10.8-km) swim, a 15-mile (24-km) hike, and a 4-mile (6.4-km) run. (Sandestin, Emerald Coast Parkway, Destin 32541. Tel: 904/267-8135.)

DECEMBER: Tallahassee Ultra Distance Classic – Wakulla Springs. The event includes a 50 kilometer and 100 kilometer ultra distance run. (Wakulla Springs Lodge and Conference Center, 1 Springs Drive, Wakulla Springs 32305. Tel: 904/224-5950.)

RODEO

FEBRUARY: Homestead Championship Rodeo – Homestead. This is one of the top three rodeos in Florida. It normally attracts championship cowboys from throughout the US. Entertainment includes bronc riding, steer wrestling, clown acts, mounted drill teams and more. (Susan Neuman Inc., 555 N.E. 15th St, Suite 25-K, Miami 33132-1450. Tel: 305/372-9966.)

Silver Spurs Rodeo – Kissimmee. (Always third weekend in February.) The first Silver Spurs was held in 1944 to benefit war bonds. It has since developed into a twice-yearly 3-day celebration in Osceola County. Professional cowboys from the United States and Canada come to compete for the thousands of dollars in one of the oldest and largest professional rodeos in the Southeast. (Carlman Booker Public Relations, 520 S. Maitland Road, Maitland 32751. Tel: 407/628-2280.)

MARCH: Chalo Nitka Festival & Rodeo – Moore Haven. (Always held the first weekend in March.) Chalo Nitka means "day of the bass" in Seminole language, and the festival features an 8-week bass fishing contest that culminates in a Seminole Indian program and rodeo. Also featured are a parade, King and Queen of Bass Dinner, and a showboat dinner cruise with live entertainment. (Chamber of Commerce, Box 490, Moore Haven 33471. Tel: 813/946-0440.)

All-Florida Championship Rodeo – Arcadia. Held since 1929, Florida's oldest rodeo features calf roping, calf scramble, quadrille, cloverleaf barrel racing, saddle bronc riding, bare-back riding and bull riding. (All-Florida Championship Rodeo Association, Box 591, Arcadia 33821. Tel: 813/494-3773.)

JULY: **Silver Spurs Rodeo – Kissimmee.** (Always July 4 weekend.) What began as a Sunday afternoon get-together between ranchers in the "cow town" of Kissimmee more than 35 years ago, has turned into Florida's oldest continuous professional rodeo. Cowboys compete for thousands of dollars and national points in bull riding, bronc riding, cow roping and steer wrestling. (Carlman Booker Public Relations, 520 S. Maitland Ave, Maitland 32751. Tel: 407/628-2280.)

SEPTEMBER: **North Brevard Area Rodeo – Titusville** The cowboys gather at the Space Center Executive Airport for a PRCA-sanctioned event that includes bronc riding, steer wrestling, barrel racing and more. (Titusville Chamber of Commerce, 2000 S. Washington Ave, Titusville 32780. Tel: 407/267-3036.)

PARI-MUTUELS

HORSE TRACK

January–March: **Gulfstream Park**, Hallandale
March–May: **Hialeah Park**, Hialeah
November–January: **CalderRace Track**, Opa-Locka (Miami)
December–April: **Tampa Bay Downs**, Oldsmar

HARNESS TRACKS

November–May: **Pompano Park Harness Racing**, Pompano Beach

QUARTER HORSE RACING

June–August: **Tourist Attraction, Inc.**, Pompano Park

JAI-ALAI FRONTONS

January–December: **Orlando Jai-Alai**, Orlando
January–June: **Tampa Fronton**, Tampa
January–July: **Fort Pierce Jai-Alai**, Fort Pierce
January–July: **Palm Beach Jai-Alai**, West Palm Beach
January–March, June–September: **Ocala Jai-Alai**, Ocala

February–July: **Volusia Jai-Alai**, Daytona Beach
September–January: **Sports Palace**, Melbourne
November–April: **Dania Jai-Alai**, Dania
November–May: **Big Bend Jai-Alai**, Chattahoochee
November–September: **Miami Jai-Alai**, Miami

GREYHOUND TRACKS

January–December: **Pensacola Greyhound Park**, Pensacola
January–May: **St Petersburg Kennel Club**, St Petersburg
March–April, September–October: **St Johns County Greyhound**, Jacksonville
March–October: **Jefferson County Kennel Club**, Monticello
March–September: **Washington County Kennel Club**, Ebro
May–September: **Super Seminole**, Casselberry
May–September: **Sarasota Kennel Club**, Sarasota
June–September: **Flagler Kennel Club**, Miami
November–March: **Orange Park Kennel Club**, Jacksonville
December–May: **Key West Kennel Club**, Key West
December–May, June–September: **Palm Beach Kennel Club**, West Palm Beach
December–May: **Sanford-Orlando Kennel Club**, Longwood
December–August: **Bonita Springs Kennel Club**, Bonita Springs

MISCELLANEOUS EVENTS

JANUARY–APRIL: **Palm Beach Polo And Country Club Season – West Palm Beach.** The Glenlivet Scotch Polo Team, Palm Beach Polo and Country Club's official home team, plays a full season of matches including the Father-Son Holiday Tournament, late December–January 10; the Gold Coast League, January 3–February 28; the USPA Gold Cup, March 3–14; the Cartier International Open, March 16–April 4; and the Coca-Cola Challenge Cup, April 7–25. (Palm Beach Polo and Country Club, 13198 Forest Hill Blvd, West Palm Beach 33414. Tel: 407/798-7040.)

FEBRUARY–MARCH: **Winter Equestrian Festival – Statewide.** This series of 6 week-long hunter and jumper shows in the Florida winter horse show circuit offers spectators the opportunity to enjoy Olympic and World Cup qualifying competition. The Festival includes the Palm Beach Classic, West Palm Beach; the Palm Beach Masters, West Palm Beach; the Golden Hills International Charity Horse Show, Ocala; the Jack-Sun-Ville Internationale, Tampa; the Tallahassee Spring Horse Show; the Delta Air Lines International, Tampa; the Tournament of Champions, Tampa; and the American Invitational Tampa. (Tully-Menard, Inc., 2207 S. Dale Mabry, Tampa 33609. Tel: 813/253-0047.)

APRIL: United States/International Challenge Cup – Palm Beach Gardens. A world-class croquet event bringing together the international team and United States Croquet Association's National Team. (PGA Sheraton Resort, 400 Avenue of the Champions, Palm Beach Gardens 33418. Tel: 407/627-2000.)

NOVEMBER: Breeder's Cup – Hallandale. This is the year-end championship of thoroughbred racing at Gulfstream Park. (Gulfstream Park Racing, Gulfstream Park, Hallandale 33009. Tel: 3035/454-7000.)

DECEMBER: Winter Enduro Olympics, World Karting Association – Daytona Beach. Traditionally held between Christmas and New Year's Day, this 4-day festival of go-kart racing presents scores of trials on the same 3.56-mile (5.7-km) course as do the "big boys" at Daytona International Speedway. The course combines 31-degree-high embankments with a twisting infield pattern. (Daytona International Speedway, P.O. Drawer S, Daytona Beach 32015. Tel: 904/253-6711.)

FURTHER READING

HISTORICAL/POLITICAL/ CULTURAL

Andrews, Evangeline W., and Andrews, Charles McLean (editors). *Jonathan Dickinson's Journal; or God's Protecting Providence*. New Haven: Yale University Press, 1945.

Apple, Max. *Propheteers*. Harper & Row, 1987.

Barbour, George, M. *Florida for Tourists, Invalids and Settlers, 1882*. Floridiana Facsimile Reprint Series, Gainesville: University of Florida Press, 1964.

Barcia, Carvallido y Zuniga, Andre G. de. *Chronological History of the Continent of Florida, 1512–1722*. Translated by Anthony Kerrigan. Gainesville: University of Florida Press, 1951.

Barrientos, Bartolome. *Pedro Menendez de Aviles, Founder of Florida*. Translated by Anthony Kerrigan. Floridiana Facsimile and Reprint Series, Gainesville: University of Florida Press, 1965.

Bartram, William. *Travels of William Bartram*. Edited by Mark Van Doren. New York: Dover Publications, 1951.

Bennett, Charles E. *Laudonniere and Fort Caroline: History and Documents*. Gainesville: University of Florida Press, 1964.

Bennett, Charles E. *Settlement of Florida*. Gainesville: University of Florida Press, 1968.

Bennett, Charles E. *Three Voyages*. Gainesville: University of Florida Press, 1975.

Bickel, Karl. *The Mangrove Coast*. New York: Coward McCann, 1942.

Bill, Ledyard. *A Winter in Florida*. New York: Wood and Holbrook, 1870.

Bourne, Edward G. *Narratives of the Career of Hernando de Soto*. Two volumes. London: David Nutt, 1905.

Boyd, Mark F., Smith, Hale G., and Grifin, John W. *Here They Once Stood: The Tragic End of the Apalachee Missions*. Gainesville: University of Florida Press, 1951.

Brevard, Caroline. *A History of Florida*. Edited by James A. Robertson. Two volumes. DeLand: Florida State Historical Society, 1924–25.

Brinton, Daniel G. *A Guide-Book of Florida and the South for Tourists, Invalids and Emigrants*. Philadelphia: G. Maclean, 1869.

Brinton Daniel G. *Notes on the Florida Peninsula*. Philadelphia: J. Sabin, 1859.

Browne, Jefferson B. *Key West, The Old and the New*. St Augustine: The Record Co., 1912.

Burnett, Gene M. *Florida's Past: People and Events That Shaped the State*. Pineaple Press, 1986

Cabeza de Vaca. Alvar Nunez. *The Journey of Alvar Nunez Cabeza de Vaca and His Companions from Florida to the Pacific, 1528–1536.*

Campbell, A Stuart. *The Cigar Industry of Tampa*. Gainesville: University of Florida Press, 1939.

Canova, Andrew P. *Life and Adventures in South Florida*. Tampa: Southern Sun Publishing House, 1885.

Carson, Ruby Leach, and Tebeau, Charlton W. *Florida: From Indian Trail to Space Age*. Three volumes. Delray Beach: Southern Publishing Co., 1966.

Cash, W.T. *The Story of Florida*. New York: American Historical Society, Inc., 1938.

Caughey, John W. *McGillivray of the Creeks*. Norman: University of Oklahoma Press, 1938.

Chandler, David Leon. *Henry Flagler – The Astonishing Life and Times of the Visionary Robbery Baron Who Founded Florida*. MacMillan, 1986.

Coe, Charles H. *Red Patriots: The Story of the Seminoles*. Cincinnati: The Editor Publishing Co., 1868.

Cohen, M.M. *Notice of Florida and the Campaigns, 1836*. Edited by O.Z. Tyler, Jr. Floridiana Facsimile and Reprint Series, Gainesville: University of Florida Press, 1964.

Corse, Carita Doggett. *Key to the Golden Islands*. Corse Hill: University of North Carolina Press, 1931.

Crews, Harry. *Florida Frenzy*. University Presses of Florida, 1982.

Davis, William Watson. *The Civil War and Recon-*

struction in Florida. New York: Columbia University Press, 1913.

Deland, Margaret. Florida Days. Boston: Little Brown and Co., 1889.

Dickison, Mary Elizabeth. Dickison and His Men: Reminiscences of the War in Florida, 1890. Edited by Samuel Proctor. Floridiana Facsimile and Reprint Series, Gainesville: University of Florida Press, 1962.

Dodd, Dorothy. Florida Becomes a State. Tallahassee: Florida Centennial Commission, 1945.

Dodson, Pat. (editor) Journey through the Old Everglades: The Log of the Minnehaha. Tampa: Trend House, 1973.

Doherty, Herbett J. Jr. Richard Keith Call: Southern Unionist. Gainesville: University of Florida Press, 1961.

Douglas, Marjory Stoneman. The Everglades: River of Grass. New York: Rinehart, 1947.

Douglas, Marjory Stoneman. Florida: the Long Frontier. New York: Harper & Row, 1967.

Douglas, Marjory Stoneman. Hurricane. New York: Rinehart & Co., 1958.

Eppes, Susan Bradford. Through Some Eventful Years, 1926. Edited by Joseph D. Cushman, Jr. Floridiana Facsimile and Reprint Series, Gainesville: University of Florida Press, 1967.

Forbes, James Grant. Sketches, Historical and Topographical, of the Floridas: More Particularly of East Florida, 1821. Edited by James W. Covington. Floridiana Facsimile and Reprint Series. Gainesville: University of Florida Press, 1964.

Fuller, Walter P. This Was Florida's Boom. St Petersburg: Times Publishing Co., 1954.

Gannon, Michael. The Cross in the Sand. The Early Catholic Church in Florida, 1513–1870. Gainesville: University of Florida Press, 1965.

Garcilaso de la Vega. The Florida of the Inca. Translated by John Grier Varner and Jeannette Johnson Varner. Austin: University of Texas Press, 1951.

Gill, Joan E., and Read, Beth R. (editors) Born of the Sun: The Official Florida Bicentennial Commemorative Book. Hollywood, Fla.: Worth International Communications Corp., 1975.

Goggin, John M. Indian and Spanish Selected Writings. Coral Gables: University of Miami Press, 1964.

Gonzalez, Thomas A. The Caloosahatchee, Estero. Fla: Koreshan Unity Press, 1932.

Gonzalo Solis de Meras. Pedro Menendez de Aviles. Translated and edited by Jeanette Thurber Conner. Deland: Florida Historical Society, 1923.

Griffith, Leon Odell. Ed Ball: Confusion to the Enemy. Tampa: Trend House, 1975.

Grismer, Carl. The Story of St Petersburg. St Petersburg: P.K. Smith and Co., 1948.

Grismer, Karl H. Tampa: History of the City of Tampa Region of Florida. Edited by D.B. McKay. St Petersburg: St Petersburg Printing Co., 1950.

Hanna, Alfred Jackson. A Prince in Their Midst: The Adventurous Life of Achille Murat on the American Frontier. Norman: University of Oklahoma Press, 1946.

Hanna, Alfred Jackson and Cabell, James Branch. The St Joh's: A Parade of Diversities. New York: Farrar and Rinehart, 1943.

Hanna, Alfred Jackson, and Hanna, Kathryn T. Abbey. Lake Okeechobee, Wellspring of the Everglades. Indianapolis: Bobbs-Merrill, 1948.

Hanna, Kathryn T. Abbey. Florida, Land of Change. Chapel Hill: University of North Carolina Press, 1948.

Hardy, Iza Duffus. Oranges and Alligators, London: Ward and Downey, 1887.

Hartley, William and Hartley, Ellen. Osceola. New York: Hawthorn Books, 1973

Heather, Basil. "Wreck Ashore!" New York: Farrar, Straus and Giroux, 1969.

Howard, Clinton N. The British Development of West Florida,1763–1769. Berkeley: University of California Press, 1947.

Jahoda, Gloria. Florida: A Bicentennial History. New York: W.W. Norton and Co., Inc., 1976.

Jahoda, Gloria. The Other Florida. New York: Charles Scribner's Sons, 1967.

Jahoda, Gloria. River of the Golden Ibis. New York: Holt, Rinehart and Winston, 1973.

Jahoda, Gloria. The Road To Samarkand: Frederick Delius and His Music. New York: Charles Scribner's Sons, 1969.

Johnson, James Weldon. Along This Way. New York: Viking, 1933.

Johnston, Alva. The Legendary Mizners. New York: Strauss and Young, 1953

Kelly, Wlliam E. The Franciscans in Florida. Ithaca: Cornell University Press, 1946.

Kendrick, Baynard. Florida Trails to Turnpikes, 1914–1964. Gainesville: University of Florida Press, 1964.

Kennedy, Stetson. Palmetto Country. New York: Duell, Sloan and Pearce, 1942.

Kersey, Jr., Harry A. Pelts, Plumes and Hides: White Traders Among the Seminole Indians, 1870–1930. Gainesville: University of Florida Press, 1975.

Kofoed, Jack. Moon Over Miami. New York: Random House, 1955.

Lanier, Sidney. Florida: Its Scenery, Climate and History. Philadelphia: J.B. Lippincott and Co., 1876.

Laumer, Frank J. Massacre! Gainesville: University of Florida Press, 1968.

Lazarus, William C. Wings in the Sun: the Annals of Aviation in Forida. Orlando: Tyn Cobb's Florida Press, 1951.

Lockey, Joseph Bryne. (editor and translator) East Florida, 1783–1785. Berkeley: University of California Press, 1943.

Long, Ellen Call. Florida Breezes, or Florida: New and Old,1883. Edited by Margaret S. Chapman. Floridiana Facsimile and Reprint Series, Gainesville: University of Florida Press, 1962.

356

Lowery, Woodbury. *The Spanish Settlements within the Present Limits of the United States.* Two volumes. New York: Russel and Russel, 1959.

Lummus, John N. *The Miracle of Miami Beach.* Miami: The Teacher Publishing Co., 1940.

Lyon, Eugene. *The Enterprise of Florida: Pedro Menendez de Aviles and the Spanish Conquest of 1565–1568.* Gainesville: University Presses of Florida, 1976.

Lyon, Eugene. *The Search for the Atocha.* New York: Harper & Row, 1979.

MacCauley, Clay. *The Seminole Indians of Florida.* Smithsonian Institution Bureau of American Ethnology, Fifth Annual Report, 1883, 1884. Washington, DC, 1887.

Mahon, John K. *The Second Seminole War.* Gainesville: University of Florida Press, 1968.

Maloney, Walter C. *A Sketch of the History of Key West, Florida, 1876.* Edited by Thelma Peters. Floridiana Facsimile and Reprint Series, Gainesville: University of Florida Press, 1968.

Manach, Jorge. *Marti.* Translated by Coley Taylor. New York: Devia-Adair, 1950.

Marban, Jorge A. *La Florida: Cinco Siglos de Historia Hispanica.* Coleccion De Estudios Hispanicos: Ediciones, 1979.

Martin, Sidney Walter. *Florida's Flagler.* Athens: University of Georgia Press, 1949.

Marx, Robert F. *Spanish Treasure in Florida Waters: A Billion Dollar Graveyard.* Boston: Mariners, 1978.

Matschat, Cecile. *Suwannee River: Strange Green Land.* New York: Farrar and Rinehart, 1938.

McReynolds, Edwin C. *The Seminoles.* Norman: University of Oklahoma Press, 1957.

Motte, Jacob Rhett. *Journey Into Wilderness: An Army Surgeon's Account of Life in Camp and Field During the Creek and Seminole Wars, 1836–1838.* Edited by James F. Sunderman. Gainesville: University of Florida Press, 1953.

Mowatt, Charles L. *East Florida as a British Province, 1763–1785.* Berkeley: University of California Press, 1943.

Nash, Charles. *The Magic of Miami Beach.* Philadelphia: David McKay Co., 1938.

Neill, Wilfred T. *The Story of Florida's Seminole Indians.* St Petersburg: Great Outdoors Publishing Co., 1964.

Ney, John. *Palm Beach.* Boston: Little, Brown, 1966.

Neyland, Leedell W. *Twelve Black Floridians.* Tallahassee: Florida A & M University Foundation, Inc., 1970.

Nolan, David. *Fifty Feet in Paradise: The Booming of Florida.* Harcourt Brace Jovanovich, 1984.

Ober, Frederick A. *The Knockabout Club in the Everglades.* Boston: Estes and Lauriat, 1887.

Ober, Frederick A. *"Rambler," Guide to Florida, 1875.* Edited by Rembert W. Patrick. Floridiana Facsimile and Reprint Series, Gainesville: University of Florida Press, 1964.

Olsen, Stanley J. *Fossil Mammals of Florida.* Florida Geological Survey. Special Publication #6. Tallahassee: Florida Geological Survey, 1959.

Osterbind, Carter C., and Angela O'Rand. (editors) *Older People in Florida: A Statistical Abstract for the Elderly.* Gainesville: University Presses of Florida, 1979.

Parks, Pat. *The Railroad That Went To Sea.* Stephen Greene, 1968.

Patrick, Rembert W. *Florida Under Five Flags.* Gainesville: University of Florida Press, 1960.

Peters, Virginia B. *The Florida Wars.* Shoe String, 1979.

Pettengill, George W. *The Story of Florida Railroads 1834–1903.* The Railway and Locomotive Historical Society, Bulletin No. 86. Boston: Railway and Locomotive Historical Society, 1952.

Pizzo, Anthony. *Tampa Town.* Tampa: Trend House.

Pollack, Martin. *Welcome to Florida: The Sunshine State.* Southern Progress Alliance, 1979.

Pratt, Theodore. *That Was Palm Beach.* St Petersburg: Great Outdoors Publishing Co., 1968.

Pratt, Theodore. *Story of Boca Raton.* St Petersburg: Great Outdoors Publishing Co.

Reaver, J. Russell. (editor) *Florida Folktales.* University of Florida Press, 1987.

Redford, Poly. *Billion Dollar Sandbar: A Biography of Miami Beach.* New York: Dutton, 1970.

Reynolds, Ray. *I Declare!* Tallahassee Democrat, 1983.

Ribaut, Jean. *The Whole and True Discovery of Tera Florida. A Facsimilie Reprint of the London Edition of 1563.* Edited by David L. Dowd, 1927. Ribaut biography by Jeannette Thurber Connor. Floridiana Facsimile and Reprint Series, Gainesville: University of Florida Press, 1964.

Richardson, Joseph M. *The Negro in the Reconstruction of Florida.* Tallahassee: Florida State University Press, 1965.

Robbins, Sarah Stuart. *One Happy Winter: Or, A Visit to Florida.* Boston: Buller Bros., 1878.

Roberts, Kenneth L. *Florida.* New York: Harper and Brothers, 1926.

Roberts, Kenneth L. *Sun Hunting.* Indianapolis: Bobbs-Merrill, 1922.

Romans, Bernard A. *A Concise and Natural History of East and West Florida, 1775.* Edited by Rembert W. Patrick. Floridiana Facsimile and Reprint Series, Gainesville: University of Florida Press, 1962.

Rose, Rufus E. *The Swamp and Overflowed Lands of Florida: The Disston Contract and Sale.* Tallahassee: 1916.

Roosevelt, Theodore. *The Rough Riders.* New York: Charles Scribner's Sons, 1906. Schell, Rolfe F. *DeSoto Didn't Land at Tampa.* Island Press, 1974.

Schell, Rolfe F. *History of Fort Myers Beach, Fla.* Island Press, 1980.

Shepard, Birse. *The Love of the Wreckers.* Boston: Beacon Press, 1961.

Shipp, Barnard. *Record of the Events of Fifty-six*

Years from 1512 to 1568. Philadelphia: Collins, Printer, 1881.

Shofner, Jerrel H. *Daniel Ladd: Merchant Prince of Frontier Florida.* Gainesville: University of Florida Press, 1978.

Shofner, Jerrel H. *Nor Is It Over Yet: Florida in the Era of Reconstructions, 1863–1877.* Gainesville: University Presses of Florida, 1974.

Shoumatoff, Alex. *Florida Ramble.* New York: Harper & Row, 1974.

Simpson, George S. "Extinct Land Mammals of Florida." Florida Geological Survey, 20th Annual Report. Tallahassee: 1929.

Smith, Buckingham. (translator) *Relation of Alvar Nunez Cabeza de Vaca.* New York: Printed by J. Munsell for H.C. Murphy, 1871.

Stork, William. *An Account of East Florida, with a Journal kept by John Bartram of Philadelphia, Botanist to his Majesty for the Floridas, upon a Journey from St Augustine up the River St Johns.* London: W. Nicoll and G. Woodfall, 1766.

Stowe, Harriet Beecher. *Palmetto Leaves, 1873.* Edited by Mary B. Graff. Introduction by Edith Cowles. Floridiana Facsimile and Reprint Series, Gainesville: University of Florida Press, 1968.

Tebeau, Charlton. *A History of Florida.* Coral Gables: University of Miami Press, 1971.

Thompson, Arthur W. *Jacksonian Democracy on the Florida Frontier.* Gainesville: University of Florida Press, 1961.

Townshend, F. Trench. *Wild Life in Florida, With a Visit to Cuba.* London: Hurst and Blackett, 1875.

Weigall, Theyre Hamilton. *Boom in Paradise.* New York: A.H. King, 1932.

Will, Lawrence E. *A Cracker History of Lake Okeechobee.* St Petersburg: Great Outdoors Publishing Co., 1965.

Will, Lawrence E. *A Dredgement of Cape Sable.* St Petersburg: Great Outdoors Publishing Co., 1967.

Will, Lawrence E. *Okeechobee Boats and Skippers.* St Petersburg: Great Outdoors Publishing Co., 1965.

Williams, John L. *A View of West Florida, Embracing Its Geography, Topography, Etc. with an Appendix Treating of Its Antiquities, Land Titles, & Canals & Containing a Map Exhibiting a Chart of the Coast, a Plan of Pensacola, & an Entrance of the Harbour, 1827.* Floridiana Facsimile and Reprint Series, Gainesville: University of Florida Press, 1964.

Williams, Joy. *Florida Keys – History and Guide,* Random House, 1987.

Young, June Hurley. *Florida's Pinellas Peninsula.* St Petersburg: Byron Kennedy & Co., 1984.

GUIDES, REFERENCES, SPECIAL INTEREST

AAA Tour Book: Florida. Falls Church, Va.: The American Automobile Association, revised annually.

Birnbaum, Steve. *Walt Disney World: The Official Guide.* Boston: Houghton Mifflin, 1984. Authorized by Walt Disney World. (Revised annually.)

Brookfield, Charles M. and Griswold, Oliver. *They All Called It Tropical: True Tales of the Romantic Everglades, Cape Sable and the Florida Keys.* Miami: Historical Association of southern Florida and Banyan Books, 1977. Reprint of 1949 edition.

Brown, Robin C. *Florida's Fossils – Guide to Location, Indentification and Enjoyment.* Pineapple Press, 1988.

Burt, Alvin. *Florida: A Place in the Sun.* Burda, 1974.

Craighead, Frank C. *Orchids and Other Air Plants of the Everglades National Park.* Coral Gables: University of Miami Press, 1963.

Craighead, Frank C. *The Trees of South Florida, Vol. One, The Natural Environments and Their Succession.* Coral Gables: University of Miami Press, 1971.

Dasman, Raymond F. *No Further Retreat: The Fight To Save Florida.* New York: the Macmillan Co., 1971.

Densmore, Francis. *Seminole Music.* Smithsonian Institution Bureau of American Ethnology, Bulletin 161. Washington: US Government Printing Office, 1956.

DeWire, Elinor. *Guide to Florida Lighthouses.* Pineapple Press, 1987.

Disney's Children's Adventure Travel Guide to Florida. Fodor's Modern Travel Guides Series. New York: McKay, 1980. Strictly for the kids.

Fernald, Edward O. *Florida: Its Problems and Prospects.* Tampa: Trend Publications, 1972.

Fichter, George S. *Birds of Florida.* Miami: E.A. Seemann Publishing, 1971. The definitive guide to Florida's feathered inhabitants.

Firestone, Linda and Morse, White. *Sanibel and Captiva: The Firestone/Morse Guide to Florida's Enchanting Island.* Richmond: Good Life Publishers, 1976 (Regularly revised.) A detailed handbook for exploring Florida's favorite shell-hunting (shunting) grounds.

Fleming, Glenn; Genelle, Pierre; and Long, Robert W. *Wild Flowers of Florida.* Miami: Banyan Books, 1976.

Fletcher, Leslie. *Florida's Fantastic Fauna and Flora.* Beau Lac, 1977.

Ford, Norman D. *Florida.* Harian, 1979 (Regularly revised).

Frisbie, Louise K. *Florida's Fabled Inns.* Imperial Publishing Co., 1980.

Gantz, Charlotte Orr. *A Naturalist in Southern*

Florida. Coral Gables: University of Miami Press, 1971.

Geneva. *The Florida Keys Gourmet Guide*. Key West: Island Graphics, 1979.

George, Jean Craighead. *Everglades Wildguide*. Washington: US Government Printing Office, 1972.

Grimm, Tom, and Grimm, Michel. *Florida*. This Beautiful World Series: Volume 59. Tokyo: Kodansha International, 1977.

Guide to Florida. Chicago: Rand McNally, 1984 (Regularly revised.) Includes comprehensive campgrounds listings.

Hill, Jim and Hill, Miriam. *Fabulous Florida*. Ambassador Publishing, 1976.

Hill, Jim. *Beyond the Beaten Path: A See More Spend Less Guide to Orlando, Walt Disney World and 50-Mile Vicinity*. Ambassador Publishing, 1976.

Hoffmeister, John Edward. *Land From the Sea: The Geologic Story of South Florida*. Coral Gables: University of Miami Press, 1974.

Holland, Claude V. *Tortugas Run*. Holland Books, 1973.

Hudson, L. Frank, and Prescott, Gordon R. *Lost Treasures of Florida's Gulf Coast*. St Petersburg: Great Outdoors, 1973.

Key West Women's Club. *The Key West Cookbook*. New York: Farrar, Straus and Giroux, 1949.

Kosoy, Ted. *Kosoy's Travel Guide Series*. Washington: Acropolis Books, 1979.

Koukoulis, Andrew. *Poisonous Snakes of Florida*. Silver Springs: International Graphics, 1972.

Lakela, Olga, and Long, Robert W. *Ferns of Florida*. Miami: Banyan Books, 1976.

Lewis, Gordon. *Florida Fishing: Fresh and Salt Water*. St Petersburg: Great Outdoors, 1957.

Luer, Carlyle A. *The Native Orchids of Florida*. New York: The New York Botanical Garden, 1972.

Marks, H.S., and Riggs, Gene B. *Rivers of Florida*. Southern Printing, 1974.

Marsh, Richard. *Key West Ghosts*. Pocket Poetry, 1976.

Marth, Del, and Marth, Martha. *Florida Almanac*. St Petersburgh: A.S. Barnes, 1980. (Revised regularly.) Florida facts at your fingertips and hundreds of fascinating snippets about Florida subjects.

Matschat, Cecile H. *Suwannee River: Strange Green Land*. Gainesville: University of Florida Press, 1980.

McLean, Will. *Florida Sand, Original Songs and Stories of Florida*. Orlando: Curry's Printing Co., 1969.

Mesouf, Hank, and Cleo, June. *Florida: Polluted Paradise*. Philadelphia: Chilton Books, 1964.

Mobil Travel Guide: Southeastern States. Chicago: Rand McNally, 1981. (Revised annually.) Detailed listings and ratings of hotels, motels and restaurants in Florida cities, accompanied by brief descriptions of attractions, parks, etc. Includes money-saving guest certificates to some attractions.

Morris, Allen. *Florida Place Names*. Coral Gables: University of Miami Press, 1974. The fascinating stories behind the dozens of names of Florida cities, countries, rivers, etcetera.

Morris, Allen. *The Florida Handbook*. Tallahassee: Peninsula Publishing Co. Published bienially since 1947. A standard Florida reference book.

Morris, Alton C. (collector/editor) *Folksongs of Florida*. Gainesville: University of Florida Press, 1950.

Morton, Julia. *Plants Poisonous to People in Florida and Other Warm Areas*. Miami: Fairchild Tropical Gardens, 1971, 1977.

O'Reilly, John. *Boater's Guide to the Upper Florida Keys: Jewfish Creek to Long Key*. Coral Gables: University of Miami Press, 1970.

Osler, Jack. *Fifty Great Mini-Trips for Florida*. Media Ventures, 1977.

Perrero, Laurie, and Perrero, Louis. *Disney World and the Sun and Fun Belt*. Miami: Windward Publishing.

Pollack, Martin. *Eating-Out: Guide to the Restaurants of South Florida*. Southern Progress Alliance, 1980.

Poole, Susan. *Arthur Frommer's Dollarwise Guide to the Southeast and New Orleans*. New York: Frommer/Pasmantier, 1980. (Regularly revised.) Attempts to cover too much ground in too little space.

Rabkin, Richard, and Rabkin, Jacob. *Nature Guide to Florida*. Miami: Banyan Books, 1978.

Rackleff, Robert B. *Close to Crisis: Florida's Environmental Problems*. Tallahassee: New Issues Press, 1972.

Raisz, Erwin and associates (editors), and Dunkle, John (text). *Atlas of Florida*. Gainesville: University of Florida Press, 1964.

Read, W.A. *Florida Place Names of Indian Origin and Seminole Personal Names*. Gordon Printing, 1977.

Rhodes, William W. *Rhodes Travel Guide – Florida*. Lualdi, Anthony (editor). Rhodes Geography Library, 1979.

Robertson, William B. *Everglades – The Park Story*. Coral Gables: University of Miami Press, 1959.

Rouse, Irving. *A Survey of Indian River Archaeology, Florida*. Yale University: Publications in Anthropology, No. 44, 1977. Reprint of 1951 edition.

Rowan, Tom. *Newcomers Guide to Florida*. St Petersburg: Great Outdoors, 1979.

Smiley, Nixon. *Florida: Land of Images*. Miami: E.A. Seemann, 1977. A Miami newspaper columnist recalls colorful Florida events and anecdotes.

Stachowicz, Jim. *Diver's Guide to Florida and the Florida Keys*. Miami: Windward Publishing, 1976. A good guide to underwater Florida.

Stachowicz, Jim. *Guide to Florida Campgrounds*. Edited by Sandra Romanshko. Miami: Windward Publishing, 1980. A guide to camping in the state.

Stevenson, George B. *Keyguide*. Miami: Banyan Books, 1970. Dated, but still provides interesting, little-known information about even the tiniest of Florida's Keys.

Stevenson, George B. *Trees of Everglades National Park and the Florida Keys.* Miami: Banyan Books (distributor), 1969.

Tebeau, Charlton W. *Man in the Everglades National Park.* Coral Gables: University of Miami Press, 1969.

Tolf, Robert W. *Best Restaurants, Florida's Gold Coast.* San Francisco: 101 Productions, 1979. Excellent reviews of South Florida eateries.

Tolf, Robert W. *How to Survive Your First Six Months in Florida and Love Every Minute of It.* Tampa: Trend House, 1979.

Toner, Mike, and Toner, Pat. *Florida By Paddle and Pack,* Miami: Banyan Books, 1979. A must for hikers, tubers, canoers and nature-lovers. Detailed descriptions and maps of Florida's exotic land and water trails by the former environment writers of the *Miami Herald* and *Fort Lauderdale News.* Provides lengths, times, etc.

Triplett, Kenneth E., and Triplett, Mary R. *Free Camping in Florida.* Triplett Enterprises, 1973.

Truesdell, William G. *Guide to the Wilderness Waterway of the Everglades National Park.* Coral Gables: University of Miami Press, 1969.

Ward, Bill. *Miami Herald Outdoor Guide.* Published annually by the Miami Herald.

Warnke, James R. *Balustrades and Gingerbread: Key West's Handcrafted Homes and Buildings.* Miami: Banyan Books, 1978.

Woodall's Florida Campground Directory. Highland Park III: Woodall Publishing Co. Revised annually.

Ziegler, Louis W., and Wolfe, Herbert S. *Citrus Growing in Florida.* Gainesville: University of Florida, 1961.

Zim, Herbert S. *A Guide to Everglades National Park and the Nearby Florida Keys.* New York: Golden Press, 1960.

PHOTOGRAPHIC

Bowe, Richard J. *Pictorial History of Florida.* Tallahassee: Historical Publications, Inc., 1965.

Carr, Archie. *The Everglades.* The American Wilderness Series. New York: Time-Life Books, 1973.

Dunn, Hampton. *Yesterday's Clearwater.* Miami: E.A. Seemann, 1973.

Dunn, Hampton. *Yesterday's St Petersburg.* Miami: E.A. Seemann, 1973.

Dunn, Hampton. *Yesterday's Tallahassee.* Miami: E.A. Seemann, 1974.

Dunn, Hampton. *Yesterday's Tampa.* Miami: E.A. Seemann, 1977.

Frisbie, Louise K. *Yesterday's Polk County.* Miami: Seemann, 1976.

Godown, Mariam, and Rawchuck, Alberta. *Yesterday's Fort Myers.* Miami: E.A. Seemann, 1975.

Golia, Jack de. *Everglades: The Story Behind the Scenery.* Las Vegas: KC Publications, 1979.

Harvey, Karen G. *St Augustine and St Johns County: A Pictorial History.* Donning Co., 1980.

Lewis, Paul M. *Beautiful Florida.* Edited by Robert D. Shangle. Beautiful America Series, 1979.

Linn, Christopher. *The Everglades: Exploring the Unknown.* Mawah, N.J., Troll Associates, 1976.

Marth, Del. *Yesterday's Sarasota.* Miami: E.A. Seemann, 1977.

Parks, Arva Moore. *The Forgotten Frontier: Florida through the Lens of Ralph Middleton Munroe.* Miami: Bunyan Books, 1977. A fine selection of recently released plates by Coral Gables pioneer and photographer, Ralph Middleton Munroe. A superb look at South Florida just before the turn of the century.

Russell, Franklin. *The Okefenokee Swamp.* The American Wilderness Series. New York: TimeLife Books, 1973.

Schofield, Arthur C. *Yesterday's Bradenton.* Miami: E.A. Seemann, 1975.

Smiley, Nixon. *Yesterday's Florida.* Miami: E.A. Seemann, 1974. The overview book in series of books that utilizes many pictures from the State Photographic Archives and other sources of old photographs of Florida's cities and counties.

Smiley, Stan, and Langley, Wright. *Yesterday's Key West.* Miami: E.A. Seemann, 1973.

Windhorn, Stan, and Langley, Wright. *Yesterday's Florida Keys.* Miami: E.A. Seemann, 1974.

THE SPACE PROGRAM & CAPE CANAVERAL

Armstrong, Neil. *First on the Moon: The Astronauts' Own Story.* Little, 1970.

Branley, Franklyn M. *Columbia and Beyond: The Story of the Space Shuttle.* Philomel, 1979.

Carr, Harriet. *Cape Canaveral, Cape of Storms and Wild Cane Fields.* St Petersburg: Valkyrie Press, 1974.

Cromie, William. *Skylab: The Story of Man's First Station in Space.* New York: McKay, 1976.

Freeman, Michael. *Space Traveller's Handbook: An Everyday Guide for the Experienced Astronaut and the Layman Space Traveller.* Sovereign Books, 1979.

Hallion, Richard P., and Crouch, Tom D. (editors) *Apollo: Ten Years Since Tranquility Base.* Washington: Smithsonian, 1979.

Kennedy Space Center Story. John F. Kennedy Space Center, Cape Canaveral: NASA, undated.

Langworthy, Fred H. *Thunder at Cape Canaveral.* New York: Vantage Books, 1962.

Mailer, Norman. *Of a Fire on the Moon.* Boston: Little, Brown, 1971.

Olney, Ross R. *They Said It Couldn't Be Done.* New York: Dutton, 1979.

Ross, Frank, Jr. *The Space Shuttle: Its Story and How to Make a Flying Paper Model.* Lothrop, 1979.

US News and World Report. *US on the Moon.* New York: Macmillan, 1970.

.Verne, Jules. *From the Earth to the Moon.* Available in a variety of hardcover and paperback editions since it was first published in 1865.

Wolfe, Tom. *The Right Stuff.* Bantam, 1980.

FICTION & WRITERS OF FICTION

Bigelow, Gordon E. *Frontier Eden: The Literary Career of Marjory Kinnan Rawlings.* Gainesville: University of Florida Press, 1966.

Frederiksen, Alan Ryle. *Red Roe Run.* Green Key Press, 1983.

Hemingway, Ernest. *Islands in the Stream.* New York: Charles Scribner's Sons, 1970.

Hemingway, Ernest. *To Have and Have Not.* New York: Charles Scribner's Sons, 1937. While many of Hemingway's novels and short stories were written during the 10 years he lived at Key West, this one is set in a town at Florida's southern tip.

Hemingway, Ernest. *Collected Letters (1918–1961).* New York: Charles Scribner's Sons, 1981.

Hirschfeld, Burt. *Key West.* Corgi. A steamy, seamy novel written by an esteemed pulp paperback king.

Hurston, Zora Neale. *Their Eyes Were Watching God.* Philadelphia: Lippincott, 1936. A novel about the devastating 1928 hurricane by one of the state's leading black authors.

Kaufelt, David A. *American Tropic.* Poseidon Press, 1986.

MacDonald, John D. *Condominium.* Lippincott, 1977. This fine novel deals with the effects of a hurricane on a shoddily-constructed condominium complex.

MacDonald, John D. *The Travis McGee Series.* Hardcover, Lippincott; paperback, Fawcett. Various publication dates. *The Deep Blue Goodby* (1979), *The Dreadful Lemon Sky* (1975), *Dress Her in Indigo* (1971), *The Empty Copper Sea* (1978), *The Long Lavender Look* (1972), *and A Tan and Sandy Silence* (1979) are only a few of the titles by Florida's most prolific novelist, about his detective, McGee.

McGuane, Thomas. *Ninety-two in the Shade.* New York: Farrar, Straus and Girous, 1973. The sea and the seedy side of Key West play an integral role in this superb tale of treachery.

McLendon, James. *Papa Hemingway in Key West.* Miami: E.A. Seemann, 1972.

Norman, Geoffrey. *Midnight Water.* Dutton, 1983.

Pratt, Theodore. *The Barefoot Mailman.* New York: Duell, Sloan and Pearce, 1943.

Rawlings, Marjorie Kinna. *Cross Creek.* New York: Charles Scribner's Sons, 1942. The tales here reek of Deep South rural Florida and are probably more fact than fiction.

Rawlings, Marjorie Kinna. *The Yearling.* New York: Charles Scribner's Sons, 1939. The Pulitzer prize-winning story of a boy and his young deer.

Slaughter, Frank. Various novels, publishers and dates. Try *Storm Haven* (1953), *Fort Everglades, East Side General* (1952), *The Golden Isle* and *In*

a Dark Garden (1946); novels with a Florida backdrop from another of the state's prolific tale-spinners.

Wilder, Robert. *Flamingo Road.* New York: Grosset and Dunlap, 1942. Happenings in Truro, the Peyton Place of Florida.

Williams, Tennessee. *Memoirs.* New York: Doubleday, 1975. The dean of American playwrights tells about his life in Key West and elsewhere.

Williams, Tennessee. Various plays. Many of William's plays convey the mood of a steamy night in the South. Try *Three by Tennessee: Sweet Bird of Youth, The Rose Tattoo* and *Night of the Iguana.* Signet Classics: New American Library, 1976.

MUSIC

The following brief listing of music does not profess to be a comprehensive guide to melodies written about, inspired by or composed in the Sunshine State. It does, however, provide a sampling of music for a variety of tastes – including classical, jazz, Bahamian-flavored ballads, classic American folksongs, and hard Southern rock and roll – all in some way connected with Florida. Try listening to your choice while reading *Insight Guide: Florida,* or on your car stereo while driving along the state's byways and highways.

Buffet, Jimmy, A-1-A MCA 37027.
– *Changes in Latitudes, Changes in Attitudes.* MCA AB-990.
– *Coconut Telegraph.* MCA 5169.
– *Havana Daydreamin'.* MCA 37023.
– *Living and Dying in Three-Quarter Time.* MCA 37025.
– *Son of a Son of a Sailor.* MCA 37024.
– *White Sport Coat and Pink Crutaseans.* MCA 37026.
– *You Had to Be There.* MCA AK2-1008.
"Woman Goin' Crazy on Caroline Street," "Ringling, Ringling," and "Banana Republics," are some of the titles of songs composed by Buffet, who got his start playing bars in Key West. He now divides his time between Florida and Colorado. His Florida concerts are usually sell-outs.

Charles, Ray, Best. At. 1543.
– *Genius* (12–59). At. 1312.
– *Great.* At. 1259.
– *Greatest.* At. 8054.
– *Live.* (Double album). At. 2-503.
Born in the small Florida town of Greenville near the Georgia border, Charles went blind at an early age after a futile attempt to save his brother from drowning. He grew up here and began piano training at the Florida School for the Deaf and Blind in St Augustine. before leaving the state to set out to become a legend. The trauma of those early days in Florida is still evident in the soulful stylings of Charles' compositions and interpretations.

Delius, Frederick
Florida Suite, Dance Rhapsody #2, Over the Hills and Far Away. The Beecham Royal Philharmonic, Seraphim 5-60212.

Florida even has its own resident composer, Delius, who moved to a small farm on the banks of the St Johns. The songs and melodies sung by plantation slaves are evident in his plantation suites. Also try *Summer Night on the River, Song Before Summer, In A Summer Garden*, etc. Barbirolli, Halle Orchestra, Angel S-36588; and *Walk To the Paradise Garden* (1910), *Song of Summer*. Barbirolli, Angel S-36415.

Foster, Stephen
Old Folks at Home and other songs.
– The Florida Concert Society, Request 10035.
– Mormon Tabernacle Choir, Columbia MS-7149.
– Rogers Orchestra and Choir, London 44050.
– Gregg Smith Singers with the New York Vocal Arts Ensemble, Turn. 34609.

Although Foster never set foot in Florida, the state has adopted him as a favorite son for his use of the famous refrain "Way down upon the S'wanee River" in his "Old Folks at Home." "The Camptown Races," "Jeannie With the Light Brown Hair," "Oh! Susanna," and "My Old Kentucky Home" are only a few of his classics.

Lynyrd Skynyrd
– *Bullets*, MCA 37070.
– *First and Last*. MCA 37071.
– *Nuthin' Fancy*. MCA 37069.
– *One From the Road*. (Double album), MCA 8011.
– *Pronounced Leh-nerd*. MCA 3019.
– *Second Helping*. MCA 3020.
– *Street Survivors*. MCA 3029.

They were the pioneers of deep-fried southern rock and roll until most of the band members died in a plane crash. But you would never know they were gone if you drive through Florida listening to stereo FM stations (which play their classic "Free Bird" as often as they play contemporary hits).

Molly Hatchet
– *Beatin' The Odds*. Epic FE-36572.
– *Flirtin' With*. Epic JE-35110.

Current practitioners of the art of southern rock and roll. Many of the band members hail from Jacksonville and other Florida cities.

USEFUL ADDRESSES

AIRLINES

Airlines with Florida service:

Aer Lingus-Irish Airlines: Tel:	1-800-223-6537
Aerolineas Argentinas:	1-800-327-0276
Aeromexico:	1-800-776-3000
Air Canada:	1-800-422-6232
Air Jamaica:	1-800-523-5585
Alitalia Airlines:	1-800-223-5730
American Airlines:	1-800-443-7300
British Airways:	1-800-247-9297
Delta Air Lines:	1-800-638-7333
Eastern Airlines:	1-800-327-8376
Iberia Air Lines of Spain:	1-800-221-9741
Japan Air Lines:	1-800-525-3663
KLM-Royal Dutch Airlines:	1-800-556-7777
Lan-Chile Airlines:	1-800-255-5526
Northwest Orient:	1-800-447-4747
Pan Am:	1-800-221-1111
Piedmont Airlines:	1-800-251-5720
Sabena Belgian:	1-800-645-3790
Scandinavian Airlines:	1-800-221-2350
Swissair:	1-800-221-4750
TAP Air Portugal:	1-800-221-7370
Trans World Airlines:	1-800-221-2000
USAir:	1-800-428-4322
United Airlines:	1-800-521-4041
Varig Brazilian Airlines:	1-800-468-2744
Viasa Venezuelan International:	1-800-432-9070
Wardair Canada 1975 Ltd:	1-800-282-4751

CHAMBERS OF COMMERCE

This list also includes addresses of convention and visitors' bureaux.

Alachua Chamber of Commerce, P.O. Box 387, Alachua, FL 32615. Tel: 904/462-3333
Alachua County Tourist Development Council, P.O. Drawer CC, Gainesville, FL 32602. Tel: 904/374-5210
Amelia Island Chamber of Commerce, P.O. Box 472, Fernandina Beach, FL 32034. Tel: 904/261-3248
Anna Maria Island Chamber of Commerce, 503 Manatee Ave, Suite A, Holmes Beach, FL 34217. Tel: 813/778-1541
Apalachicola Bay Chamber of Commerce, 128 Market St, Apalachicola, FL 32320. Tel: 904/653-9419

Apopka Area Chamber of Commerce, 180 E. Main St, Apopka, FL 32703. Tel: 407/886-1441

Auburndale Chamber of Commerce, 111 E. Park St, Auburndale, FL 33823. Tel: 813/967-3400

Avon Park Chamber of Commerce, P.O. Box 1330, Avon Park, FL 33825. Tel: 813/453-3350

Baker County Chamber of Commerce, 20 E. Macclenny Ave, Macclenny, FL 32063. Tel: 904/259-6433

Bartow Chamber of Commerce, P.O. Box 956, Bartow, FL 33830. Tel: 813/533-7125

Bay County Chamber of Commerce, P.O. Box 1850, Panama City, FL 32402. Tel: 904/785-5206

Belleview-South Marion Chamber of Commerce, 5301 S.E. Abshier Blvd, Belleview, FL 32620. Tel: 904/245-2178

Belle Glade Chamber of Commerce, 540 S. Main St, Belle Glade, FL 33430. Tel: 407/996-2745

Bonita Springs Chamber of Commerce, P.O. Box 1240, Bonita Springs, FL 33959. Tel: 813/992-2943

Brandon Chamber of Commerce, 408 W. Brandon Boulevard, Brandon, FL 33511. Tel: 813/689-1221

Brevard County Tourist Development Council, 2235 North Courtenay Parkway, Merritt Island, FL 32953. Tel: 407/453-2211

Calhoun County Chamber of Commerce, 314 E. Central Ave, Blountstown, FL 32424. Tel: 904/674-4519

Cedar Key Area Chamber of Commerce, Second St, Cedar Key, FL 32625. Tel: 904/543-5600

Chamber of Commerce of South Brevard, 1005 E. Strawbridge Ave, Melbourne, FL 32901. Tel: 407/724-5400

Chamber of Commerce of the Palm Beaches, 501 N. Flagler Drive, West Palm Beach, 33401. Tel: 407/833-3711

Chamber of S.W. Florida, P.O. Box CC, Fort Myers, FL 33902. Tel: 813/334-1133

Chamber of S.W. Florida-Cape Coral, 2051 Cape Coral Parkway, Cape Coral, FL 33904. Tel: 813/542-3721

Charlotte County Chamber of Commerce, 2702 Tamiami Trail, Port Charlotte, FL 33952. Tel: 813/627-2222

Citrus County Chamber of Commerce, 208 W. Main St, Inverness, FL 32650. Tel: 904/726-2801

Citrus County Commission and Tourist Development Council, 110 N. Apopka St, Inverness, FL 32650. Tel: 904/726-8500

Clay County Chamber of Commerce, P.O. Box 1441, Orange Park, FL 32607-1441. Tel: 904/264-2651

Clermont Area Chamber of Commerce, P.O. Box 417, Clermont, FL 32711. Tel: 904/394-4191

Clewiston Chamber of Commerce, P.O. Box 275, Clewiston, 33440. Tel: 813/983-7979

Cocoa Beach Area Chamber of Commerce, 400 Fortenberry Road, Merrit Island, FL 32952. Tel: 407/459-2200

Coconut Grove Chamber of Commerce, 2820 McFarlane Road, Coconut Grove, 33133. Tel: 305/444-7270

Columbia County Chamber of Commerce, P.O. Box 566, Lake City, FL 32056. Tel: 904/752-3690

Coral Springs Chamber of Commerce, 7305 W. Sample Road, #110, Coral Springs, 33065. Tel: 305/752-4242

Crestview Area Chamber of Commerce, 502 S. Main St, Crestview, FL 32536. Tel: 904/682-3212

Crystal River Chamber of Commerce, 28 N. US Hwy, 19, Crystal River, FL 32629. Tel: 904/795-3149

Dade City Chamber of Commerce, 402 E. Meridian Ave, Dade City, FL 33525. Tel: 904/567-3769

Dania Chamber of Commerce, P.O. Box 838, Dania, 33004. Tel: 305/927-3377

Davie-Cooper City Chamber of Commerce, 4185 S.W. 64 Ave, Davie, 33314. Tel: 305/581-0790

Daytona Beach Shores Chamber of Commerce, 3048 S. Atlantic Ave, Daytona Beach, FL 32018-6102. Tel: 904/761-7163

DeBary Area Chamber of Commerce, P.O. Box One, DeBary, FL 32713. Tel: 407/668-4614

DeLand Area Chamber of Commerce, P.O. Box 629, DeLand, FL 32721-0629. Tel: 904/734-4331

Deltona Area Chamber of Commerce, P.O. Box 5152, Deltona, FL 32728. Tel: 407/574-5522

DeSoto County Chamber of Commerce, P.O. Box 149, Arcadia, FL 33821. Tel: 813/494-4033

Destin Chamber of Commerce, P.O. Box Eight, Destin, Fl 32541. Tel: 904/837-6241

Destination Daytona, P.O. Box 2775, Daytona Beach, FL 32015. Tel: 904/255-0981

Dunnellon Area Chamber of Commerce, P.O. Box 868, Dunnellon, FL 32630. Tel: 904/489-2320

East Orange Chamber of Commerce, P.O. Box 677027, Union Park Branch, Orlando, FL 32867-7027. Tel: 407/277-5951

Englewood Area Chamber of Commerce, 601 S. Indiana Ave, Englewood, FL 34223. Tel: 813/474-5511

Eustis Chamber of Commerce, P.O. Box 1210, Eustis, FL 32727-1210. Tel: 904/357-3434

Everglades Area Chamber of Commerce, P.O. Box 130, Everglades City, FL 33929. Tel: 813/695-3941

Flagler County Chamber of Commerce, Star Route 18-N, Bunnell, FL 32010. Tel: 904/437-0106

Fort Meade Chamber of Commerce, P.O. Box 91, Fort Meade, FL 33841. Tel: 813/285-8253

Fort Myers Beach Chamber of Commerce, P.O. Box 6109, Fort Myers, FL 33932. Tel: 813/463-6451

Frostproof Chamber of Commerce, P.O. Box 968, Frostproof, FL 33843. Tel: 813/635-9112

Gadsden County Chamber of Commerce, P.O. Box 389, Quincy, FL 32351. Tel: 904/627-9231

Gainesville Area Chamber of Commerce, Inc., P.O. Box 1187, Gainesville, FL 32602. Tel: 904/372-4305

Gilchrist County Chamber of Commerce, P.O. Box 186, Trenton, FL 32693. Tel: 904/463-6327

Glades County Chamber of Commerce, P.O. Box 490, Moore Haven, FL 33471. Tel: 813/946-0440

Greater Boca Raton Chamber of Commerce, 1800

N. Dixie Hwy, Boca Raton, FL 33432. Tel: 407/395-4433

Greater Boynton Chamber of Commerce, 639 E. Ocean Ave, #108, Boynton Beach, FL 33435. Tel: 407/732-9501

Greater Clearwater Chamber of Commerce, P.O. Box 2457, Clearwater, FL 33517. Tel: 813/461-0011

Greater Deerfield Beach Chamber of Commerce, 1601 E. Hillsboro Blvd, Deerfield Beach, FL 33441. Tel: 305/427-1050

Greater Delray Beach Chamber of Commerce, 64 S.E. Fifth Ave, Delray Beach, FL 33483. Tel: 407/278-0424

Greater Dunedin Chamber of Commerce, 434 Main St, Dunedin, FL 34698. Tel: 813/736-5066

Greater Fort Lauderdale Chamber of Commerce, P.O. Box 14516, Fort Lauderdale, FL 33302. Tel: 305/462-6000

Greater Fort Lauderdale Convention & Visitors' Bureau, 500 E. Broward Blvd, # 104, Fort Lauderdale 33394. Tel: 305/765-4466

Greater Fort Walton Beach Chamber of Commerce, P.O. Drawer 640, Fort Walton Beach, FL 32549. Tel: 904/244-8191

Greater Gulf Breeze Chamber of Commerce, 913 Gulf Breeze Pkwy, Suite 17, Gulf Breeze, FL 32561. Tel: 904/932-7888

Greater Hollywood Chamber of Commerce, P.O. 2345, Hollywood, FL 33022. Tel: 305/920-3330

Greater Homestead-Florida City Chamber of Commerce, 650 US Hwy One, Homestead, FL 33030. Tel: 305/247-2332

Greater Key West Chamber of Commerce, 402 Wall St, Key West, FL 33040. Tel: 305/294-2587

Greater LaBelle Chamber of Commerce, P.O. Box 456, LaBelle, FL 33935. Tel: 813/675-0125

Greater Lake Placid Chamber of Commerce, P.O. Box 187, Lake Placid, FL 33852. Tel: 813/465-4331

Greater Lake Worth Chamber of Commerce, 1702 Lake Worth Road, Lake Worth, FL 33460. Tel: 407/582-4401

Greater Largo Chamber of Commerce, 395 First Ave, S.W. Largo, FL 34640. Tel: 813/584-2321

Greater Miami Convention & Visitors' Bureau, 701 Brickell Ave, Miami 3313. Tel: 305/539-3000

Greater Mulberry Chamber of Commerce, P.O. Box 254, Mulberry, FL 33860. Tel: 813/425-1215

Greater Orange City Area Chamber of Commerce, 520 N. Volusia Ave, Orange City, FL 32763. Tel: 904/775-2793

Greater Orlando Chamber of Commerce, P.O. Box 1234, Orlando, FL 32802. Tel: 407/425-1234

Greater Palm Harbor Area Chamber of Commerce, 1000 US 19 North, Suite 300, Palm Harbor, FL 34684. Tel: 813/785-5205

Greater Pine Island Chamber of Commerce, P.O. Box 525, Matlacha, FL 33909. Tel: 813/283-0888

Greater Pinellas Park Chamber of Commerce, 5851 Park Blvd, Pinellas Park, FL 34665. Tel: 813/544-4777

Greater Plant City Chamber of Commerce, P.O.

Drawer CC, Plant City, FL 33566. Tel: 813/754-3707

Greater Riverview Chamber of Commerce, P.O. Box 18, Riverview, FL 33569. Tel: 813/677-26074

Greater Sanford Chamber of Commerce, P.O. Drawer CC, Sanford, FL 32772-0868. Tel: 407/322-2212

Greater Sebring Chamber of Commerce, 309 South Circle, Sebring, FL 33870. Tel: 813/385-8448

Greater Seminole Area Chamber of Commerce, P.O. Box 3337, Seminole, FL 34642. Tel: 813/392-3245

Greater Seminole County Chamber of Commerce, P.O. Box 784, Altamonte Springs, FL 32715-0784. Tel: 407/834-4404

Greater Tampa Chamber of Commerce, P.O. Box 420 Tampa, FL 33601. Tel: 813/228-7777

Greater Tarpon Springs Chamber of Commerce, 210 S. Pinellas Ave, #120, Tarpon Springs, FL 34689. Tel: 813/937-6109

Groveland/Mascotte Chamber of Commerce, P.O. Box 115, Groveland, FL 32736. Tel: 904/429-3678

Gulf Beaches Chamber of Commerce, P.O. Box 273, Indian Rocks Beach, FL 34635. Tel: 813/595-4575

Haines City Chamber of Commerce, P.O. Box 986, Haines City, FL 33844. Tel: 813/422-3751

Halifax Area Chamber of Commerce, P.O. Box 2775, Daytona Beach, FL 32015. Tel: 904/255-0981

Hamilton County Chamber of Commerce, P.O. Drawer P, Jasper, FL 32052. Tel: 904/792-1300

Hardee County Chamber of Commerce, P.O. Box 683, Wauchula, FL 33873. Tel: 813/773-6967

Hawthorne Area Chamber of Commerce, P.O. Box 125, Hawthorne, FL 32640. Tel: 904/481-2433

Hernando County Chamber of Commerce, 101 E. Fort Dade Ave, Brooksville, FL 34601. Tel: 904/796-2420

High Springs Chamber of Commerce, P.O. Box 863, High Springs, FL 32643. Tel: 904/454-3120

Hobe Sound Chamber of Commerce, P.O. Box 1507, Hobe Sound, FL 33455. Tel: 407/546-4724

Holly Hill Chamber of Commerce, P.O. Box 615, Holly Hill, FL 32017. Tel: 904/255-7311

Holmes County Chamber of Commerce, P.O. Box 1977, Bonifay, FL 32425. Tel: 904/547-4682

Homosassa Springs Area Chamber of Commerce, P.O. Box 1098, Homosassa Springs, FL 32647. Tel: 904/628-2666

Immokalee Chamber of Commerce, 907 Roberts Ave, Immokalee, FL 33934. Tel: 813/657-3237

Jacksonville Chamber of Commerce Beaches Development Department, 413 Pablo Ave, Jacksonville Beach, FL 32250. Tel: 904/249-3868

Jackson County Chamber of Commerce, P.O. Box 130, Marianna, FL 32446. Tel: 904/482-8061

Jacksonville and its Beaches Convention & Visitors' Bureau, 6 E. Bay St, Suite 200, Jacksonville, FL 32202. Tel: 904/353-0736

Jacksonville Chamber of Commerce, 3 Independent Drive, Jacksonville, FL 32201. Tel: 904/353-0300

Jensen Beach Chamber of Commerce, 1910 N.E.

Jensen Beach Blvd, Jensen Beach, FL 34957. Tel: 407/334-3444

Kissimmee-Osceola County Chamber of Commerce, 320 E. Monument Ave, Kissimmee, FL 32741. Tel: 407/847-3174

Kissimmee/St Cloud Convention & Visitors' Bureau, P.O. Box 2007, Kissimmee, FL 32742-2007. Tel: 407/847-5000

Lake Alfred Chamber of Commerce, P.O. Box 956, Lake Alfred, FL 33850. Tel: 813/956-1334

Lake City-Columbia County Chamber of Commerce, 15 E. Orange St, P.O. Box 566, Lake City, FL 32056-0566. Tel: 904/752-3690

Lake County Tourist Development Council, 315 W. Main St, Tavares, FL 32778. Tel: 904/343-9850

Lake Wales Area Chamber of Commerce, 340 W. Central Ave, Lake Wales, FL 33859-0191. Tel: 813/676-3445

Lakeland Area Chamber of Commerce, 35 Lake Morton Drive, Lakeland, FL 33802. Tel: 813/688-8551

Land O' Lakes Chamber of Commerce, P.O. Box 98, Land O'Lakes, FL 34639. Tel: 813/949-1582

Lee County Visitor & Convention Bureau, 2180 W. First St, Fort Myers, FL 33901. Tel: 813/335-2631

Leesburg Area Chamber of Commerce, P.O. Box 269, Leesburg, FL 32749. Tel: 904/787-2131

Lehigh Acres Chamber of Commerce, Inc., P.O. Box 757, Lehigh Acres, FL 33970-0757. Tel: 813/369-3322

Liberty County Chamber of Commerce, P.O. Box 523, Bristol, FL 32321. Tel: 904/643-2359

Longboat Key Chamber of Commerce, 510 Bay Isles Road, Longboat Key, FL 34228. Tel: 813/383-2466

Longwood-Winter Springs Area Chamber of Commerce, P.O. Box 520963, Longwood, FL 32752-0963. Tel: 407/831-9991

Madeira Beach Chamber of Commerce, 501 150th Ave, Madeira Beach, FL 33708. Tel: 813/391-7373

Madison County Chamber of Commerce, 105 North Range, Madison, FL 32340. Tel: 904/973-2788

Maitland-South Seminole Chamber of Commerce, 110 N. Maitland Ave, Maitland, FL 32751. Tel: 407/644-0741

Manatee Chamber of Commerce, 222 10th St West, Bradenton, FL 34205. Tel: 813/748-3411

Manatee County Convention & Visitors' Bureau, P.O. Box 788, Bradenton, FL 34206-0788. Tel: 813/746-5989

Marco Island Area Chamber of Commerce, P.O. Box 913, Marco Island, FL 33969. Tel: 813/394-7549

Mayo-Lafayette Chamber of Commerce, P.O. Box 416, Mayo, FL 32066. Tel: 904/294-2705

Monroe County Tourist Development Council, P.O. Box 866, Key West, FL 33041. Tel: 305/296-2228

Monticello-Jefferson County Chamber of Commerce, 420 W. Washington St, Monticello, FL 32344. Tel: 904/997-5552

Mount Dora Chamber of Commerce, P.O. Box 196, Mount Dora, FL 32757. Tel: 904/383-2165

Naples Area Chamber of Commerce, 1700 N. Tamiami Trail, Naples, FL 33940. Tel: 813/262-6141

Navarre Beach Chamber of Commerce, P.O. Box 5336, Navarre, FL 32569-5336. Tel: 904/939-3267

New Smyrna Beach-Edgewater-Oak Hill Chamber of Commerce, P.O. Box 129, New Smyrna Beach, FL 32070. Tel: 904/428-2449

Newberry Area Chamber of Commerce, P.O. Box 1004, Newberry, FL 32669. Tel: 904/472-4121

North Fort Myers Chamber of Commerce, 13180 N. Cleveland Ave, Suite 115, North Fort Myers, FL 33903. Tel: 813/997-9111

North Tampa Chamber of Commerce, P.O. Box 271629, Tampa, FL 33688. Tel: 813/960-9344

Ocala-Marion County Chamber of Commerce, P.O. Box 1210, Ocala, FL 32678. Tel: 904/629-8051

Okeechobee County Chamber of Commerce, 55 S. Parrot Ave, Okeechobee, FL 34972. Tel: 813/763-6464

Oldsmar Chamber of Commerce, P.O. Box 521, Oldsmar, FL 34677. Tel: 813/855-4233

Orlando/Orange County Convention & Visitors' Bureau, 7680 Republic Drive, Suite 200, Orlando, FL 32819. Tel: 407/345-8882

Ormond Beach Chamber of Commerce, P.O. Box 874, Ormond Beach, FL 32074. Tel: 904/677-3454

Palm Bay Area Chamber of Commerce, 4100 Dixie Hwy, N.E., Palm Bay, FL 32905. Tel: 407/723-0801

Palm Beach County Convention & Visitors' Bureau, 1555 Palm Beach Lakes Blvd, #204, West Palm Beach, FL 33401. Tel: 407/471-3995

Palm City Chamber of Commerce, P.O. Box 530, Palm City, FL 33490. Tel: 407/286-8121

Panama City Beach Convention & Visitors' Bureau, P.O. Box 9473, Panama City Beach, FL 32407. Tel: 904/234-6575

Pensacola Chamber of Commerce, P.O. Box 550, Pensacola, FL 32593. Tel: 904/438-4081

Pensacola Convention & Visitors' Information Center, 1401 E. Gregory St, Pensacola, FL 32501. Tel: 904/434-1234

Perry-Taylor County Chamber of Commerce, P.O. Box 892, Perry, FL 32347. Tel: 904/584-5366

Pinellas County Tourist Development Council, 4625 E. Bay Drive, Suite 109A, Clearwater, FL 34624. Tel: 813/530-6452

Polk County Tourism Development Council, P.O. Box 1909, Bartow, FL 33830. Tel: 813/533-1161

Ponce de León Area Chamber of Commerce, P.O. Box 36, Ponce de León, FL 32455. Tel: 904/836-4747

Port Orange-South Daytona Chamber of Commerce, 3431 Ridgewood Ave, Port Orange, FL 32019. Tel: 904/761-1601

Port St Joe-Gulf County Chamber of Commerce, P.O. Box 964, Port St Joe, FL 32456. Tel: 904/227-1223

Port St Lucie Chamber of Commerce, 1626 S.E.

Port St Lucie Blvd, Port St Lucie, FL 33452. Tel: 407/335-4422

Putnam County Chamber of Commerce, P.O. Box 550, Palatka, FL 32078. Tel: 904/328-1503

Safety Harbor Chamber of Commerce, 200 Main St, Safety Harbor, FL 34695. Tel: 813/726-2890

Sanibel-Captiva Island Chamber of Commerce, P.O. Box 166, Sanibel, FL 33957. Tel: 813/472-3232

Santa Rosa County Chamber of Commerce, 501 Stewart St S.W., Milton, FL 32570. Tel: 904/623-2339

Sarasota Convention & Visitors' Bureau, 655 N. Tamiami Trail, Sarasota, FL 34236. Tel: 813/957-1877

Sarasota County Chamber of Commerce, P.O. Box 308, Sarasota, FL 34230. Tel: 813/955-8187

Sebastian River Area Chamber of Commerce, P.O. Box 780385, Sebastian, FL 332978-0385. Tel: 407/589-5969

Siesta Key Chamber of Commerce, 5263 Ocean Blvd, Sarasota, FL 34242. Tel: 813/349-3800

South Hillsborough County Chamber of Commerce, 315 S. Tamiami Trail, Ruskin, FL 33570. Tel: 813/645-3808

St Augustine-St Johns Chamber of Commerce, P.O. Drawer O, St Augustine, FL 32085. Tel: 904/829-5681

St Cloud Area Chamber of Commerce, P.O. Box 5, St Cloud, FL 32769. Tel: 407/892-3671

St Lucie County Chamber of Commerce, 2200 Virginia Ave, Fort Pierce, FL 34982. Tel: 407/461-2700

St Petersburg Area Chamber of Commerce, P.O. Box 1371, St Petersburg, FL 33731. Tel: 813/821-4069

St Petersburg Beach Chamber of Commerce, 6990 Gulf Blvd, St Petersburg, FL 33706. Tel: 813/360-6957

Starke-Bradford County Chamber of Commerce, P.O. Box 576, Starke, FL 32091. Tel: 904/964-5278

Stuart-Martin County Chamber of Commerce, 1650 S. Kanner Hwy, Stuart, FL 33494. Tel: 407/287-1088

Sumter County Chamber of Commerce, P.O. Box 550, Bushnell, FL 33513. Tel: 904/793-3099

Sun City Center Chamber of Commerce, 1651 Sun City Center Plaza, Sun City, FL 33570. Tel: 813/634-5111

Suwannee County Chamber of Commerce, P.O. Box C, Live Oak, FL 32060. Tel: 904/362-3071

Tallahassee Convention & Visitors' Bureau, P.O. Box 1639, Tallahassee, FL 32302. Tel: 904/224-8116

Tampa/Hillsborough Convention & Visitors' Association, 100 S. Ashley Drive, Suite 850, Tampa, FL 33602. Tel: 813/223-1111

Tavares Chamber of Commerce, P.O. Box 697, Tavares, FL 32778. Tel: 904/343-2531

Titusville Chamber of Commerce, 2000 S. Washington Ave, Titusville, FL 327800. Tel: 407/267-3036

Treasure Island Chamber of Commerce, 152–108 Ave, Treasure Island, FL 33706. Tel: 813/367-4529

Umatilla Chamber of Commerce, P.O. Box 300, Umatilla, FL 32784. Tel: 904/669-3511

Venice Area Chamber of Commerce, 257 N. Tamiami Trail, Venice, FL 34285. Tel: 813/488-2236

Vero Beach-Indian River County Chamber of Commerce, 1216 21st St, Vero Beach, FL 32960. Tel: 407/567-3491

Walton County Chamber of Commerce, Chautauqua Bldg, Circle Drive, Defuniak Springs, FL 32422. Tel: 904/267-3511

Washington County Chamber of Commerce, P.O. Box 457, Chipley, FL 32428. Tel: 904/636-4157

West Hernando Chamber of Commerce, 2563 Commercial Way, Spring Hill, FL 34606. Tel: 904/683-3700

West Nassau Chamber of Commerce, P.O. Box 98, Callahan, FL 32011. Tel: 904/879-1441

West Orange Chamber of Commerce, P.O. Box 522, Winter Garden, FL 32787. Tel: 407/656-1304

West Pasco Chamber of Commerce, 407 W. Main St, New Port Richey, FL 34652. Tel: 813/842-7651

West Pasco Chamber of Commerce-Hudson Office, 13740 Old Dixie Hwy, Hudson, FL 34667. Tel: 813/868-9395

West Tampa Chamber of Commerce, 3005 W. Columbus Drive, Tampa, FL 33607. Tel: 813/879-2866

Winter Haven Area Chamber of Commerce, P.O. Drawer 1420, Winter Haven, FL 33882-1420. Tel: 813/293-2138

Winter Park Chamber of Commerce, P.O. Box 280, Winter Park, FL 32790. Tel: 407/644-8281

Ybor City Chamber of Commerce, P.O. Box 5055, Tampa, FL 33675-5055. Tel: 813/248-3712

Zephyrhills Chamber of Commerce, 691 Fifth Ave, Zephyrhills, FL 34248. Tel: 813/782-1913

DAILY NEWSPAPERS

Boca Raton News, 33 S.E. Third St, 33432.

Bradenton Herald, 102 Manatee Ave W., 33505

Brooksville Sun-Journal, 703 Lamar Ave, 34601

Cape Coral Daily Breeze, P. O. Box 846, 33904

Charlotte Harbor Sun, 23170 Harborview Road, 33980

Clearwater Sun, 301 S. Myrtle Ave, 33515

Daytona Beach News-Journal, 901 Sixth St, 32015

Deland Sun News, 111 S. Alabama, 32724

Deland News-Sentinel, 101 N. New River Drive, Ft. Lauderdale 33302

Delray Beach News, 34 S.E. Second Ave, 33432

Deltona Voulusian, P.O. Box 5339, 32728

Ft. Lauderdale News, 101 N. New River Drive, 33302-2297

Ft. Myers News-Press, 2442 Anderson Ave, 33901-3987

Ft. Pierce News-Tribune, P.O. Box 69, 33454

Ft. Walton Beach Playground Daily News, P.O. Box 2949, 32548

Gainesville Sun, Drawer A, 32602

Hollywood Sun-Tattler, 2600 N. 29th Ave, 33022

Homestead South Dade News Leader, P.O. Box 339, 33090

Inverness Citrus County Chronicle, 130 Heights Ave, 32652

Jacksonville Florida Times Union, One Riverside Ave, 32201

Key West Citizen, P.O. Box 1800, 33040

Lake City Reporter, P.O. Box 1709, 32056

Lakeland Ledger, P.O. Box 408, 33802

Lake Wales Highlander, P.O. Box 872, 33853

Leesburg Commercial, Drawer 7, 32749-0600

Marianna Jackson County Floridian, P.O. Box 520, 32446

Melbourne Florida Today, P.O. Box 363000, 32936

Miami Herald, One Herald Plaza, 33132-1693

Naples Daily News, 1075 Central Ave, 33940

New Smyrna Beach News & Observer, Drawer B, 32069

Ocala Star-Banner, P.O. Box 490, 32678-0490

Orange Park Clay Today, P.O. Box 1209, 32067-1209

Orlando Sentinel, 633 N. Orange Ave, 32801-1349

Palatka Daily News, P.O. Box 777, 32078-0777

Palm Beach Daily News, 265 Royal Poinciana Way, 33480

Panama City News-Herald, P.O. Box 1940, 32402-1940

Pensacola News-Journal, P.O. Box 12710, 32574

Punta Gorda Charlotte Herald-News, 114 W. Olympia Ave, 33951-1808

Sanford Herald, 300 N. French Ave, 32771

Sarasota Herald-Tribune, P.O. Box 1719, 33578-1719

St Augustine Record, Drawer 1630, 32085

St Petersburg Times, P.O. Box 1121, 33731

Stuart News, P.O. Box 9009, 34995

Tallahassee Democrat, P.O. Box 990, Tallahassee 32302-0990

Tampa Tribune, P.O. Box 191, 33601-0191

Vero Beach Press-Journal, P.O. Box 1268, 32961-1268

West Palm Beach Post, Drawer T, 33402

ART/PHOTO CREDITS

INDEX

A

accommodation 40, 43, 117, 93, 95, 108, 207, 243, 257, 267
airlines 44, 165
airports 121, 153
Alligator Alley 146
alligators 51, 73, 183, 187, 205, 233, 241, 242, 245, 246, 263, 308
Amelia Island 208
Apalachicola 38, 223–224
    National Forest 225
    River 219
Apopka 112
Arcadia 112
archaeology 21, 22, 136, 146, 184
Art Deco 165, 166–168
auto racing 112, 199, 201, 293–297
Avilés, Pedro Menendez de 28, 30, 204

B

Bagdad 220
Bahia Honda 262
Bardin 234
Bartow 112
baseball 78, 287–291
basketball 156
Bay Lake 91, 93, 102
beaches 19, 129, 130, 146, 169, 171, 196, 199, 201, 208, 213, 220, 221, 262, 275
Bear Lake 22
Big Cypress Swamp 38, 52, 53, 146, 246
Big Pine Key 262
Billy Bowlegs, Chief 33, 38, 52
"Bimini" 25
Bird Key 130
birds 96, 128, 130–131, 144, 146, 193–194, 196, 243, 244, 246, 260, 275, 308
Biscayne Bay 25, 40, 42, 151, 153
blacks 39, 49, 61, 63–66, 155, 160
Blue Angels 216, 217
Boca Grande 143
Boca Raton 43, 174
Bone Valley 112
Bowles, William Augustus 34
bowling 77
Braden Castle 140
Bradenton 139
Brighton Indian Reservation 52, 53, 187
British 28, 31, 33, 34–35, 315
Brooksville 123
Busch Gardens 45, 121–122
Bush Key 275

C

Cabeza de Vaca, Alvar Nunez 27
Cabot, John (Giovanni Caboto) 25
Caloosahatchee River 144, 184
canoeing 111, 146, 233, 243, 244
Cape Canaveral 25, 44, 192, 307, 309
Captiva Island 144, 145
Carrabelle 224
Castillo de San Marcos 33, 204
Castro, Fidel 44, 59, 155
cattle 53, 110, 117, 186, 195–196
Cedar Key 38, 136
Charlotte County 75
Charlotte Harbor 26, 143
Chassahowitzka 135–136
Church of Scientology 132
citrus fruits 33, 39, 40, 108–109, 117, 140, 182, 184, 195
Civil War 38–39, 66, 228–229
Clearwater 75, 132, 290, 291
    Beach 131
Clermont 109
Clewiston 186
climate 21, 207, 289
clowns 142
Cocoa Beach 192, 195, 291
Coconut Grove 49, 159–161
Columbus, Christopher 23, 25
concerts 56, 127, 162
conches 21, 255
Coral Beach 153
Coral Gables 42, 161–162
crabs 21, 136
Crackers 49, 69–71, 72
crime 43, 77, 155
croquet 182
cruises 106, 144, 173, 184, 203, 232, 246
Crystal River 136
Cuba 18, 31, 33, 44, 126
Cubans 39, 42, 49, 57–61, 66, 118, 151, 155, 156–158, 265, 274
Cumberland Island 208
Cypress Gardens 106

D

Dade County 53, 60, 151, 169
Dade, Francis L 36, 123
Dali, Salvador 126
Dania 173, 302
Daytona Beach 66, 188–189, 199–200, 288, 293–297
De Land 109
Dead Lakes 219
deer 262–263
Delius, Frederick 207
Delray Beach 49, 174
Destin 220–221
Disney World see Walt Disney World Vacation Kingdom
diving 233, 255, 256, 263
Drake, Sir Francis 30
Dunedin 132, 290

E

Eatonville 65
Edison, Thomas 75, 143–144
Ellenton 139
EPCOT Center 93, 99–102
Estero 146
Everglades 19, 22, 38, 43, 51, 52, 60, 144, 146, 151, 186, 236–246
   City 146, 246
   National Park 53, 146, 239, 241, 242–246

F

Fernandina Beach 38, 208
festivals 54, 59, 108, 127, 136, 141, 158, 160, 186, 187, 208, 214, 232
fishing 131, 135, 146, 169, 171, 187, 194, 218, 221, 224, 228, 230, 231, 234, 244, 257, 258
Flagler, Henry Morrison 40, 71, 151, 178, 180, 203, 261
Flamingo 242, 243, 244
Florida Keys 18, 22, 25, 244, 253–263, 264–275, 282
football 122, 162, 207, 230
forests 111, 123, 225, 234
Fort Barrancas 216
Fort Caroline 206
Fort Clinch 208
Fort Dallas 151, 152
Fort De Soto 128
Fort George 215
Fort Jefferson 274–275
Fort King 36
Fort Lauderdale 64, 76, 171–173, 289, 290, 291
Fort Myers 21, 26, 53, 75, 76, 143–144
Fort Pickens 215–216
Fort Pierce 184, 302
Fort Walton Beach 220
fossils 18, 19, 112
French 19, 28, 30, 206, 260

G

Gadsden County 64
Gainesville 213, 234
gambling 43, 298–302
gardens 45, 112, 121–122, 128, 131, 140, 142, 146, 162, 169, 201, 229
Gasparilla Invasion 119–120
Gasparilla Island 143
Gatorland 187
geology 18–19, 110, 152, 262
Geronimo 216
Gibsonton 49, 123
golf 105, 132, 142, 169, 181–182, 208, 229, 257
Gorrie, Dr John 38, 224
Grassy Key 261
Greeks 49, 197
Green Corn Dance 54
Gretna 64–65
Grey, Zane 260
greyhound racing 43, 127, 222, 230, 298, 301–302
Gulfstream Park 299, 300

H

Haitians 33, 61, 151
Hemingway, Ernest 267, 268–269
Hernando County 135
Hialeah 54
Hialeah Park 298–299, 300
Hillsborough River 117
   State Park 123
Hollywood 52, 53, 173–174
Homestead 40, 169
Homossassa Springs 19, 136
horses 43, 110–111, 122, 298–301
Hurricane Andrew 44, 45, 169
Hutchinson Island 184

I

Indian Key 260
Indian River 109, 192
Indian Rocks Beach 131
Indians 21, 22, 26, 27, 28, 29, 30, 31, 34, 136, 196, 197, 208, 216, 218, 228, 234
   Ais 23, 184, 191, 308, 309
   Apalachee 23, 31, 228
   Apalachicola 23
   Calusa 23, 26, 146, 241, 260, 265
   Chtot 23
   Creek 31, 33, 34, 35, 53
   Jeaga 23
   Mayaimi 23, 26, 241
   Miccosukee 35, 51–52, 53, 146
   Pensacola 23
   Seminole 31, 33, 35, 36, 38, 49, 51–55, 65, 117, 151, 162, 187, 197, 230
   Talasi 35
   Tequesta 23, 151, 241
   Timucuan 23, 28, 31, 109, 132, 191
   Tocobega 23
Innisbrook 134
insects 242, 255
Iron Mountain 112

J

J.N. "Ding" Darling National Wildlife Refuge 144
Jackson, Andrew 35, 36, 215
Jacksonville 38, 64, 66, 76, 206–208
jai-alai 298, 302
Japanese 49
jazz 105, 119, 214
Jensen Beach 184
Jews 49, 61, 76, 166, 169
John Pennekamp Coral Reef State Park 255–256
Jupiter 182–183

K – L

Kennedy Space Center 44, 190, 192–193, 307–311
Key Biscayne 61
Key Largo 254–257
Key West 40, 49, 118, 264–275, 281, 301
Kingsley, Zephaniah 34
Kissimmee 110
Lake Apopka 112
Lake Buena Vista 91, 95, 102
Lake City 233
Lake County 112

Lake Eola 108
Lake Jackson 228
Lake Maggiore 128, 297
Lake Okeechobee 22, 23, 151, 186, 239, 241
Lake Tarpon 134
Lake Wales 109, 112
Lake Weir 111
Lakeland 44, 112
lakes 19, 112, 127
Lantana 174
Lignumvitae Key 260
Little Havana 57, 60, 157–158
Long Key 260–261
Lue Gim Gong 39, 109
Luna y Arellano, Tristan de 28
Lutz 123

M

"Ma" Barker 111
Madison 213, 232
Magic Kingdom see Walt Disney World Vacation Kingdom
Malabar 22
Manatee River 139
manatees 136, 269, 308
Marathon 261
Marco Island 146
Marquesas 274
Marti, José 42, 118
Masaryktown 123
Matanzas Bay 30, 203, 204
Matecumbe Keys 22, 257–260
Mayport Naval Station 206
McGillivray, Alexander 34
Melbourne 191–192, 194
Mennonites 139
Merrick, George Edgar 42, 161
Merritt Island 192, 193–194, 308, 309
Miami 40, 43, 54, 57, 59, 60, 64, 66, 71, 76, 151–162, 301, 302
  Port of 152, 156
  River 153
Miami Beach 43, 49, 76, 151, 153, 165–169
Miami Dolphins 58, 162
Micanopy 234
Mickey Mouse 44, 91
Milton 220
mining 19, 112, 113
Minorcans 49, 197
Mizner, Addison 43, 174
Monticello 231–232, 301
Moore Haven 186
movies 95, 119, 125
museums 110, 118, 119, 126, 127, 130, 132, 136, 140, 142, 143, 144, 153, 156, 159, 171, 184, 187, 191–192, 203, 204, 205, 214, 217, 218, 222, 224, 227, 230, 273

N

Naples 53, 146
Narváez, Pánfilo de 27, 65, 117
nature trails 128, 216, 242, 245, 263
New Port Richey 135
New Smyrna Beach 49, 196–197
nightlife 162, 200, 214–215
nudism 123

O

Ocala 110, 111, 302
Ochlockonee River 225
Okeechobee 187
  Waterway 184
Oklawaha River 111
Orange County 109
Orlando 64, 91, 108, 290
Ormond Beach 200
Ortiz, Juan 28
Osceola 36, 37, 38, 52
Osceola National Forest 234
oysters 21, 223, 230, 272

P

Palatka 234
Palm Beach 40, 43, 76, 177–182, 291
Panama City 222
  Beach 221
Panhandle, the 22, 23, 64, 213–225
parachuting 123
parks 53, 112, 123, 128, 132, 135, 142, 143, 146, 152, 157, 159–160, 162, 165, 168, 169, 174, 183, 184, 201, 208, 219, 229, 232, 233, 239, 241, 242–246
Pass-a-Grille 129
Payne's Prairie 234
Pelican Island 184
pelicans 135, 184, 308
Pensacola 33, 35, 54, 65, 76, 213–218, 227
  Bay 26, 28
Perry 230
phosphates 19, 112, 117
Pine Island 52
Plant, Henry B. 40, 71, 117, 118
Point Washington 221
politics 77
Polk County 109
polo 174, 175, 181
Pompano Beach 174, 291, 300
Ponce de León, Don Juan 25–27, 143, 196–197, 203, 275, 308
population 21, 35, 39, 43, 64, 71, 72, 75, 117, 143, 207, 214, 266, 271
Port Richey 123
Port St Joe 222–223
prehistory 18, 19, 21

R

railroads 38, 40, 71, 117, 146, 171, 178, 207, 266
ranches 111, 195–196
Rawlings, Marjorie Kinnan 234
religion 58–59
restaurants 95, 102, 108, 112, 119, 120, 122, 125, 131, 132, 133–134, 136, 157–158, 166, 174, 179, 231, 257, 258, 272
retirees 49, 71, 75–78
Ribaut, Jean 19, 28, 30
Ringling, John 43, 123, 140–141, 142
rodeos 110, 187

S

Safety Harbor 22, 127, 132
St Augustine 28, 30, 33, 40, 65, 66, 203–205, 213, 227
St George Island 224
St Johns River 21, 25, 28, 206, 234
St Leo 123
St Lucie River 23, 184
St Marks 33, 34, 230
St Petersburg 21, 42, 64, 76, 77, 125–129, 288, 290, 301
St Vincent Island 223
Salt Springs 111
Sand Key 131
Sanibel Island 144, 145
Santa Fe River 232, 233
Santa Rosa Island 213, 217–218
Sarasota 43, 140–142, 290
Sea World 105
Sebring 112, 297
Seminole Wars 35, 36, 38, 52, 66, 144, 171, 199, 220
Seven Mile Bridge 44, 261, 262
Shark River 244
shells 108, 142, 144, 145
shopping 102, 108, 119, 156, 158, 205, 274
shrimps 117, 158, 208, 224, 243, 267
shuffleboard 77, 127
Silver Springs 106
sinkholes 108, 128
slaves 31, 33, 34, 38, 49, 63
snakes 106, 187, 224, 246
snorkeling 256, 275
Sopchoppy 220
Soto, Hernando de 27, 139, 140, 227–228
souvenirs 95, 96, 101, 274
Spaniards 25, 27, 31, 33, 34, 35, 65, 117, 204, 205, 206, 214, 215, 228, 281–283
Spanish-American War 42, 118
Spoil Islands 162
sponges 132, 133, 265
Spring Creek 224
Spring Hill 123
springs 21, 105, 106, 111, 135, 142, 203, 232
Steinhatchee 231
Stock Island 263
Stowe, Harriet Beecher 39, 40, 234
Sugar Loaf Key 263
Sumatra 220
Sun City Center 77
Sunset Beach 130
Sunshine Skyway 44, 136
surfing 184
Suwannee River 19, 232–233

T

Tallahassee 35, 38, 66, 227–230
Tamiami Trail 51, 53, 146, 245
Tampa 39, 40, 42, 43, 64, 117–123, 289, 291
Tampa Bay 23, 27, 28, 44, 76, 117
Tarpon Springs 49, 132–134
Tate's Hell Swamp 224–225
Ten Thousand Islands 52, 146, 246
Terra Ceia Island 136
theater 112, 125, 140, 141, 182–183
Tierra Verde 129
tobacco 39, 42, 64, 117, 118, 265

Tortugas 25, 274, 275
Treasure Island 130
treasure-hunting 274, 281–283
trees 19, 144, 208, 216, 219, 241, 242, 246, 253, 260
Tupperware 110
Turtle Mound 196, 197
turtles 136, 184, 194–195, 223, 275
Tuttle, Julia D. 40, 151–152

U – V

Universal Studios 91, 105
universities 112, 118, 121, 125, 141, 153, 204, 207, 230, 234
Venice 142–143
Vero Beach 21, 184, 290
Vietnamese 33, 44, 49
Vizcaya 159

W

Wakulla Springs 230
Walt Disney World Vacation Kingdom 44, 91–99
Warm Springs 21, 142
water parks 92, 105, 122
Weeki Wachee Spring 19, 135
Wet 'N' Wild 105
White Springs 232
wildlife sanctuaries 130, 136, 142, 144, 184, 192, 193–194, 223, 225, 255–256, 262, 263
Williams, Tennessee 44, 263, 267, 269
Windley Key 257
Winter Park 108
Wright, Frank Lloyd 44, 112

Y – Z

Yankees 49, 69, 71, 72
Ybor City 117–119
Ybor, Vicente Martinez 39, 42, 118
zoos 108, 122, 146, 162, 182, 183, 191, 208

A
B
D
E
F
G
H
I
J
a
b
c
d
e
f
g
h
i
j
I